Lenin's Interventionist Marxism

Tom Freeman was a lifelong revolutionary and a member of the International Socialist Tendency for nearly 30 years. He died in 2005.

Lenin's Interventionist Marxism

— 🌙 —

Tom Freeman

Edited and introduced by Sandra Bloodworth

Originally submitted as PhD thesis
"Lenin's conception of the party: organisational
expression of an interventionist Marxism"
University of Melbourne, 1999

INTERVENTIONS
MELBOURNE

© Tom Freeman 1999

Published in 2017 by Interventions

Interventions is a not-for-profit, independent left wing book publisher. For further information:
    www.interventions.org.au
    admin@interventions.org.au
    Trades Hall Suite 68
    54 Victoria Street
    Carlton VIC 3053

Design and layout by Viktoria Ivanova
Printed and bound in Australia by ImpactDigital

National Library of Australia Cataloguing-in-Publication entry

Creator: Freeman, Tom, 1953-2005 author

Title: Lenin's interventionist Marxism / by Tom Freeman; edited by Sandra Bloodworth.

    ISBN: 9780994537812 (paperback)

Notes: Includes bibliographical references and index

Subjects: Lenin, Vladimir Il'ich, 1870-1924
Philosophy, Marxist--Russia (Federation)--Case studies
Labor unions Russia (Federation)--Saint Petersburg--Case studies
Labor movement--Russia (Federation)--Saint Petersburg--Case studies
Communist strategy--Case studies

Other Creators/Contributors:
Bloodworth, Sandra, editor

Contents

	Editor's introduction	**1**
1	Introduction: Economic determination and conscious intervention in Marxist theory and the advance of St. Petersburg between 1861 and 1907	**23**
2	Economic determination and conscious intervention in recent Western scholarship on Lenin	**47**
3	St. Petersburg 1861–1905: Formation, emergence and containment of a "worker intelligentsia"	**77**
4	St. Petersburg 9 January 1905–3 June 1907: Formation, rise and containment of a layer of "worker activists"	**108**
5	St. Petersburg 1861–1905: Formation, emergence and containment of Marxism as the most class conscious section of the "worker intelligentsia"	**141**
6	St. Petersburg 9 January 1905–3 June 1907: Formation, rise and containment of the Bolsheviks as the most class conscious element of the "worker activists"	**177**
7	1893–1905: Lenin's conception of the party as a "worker intelligentsia"	**215**
8	9 January 1905–3 June 1907: Lenin's conception of the party as an organisation of "worker activists"	**249**
9	Conclusion	**292**
	References	**300**
	Bibliography	**307**
	Index	**330**

Acknowledgements

This thesis owes much to individuals and institutions in three countries. In Australia Professor Leslie Holmes showed great optimism, perseverance, attention to detail and enthusiasm in reading drafts and seeking grants. Professor Graeme Gill read and commented on a substantial section of the preliminary work and was always encouraging. Professor Harry Rigby allowed me to use his extensive personal library for primary and secondary sources, and was sympathetic to my endeavour despite our differences on the topic. I am also indebted to the staffs of the Baillieu and Borchardt Libraries in Melbourne, as well as the National Library and the library of the Australian National University in Canberra for their assistance in finding and supplying what were often very obscure materials.

In England Professors Robert Service and Neil Harding offered me great hospitality and useful discussion. John Molyneux did not agree with some of my pointed comments on his own work, but his reply has had a considerable influence on the form of my argument. Perhaps more than any other writer this thesis builds on his earlier writings concerning the party. Geoffrey Swain discussed his own work that overlapped my topic and supplied relevant sections of his doctoral thesis. In addition I was assisted by the overworked staff of the British Library and the library of the School of Slavonic and East European Studies at the University of London in finding and examining materials.

In Russia I was most of all indebted to the colleagues of the Section on the History of the Russian Revolution and Workers' Movement, of the St. Petersburg Branch of the Institute of Russian History, Russian Academy of Sciences, where I was a temporary postgraduate for four months in mid-1995, and was able to present a seminar on my work in mid-1997. These colleagues, and especially the head of the section who acted as my supervisor, Sergei Ivanovich Potolov, showed great hospitality and engaged in many penetrating discussions at a time when their own circumstances were parlous and precipitously declining. In St. Petersburg I was helped by the staff of the Central State Archive of St. Petersburg, the Russian State Historical Archive, and especially the Central State Archive of Historico-Political Documents of St. Petersburg, who provided me with material concerning the workers' movement and political parties from the pre-revolutionary period. At the latter archive Tasiia Pavlovna Bondarevskaia, whose own extensive empirical research provided a section of the base for my own argument, was always anxious to discuss issues and helpful in identifying and interpreting documents. To a lesser extent I was assisted by the staff of the Centre for the Preservation and Utilisation of Contemporary Documents, the Russian State Library, the Russian State Historical Library and the Historico-Political Library, all located in Moscow, in finding and interpreting primary and secondary sources.

Perhaps most of all I owe a debt to someone who cannot be thanked personally and will not be able to read the thesis – he died some fifteen months before the final submission. Lloyd Churchward spent many hours listening to chapters read out on tape and in person, as he had gone blind some years before I began my work. He stubbornly persisted in this time consuming and exhausting effort even as his health gave way and it became clear that his own time was running out. This commitment reflected the two concerns that had earlier come to dominate his life – the reform of the Soviet Union and the establishment of a political science of Soviet-type societies. He lived to see both these dreams reduced to ashes, yet a basic humanistic instinct and intellectual integrity seemed to be encouraged by the progress of this thesis. While I haven't dedicated the thesis to Lloyd, I thought, as I was writing the final chapters without him, that he would have found the work a fitting testimonial.

For Ian, John and Dianne, who were right on 22 April 1984,
and for Cliff, who, like me, was so fundamentally wrong, and
with such enduring consequences.

Editor's introduction

Sandra Bloodworth

Tom Freeman was a lifelong revolutionary and a member of the International Socialist Tendency (IST) for nearly 30 years. Although he died at the young age of 51 in 2005, he brought to life a history of radical organising which deserves to be better known. So the opportunity to introduce this work is most welcome.[1] His PhD thesis, completed at Melbourne University in 1999, makes a valuable contribution to our knowledge of the early revolutionary movement in tsarist Russia and Lenin's theory and politics. Freeman visited Russia several times to undertake original research in Russian-language archives. So simply from the point of view of historical accuracy, but also as a contribution to debates among socialists and others wanting to understand Lenin's theory of the revolutionary party, his work deserves a wider readership.

As well as his own detailed research, Freeman draws on histories written by specialists and academics, which are not widely known, creating a rich tapestry of activism, of theoretical and political debates, of industrial and social struggle. This provides the framework with which to show how Lenin developed his ideas as he participated in the struggles of the working class. Freeman shows clearly the interpretation of Marxism Lenin developed, which underpinned his commitment to building a revolutionary party consisting of

---

1   I want to thank Janey Stone for inviting me to edit Tom's thesis and to write the introduction. When I first read his thesis about ten years ago I hoped someone might publish it. A note on editing: I am committed to the politics and ideas to which Tom devoted his life, and have edited the thesis only to reduce the repetition which is an inevitable result of the requirements of an academic thesis. Tess Lee Ack, sharing the same politics, copyedited it as for any work being prepared for publication. We are confident we have not altered in any way Tom's political intentions, the flow of his argumentation, or his conclusions. We have corrected errors which occurred in footnotes and the bibliography, and again, only with an eye for the accuracy Tom would have wanted. However, we are not Russian specialists and so have not changed any Russian language references. Readers can find the whole, unedited thesis online at minerva-access.unimelb.edu.au/handle/11343/38767.

the most advanced workers. This is an important contribution to the debates about what Lenin stood for. It also highlights aspects of this history with relevance for today.

As is evident from the original title, "Lenin's conception of the party: organisational expression of an interventionist Marxism", this is no simple narrative history. Freeman engages with general arguments about the relationships of class consciousness, spontaneity, activity and organisation. His arguments about Lenin's politics and how he responded to events foreshadow the widely read re-assessment of Lenin by Lars Lih, whose book *Lenin Rediscovered* was published in 2005.[2] Lih came to his conclusions by a forensic examination and rediscovery of Lenin's writings, in particular *What is to be Done? (WITBD)*. He also insisted that Lenin's arguments always need to be considered in the context in which he made them. Freeman, almost a decade earlier, was reaching the same conclusions on some key questions by his equally forensic examination of the historical context in which Lenin's politics evolved.

The experience of revolutionaries in tsarist Russia might seem a far cry from the situation faced by those who want to change society for the better today. But, in spite of the obvious differences in social and economic development and traditions, there are, I think, lessons which are still of general relevance. Until the early twentieth century, the revolutionary left was still to be built as a serious movement in the Russian empire, so revolutionaries were confined for long periods to the fringes of the working class and other oppressed layers. Today, around the world – whether it be in the most developed countries or those in the throes of industrialisation – the far left is marginalised and tiny. It's true that there are now very different circumstances, and traditions have developed in the intervening century which influence political ideas. But the far left faces the same question as in tsarist Russia: how can small, isolated groups of revolutionaries build substantial organisations capable of intervening to achieve victories when workers move into radical action? Unfortunately, many on the left today reject the strategy of building a core of revolutionaries with a view to learning how to intervene when struggles open wider layers to the arguments of the far left. Instead, there is a tendency to want influence without this step, searching for other means of building radical influence, for instance by participating in and building broad parties.[3]

This rich history reminds us that the efforts of small groups of revolutionaries – no matter how insignificant or ineffectual they seem – if they are focused on establishing a clear ideological current committed to the theory of Marxism,

---

2   Lih 2008.

3   Mick Armstrong has assessed this strategy in Armstrong 2014.

are an essential step on the road to the kind of mass party we need if capitalism is to be brought to its knees. So I am very pleased to be able to introduce this work precisely because I do think it has relevance today if interpreted with a view to the differences in context and historical experience.[4]

Freeman, as Lih would later, defends Lenin's argument that Marxist ideas originate outside the working class and are brought into the class "from outside" by intellectuals. This puts him at odds with his fellow-thinkers in the IST, in particular John Molyneux and Tony Cliff, neither of whom accepted his thesis. Cliff and Molyneux assume this means that Lenin was elitist until the experience of the 1905 revolution. Molyneux in particular argues that this concept denies workers the ability to emancipate themselves. Both Freeman and Lih convincingly argue that Lenin did not interpret this proposition in an elitist way.[5]

Freeman shows two crucial things. First, that study circles, often set up by students intersecting with the workers' movement, and which debated political theory, were important in the period this thesis covers; that workers sought out intellectuals, intervened in their debates, and drew their own conclusions about their struggles. Out of this layer the beginnings of the Marxist movement of workers and students emerged. Second, that the usual debates about the relationship between spontaneity and organisation and the related argument about ideas being introduced "from outside" the working class are usually misplaced and lacking in an understanding of what Lenin was actually doing. There was no "break" in his thought because, from his earliest days as a Marxist, Lenin understood the importance of intervention, precisely because the ideas workers would act on were introduced to them by intellectuals of all persuasions. The economic struggle was insufficient in itself, especially short of revolution, for workers to develop a clear Marxist analysis of society and how to overthrow it. Therefore, Lenin's practice and theory constitute a break from the determinism which had gained prominence in the Second International. Accordingly, Lenin intervened consistently in changing circumstances.

The political arguments

Marxism is the theory of working class revolution. But students and intellectuals have always played an important role in building Marxist organisation and spreading theory among workers, a fact that seems counter-intuitive. In fact, it is common these days for radicals and leftists to dismiss

---

4   I summarised what I think we can take from Lenin in Bloodworth 2013 and Bloodworth 2014.

5   Lih 2008, pp529-44.

student-based groups as something of an irrelevancy in the mammoth task of building influence among the mass of workers. Freeman's detailed study of the beginnings of the revolutionary movement in Russia shows quite clearly how mistaken this view is.[6] Even those who recognise that students can provide a layer of radicals and revolutionaries tend to notice them when they are in motion, demonstrating or adding a militant edge to movements rather than in their role as theorists and propagandists. In Tony Cliff's biography of Lenin covering the period of this study, students appear when mobilised into protest, while their role in influencing and educating workers in Marxism is much underplayed.

This reluctance to treat the students' and intellectuals' interventions seriously reflects Cliff and others' rejection of the argument in *WITBD* which Lenin took from Kautsky: that Marxist ideas will not develop spontaneously among workers, but will be introduced "from outside". In chapter two, Freeman critiques these arguments against Lenin, beginning with the influential theorist Alfred G. Meyer, who, he says, "sees a counter position in Lenin between 'spontaneity' (among workers) and 'consciousness' (among bourgeois intellectuals). The organisational consequence of this view is that for Lenin the party must remain a narrow contained and small group of intellectuals whatever the context". Freeman points out that Meyer cannot account for statements by Lenin that occur in periods of revolutionary struggle, and which contradict this assessment, because he "does not have any conception of class consciousness emerging in struggle, or the role of conscious intervention in catalysing that rise" – which is the essence of Lenin's theory of class consciousness.

In the introduction, Freeman concludes that Marx's ideas on political consciousness were insufficiently developed: "Marx outlined his own ideas over a period when revolutionary struggles, indeed any struggles of a large scale, were separated by long passages of relative stability. This meant that the necessary role he gave to conscious intervention was not, and could not have been, fully consistent and thoroughgoing". The casual use of the word "inevitable" by Marx opened the door to determinist interpretations that understated the importance of conscious intervention and which became widely accepted in the Second International. A failure to recognise Lenin's clearer understanding of both spontaneous, mass struggles and intervention by revolutionaries led to misunderstandings about his changing positions. For Lenin, the political arguments and tasks at any one time had to be grounded in the actual situation. Lenin's determined calls to build a well-organised,

---

6   Mick Armstrong has argued that students are often the means to build the beginnings of revolutionary organisation in Armstrong 2007.

disciplined party are interpreted as authoritarian and elitist, rather than the response they were to the repressive conditions of tsarist Russia.

Marcel Liebman was one writer who partially broke with this view of Lenin. However, Freeman argues that, like many others, Liebman incorrectly assumed that Lenin's view of the party was that it and not the working class as a whole should take power. This leads Liebman to an unduly programmatic view of the party:

> Liebman's overwhelming focus on formal organisational structures prevented him from making a comprehensive critique of the mainstream. For such a focus does not encompass the transformation of worker consciousness in struggle that was central to Lenin's understanding of the advance to power by the working class.

In his discussion of Tony Cliff's critique of Lenin, Freeman argues that in spite of recognising the need for a different kind of organisation in different circumstances, there is still a weakness in Cliff's reading. He objects that Lenin's statement about ideas being introduced into the class "overemphasised the difference between spontaneity and consciousness". And so a break was necessary in 1905 for Lenin to embrace the radicalism of the working class. As well, "Cliff, like Liebman, does not explicitly acknowledge Lenin's role for the party in leading the class in a struggle to impose its own state power, rather than inheriting the existing state power in the wake of struggle by the class". In neither Cliff's discussion of the armed struggle nor the dictatorship of the proletariat "is a direct relation shown between his conception of the working class in power and the role of conscious intervention in the seizure of that power", a serious "omission of a non-determinist role for conscious intervention" by Cliff.

Molyneux's critique differs from Cliff's, but he concludes that if it were to be accepted that ideas are introduced to the class by intellectuals, then "precious little is left of Marx's fundamental dictum that 'the emancipation of the working class is the act of the working class itself'". As a result, the revolutionary class would now become discontented intellectuals, the division of material and mental labour in capitalist society would be "sanctified in the revolutionary party", [7] and science would be seen as developing in isolation from workers' struggle. Freeman replies:

> These are substantial claims, and cannot be supported even by
> the passages from *WITBD* that Molyneux has cited, let alone
> the book as a whole or the polemic against the Economists of

---

7   Quoted in chapter two.

which it was the culmination. In reacting against what might be taken – indeed what almost universally has been taken – as a statement of the idealist elitism in Lenin's conception of the party, Molyneux has himself incorporated an element of determinism into his understanding of the growth of the labour movement and revolutionary consciousness.

What does he mean by this? He points out that Molyneux ignores the fact that "Lenin explicitly proposes that workers could become such intellectuals" and developed a conception of a worker intelligentsia similar to that of Gramsci's concept of organic intellectuals. Those who reject the formulation at issue fail to see the ability of workers to study the ideas being introduced into their ranks by the educated radicals, to debate and assess them, and to draw their own conclusions. So some workers became Marxists in the 1880s and 1890s, others followed the populists and so on. Freeman shows that, contrary to Cliff and Molyneux's argument, there is no sharp break in Lenin's thinking in 1905 when he supposedly had to break from his elitist attitude in order to respond to the revolutionary upheaval. In fact, it was Lenin's confidence that workers *were* capable of self emancipation, as Marx had argued, which made him the leader most capable of intervening successfully and relating to the revolutionary spirit of the masses. Freeman concludes:

> [I]f this role of those "outside" the class was the entirety of Lenin's argument, then the view of Lenin as at least in part an authoritarian would indeed be valid, for the basic initiative in the development of class consciousness would lie outside the class, and workers could be seen as the object rather than the subject of history. However, just as Lenin posed the reality of a "worker intelligentsia" throughout his polemic against the Economists, so even in these earliest interactions it is clear that worker leaders were active and critical in their acquisition of a critique of tsarism "from outside", rather than passive and uncritical in the sense that is usually taken from Lenin's polemic.[8]

Freeman emphasises that the worker "intelligents" need to be cohered and organised in order to become capable of leading the mass of workers in revolution. He also documents how, when the revolution does break, Lenin throws every effort into convincing that layer of worker "intelligents" of how to cohere a much broader layer of "activist" workers. In fact, Freeman argues, the

8   Chapter three.

implication of Lenin's theory about worker intellectuals "is that workers could become socialist theorists themselves – as long as revolutionary intellectuals did not adopt a determinist passivity in relation to this possibility".[9]

Lars Lih's work backs up Freeman on these points: "The two upsurges of 1905 and 1912 are great historical landmarks for Lenin. His reaction to both can accordingly be *predicted* from *WITBD* and his political agitation articles for *Iskra*". He says Lenin felt the upsurges proved "that the revolutionising of the workers is as unstoppable as a force of nature, despite the nay-saying of intellectuals whose weak faith was shaken by intervening months and years of worker quiescence".[10] His description of the Bolsheviks, under Lenin's influence, gives a flavour of how they understood the relationship of intellectuals and students to workers.

> The workers are presented throughout as students who need the education provided by the Social Democrats…adult students who know what it is they do not know and why they need to know it. The Social Democrat teachers are occasionally abashed to see that the students move ahead of them in finding new methods of struggle. [11]

Alan Shandro, also writing years after Freeman, echoes Freeman's argument and even strengthens it. Shandro argues that, unlike the Erfurtian concept of a merger between the Marxist and workers' movements, it follows from Lenin's argument that workers will independently create new situations which Marxists have to both learn from and interpret. Therefore, "Marxist theory is also an object in the political struggle; failure to develop, concretise and modify it [in the context of the class struggle raising new questions] invites its revision and appropriation by forces that would disarm the working class movement" – which is the basis for Lenin's hostile critique of Bernstein and later Kautsky and the Mensheviks as "abstract, dogmatic Marxists – that is, no longer Marxists". Readers will see the congruence between Freeman's summary of Lenin's conclusions on this issue, quoted above, and Shandro's conclusion:

> [I]f the theoretical absorption of spontaneous innovations leads to significant modification in Marxist theory, it will be true, in an important sense, that the masses of workers and not just the theoreticians take an active, independent and creative part in

---

9   Chapter two.

10   Lih 2008, pp429-30.

11   This is in the *Iskra* period (1903-05). Lih 2008, p188.

elaborating socialist consciousness… Lenin would learn from mass
practice, notably from the spontaneous and proletarian initiative
in establishing the soviets, and he would modify the structure of
Marxist theory in consequence of this learning…not in spite of the
thesis of consciousness from without, but because of it.[12]

So again, an examination of Lenin's practice and theory years later
vindicates Freeman's central thesis that Lenin's view of the party was
interventionist, not passively determinist. And this was based on an
absolute absence of any elitism in Lenin's attitudes from his earliest years
– which is a refutation of the widely held views of Lenin and a contribution
to understanding Lenin's concept of the party. These arguments are very
relevant to debates today as many, if not most, critics who reject Lenin's
theory of the need for a revolutionary party do so on the basis of serious
misunderstandings of his positions. Freeman's detailed evidence, together
with the arguments of Lih and Shandro, are an important rebuff to the
standard criticisms of Lenin.

There is, in spite of many similar, reinforcing arguments by Freeman and
Lih, one aspect of Freeman's work which is a corrective to one of Lih's themes.
Lih emphasises that Lenin was essentially an "Erfurtian", meaning he had the
same politics as that of the Second International of Kautsky and the German
Social Democratic Party (SPD). However, any reader familiar with the debates
will recognise that Freeman's thesis explicitly and convincingly shows that
while Lenin may have not recognised that his approach differed from Kautsky,
he differed fundamentally from the determinism of Second International
Marxism. Freeman's project is to show that Lenin recognised that Marxism
was not mechanically determinist, that he consciously devoted his whole
life's work towards building an *interventionist* party, i.e. one which recognised
that the fate of workers' struggles, from strikes to revolution, depends on the
intervention by those with a political program. In essence, Freeman illustrates
what Chris Harman, a long-standing leader of the IST, argued in opposition
to Lih. Harman argues that Lih's rejection of the argument that Lenin did not
understand how he differed from Kautsky

fails to understand how people read texts. We do so in terms of the
context in which we find ourselves and interpret them accordingly.
This frequently means…that readers ascribe different meanings
to texts from those intended by the author…without necessarily
becoming aware of these differences. In the case of Kautsky, this
was not just a problem for Lenin. Virtually the whole of the Second

12 Shandro 2015, pp146-7.

International accepted Kautsky's version of orthodoxy until August 1914, with only a small group around Bernstein publicly dissenting on one side, and an even smaller group around Rosa Luxemburg on the other. The Bolsheviks, the Mensheviks, and those that wavered between them, all believed themselves to be "Kautskyists" until 1914. This did not stop their various practices from being very different.[13]

Freeman does not explicitly take up any of this kind of debate, as he foreshadows discussion yet to develop on the international left. He simply points out what his research indicates: that Lenin's practice and therefore his theoretical conclusions from his experience in the class struggle are a correct interpretation of Marxism as opposed to the determinism of Second International orthodoxy.

One last point to consider is the analysis of economism, against which Lenin waged a relentless polemic. How should we understand this current in the socialist movement of the time, which argued that workers should just conduct their economic struggle, without interference by intellectuals and that politics should be kept in the domain of the intellectuals? Cliff puts the rise of economism down to a flip over from an over-emphasis on the economic struggle as a corrective to an over-emphasis on theory in the earlier period. But Freeman argues (more convincingly in my opinion) that "economism is…the form which the demoralisation of both the student and 'worker intelligentsia' took in the face of apparently crippling repression and irrepressible economic growth in the late 1890s".[14]

Lih confirms this analysis: "economism was the product of a 'disenchantment' with the workers and the 'primitiveness'…of the strike movement".[15] In 1896-97, textile workers led an upturn in industrial struggle. Over the course of these strikes, some 1,000 workers were arrested in St. Petersburg, possibly the entire politicised peak of the "worker intelligentsia". The revisionist, determinist ideas coming from Bernstein in Germany helped provide an ideological justification for economism and can be found in their publications.

Many historians accept the self-definition of the economists: workers who had found their feet, were supposedly fighting for their economic demands and rejected the intervention of elitist intellectuals who wanted to artificially introduce politics into their unreceptive ranks. This suits historians who reject the idea of self-emancipation and it fits with the polemics against Lenin as an

---

13   Harman 2010, p71.

14   Chapter three.

15   Lih 2008, p239.

elitist. But Freeman points out:

> [D]espite rhetoric about "worker self-activity", as well as its supposed worker composition, the leadership of the Economist trend actually comprised both students and "worker intellectuals" who were united by the view that workers' struggle should be limited to immediate economic questions.[16]

Their paper *Rabochaia Mysl'* was founded by a worker and a teacher from the "Sunday Schools", which were run by activists and largely tolerated, sometimes even promoted by the authorities, as a cheap way to have workers educated in literacy and other basic skills. The best known figure responsible for organising the Marxist movement was K.M. Takhtarev, a medical student. But worker intellectuals and circles based in factories were prominent in opposing economism, the best known being a circle of workers around M.I. Kalinin at the Putilov plant.

Freeman deals with all these questions with much more complexity than I can in this introduction, backed up by his research into both the activity and writings of Lenin and those around him. Perhaps the most impressive thing is that he drew his conclusions almost a decade before the international left seriously engaged with similar arguments.

The historical narrative

To those unfamiliar with the period and the groups which contributed to this early development of Marxism in Russia, the kaleidoscope of their existence may be difficult to piece together, given Freeman is intent on themes rather than the narrative. So I have compiled a brief outline of the main groups and individuals, which hopefully will provide the context in an accessible way before readers embark on Freeman's most rewarding theoretical and political treatment of this history.

Tony Cliff says of the Russian Emancipation of Labour Group (ELG) in exile in the decade 1883 to 1893: "It *was* practically the whole of the Marxist movement". Samuel H. Baron doesn't qualify it at all: "It was not only prominent in the movement, it was the movement". Cliff paints a picture of the ELG existing in grand isolation until an upturn in industrial struggle in the early 1890s in which they could intervene and win support. He quotes a historian approvingly to say that until 1893 labour unrest in Russia "had no connections whatsoever with any of the Social Democratic units". Mick Armstrong is less

---

16   Chapter three.

categorical; he says that in the 1880s "the ELG lost all organised contact in Russia, though unknown to them some Marxist groups did develop". Because of his emphasis on the importance of the path-breaking work of Plekhanov and the ELG he leaves it at that.[17]

The evidence assembled by Freeman points to a much richer experience and more complicated processes by which a layer of revolutionary workers and students developed. He writes a history of young students and workers, remarkable for their courage, determination and suffering inflicted by the viciously repressive tsarist state in the late nineteenth century, as they struggled to understand how to fundamentally change society.

It's not surprising that the small groups which laid the basis for a revolutionary movement were hidden from history for many long years. The names of individuals are often only recorded in secret police files which for decades were closed. They operated in a situation of extreme state repression, and relied on strict secrecy to protect members from jail and exile. Nevertheless, a picture of their activities and the identities of many individuals can now be painted by drawing on various sources.

The earliest workers' group was the Southern Workers' Union, formed about 1874 in Odessa out of workers' circles organised by the son of a noble disillusioned with radical political work among the peasantry. After a short period of rapid growth it was smashed by security forces. A more substantial underground group, set up in St. Petersburg in the autumn of 1877, was the Northern Union of Russian Workers. It was soon headed by two workers, Stepan Khalturin and Victor Obnorskii. From these earliest days, there was a fertilisation of ideas through contact with anti-tsarist intellectuals and the European socialist movements. Khalturin, at the age of 15 or 16, had been in contact with revolutionary intellectuals in exile where he grew up in the Orlov district. Both had travelled abroad as skilled workers (Obnorskii travelled as a sailor for some time as well). They were influenced by German Social Democracy as well as the leading lights of the Narodnik movement such as Plekhanov, Axelrod and Lavrov.[18] Obnorskii also made contact with a workers' group in Warsaw. Alan Woods, the Trotskyist historian, says: "Khalturin was an outstanding representative of a type: the worker-propagandist active in the circles in the first period of the Russian labour movement".[19]

---

17   To be fair, Cliff and Baron wrote their books before the records Freeman (and other historians) accessed were open. Cliff 1986, p30, Baron 1963, p117, Armstrong 2007, p28.

18   The Narodniks were the earliest revolutionaries. They saw the peasantry as *the* revolutionary class and were known for "going to the people". For a fuller explanation see marxists.org/glossary/orgs/n/a.htm.

19   Woods 1999, pp43-4.

The Northern Union's charter and program was published as a leaflet titled "To the Russian Workers!" as part of their intervention in textile workers' strikes in January 1879. They opened branches in working class areas of the capital, organised an illegal library and a fund, opened an underground printing office in February 1880, and printed leaflets and possibly two issues of the newspaper *Rabochaia Zarya* (*Workers' Dawn*) in a print shop set up by Khalturin. The membership of about 200 tried to organise walk-outs and swiftly turned the Union into an All-Russian organisation. As numerous arrests led to its dissolution in 1880, a number of its members joined the populist *Narodnaia Volia* (The People's Will) with its emphasis on terrorist attacks on officials. In 1882, Khalturin was hanged by the Odessa military court for involvement in one such assassination.[20]

Freeman comments "in fact almost all the worker leaders of the 1870s were involved with the liberal intelligentsia, and in particular its most radical elements, the populists", whose ideas and debates influenced the political ideas that dominated the worker leaders.[21]

In the mid-1880s a number of strikes, some of the most notable in the Nevskii district of St. Petersburg, articulated demands in written form, used advanced methods of organising and won solidarity. Freeman says about one of them: "echoing the earlier period, the strikers' demands were formulated 'from outside' [the working class] by a Narodnik, and 200 workers demonstrated to present their demands".[22]

But a tiny number of worker "intelligents", as Freeman calls them, along with some intellectuals, came to question populism, eventually turning to Marxism. And out of the study circles set up by students and intellectuals, worker intellectuals capable of leading other workers developed, often in paradoxical ways. Obnorskii became the worker leader he was via running a workers' library set up by the populists who oriented to the peasantry. And this is not atypical.

Take the student Blagoev's circle, one of the first Social Democratic groups in Russia, founded in 1883 with about 30 students. They independently developed a commitment to Marxism and contacted the ELG in 1884. By 1885, now known as the Petersburg Group of the Party of Russian Social Democrats, they organised possibly 140-150, mostly metal workers and printers, in 15 circles. They ran benefit societies, a central library and several mobile district libraries; they distributed educational and revolutionary literature and published two issues of the illegal paper *Rabochy* (*The Worker*) which included

---

20 *The Great Soviet Encyclopedia* 1979, encyclopedia2.thefreedictionary.com/Stepan+Khalturin.

21 Chapter three.

22 Chapter three.

articles from the ELG and was printed in one of their apartments.[23] The group had eclectic ideas, but Blagoev unequivocally declared himself a Marxist, and his circle between 1884 and 1887 helped disseminate the ideas of the ELG. Norman Naimark concludes: "they shared [with *Narodnaia Volia* workers] an infatuation with Marxism and an awareness of the revolutionary significance of the industrial proletariat".[24] The group dissolved after its leaders were arrested in 1885-87.

In a month-long strike by 11,000 workers in the Morozov cotton mill in the province of Vladimir in 1885, the presence in the factory of experienced agitators was critical – two had been involved in the Northern Union, one of whom was in the famous Kazan demonstration of December 1876, the first political demonstration in Russia and the first time workers raised the red flag.[25] The strike made a huge impact because of its militancy and the revelations of the conditions in the factory, which came out in the trial of 33 workers (who were acquitted, to the horror of the conservative press). This strike appears to have played a role in convincing intellectuals, including Plekhanov, of the revolutionary potential of the working class. On the other hand, the workers learned that they needed the help of the intellectuals to write leaflets and raise funds. And it played a role in turning the tide towards the upturn in industrial struggles of 1889-90. Six hundred were exiled from the area – many of whom would have set up or joined groups wherever they went. That was the nature of the revolutionaries of those times.

In spite of confusions and the enduring softness on terrorism, the circles that emerged from the 1880s provided fertile ground for ideological clarification, spurred on by events. Derek Offord says, correctly, that apart from the specific lessons of theory (seeing the potential of workers as a social force) and organisation, the most fundamental point to make about the groups of the 1880s, obscure as they may seem, is "that these groups simply existed and functioned, thus keeping alive a revolutionary tradition that could be reinvigorated in the 1890s when conditions were again propitious".[26] We can add that the importance of the ELG cannot be overstated. Its publications turn up everywhere. It played a role in the desperate need for clarification out of the theoretical muddle caused by the rise and decline of populism.

Another of the earliest Marxist circles was founded by Pavel Varfolomeivich Tochiiskii in 1885. He was notable for his strong opposition to populism, downplaying the role of intellectuals within the workers' movement, and

---

23   Offord 1986, pp131-4.

24   Naimark 1983, p78.

25   The Presidential Library, prlib.ru/en-us/History/Pages/Item.aspx?itemid=758.

26   Offord 1986, p164.

emphasising that workers had to build their own independent organisations with their own leadership. By 1886, when his circle had adopted the name Partnership of St. Petersburg Artisans and recruited a number of workers, it formed a network of circles and produced propaganda to distribute outside industrial plants, inside the State Dispatch Office and at a number of factories, one of which was the Putilov works, later famous as a centre of radical militancy which helped spark the 1917 February revolution.

Offord says that "workers' circles proliferated [in St. Petersburg] more or less independently of the intelligentsia by the end of the decade" of the 1880s.[27] However, Freeman says these last years of the 1880s were the lowest ebb of the revolutionary movement. Mass arrests broke up Tochiiskii's organisation during autumn 1888. Survivors joined a group formed by Brusnev, a Bulgarian student. Brusnev appears to have organised a Central Students' Circle for some time, and he and Tochiiskii helped set up a Central Workers' Circle, a city-wide organisation at the centre of 20 circles. Brusnev's group was the base from which came those who made the turn to intervention in the early 1890s, representing the culmination of Plekhanov's work in setting up the ELG.[28] They helped organise or support a number of important strikes and political demonstrations, including the first May Day demonstrations in Russia in 1891 and 1892. Freeman says they "pioneered the organisation of Marxists within the 'worker intelligentsia' of St. Petersburg".[29]

The remnants of both these student and worker intellectual milieux, which at their height had organised possibly up to 2,000 workers in St. Petersburg, influenced Lenin when he arrived in 1893. He joined a circle led by Stepan Ivanovich Radchenko, one of a couple of leaders of Brusnev's student circle who had escaped arrest and who was leading workers' circles in the Nevskii district. Radchenko was helped by Vasilii Andreevich Shelgunov, one of the founders of the Tochiiskii circle and an activist in the Central Workers' Circle, who went on to be a Bolshevik of some standing.[30]

If Lenin took anything from the milieu he entered in 1893, it would have been the dynamic interaction between intellectuals and workers and the ability of the workers for critical thought and action. Unfortunately, Cliff's and others' emphasis on the instability and short-lived existence of such circles obscures the fact that there were many links between circles, often because revolutionaries moved, or organised when in exile. Freeman argues persuasively that in the decade 1885 to 1895, workers' struggles were

---

27   Offord 1986, p.156.

28   Chapter five.

29   Chapter five.

30   Chapter three.

developing a new sophistication facilitated by "a growing involvement by the worker 'intelligents' with the general anti-tsarist intelligentsia, and the consequent consideration of disputes within that milieu".[31]

In the first half of the 1890s, a tiny but cohered layer of radicalising workers is evident. By 1891, students had formed new circles among workers in St. Petersburg after a round of repression. Naimark says that after a period of growth from 1888 to 1891, workers' circles began to clarify their ideas more seriously. For instance, the Central Workers' Circle in St. Petersburg organised debates.[32] Of the 1,000 who participated in the funeral of the beloved populist writer N.V. Shelgunov on 24 April 1891, 100 were workers mobilised by this circle. They projected an independent class presence, sending a delegation to the dying poet to thank him for his work in teaching them and exposing their conditions in his writing. They led the funeral procession carrying a banner and a wreath. And they organised the first May Day demonstration a week later, as a direct response to a call by Marx's First International.[33]

Freeman says: "The leadership of the Central Workers' Circle…came from within a layer of some 1,000 self-educated workers which could now be regarded as the core of the 'worker intelligentsia'"[34] that, according to one estimate, numbered up to 100,000 workers in study circles in St. Petersburg. In 1892, when one of the participants, Aleksandr Potresov, brought back publications by the ELG, a circle of students, including Martov (a future collaborator of Lenin, who later became a Menshevik), adopted the name Petersburg ELG.

Freeman's thesis is about St. Petersburg, but Naimark's study of police records reveals a vivid picture of revolutionary activity far and wide. Between 1887 and 1892 there were social democratic groups in Kharkov, Odessa, Kazan, Kiev, Riga, in the industrial towns of Ivanovo-Vosnesensk, Orekkhovo-Zuevo and in several backwaters. Lenin became a Marxist in Samara after participating in a *Narodnaia Volia* group in Kazan. In some places these circles had lasting influence. In Saratov in 1901-02, workers published ten issues of their paper, *Rabochaia Gazeta* (*Workers' News*) – a remarkable achievement – without any involvement by intellectuals. Semen Kanatchikov, who became a Bolshevik, later recalled their work with pride:

> From a *konspiratsiia* standpoint [meaning the ability to avoid arrest and maintain security], the printing and publication of *The Workers'*

---

31 Chapter three.
32 Naimark 1983, p172.
33 Chapter three.
34 Chapter three.

Newspaper were so well organised that, when many of us were later arrested, and the gendarmes charged some of us with direct or indirect participation in putting out the newspaper, they were incapable of proving anything. And today, when we find ourselves in possession of the archives of the gendarme office, we can see how little was revealed there about the identities of the paper's organisers and collaborators.[35]

A source of Marxist ideas in many of the provinces was the Polish Marxist organisation set up by Rosa Luxemburg, Leo Jogiches and Felix Dzierzynski. Jewish radicals often played a key role in promoting Marxism or versions of socialist ideas in Odessa, Ekaterinoslav, Kiev, Minsk and Vilna, reflected in the fact that while they were four percent of the population, they made up one-third of the delegates to the 1903 Congress of the Russian Social Democratic Labour Party (RSDLP). Tochiiskii ended up in Odessa in exile, as did many Jewish revolutionaries, where they played a role in organising circles.[36]

Poles, Ukrainians and other nationalities were prominent in circles in many provinces. This is not the place to go into all the detail that is available, but it is worth listing some that give a taste for the extent of organisations which identified as Social Democrats. There was a rich library of Social Democratic literature housed *inside* the Pavlov textile plant in a town in the Caucasus. The career of Nikolai Fedoseev is typical but also individual. In Kazan in the late 1880s, like most revolutionary students, he was interested in incorporating the ideas of Marx into a broad ideology to attract all currents of radicalism to a liberation movement. His group's main contribution to the development of a Marxist movement was its publication program. It assembled, according to Naimark, "one of the most impressive underground libraries in Russia"; including works of Marx and Engels, Plekhanov, Kautsky and Narodnik literature. In January 1892, Fedoseev, after becoming a Marxist during a 15-month stint in jail, was exiled to Vladimir, where he wrote programmatic pieces for a workers' circle in the Morozov textile factory, hammering one basic theme: the tsar is not a friend of the workers, but of the capitalist factory owners, who are determined to suppress every aspiration of workers.

In Kharkov and Rostov-on-Don, in Kazan and Vladimir, students and workers were debating, organising, making links, collecting libraries – eclectic to be sure, but which made Marxist literature available to those searching for political solutions to their problems. They often wrote programs to clarify

---

35   Lih 2008, pp450-1.

36   Naimark 1983, p210.

what they stood for. One such program in Kharkov began: "We are socialists, because we think that the best structure of society is one in which the means of production belong to the producers", and they described themselves as "revolutionaries". They agreed that political terror was justified as long as it "carries a propagandistic character"; in self-defence it was always permissible.

It is clear that the development of worker intellectuals depended heavily on the work of students. Their untiring efforts, punctuated by arrest and exile, helped disseminate the ideas not just of the ELG, but of all the Marxists of the time. In Moscow, we have the clearest profile of the role of students. In the early 1880s, a number of revolutionary students tried to set up groups in the military, one of the earliest being Vasilii Trifonovich Raspopin, a Moscow University student described as "one of the leading early propagandists of the works of Marx and Engels in Russia". The Society of Translators and Publishers translated Marxist and other socialist material because military officers didn't read other languages. Their translations, including Engels' *Condition of the Working Class in England* and his *Socialism, Utopian and Scientific* – two works that crop up regularly in libraries and parcels – were distributed in Kharkov, St. Petersburg and Warsaw as well as Moscow. Their own written material emphasised the working masses by 1884, and they were said to support and have good contact with the ELG.

Some of the students referred to the worker intelligentsia and talked of workers needing to develop their own conscious leadership. Another Shelgunov, this time N.N., made links with Blagoev in St. Petersburg in 1886. And at least one of these leaders attended the first congress of the Second International in 1889, returning with a pretty complete library of ELG works. In 1891, Brusnev went to Moscow to organise circles.

But, as elsewhere, the confusion between populism and Marxism would not be settled for some time. For instance, V.K. Kurnatovskii, while still a member of *Narodnaia Volia*, taught Marxism and later went on to be a leading Bolshevik. Throughout the late 1880s into the early 90s, there was regular contact with the Polish Marxists; representatives visited a small, reportedly "highly sophisticated" circle of Marxists at the Polytechnic school in Riga, returning with Plekhanov's writings. Out of this ferment, one of the workers' circles decided to form a Russian revolutionary party which included circles in the Caucasus and Kharkov, later establishing contact with Kiev circles. So when an envoy from the ELG arrived in April 1892, they had a ready audience for their material, although the three who met him (one of whom was Brusnev) typically did not reveal any names of their contacts; another reason why unearthing their history is so difficult.

While workers might be in separate circles, they quite unselfconsciously sought out students and intellectuals to provide leaders and written material.

In the 1870s, according to Plekhanov, Khalturin "willingly met students and tried to make their acquaintance, getting every kind of information from them and borrowing books. He often stayed with them until midnight… [T]here was always an element of irony in his relations with the students…he looked upon the [workers] as more solid, and so to speak, more natural revolutionaries", which was a common view.

Some historians assume that workers had separate circles because of hostility to the students and intellectuals. However, there is abundant evidence that the separate circles rarely implied ideological or social hostilities. Some students thought they were the theoreticians and workers the receivers of their wisdom. But the most common reason for workers to keep separate from intellectuals was the question of security. Often the police targeted the students. The circle Lenin joined in St. Petersburg in 1893 was limited to intellectuals because Radchenko imposed strict security which included staying apart from workers' circles.

A layer of worker intellectuals was gradually developed from the small, unstable and often unclear worker and student circles. It was into this layer, tiny as it was, of worker "intelligents", that Marxists had to intervene, which is a theme of Freeman's thesis. The role of Plekhanov and the ELG was critical in developing a tiny layer of student and worker intellectuals committed to genuine Marxism out of the confusing experiences of the newly-emerging working class and its efforts to find a voice, to say nothing of the muddle among anti-tsarist intellectuals. By the time Lenin joined the circles in St. Petersburg in 1893, this layer was a ready audience into which he made his own unique intervention.

Lenin's achievement in establishing the Bolsheviks was a final tribute to, but also only possible because of, the incredible suffering, sacrifice and resolute determination of astonishingly inspirational individuals and groups, some of whose names are recorded only in police files, some in memoirs. Most of them remain nameless. As Freeman argues: "In the subsequent growth of Marxism from a small number of isolated 'intelligents' to a significant layer of leading 'activists'…this defensive struggle by the exiled leaders was vindicated".[37]

Conclusion

The 1880s, usually seen as a desert for the Marxist movement in the Russian empire, was actually a time of clarification and tentative experience for a layer of students and workers groping their way towards political understanding.

---

37   Chapter nine.

Circles across the breadth of Russia, especially in industrial centres, were regularly impacted by the ideas of the ELG, Marx and Engels, Kautsky and the Polish Marxists. Workers constantly sought out revolutionary literature, and participated in all the debates among anti-tsarist intellectuals. As Offord says, it is clear from a range of sources that "by the 1890s hardly a provincial town of any importance was without its revolutionary propagandists and sympathisers". Students, Jewish intellectuals, Polish Marxists and worker leaders sent into exile took their ideas across the expanse of Russia. And through the circles, both of Narodniks and those groping for Marxism in the factories in all the major industrial centres, revolutionaries, he says,

> maintained a connection with the masses and thereby facilitated
> the building of a working-class movement when the pace of
> industrialisation quickened in the 1890s and when the growth of
> unrest among the urban workers made it more than ever desirable
> for the revolutionaries to cultivate them.[38]

Economism took its toll, becoming influential among the 400 members of the Union of Struggle for the Liberation of the Working Class of St. Petersburg which Lenin had helped establish. But a breakaway group, Workers' Flame, with 25 members, organised 18 circles and stayed in touch with Plekhanov between 1897 and 1900. The disintegration of the revolutionary intellectual circles and the decline in struggle led them to increasingly abstract propaganda, even to renouncing strikes. But in spite of incredible odds, there was some continuity through two decades of theoretical debates and struggles. In 1900, there was a number of propagandist groups composed of students and workers, which provided the base for Lenin's projected new paper when he again attempted to make contacts in St. Petersburg. Freeman says "1900-05 was [a period] of dogged struggle to re-establish a Marxist current intervening concretely within workers' struggles". With the formation of the pro-*Iskra* "Petersburg Committee", for the first time since the mid-1890s most Social Democrats were in one organisation, but they split in 1903 at the Second Congress of the RSDLP.

Lenin had to complete the task of clarifying the theory and political program of a genuinely revolutionary organisation against Plekhanov, and against Martov, who had been Lenin's collaborator in establishing *Iskra*. Lenin's polemics against these two and his determination to establish a serious, Russia-wide organisation of revolutionary worker intellectuals, was the final act in the establishment of the Bolsheviks. This project was not

---

38   Offord 1986, p165.

completed until they had been through the test of the 1905 revolution, the savage reaction which followed it, and their determined intervention in the upturn of struggle which followed. It was only in 1912 that the Bolsheviks can definitively be said to have established the kind of party Lenin had fought for, clearly separate from the Mensheviks.

The Bolsheviks had about 3-400 members of 800 Social Democrats in St. Petersburg at the time of Bloody Sunday in January 1905, probably no more than in 1895, but significantly clearer theoretically. They were still marked by the abstract propaganda common in the difficult times. "And yet", says Freeman, "for all these limitations, the Committee responded to the rising movement with an energy and enthusiasm that would allow it to advance and transform itself over the next two years".[39] Shelgunov, the long-term worker intellectual and labour movement leader, played a critical role at a joint meeting of Putilov and Semiannikov workers on 2 January 1905, representing the best of the results of two decades of what at times seemed fruitless endeavour.

Tom Freeman argues that while the crises of tsarism were relatively shallow, Marxism could only take the form of an abstract defence of ideas among an "intelligentsia of various class backgrounds". Prior to 1900, this "intelligentsia" in St. Petersburg was formed through the propaganda of dissident students and young professionals among a layer of worker "intelligents". In the re-formation of an orthodox movement after 1900 the central role of such elements was even more pronounced than it had been earlier.

> Thus social democratic organisation was centred on a number of
> prominent higher educational institutions, the secretary of the St.
> Petersburg Committee became the focus of student activity, and
> general political activity reflected the cycle of the student year. With
> class struggle and opportunities for concrete intervention limited,
> students predominated within the social democratic movement.[40]

Marxism could only take root on a mass scale in the context of a generalised crisis of tsarism. "Thus the struggle by Lenin, first against the Economists and then the Mensheviks, marked the culmination of a long process of theoretical clarification by identifiable exile leaders 'outside' the working class."[41]

If the far left is to rebuild after three decades of defeat and retreat in the West, and to break out of the margins in other countries, we will do well to take these lessons to heart and use them creatively in the modern context.

---

39   Chapter five.

40   Chapter five.

41   Chapter five.

References

Armstrong, Mick 2007, *From Little Things Big Things Grow*, Socialist Alternative (Australia).

Armstrong, Mick 2014, "A critique of the writings of Murray Smith on broad left parties", *Marxist Left Review*, 7, Summer.

Baron, Samuel H. 1963, *Plekhanov, the Father of Russian Marxism*, Stanford University Press.

Bloodworth, Sandra 2013, "Lenin vs 'Leninism'", *Marxist Left Review*, 5, Summer.

Bloodworth, Sandra 2014, "Lenin and a theory of revolution for the West", *Marxist Left Review*, 8, Winter.

Cliff, Tony 1986 [1975], *Lenin: Building the Party 1883-1914*, Bookmarks.

Harman, Chris 2010, "Lenin Rediscovered?", *Historical Materialism*, 18.

Lih, Lars 2008, *Lenin Rediscovered. What is to be Done? In Context*, Haymarket Books.

Naimark, Norman N. 1983, *Terrorists and Social Democrats. The Russian Revolutionary Movement Under Alexander III*, Harvard University Press.

Offord, Derek 1986, *The Russian Revolutionary Movement in the 1880s*, Cambridge University Press.

Shandro, Alan 2015 [2014], *Lenin and the Logic of Hegemony. Political Practice and Theory in the Class Struggle*, Haymarket Books.

Woods, Alan 1999, *Bolshevism. The Road to Revolution*, Wellred Books.

Chapter 1

INTRODUCTION: ECONOMIC DETERMINATION AND CONSCIOUS INTERVENTION IN MARXIST THEORY AND THE ADVANCE OF ST. PETERSBURG BETWEEN 1861 AND 1907

In the social production of their life, men enter into definite relations that are independent of their will, relations of production which correspond to a definite stage of development of their material productive forces. ... At a certain stage in their development the material forces of society come into conflict with existing relations of production, or – what is but a legal expression for the same thing – the property relations within which they have been at work hitherto. From forms of development of the productive forces, these relations turn into fetters. Then begins an epoch of social revolution.

> – Karl Marx, Preface to *A Contribution to the Critique of Political Economy.*[1]

The ruling ideas of each age have been the ideas of its ruling class.

> – Karl Marx, Friedrich Engels, *Manifesto of the Communist Party.*[2]

We have said that *there could not have been* social democratic consciousness amongst the workers. It could only have been brought to them from without. The history of all countries shows that the working class exclusively by its own effort is able to develop only trade union consciousness... The teachings of socialism, however, grew out of the philosophic, historical, and economic theories elaborated by educated representatives of the propertied classes, by the intelligentsia.

> – V.I. Lenin, *What is to be done?*[3]

---

1   Cited in Burns 1982, pp267-8.

2   Marx and Engels 1977, p57.

3   Lenin, *Collected Works* 1977-78 (hereafter *CW*), vol. 5, pp 347-531.

... nothing will ever compare in importance with the direct training that the masses receive in the course of the revolutionary struggle itself.

– V.I. Lenin, *What is Happening in Russia?*[4]

Workers have the class instinct, and, given some political experience, they pretty soon become staunch Social-Democrats.

– V.I. Lenin, *Speech on the Question of the Relations Between Workers and Intellectuals Within the Social-Democratic Organisations April 20* in *The Third Congress of the R.S.D.L.P.*[5]

These pairs of quotations embody an apparent contradiction in the Marxist understanding of working class consciousness and its transformation.[6] On the one hand Marxism analyses society as divided into classes in which the rulers ideologically dominate the ruled. Yet at the same time Marx analysed human history as a series of revolutions in which ruled classes rose against their rulers and imposed a new order on society. This thesis is a case study to show how Lenin resolved this apparent contradiction through the role of struggle between the classes of capitalism in transforming workers' consciousness.

By setting Lenin's comments on worker consciousness and party organisation within the context of the class struggle which they addressed, I seek to show their relation to Marx's fundamental conception of the working class as its own liberator. Due to its pivotal role, as well as the resource confines of a thesis, this case study is focused on the city of St. Petersburg[7] between 1861 and 1907 – its economy and labour movement, the Marxist current within that movement, Lenin's relations with that current, and finally the consequent conclusions he drew for workers' class consciousness as

---

4   ibid., vol. 8, p104.

5   ibid., vol. 8, p408.

6   This contradiction has been broadly recognised for some time, though how it can be resolved has been discussed at length only more recently. Thus the Marxist Chris Harman begins a significant article "There is a confusion at the very centre of Marxism" (Harman 1986, p3). Tony Cliff opens the conclusion of his discussion of the break between Lenin and Trotsky after the Second Congress of the RSDLP: "Marx stated that the emancipation of the working class is the act of the working class. At the same time he also stated that the prevailing ideas in every society are the ideas of the ruling class. There is a contradiction between these two statements, not in Marx's head but in social reality." (Cliff 1989, p77.) For a discussion of the problem of transition within a perspective that is not sympathetic to the political aims of Marx see Alan Carter, "Marxism/ Leninism: The Science of the Proletariat?", in *Studies in Marxism*, no. 1, 1994, pp125-41.

7   See for example the opinion of Lenin cited at the opening of the Introduction in Bondarevskaia et al. 1986, p5.

well as the party organisation of Marxists. Yet such an argument presumes a framework concerning the relation between economic determination and conscious intervention in the Marxist understanding of historical transformation. That basic framework is outlined here, together with some preliminary observations concerning the economic development of the Russian empire over the period of the study, as well as the role of St. Petersburg within that development. Finally the overall structure of the thesis is outlined.

Marx and Engels on determination

Among Marxists there would be widespread agreement with the view that Marx saw the overall sweep of human history, and hence the consciousness of humans within that sweep, as being ultimately determined by the advance of the instruments they collectively use to secure their physical survival.[8] This basic correspondence between the "forces of production", the "relations of production" humans enter into in that production, and the general pattern of human relations in society, was plainly asserted by Marx in the well-known declaration:

> In acquiring new productive forces men change their mode of production; and in changing their mode of production, in changing their way of earning a living, they change all their social relations. *The handmill* gives you society with a *feudal lord; the steam mill* society with an *industrial capitalist.* [my emphasis][9]

Most of those who call themselves Marxists would accept that the "absolute" determinism, which has usually been taken from this sweeping declaration, has a growing validity as the historical and geographical focus broadens.[10]

It would also be widely accepted that Marx's view emerged as the critique of a long predominant conservative materialism on the one hand, as well as the challenge to that view by the idealism of the Enlightenment and in particular Hegel's idealist version of the dialectic.[11] Within the former view human

---

8   See for example the discussion in Harman 1986, pp9-18 and Molyneux 1995, pp37-74.

9   Marx and Engels, *Collected Works* 1975– (hereafter *CW*), vol. 6, p166.

10   Here I am taking the meaning of "absolute" determinism from the discussion in Molyneux 1995, pp37-74, especially the section "Determinism: absolute and relative" pp41-6. I am also taking the meaning of "forces of production" and "relations of production" from the section "Forces and Relations of Production" in the same article, pp46-53. Additional discussion of these two conceptions and their relation in Harman1986, pp9-18.

11   For a discussion of Marx's relation to his philosophical forebears and particularly Hegel see Rees 1998, pp13-60, Jakubowski 1990, pp13-29 and Callinicos 1983, pp52-64. For Marx and

nature was regarded as negative and static due to its physical connection to nature. Within the latter, human nature was positive and changeable – but this change occurred through the mental activity of an elite among its members. Marx developed a materialist view that rejected both the earlier conservatism, but of even greater significance for the later development of Marxist ideas, as well as the argument of this thesis, also rejected the view that historical change could only result from the action or thought of an elite. For Marx such change must occur through the mobilisation of the majority of society, and involve humans changing themselves and hence the social structures through which they interacted.[12] Such mobilisation must be premised on the prior development of a productive base sufficient to sustain a new type of society.

> These most basic premises concerning human nature and historical change that were developed by Marx have generally not been controversial among subsequent Marxists. Yet such a broad framework provides little guidance to understanding the detail of transition between particular historical epochs. As such it provides little direct guidance to those Marxists seeking to understand the present transition from capitalism to socialism. In particular it leaves vague the organisational forms through which Marxists seek to facilitate that transition – what has become known as party organisation. The initial response of Marxists to this lack of clarity was to apply Marx's general principles very directly and crudely to the detail of mobilisation within the present transition.

Thus the predominating position of Marx's immediate heirs in the Second International became one of "absolute determination" in relation to the class struggle, based on an overriding primacy given to the "forces of production". Based mainly on the writings of the recognised theoretical heir to Marx and Engels, Karl Kautsky, as well as the practice of the first mass Marxist party, the German Social Democratic Party (SPD), this position set a framework that was formally accepted by almost all other Marxists from the mid-1890s until the First World War, including those within the Russian Social Democratic and Labour Party (RSDLP). Reflecting a prolonged period of economic expansion, as well as relative peace between the classes, the role of class struggle was steadily reduced for Kautsky, and socialism came to

---

Engels' critique of Hegel see Rees 1998, pp63-9.

12   This position basic to Marx's philosophy is evident in many of his early statements, most notably in the Theses on Feuerbach, which could be considered a summation of the position developed in The German Ideology (reprinted in Tucker 1978, pp143-5 and pp146-202 respectively).

be seen in practice as arising directly from the growing productive power of capitalism itself. This framework led most Marxists to see the rise of socialist consciousness as an inevitable process, and consequently confined their own role to that of abstracted propaganda divorced from direct intervention within the struggle of workers.

That Marx himself would not have drawn such passive conclusions from his own basic framework seems indisputable. "The history of all hitherto existing society is the history of class struggles"[13] opens the *Communist Manifesto*, Marx and Engels' best known political declaration. In the following paragraph they make clear that the outcome of these struggles was not predetermined but could be either "a revolutionary reconstruction of society at large, *or the common ruin of the contending classes*" [my emphasis]. Further, while they were still alive Marx and Engels expressed concern about the direction in which the German SPD was developing.[14] Thus Marx wrote in a private letter of Kautsky:

> He is a mediocrity with a small-minded outlook, superwise (only 26), very conceited, industrious in a certain sort of way, he busies himself a lot with statistics but does not read anything very clever out of them, belongs by nature to the tribe of philistines but is otherwise a decent fellow in his own way. I turn him over to friend Engels as much as possible.[15]

And Engels began his best known declaration against determinism in a letter to the German Bloch:

> According to the materialist conception of history, the *ultimately* determining element in history is the production and reproduction of real life. More than that Marx nor I have *never* asserted. Hence if somebody twists this into saying that the economic element is the *only* determining one, he transforms that proposition into a meaningless, abstract, senseless phrase. [my emphasis][16]

In the late 1870s Marx and Engels intervened strongly against the drift of the SPD following unification between their own supporters and the reformist

---

13 Marx and Engels 1977, p35.

14 Molyneux 1978, pp31-3.

15 Letter from Marx to his daughter Jenny, 11 April 1881, in Marx and Engels 1941, p389.

16 "To Joseph Bloch", in Tucker 1978, pp760-8.

Lassalleans in 1875.[17] Thus there was much in the writings of Marx and Engels that figures like Lenin and Luxemburg could draw on to support an emerging interventionist critique of the passivity that came to predominate within the Second International.

In the interpretation of his overall historical approach, Marx could be seen as formally opposing "absolute determination" and recognising the possibility of human stagnation, or even degeneration, as well as advance. Yet his views were developed as a critique of the elitism and voluntarist idealism of the Enlightenment, and particularly its culmination in the work of Hegel. Marx outlined his own ideas over a period when revolutionary struggles, indeed any struggles of a large scale, were separated by long passages of relative stability. This meant that the necessary role he gave to conscious intervention was not, and could not have been, fully consistent and thoroughgoing. Thus Marx's use of the term "inevitable" may be dismissed as "occasional rhetorical flourishes".[18] Yet at times the use of such a sweeping term appears considered and with a significant intent. Thus even in the *Manifesto* the first section concludes:

> What the bourgeoisie therefore produces, above all, are its own grave-diggers. *Its fall and the victory of the proletariat are equally inevitable.*[19] [my emphasis]

And at the end of the revolutionary wave that the *Manifesto* had foreshadowed, Marx commented in an editorial:

> A new revolution is possible only in consequence of a new crisis. *It is, however, just as certain as this crisis.*[20] [emphasis in original]

This partial inconsistency in Marx's understanding of the overall dynamic of the current historical transition became more marked as he narrowed his focus to the role of political leadership, as well as the transformation of workers' consciousness, within that transition. For it was precisely with this narrowing that the role of conscious intervention became greater, and hence there was a decreased predictability in the outcome of events. Thus Marx saw the emergence of an organised labour movement as flowing very directly from workers' experience of struggle, as he could not have witnessed the role of

---

17 Molyneux 1978, p33, Geary 1987, p1.

18 Rees 1998, p81.

19 Marx and Engels 1977, p48.

20 Marx and Engels, *CW*, vol. 10, p510.

palliatives, ideological influence and repression in containing that movement.[21]

This tendency toward excessive determinism in relation to the rise of a labour movement became more marked in relation to the broader consciousness and organisation embodied in a revolutionary party. Flowing from his basic materialism, as well as his inexperience with the development of workers' political organisation, Marx saw the party reflecting the class and, like the labour movement of which it was an indistinguishable part, flowing directly from the rising class struggle. Thus in the *Manifesto* he and Engels declared:

> Now and then the workers are victorious, but only for a time. The real fruit of their battle lies, not in the immediate result, *but in the ever expanding union of the workers...* This organisation of the proletariat into a class, *and consequently into a political party*, is continuously being upset again by the competition between the workers themselves. *But it ever rises up again, stronger, firmer, mightier.*[22] [my emphasis]

Such comments might also be dismissed as rhetoric written by Marx and Engels early in their political activity. Yet in relation to the First International as well as the German SPD Marx and Engels sought the broadest organisational unity across divergent political views. Indeed they refrained in principle from a formal organisational split despite the trenchancy of their critique of the views they opposed.[23]

The Second International

In their writings on historical transition Marx and Engels were immediately concerned to counter an elitist and voluntarist idealism. As a result, despite seeing this transition occurring overall through class struggle, they tended to an excessive determinism, particularly as their focus narrowed to the rise of the labour movement and the role within it of revolutionary leadership. Within the Second International this leaning to determinism broadened and hardened to the point of rejecting any role for conscious intervention in historical transition, and this ultimately led to a rejection of Marx's basic role for the class struggle. Thus for Karl Kautsky Darwin's supposedly peaceful evolutionism provided the model for transition,[24] while the more far-reaching

---

21   Molyneux 1978, p30.

22   Marx and Engels 1977, p45.

23   Molyneux 1978, pp27-8, 33.

24   Rees 1998, pp132-3, 137; Geary 1987, p106.

Bernstein[25] went so far as to reject the dialectical basis of Marx's philosophy as well as the revolutionary intent of the *Manifesto*.[26]

Within such an "absolutely determined" framework the advance of the labour movement and socialist consciousness became a process of uninterrupted, if perhaps gradual, accretion which reflected the irresistible advance of productive forces within capitalism. Thus deep economic crisis, generalised class struggle, and dramatic shifts in consciousness would not re-occur because capitalism had ameliorated its contradictions.[27] Such a view led the more consistent and thorough-going Bernstein to reject Marx's theory of crisis as well as the labour theory of value. The "centrist" Kautsky, who at this stage offered limited opposition to Bernstein in order to placate the left wing of the Second International, would later develop the theory of "ultra-imperialism".[28]

Ultimately Bernstein's determinism led him back to the idealism that Marx had originally broken from. For him the oppression of the working class under capitalism meant that it could no longer be the subject of a transition to socialism. Rather, that role was now to be taken by the educated members of other classes.[29] Such a conclusion could also be drawn from Kautsky's formulation of the educated bourgeois as the source of socialist theory. Corresponding with this return to historical transition as the result of the idealism of an elite was the indefinite "absolutely determined" passivity of the mass of the working class.[30] As one scholar of Kautsky has concluded:

> The proletariat invariably had to *wait* upon the laws of Capitalist development. In Kautsky's hands, therefore, Marxism was not, as it was for Lenin, "a guide to action" but rather a recipe for "inaction".[31]
> [italics in original]

25   On the differences between Kautsky and Bernstein, as well as their limited character, see Geary 1987, pp33-45, especially pp37-40, Rees 1998, pp138, 153.

26   Rees 1998, pp129, 130.

27   ibid., p153.

28   Geary 1987, pp52-9.

29   Rees 1998, pp133-4.

30   For some discussion of Kautsky's position see Rees 1998, pp139-40. An equation is usually made here with Lenin's own position prior to 1905. Indeed the Marxist writer John Molyneux uses the phrase "the 'Lenin-Kautsky' theory of 'separate development'" (Molyneux 1978, p49). That such an interpretation of Lenin's position is overdrawn will be argued in the next chapter.

31   Geary 1987, p106. See also a comparable citation from Anton Pannekoek, p71, and Franz Naumann, p92.

The passivity that flowed from an "absolutely determined" interpretation of Marx went furthest in relation to party organisation. If the growth of the labour movement in general was the determined consequence of the growth of capitalist productive power, then the growth of the party was a direct result of the movement's growth. Hence the growth of the party reflected the advancing consciousness of the class as a whole, and any need to deliberately intervene within that consciousness was eliminated. Flowing from the determined passivity of the class, the party would take over the capitalist state on behalf of the workers, rather than lead them in smashing that state.[32] As a result of these strategic conceptions Kautsky in practice always argued for the party to avoid decisive confrontation, and in particular to avoid the example of the "mass strike" from the Russian empire.[33]

An interventionist alternative to Second International determinism

The "absolute determinism" of the Second International was subjected to a trenchant critique by figures such as Luxemburg,[34] Trotsky,[35] Lukács[36] and Lenin,[37] who argued for the role of conscious intervention in determining the outcome of decisive class confrontations. For Marxists it could be seen to have been criticised with even greater force, indeed finality, by the subsequent history of the twentieth century.[38] That history could be analysed as a series of economic crises, local and generalised wars, and revolutionary upsurges, yet workers have yet to seize and hold power on a global scale in the way that Marx had envisaged.[39] Confronted with the evident inadequacy of the

---

32 Molyneux 1981, pp6-7, Geary 1987, pp18-9, 76-7.

33 Geary 1987, pp62-3, 65.

34 Through her writing against revisionism and in particular the pamphlet *Reform or Revolution*.

35 Most particularly through the example of his *History of the Russian Revolution*, and particularly his discussion of Lenin's role during October 1917.

36 Most particularly in Lukács 1971.

37 In particular through his philosophical writings in the wake of the beginning of World War I.

38 See for example comments by Molyneux in Molyneux 1995, p64.

39 I am using the phrase "Marx had envisaged" advisedly to deal with the question of the many states calling themselves socialist that were established in the wake of World War II. To summarily deal with an enormous issue I am following the view that these states represented not a transfer of power to workers but the centralisation of capital. Similarly, while the 1917 revolution did represent such a transfer of power, the consolidation of Stalin's rule represented the loss of that power and the consolidation of a new capitalist class based on direct control of the state rather than private or joint ownership of property. Such a view of a new class society,

"absolute determinism" of the Second International Marxists have attempted, and continue to attempt, to integrate an apparently necessary element of conscious intervention into the Marxist understanding of historical transition. Yet in doing so they have sought to avoid reverting to a pre-Marxist elitist or voluntarist idealism.[40] Drawing on these attempts, such an integrated model of historical transition will be outlined here, and forms the theoretical framework for the case study developed in this thesis.

An integrated Marxist understanding of historical transition must return to Marx's own starting point in the *Manifesto* – the basic role of struggle between classes in transforming consciousness and hence enabling that transition. Contrary to the passive conclusions flowing from the "absolute determinism" of the Second International, Marx himself argued that such a struggle had occurred continuously and pervasively since the inception of classes. While generally such struggles are only recognised when they rise to the point of threatening the power of an old ruling class, such highpoints draw on an unceasing though lesser underlying conflict. Yet to initiate and maintain such a lesser, supposedly "spontaneous" confrontation, no matter how limited that may be, still requires a conscious intervention against an order reflecting the will of the ruling class. Thus a case of conscious intervention often cited, that of Lenin in October 1917,[41] presupposed a chain of lesser "links" in which Lenin, other Bolsheviks and the leaders of the labour movement in general had intervened to promote a workers' struggle that had risen to the point of an assault on state power.

The development of the productive forces is most certainly the "necessary but not sufficient" condition for workers' struggle[42] and will have a profound influence on the probability, form and outcome of that struggle. Indeed the possibility of class consciousness, and therefore the scope for conscious intervention, must always be constrained by the material reality of the existing productive forces. Yet waging such a struggle is a conscious process by both ruled and rulers, and its outcome therefore cannot be determined in the way that the advance of the productive forces can. In setting this vital catalytic role for conscious intervention within the determination of history, Marxism remains a form of humanism – but one ultimately based on humans' potential to transform their material connection to the rest of nature, rather than the

---

or more precisely "state capitalism" has been developed by a number of writers, perhaps most systematically by Cliff in Cliff 1988.

40 For a limited discussion of reactions against determinism that did not avoid reverting to idealism see Harman 1986, pp7-9.

41 For example in Molyneux 1995, p65, Harman 1986, pp40-1.

42 Molyneux 1995, p52.

resolution of contradiction through the thought of an elite.[43]

A consciously-led class struggle must be central to an integrated Marxist understanding of historical transition because, contrary to the implicit conclusion of Second International "absolute determinism", established ruling classes do not disperse or transform themselves in response to the advance of "productive forces". Rather, the struggle they themselves had earlier waged as a class rising to power is continued in the consolidation of their rule against the remnants of the defeated ruling class. Once consolidated that rule is again defended against new classes that rise with the further advance of "productive forces". To make a conscious intervention in defence of their own power and privilege the new ruling class creates a "superstructure",

> political forms of the class struggle and its results, to wit:
> constitutions established by victorious classes after a successful
> battle, etc., juridical forms, and even the reflexes of these actual
> struggles in the brains of the participants, political, juristic,
> philosophical theories, religious views and their further development
> into systems of dogmas.[44]

That superstructure is normally associated with the repressive arm of the state, but as this citation suggests, the institutions which take a role in the ideological domination of the working class can extend far beyond those of direct physical repression. For a period the productive forces can advance relatively unfettered by the new relations of production. Consequently class conflict is relatively limited, and this struggle can be contained through the largely peaceful imposition of ruling class ideology by the "superstructure".

After a certain period, however, the new relations of production begin to severely hinder any further advance in productive forces. As a result wholly ideological methods prove to be less effective in containing the increasingly generalised struggle that is precipitated by this stagnation. Consequently the superstructure is forced to augment such "peaceful" methods with the direct physical repression of the forces rising against it, and particularly those elements consciously intervening to cohere these forces. As the struggle broadens and deepens, the clarity of conscious intervention from both ruled and ruling classes takes on greater significance in determining its outcome.[45] Indeed it is possible for the rising class to be defeated for a shorter or longer

---

43   Compare with the absence of a role for human initiative in Kautsky's Marxism (Geary 1987, pp91, 93, Rees 1998, p140).

44   "To Joseph Bloch", in Tucker 1978, p780.

45   For the understanding of this point by Luxemburg, see Rees 1998, p160.

period[46] as the now established ruling class may inadvertently or deliberately retard the progress of, or even destroy part of, its productive base in order to defeat the class rising against it. Thus it is only as the framework becomes more global and historical that human advance can be seen as becoming more determined.[47]

The necessary role of conscious intervention can be seen in the rise of the labour movement against the current capitalist ruling class – a class that Marx himself saw as the most dynamic, centralised and flexible in history.[48] The conscious intervention to launch the labour movement is premised upon and conditioned by certain necessary material prerequisites – most notably the rise of industry, the concentration of workers and the population in general, as well as the establishment of extensive means of communication. The conscious intervention of those confronting capitalism, as well as the response it receives from the rest of those exploited within the system, ultimately reflects the hindrance of the rising productive forces by the current relations of production. Initially the intervention will be narrow and the response limited, due to the as yet mild fettering of productive forces. Consequently the labour movement will be contained relatively easily – largely by ideological means through the various arms of the "superstructure". Yet as the fettering becomes more severe the conscious intervention of labour leaders,[49] as well as the response it evokes among workers in general, becomes more general and the reply of the "superstructure" must become more directly repressive.

Whether the labour movement achieves the seizure of state power depends on how clearly and widely class consciousness develops within it. For this reason the ideas and effectiveness of those consciously intervening to lead the labour movement now decides the outcome of the workers' struggle. The workers may be victorious if their leaders are sufficiently clear and concrete in their revolutionary understanding. But they may also be defeated by the capitalist "superstructure" if their leadership is confused, uneven or vacillating.[50] Thus the germination and growth of a clearly revolutionary party

---

46   Harman 1986, p18.

47   Harman 1986 makes the point that while in most cases pre-capitalist ruling classes were able to suppress those rising against them, the fact that a breakthrough was made in at least one case led to eventual domination of the world by capitalism.

48   For example, "The bourgeoisie, historically, has played a most revolutionary part", Marx and Engels 1977, p38, as well as subsequent pages to p42.

49   Stated here as a determined fact. Actually this generalisation is itself a deliberate process of generalising from only certain experience under capitalism – that of struggle (Harman 1986, p37).

50   Harman 1986, p37.

is always the vital task of Marxists.

This model of the relation between economic determination and conscious intervention can be well fitted to the case of the labour movement in St. Petersburg between the so called "Emancipation" of 1861 and the "Stolypin coup" in 1907. Over that time industrial production throughout the Russian empire, and particularly in St. Petersburg, expanded enormously and the material preconditions for the formation of a labour movement were clearly evident. Yet when this movement was formed it was through the conscious intervention of individuals who acted on their own, as yet incomplete, understanding of the contradictions within the system. Up to 1905 these crises were comparatively mild and the labour movement could be contained by the tsarist "superstructure" through palliatives combined with a pervading though not extreme repression.[51]

The far greater movement after 1905 resulted from a more generalised conscious intervention that responded to the qualitatively deeper crisis that emerged from 1900. Yet, without a sufficiently large and experienced Marxist current within that labour leadership, workers failed to overcome tsarism and seize power, despite their evident potential to do so. The result was a massive setback for the labour movement, as the tsarist "superstructure" responded to this rising with overwhelming physical repression in the hope of securing its rule from any future threat.

Lenin's focus on cohering a consistently revolutionary party reflected his understanding of the role of consciousness in determining the outcome of this class struggle. Thus his formulations on organisation were themselves a conscious intervention aimed at realising the potential for the development of such a general political leadership.

1861-1907: The development of capitalism in the Russian empire as part of the emerging imperialist system

The apparently irrepressible advance of productive forces over the nineteenth century could appear to validate determinism, and by the mid-1890s almost all Marxists, including Lenin, formally accepted such a framework.

The development of industrial capitalism in Russia, for a determinist view not only a necessary but also a sufficient condition for the ultimate establishment of socialism, certainly occurred to a significant extent over the

---

51 Speaking here relative to cases of the repression of labour movements in the fascist regimes over the interwar years such as Germany, Italy and Spain, as well as the treatment of members of these movements by authoritarian regimes such as those in Latin America.

century. Yet the external stimulus [of arms competition] for this development led to a pattern of industrialisation markedly different to what could have been expected by an "absolutely determinist" interpretation of Marx.

In the earlier developing capitalist countries industrial development was promoted by a growing class of small proprietors which was driven to carry out sweeping economic and political changes. In the Russian empire this development was sponsored by an old ruling class fearful of losing its international position, but also at times even more fearful of threats to its rule from internal dissent. These threats flowed from the concentration of population and widespread communication necessary for industrial production, and had been amply demonstrated by worker uprisings in Europe, most particularly the 1848 revolutions. The nobility of the empire wished to hinder the rise of productive forces in order to maintain the archaic base of their power[52] but the advance of these forces in other powers meant that they could not do so.

Caught between imminent threats external and internal, the nobility vacillated and pursued policies concerning industrialisation that reflected whichever particular threat was felt to be greatest.[53] Consequently industrialisation advanced intermittently rather than continuously, and was associated with relatively little change within the economic and political organisation of the empire. Over the first half of the nineteenth century, while the external threat was present it was far outweighed by the internal threat, and the state pursued an extremely conservative industrial policy.[54] As a result, growth in industrial capacity, although significant in absolute terms, still fell far short of any qualitative advance.[55] That advance is usually seen as occurring in the wake of the defeat in Crimea, and being focused in particular on the freeing of the serfs in 1861.[56] Yet for the 25 years following the Emancipation the growth of industry continued to be stunted by the predominance of the

---

52   See for example the comment in Bater 1976, pp58, 65.

53   Davidheiser 1990, pp115-19, 126-32, 143-5, Gatrell 1994, p14, Blackwell 1968, pp262, 272-3, Gatrell 1986, pxi, Blackwell 1970, p22.

54   See in particular the attitude of the most prominent conservative of the period, the minister of finances over the reign of Nicholas I, Count E.F. Kankrin (Blackwell 1968, pp140-3, Guroff 1970, pp25-7).

55   See for example the table "Part 2: Russian Industry in the Early Nineteenth Century" (Blackwell 1968, pp423-6). Falkus 1972, pp31-43, outlines the growth that did occur over the period, though noting that this was largely focused on consumer industries in comparison to the Witte period and makes the significant point that over this period the empire fell further behind its rivals.

56   In fact the Emancipation was a complex and contradictory measure reflecting its contradictory motives (Blackwell 1970, p25).

fear from the internal threat.[57]

This relative stagnation gave way to a fifteen-year period of qualitative advance from 1885 that was particularly marked during the tenure of Sergei Witte as finance minister.[58] This breakthrough was both necessitated and facilitated by the concentration of capital and its association with nation states that has been analysed within the Marxist tradition as the theory of imperialism.[59] The consequent rise in international tensions, embodied in an accelerated arms race and acquisition of colonies, dramatically shifted the balance within the nobility toward industrialisation. At the same time loan capital now available from the main powers, particularly France,[60] provided the means for the establishment of a world-class arms industry.[61]

This externally motivated industrialisation had by the turn of the century established in the empire an economy and society that, perhaps more than any other of the time, confounded an "absolute" determinist expectation of a broad and consistent advance through capitalism towards socialism.[62] The empire's "combined and uneven"[63] development had spawned an arms industry containing the largest and most modern factories in the world, yet this industry was juxtaposed with an agriculture that was among the most backward. The population was dispersed between urban centres where the cultural level was among the highest in the world,[64] together with a vast rural hinterland where the great majority of the population languished in a

---

57   This conservatism was usually expressed by a preference for agriculture over industry in state policy (Davidheiser 1990, pp92-5, 147-50).

58   Tugan-Baranovsky 1970, pp274-7; Davidheiser 1990, p152; Falkus 1972, pp44-6, 51-2, 61-74; Guroff 1970, pp16, 34-6.

59   A position probably best known due to its advocacy by Lenin in his very significant pamphlet *Imperialism, the Highest Stage of Capitalism*, written in the first half of 1916 and published in mid-1917. A more comprehensive and less polemical presentation by the theorist with which the theory has been most closely identified could be found in Bukharin 1976.

60   Von Laue 1963, pp105-106. On the inflow of capital see Guroff 1970, p58, Gatrell 1986, pp222-8.

61   For the relation between the empire and international business cycles see Tugan-Baranovsky 1970, p277. For the role of rail transport see Gatrell 1986, pp150-4.

62   For a summary of Russia's contradictory status as an industrial power see Falkus 1972, pp10-13.

63   The term is taken from the best known analysis of the empire's pre-revolutionary development by Leon Trotsky. For an outline of this analysis see Trotsky 1982.

64   Guroff 1970, pp46, 82-6, 86-90 (Guroff notes that the literacy rate for men in St. Petersburg in 1910 over six years of age was 86.3 percent, for those between 12 and 19, 94.4 percent and for women of the same age, 74.3 percent, pp90-5. In the section "The Growth of Available Publications" he notes that the empire became the greatest publisher of book titles over a period of 20 years. Production rose from 18 million copies in 1887 to 58 million copies in 1901.)

backwardness that had not changed for centuries.[65]

Perhaps of greatest significance for the development of Marxism in the empire, the parliamentary and civil avenues, central to the reformist political practice flowing from a determinist interpretation of Marx, were almost completely absent. The nobility remained deeply apprehensive about the internal threat that industrialisation posed – even as its priority shifted to meeting the external threat constituted by the other powers. As a result the empire had the most pervasive surveillance and repression of civil society of all the great powers at the time. The private bourgeoisie had earlier been both the base and result of the rise of capitalism, and consequently the vehicle for the establishment of democracy. Yet the late development of capitalism in the empire stunted the growth of this class, and it was incapable of playing its former historical role. Flowing from this weakness it was the uncontested Marxist orthodoxy until the late 1890s that democracy could only be won by a revolutionary movement in which the working class took the leading role. Lenin's distinctive contribution on the party was germinated in response to the Economists, who opposed this tradition in a polemic where the implications flowing from a determinist view were very sharply drawn.

If the uncertain though relatively unhindered advance of the nineteenth century might have been drawn on to support a determinist view, then the early years of the new century starkly demonstrated the limitations of that position. For in 1900 economic growth came to an abrupt halt and the empire entered a nine-year period of decline and stagnation.[66] With the onset of this crisis society did indeed enter an "epoch of social revolution" as Marx would have prophesied. However, contrary to a determinist view, the result of this turbulence was not the smooth displacement of the old order by the rising workers and peasants. Rather, the tsarist state, after having been shaken by a series of blows of increasing magnitude, survived with its power almost entirely undiminished and the methods of its rule largely unchanged. It was in this context of assault by, and then repulsion of, a rising workers' movement that the political and organisational consequences of the determinist view, as well as Lenin's interventionist reaction against it, received their initial development.

Thus although the first major crisis of tsarism is usually seen as opening with the massacre of Bloody Sunday in January 1905, this event was in fact the culmination of five years of growing tension and spasmodic protest beginning with student and worker protests in early 1901.[67] The police-sponsored loyal trade

---

65   For a summary of this contradictory development see Blackwell 1970, pp42-54.

66   Tugan-Baranovsky 1970, pp289, 306-307, Falkus 1972, pp75-84, Gatrell 1986, p169, Guroff 1970, p50.

67   Davidheiser 1990, pp320, 338, 340, Von Laue 1983, p249.

union movement was an attempt to contain this rising wave of struggle within non-revolutionary channels, as in part also was the Russo-Japanese War. The weak position of the tsarist state relative to its rivals meant that these measures could not contain either the economic crisis or the movement of protest – indeed they exacerbated both.[68] Thus the war was lost, fundamentally undermining the authority of the tsar among all sectors of society, particularly the bourgeoisie and middle class. And the loyal trade union movement would go on to burst its bounds and become the vehicle for a perilous challenge to the power of the tsarist state. During 1905 this challenge grew to the point of a general strike in October which induced the granting of significant democratic concessions.

Such steps towards a democratic bourgeois state containing a vibrant workers' movement might have been seen as powerfully vindicating a determinism in relation to the rise of the class struggle and the labour movement. Yet the overwhelming, and for a period successful, measures taken by tsarism to crush the movement rising against it contradict that view. Indeed as the threat to it became greater, tsarism responded with greater and greater force rather than submit. Thus while the response to the strikes of the late 1890s was mass arrests and exile, the revolt of the early 1900s was met with even broader acts of repression.

Consequently Lenin's views on party organisation should not be seen as a conspiratorial alternative to Marxism reflecting conditions that were entirely peculiar to the Russian empire. Rather, they represented an attempt to develop an organisational response to the repression of the workers' movement by one of the major powers as it sought to preserve its position within the imperialist system. That workers' movement itself was not peculiar to the empire, but rather the result of production for an arms race in which all imperialist powers competed. The Russian empire was certainly the most repressive of these powers, but this repression was shared to a significant extent by all the imperialist powers of the time. Thus in the concentration and modernity of its industry, as well as the lack of civil society, the empire represented the extreme point of an essential continuity with the other powers, not a qualitative break from them.

The development of St. Petersburg – focus of contradiction in the Russian empire

If the Russian empire as a whole constituted an extreme case of the contradictions within imperialism, then the city of St. Petersburg in turn represented the focus of these contradictions within the empire.[69] Within

---

68   Davidheiser 1990, pp292-306.

69   For an account of the similarities and differences with the rest of the empire see Bonnell

a determinist framework, St. Petersburg, as the capital, would have been expected to reflect and promote the advance of the empire as a whole. Indeed periods of industrial growth across the empire resulted in disproportionate advances in the city. Yet this advance of the capital reflected above all the diplomatic ambitions and consequent military needs of the tsarist court,[70] leading to a drain of resources from the rest of the empire which deepened its rural crisis. Thus St. Petersburg's development aggravated the contradictions within tsarism, laying the basis for a generalised outburst of revolt, rather than a consistent transition to democracy and subsequently socialism.

The contradictory nature of St. Petersburg's development can be seen in the internal results of its growth. A determinist view would have suggested a fairly uniform advance in the conditions of its workers and urban poor within the context of a general rise in material and cultural circumstances. In fact while some advance did occur, this led to stark and growing disparities in the circumstances of the city's population, and particularly within the working class districts.

As its diplomatic and military centre, the advance of the productive forces in St. Petersburg was greater than in any other part of the empire.[71] Such an advance involved the attraction of the youngest and most flexible sector of the empire's population,[72] and as a result the city comprised a growing proportion of young single males.[73] Of most significance for the formation of a labour movement, the proportion of workers in the population grew dramatically.[74] Important for the formation of a conscious leadership within that movement, the greatest growth was among metal workers,[75] who were the most skilled, best paid[76] and most literate sector of the working class.[77] This growth in the number of metal workers is probably the best known and most commented upon feature of St. Petersburg's industrial advance, and flowed directly from the escalating arms race at the heart of imperialism. It was the pressure of that race that resulted in the founding and rapid growth of a number of major metal plants producing weapons and other needs of

---

1983, pp20-72. On the immediate role of the Crimean War, see Bater 1976, pp85-7.

70   Industry "born in the 'fire of war'", Bater 1976, pp40, 42.

71   For the initial impact of the Emancipation on St. Petersburg see Bater 1976, pp85-149.

72   The city grew by 11.3 percent in the 1880s, from 928,000 to 1,033,600, but by 39.3 percent in the 1890s, from 1,033,600 to 1,439,130 (McKean 1990, p3). Kochakov (ed.) 1956, vol. 2, pp175-7, 216.

73   McKean 1992, p19, Kochakov (ed.) 1956, vol. 2, pp173, 188-91, Bater 1976, pp169-71.

74   Surh 1989, p11, Kochakov (ed.) 1956, vol. 2, pp77, 188-91.

75   Surh 1989, p20, Kochakov (ed.) 1956, vol. 2, pp84, 94-107.

76   Surh 1989, pp23-5.

77   Hogan 1993, pp12-24.

national defence, principally the railway system. These plants came, by the turn of the century, to dominate the peripheral working class districts of St. Petersburg. Their workforces proved capable of mobilising the whole working class of the districts where they were located, and they were consequently pivotal to the revolutionary movement in the twentieth century.[78] In this, they most certainly fulfilled the fears of the nobility reluctant to establish industry, as well as the hopes of all those who wished for a radical transformation of the empire.

These changes in the size and composition of St. Petersburg's population were reflected in the geography of the city, producing a layout in which the realities of class became increasingly evident. Thus, around a sumptuous central district focused on a series of public buildings lay an array of vast working class slums focused on huge factories.[79] The size of these slums grew disproportionately with the general growth of the city, and continued to grow during the economic crisis after 1900 as ruined peasants continued more than ever to flood into the city.[80]

This geographical polarisation along class lines was made more apparent by the role of physical barriers in dividing the city – the Neva river to the north of the central district and a band of undeveloped land to its south. It was made more complete by poor communication outside the city centre, that isolated the working class districts from each other as well as the centre. Certainly, substantial numbers of workers did live in the central districts, but these tended to be workers outside the core of the working class, like artisans, employees of small firms and servants.[81] The sharpness of St. Petersburg's geographical polarisation had profound consequences for workers' consciousness, the forms of worker protest, and the development of revolutionary organisation. Thus the first Russian Revolution was sparked by attempts to march from the peripheral workers' districts to the centre of the city. And it was in the oldest and largest of these districts, the Nevskii side, that Lenin began his career as a propagandist among workers.

Even in the period of relative advance over the second half of the nineteenth century, factors which could hinder any straightforward advance by workers to socialism were clearly evident. The nature of St. Petersburg as an outpost of advanced industrial development in a predominantly archaic

---

78   Surh 1989, p8.

79   Hogan 1993, pp35-8, Zelnik 1971, pp59-61, 215-20. For the particularly marked class divisions prior to 1850 see Bater 1976, p74. For an outline of the development of these trends see Bater 1976, pp150-212.

80   Surh 1989, p11.

81   McKean 1992, p38.

rural empire made it especially vulnerable to the world business cycle. Thus while the city made a steady if unspectacular advance from 1861 to 1873[82] the crisis beginning that year and lasting until the early 1880s severely hindered its metal-working industry. Indeed a number of the most important plants became insolvent and had to be reconstituted with foreign assistance. In 1891 Sergei Witte was appointed minister of finance following an economic crisis characterised by famine in the countryside and great disquiet in the city.[83]

Within a determinist interpretation of Marx, the growing proportion of workers in the population would have reflected the inexorable advance of productive forces, and would have been sufficient in itself for the advance to socialism. Yet while the proportion of workers grew, so also did those members of the "superstructure" charged with defending the old order. Thus a number of elite army regiments were located in the city, the number of police per inhabitant grew dramatically, and in addition a very substantial body of caretakers, providing support to the police, was established.[84]

Within a determinist view, the advance to socialism occurred through a relatively smooth transition in the relations between the classes. Yet in St. Petersburg relations both in general society and on the factory floor were on the whole fixed in the authoritarian paternalism of Russia's feudal past.[85] The city formed one of the most advanced elements in the world's industrial system, yet the general backwardness of the empire as a whole constrained the nature of social relations within it.

Within a determinist understanding of the rise of labour, the working class should have grown in cohesion and uniformity as it grew in size. Yet St. Petersburg's dramatic and externally-stimulated growth produced a rather different result. The increase in worker numbers occurred through waves of immigration from the countryside and the level of skill, literacy, and payment of workers was closely related to their length of time in the city. Reflecting these waves was a clearly marked hierarchy within the working class which has been a major focus of study within the Soviet literature.[86] Thus over the 1890s an "elite" of young male[87] skilled, literate[88] and well paid workers

82   Zelnik 1971, pp204-15.

83   Hogan 1993, p25.

84   Kochakov (ed.) 1956, vol. 2, pp224-7. This role of the state, especially the collaboration between the police and caretakers, was very marked in the city by the early 1800s; Bater 1976., p82.

85   Hogan 1993, pp32-5.

86   McKean 1992, pp25-6.

87   Surh 1989, p31; Zelnik 1971, pp49, 53.

88   Surh 1989, p32.

emerged and grew in the large strategic metal plants.[89] It was the political consciousness of this "elite" that was pivotal to the strategic discussions on party organisation by Lenin and other Social Democrats, just as it was central to the considerations of the harassed ruling class attempting to contain the revolutionary threat.

Too much can be made of the separation of this "elite" from the working class as a whole. Thus, while there was a difference in the experience and conditions with other workers, these differences were ones of degree within the same class position. The "elite" lived alongside and worked near the "grey masses" while still maintaining a connection with, as well as an awareness of, conditions throughout the empire as a whole.[90] This awareness impelled the "elite", or "cadre", as they have been called, to lead all workers from the districts in which they lived.

If the last half of the nineteenth century could raise the prospect of an indefinitely advancing capitalism for those holding a determinist view of Marxism, then the first decade of the twentieth century must have severely undermined confidence in such an approach. For while the boom of the 1890s made a disproportionate impact on St. Petersburg and its working class, this was also the case for the slump following the turn of the century. Of great political significance, it was the advanced centres of the metal worker "elite" that suffered disproportionately.[91] Thus in the immediate wake of the slump the leading metal plants like the Putilov plant[92] and Nevskii Iron and Steel sacked one-third of their workforce. For those "cadre" workers who kept their jobs, conditions and dignity declined or stagnated after having significantly advanced in the 1890s. This unemployment and deterioration in shopfloor conditions also occurred, if to a somewhat less marked extent, throughout the rest of industry and in particular within the textile industry. Conditions in the working class districts were made even more severe by an influx of ruined peasants fleeing famine in the countryside.[93] In the first decade of the new century, then, the city was ripe for an explosion of revolt which very quickly came.

Boom conditions would not resume until 1909. While most metal plants recovered their previous production levels and workforce size from the start of the Russo-Japanese War, there was not to be a significant advance. With

---

89   Kochakov (ed.) 1957, vol. 3, p14.

90   Surh 1989, pp10-20, 35.

91   Hogan 1993, pp48-51; Kochakov (ed.) 1957, vol. 3, pp9-10, 16, 37.

92   Kochakov (ed.) 1957, vol. 3, p20.

93   Surh 1989, p11; Kochakov (ed.) 1957, vol. 3, pp105, 111.

the end of the war, a new slump began in 1906 and deepened in 1907.[94] Consequently, apart from the year of worker offensive in 1905, working class conditions continued to stagnate or decline.[95]

Advance of the labour movement in St. Petersburg – a necessary role for conscious intervention

This thesis takes the case of the labour movement in St. Petersburg between 1861 and mid-1907 to show how the rise of workers towards power both requires and develops the conscious intervention of those attempting to lead this rise. The role of that intervention is analysed at three levels of generalised understanding of class relations. At the most basic level of worker self-consciousness, the formation of a labour leadership in the ebb and flow of industrial struggle between 1861 and 1907 is outlined. Within this labour leadership the growth of a Marxist current, and eventually a Social Democratic party, reflected a broader understanding of class society. Finally Lenin's intervention on party organisation represents a further degree of generalisation aimed at enabling the intervention of this current within the labour movement. These three levels of understanding were necessarily interrelated. Thus the advance of the "productive forces" of industry had been the precondition for the establishment and development of a labour movement, and that movement in turn provided the base for the Marxist current, which was the audience for Lenin's intervention on party organisation.

The conversion of the post-1900 economic downturn into a full blown political crisis on Bloody Sunday marked a turning point in the development of the labour movement, and hence the role of conscious intervention within it. Prior to that date economic crisis in the imperial economy had been relatively shallow and brief, with the result that the class struggle remained largely sectional and spasmodic. Consequently the labour movement organised only spasmodically and its leadership was confined to a small section of what was termed the "worker intelligentsia" – a substantial proportion of the metal worker "elite" that educated themselves through a voluntary education system. In these circumstances Marxism as a current was generally confined to an isolated and small section of these leading "intelligents". Its intervention was limited to theoretically defending the Marxist vision of the labour movement against threats from radical liberalism and revisionism. Lenin's comments on party organisation at this time were an intervention among the Marxists aimed at ensuring success in this difficult defensive task. As such they argued for the

---

94 McKean 1992, p7.

95 McKean 1992, pp12, 32, 35.

party as a politically clear and rigorously centralised "worker intelligentsia".

In the intractable and generalised crisis of the "superstructure" following Bloody Sunday, there was a qualitatively greater scope for conscious intervention. In these circumstances a large layer of "activists" cohered around the "intelligents" who had formerly led the labour movement, and this "activist" leadership was able to lead workers as a whole in radical struggles. Associated with this transformation in the general labour leadership was a comparable growth of the Marxists to become the most combative and irreconcilable section of these leading "activists". Responding to these developments Lenin made a radical shift in his own intervention and sought to have his supporters intervene wholeheartedly and effectively in this new context. As such Lenin's comments now posed the party as a tactically flexible and structurally open formation of "activists".

In accordance with the structure of this argument, the thesis is divided into six substantive chapters following a discussion of the Western literature dealing with Lenin's views on party organisation. The first two chapters outline the history of the labour movement in St. Petersburg. Here the case is made for the development of the labour leadership as a section of the "intelligentsia" prior to 1905, and subsequently a layer of "activists" after Bloody Sunday. The second pair of chapters conforms to this historical schema, and outlines the emergence and development of Marxism as an organised presence in St. Petersburg. It shows how the transition from "intelligents" to "activists" in the general labour leadership also occurred among the Bolshevik supporters of Lenin's interventionist Marxism. The final two substantive chapters discuss Lenin's comments on party organisation before and after Bloody Sunday and, while showing a continuity in the task of conscious intervention, relate the contrast in his comments on structure and consciousness to the radical shift in the context of workers' struggle.

In conclusion, a study that is grounded in the empirical base of Soviet labour history, recently available archival materials, and the studies of Western "social historians", can vindicate an interventionist interpretation of Marx's understanding of historical advance. The role of conscious leadership in the advance of the labour movement, as well as the development of a Marxist party within that movement, can be convincingly demonstrated for the case of St. Petersburg between 1861 and 1907. Such a demonstration stands against the view, now very prevalent, that Marx's conception of class and workers' class consciousness has been refuted by historical experience. Finally this recognition of the role of conscious leadership leads Lenin's views on party organisation to be seen as enabling the intervention of Marxists within workers' struggle and the labour movement. As such it can be shown that Lenin's views always related to the current workers' struggle, and sought to advance that struggle to the point of power rather than incorporate the labour movement within the ambit of a new ruling elite. As a result those views do not mark a break with Marx's fundamental purpose of workers' self-emancipation, but only with an element of determinism in Marx's understanding of the rise of class consciousness in workers' struggle. The changes in Lenin's position on workers' consciousness and party structure do not flow from an inconsistency in his position, but rather represent an advance in the Marxist understanding of the contradictory nature of workers' consciousness within capitalism.

Chapter 2

ECONOMIC DETERMINATION AND CONSCIOUS INTERVENTION IN RECENT WESTERN SCHOLARSHIP ON LENIN

Western literature on the revolutionary experience of the Russian empire, and Lenin's role in particular, has always been strongly influenced by broader political circumstances. This was particularly so over the early period of the Cold War, when theoretical partisanship reflected a more general polarisation in international relations. In such circumstances, a mainstream consensus hardened that Lenin was an authoritarian in his aims, as well as a conspiracist in his methods. The sources of these traits were largely traced to the authoritarianism of the Russian empire, as well as the terrorist methods of those opposing its ruling order.[1]

From the early 1960s this international polarisation began to ease, and from the mid-1960s, for a period of perhaps ten years, most Western governments were subject to repeated challenges from movements of protest. Throughout this period of turmoil, and particularly during its opening phase, these protests were often focused on or initiated within the university. As a result an integral part of their development was a critical re-examination of the mainstream view throughout the social sciences and humanities, with a marked shift in sympathy towards a radical, if not a fully Marxist, viewpoint.[2] Probably the most significant result of this radical shift within the field of "Soviet Studies" was a critical re-examination of the revolutionary history of the Russian

---

1   The existence of such a predominating position appears to be widely accepted, especially by those critical of it. See for example Liebman 1975, pp19-22. The existence of such a position and its pre-World War II roots is probably put with most force in Harding 1976, pp366-83. Perhaps the best known advocates of the mainstream position, though clearly not its pioneers, have been the historian Richard Pipes (Pipes 1990) and the political scientist Leonard Schapiro (Schapiro 1970).

2   Perhaps the best known, though by no means the only, attempt to collate this radical critique of the mainstream was the collection of articles and bibliography *Counter Course*, edited by Trevor Pateman (Pateman 1972). A more clearly Marxist attempt at a critique of the mainstream was made by the British academic Martin Shaw (Shaw 1975).

empire.[3] This "social history" distanced itself from the assumptions that underlay the earlier mainstream consensus, and appeared to be influenced by Marxism.[4] For writers adopting this approach the revolutionary movement was seen far more as a genuine mass revolt against an authoritarian regime, and consequently consistent with a purported basic purpose of human emancipation in Marx.[5]

The work of these "social historians" could allow the circumstances within which Lenin intervened to be seen more broadly than they had been by the mainstream – he could now be analysed as a participant within a genuine mass labour movement rather than as a purely conspiratorial figure within the context of unchallenged authoritarianism.[6]

From about 1975, the broader political challenge to Western governments receded; and associated with this retreat the critical wave of writing within the

---

3   Although the relation between historical study and general world events appears obvious from publication dates, as well as in some cases non-academic political publishing, it is only Smith who explicitly identifies the "social historians" as "profoundly shaped by the political and intellectual spirit of 1968" (Smith 1994, p564).

4   While the label of Marxism was utilised by the mainstream in the critique of the critical "social historians" it seems clear that most were not consistently and rigorously Marxist in their analysis. Thus in a review article written in 1994 a major US figure, Ronald Grigor Suny, summarises the central feature of "social history" in far from exclusively Marxist terms as: "a more structuralist appreciation of the movements of social groups and a displacement of the former emphasis on leaders and high politics". An ambivalent relationship is also evident when he later comments: "Though social history has often been uncomfortable with its pedigree in Marxism, central to much of its agenda has been the concept of class and the exploration of the social and political processes that have validated (or undermined) that particular identity" (Suny 1994, pp167, 178).

5   For a summary of this development of "social history", though one written recently and hence omitting any mention of the influence of Marxism, see Acton et al. 1997, pp3-17. For perhaps the best example of the results of this approach, which was largely developed by US scholars and focused on 1917 rather than the whole revolutionary history of the Russian empire, see Kaiser 1987. Concerning the role and ideas of Lenin there was less material produced.

6   The work of the "social historians" facilitated a critical reinterpretation of Lenin, which is the basic purpose of this thesis. Yet the "social historians" themselves did not undertake such a reinterpretation, and their work is relevant to the background rather than the central issues of the thesis. For this reason a detailed discussion of development of "social history" is not included in this chapter. Perhaps even more significant for the potential rewriting of the history of the Russian revolutionary movement, as well as the reconsideration of the role of leadership within it, is the "Chronicle of the Workers' Movement in Russia" project now being undertaken by historians and archivists in the Russian Federation. The aim of this project is to catalogue all material held on all strikes, protests, movements, political parties and publications held in archives within the Russian Federation for the period 1895 to February 1917. For a discussion of this work see Kirianov et al. 1991. The major result of this work, the *Rabochee dvizheniie v Rossii: khronika*, is being produced as a year by volume series from 1895. To this date volumes have been produced for the years 1895 to 1898 inclusive.

social sciences and humanities was steadily displaced by "post-modernism".[7] This decline in radicalism reached its nadir with the events of August 1991 in the Soviet Union.[8] As much as the work of the "social historians" provided part of the means for a reconsideration of Lenin's role and ideas, they were arguably never wholly Marxist in their views, and almost all made some form of reconciliation with the mainstream through the medium of at least a partial acceptance of this approach.[9]

The conditions that led to the rise of a "social history" of the Russian revolutionary experience also resulted in a reconsideration of the role and ideas of Lenin by a smaller number of academic and non-academic writers.[10] For the mainstream, Marxism, based on the conception of economically determined classes and the historical role of the struggle between them, was inherently an authoritarian threat that could bear no relation to social reality.[11] Of all those who participated in this movement Lenin was regarded as its most significant exponent.[12] With little variation they located the sum total of Lenin's views on consciousness and organisation within a single supposedly seminal statement of organisational authoritarianism, *What is to be Done?* [hereafter *WITBD*], and analysed this polemic as a formula for all contexts.[13]

---

7   A critique of this approach to the social sciences, as a well as an argument for its base in the disillusionment of the "generation of '68", can be found in Callinicos 1989, especially pp121-71.

8   Perhaps the most significant statement of this retreat, due to the prominence of its author as well as the pivotal role of the journal in which it was published, is Blackburn 1991, pp5-67.

9   Most notably through an ambivalent attitude to post-modernism. See for example Acton et al. 1997, pp13-4.

10   The most substantial of these critical studies were by Liebman 1975, Cliff 1975-78 and Harding 1977-81. A discussion of the work of these writers forms the core of this chapter. David Lane in a book reviewing recent literature on Leninism and associated questions noted that up to the late 1970s most Western Marxists were more interested in exploring the work of the "early Marx" than that of Lenin (Lane 1981, p2).

11   Perhaps most clearly put by the prominent mainstream writer R.N. Carew Hunt, especially the chapters "The Class Struggle", pp73-90, and "The Dictatorship of the Proletariat", pp138-64 (Carew Hunt 1954). See also Carew Hunt 1957, especially the sections "The Class Struggle", pp41-3, and "The Marxist Theory of the State and of Revolution", pp70-83. For a more dispassionate critique by a writer discussed in greater detail below see Meyer 1970, especially pp103-21, 142-9.

12   Thus Carew Hunt opens the conclusion to *Marxism Past and Present* with: "The great reputation as a thinker that Marx enjoys today is largely due to Lenin". (Carew Hunt 1954, p165.)

13   A useful summation of this position, by a writer discussed in detail later in this chapter, can be found in Meyer 1964, pp37-43. See also Carew Hunt 1957, pp163-70, which mentions further statements concerning party organisation but argues that these all reworked and defended the original themes of *WITBD*. For the typical summation in passing of the role of *WITBD* by most mainstream historians of the Russian revolutionary movement see Pipes 1990, pp359-60. See also Schapiro 1970, pp39-40.

Rejecting the possibility of working class self-consciousness in the Marxist sense, writers in the mainstream could only see *WITBD* as a proposal for a new elite ruling a regime resulting from social disintegration. Such an approach leads these writers to provide little if any context for *WITBD* as well as other less extended comments by Lenin on organisation. Indeed these other formulations were usually ignored or, on the few occasions when they were noted, treated only as an opportune shift in rhetoric aimed at the incorporation of protest within the tutelage of the party.[14]

Contrary to this mainstream view the critical writers interpreted Lenin's writing as at least reflecting, if not actively seeking to achieve, a revolutionary self-consciousness among workers. However, despite their general rejection of the premises and conclusions of the mainstream, the writers who took such a position showed a marked ambivalence about the supposedly seminal comments in *WITBD*. For the mainstream, that book had marked the necessary authoritarian outcome of Marxism. Despite their hostility to the basic elements of the mainstream approach, for these critical writers the book still contained an element of elitist idealism, and this broke with what they saw as Marx's own political aim in the self-emancipation of the working class.[15]

These critical commentators on Lenin came to a conclusion that was to a limited extent comparable to that of the mainstream, because they were still inclined to examine *WITBD*, and particularly its most controversial passages, with only a limited background of the labour movement to which it was directed. However, in contrast to the method of the mainstream, the critics did not regard this book as the sum total of Lenin's comments on consciousness and organisation. For they give at least equal weight to very different formulations by Lenin on a number of other occasions, must notably during the revolutionary upheavals of 1905 and 1917.[16] For the critics these formulations are far more in keeping with their own view of Marxism.

---

14   See for example the argument in Meyer 1972, pp43-56, which will be discussed further below. A similar conclusion reached through a biographical approach can be found in Ulam 1965, p207.

15   For two of the three principal critics discussed in this chapter see Liebman 1975, pp29-37 and Cliff 1975-78, vol. 1, pp79-82. The third of the three critics, Neil Harding, is unusual in denying a break between Lenin and Marx; but in his later writing, this assertion, which was seen as denying an element of authoritarian elitism in Lenin, was the basis for asserting an authoritarianism in both. For those writers who built on the principal critics see the less critical position in Molyneux 1978, pp46-50, and a basic endorsement by Paul Le Blanc in Le Blanc 1990, pp58-68. These passages will be discussed later in this chapter.

16   For 1905 see Liebman 1975, pp84-96, Cliff 1975-78, vol. 1 pp168-83, Molyneux 1978, pp57-63; Le Blanc 1990, pp101-26 provides a more sympathetic though limited discussion of the development of Lenin's views and the development of the Bolsheviks in 1905.

Here the relation to the labour movement in which Lenin was an active participant was recognised. However this is not done with sufficient detail to convincingly relate particular formulations to the role of a consciously intervening leadership necessary if the possibilities for workers' struggle were to be realised. The result was that most critics could not break completely from the mainstream on the formation of the labour movement and the role of political leadership within it, despite their own aspirations to provide a general critique of that paradigm.

This ambivalence and abstraction in the critics' approach to *WITBD* could be seen as reflecting a residual element of determinism in their approach to the advance of class consciousness within struggle by workers. Such a determinism reflected the extreme radicalism and apparently unhindered advance of the movement that had inspired all radical social scientists and had also been very marked among the "social historians".[17] If this were accepted, an explanation is offered for the retreat of most critical commentators on Lenin, together with almost all the "social historians", back towards the mainstream in the 1990s. For the apparently spontaneous upsurge of 1968-75 was followed not by an even greater struggle, but by fifteen years of deepening passivity. With their confidence seriously weakened by this inexplicable development, the radical social scientists were then faced with the crushing spectacle of the collapse of regimes that most saw as post-capitalist, however distorted. With some notable exceptions, most "social historians", as well as those seeking to make a re-interpretation of Lenin had, by the late 1990s, completed a substantial return to the mainstream in which their former radicalism was severely attenuated or explicitly abandoned.[18]

Perhaps the most striking case of this shift in sympathy and method can be seen in the approach adopted by the political theorist and critical commentator on Lenin, Neil Harding. In the late 1970s Harding made perhaps the most acute analysis of the development of Lenin's conception of revolution in the Russian empire, as well as the associated questions of the state and party organisation.[19] He did so from a perspective that might well have been

---

17   For the case of the "social historians" it is significant that Suny speaks of the "social determinism of many social historians" (Suny 1994, p177) and cites Leopold Haimson as the pioneer of "social history" (p173). In the late 1950s and early 1960s Haimson was the principal archivist and historian of the Mensheviks with an apparent sympathy for this current which interpreted Marxism in a determinist way.

18   For a Marxist view of this retreat by the "social historians" of the Russian Revolution see Mike Haynes, "Social History and Russian Revolution" pp57-80, in Rees (ed.) 1998. For an alternative non-Marxist analysis by one of the leading "social historians" see Edward Acton, "The Revolution and its Historians", in Acton et al. 1997, pp3ff.

19   The analysis largely parallels that here, although the shift from the late 1960s is analysed as

regarded as sympathetic to Marxism, and certainly viewed the mainstream with obvious hostility.[20] Yet, in a book that could be regarded as a reworking of the second part of his major analysis of Leninism, Harding explicitly declared his hostility to Marxism[21] and was clearly influenced by post-modernism in his analysis and conclusions.[22] Here, as well as in a paper presented in 1995, he maintained his hostility to the mainstream, though now this hostility was focused on any attempt to distance a supposed authoritarianism in Lenin from Marx's own basic motivation.[23] For Harding such a view ignored the authoritarianism flowing from the Hegelian dialectics at the core of both Marx's, and subsequently Lenin's, writing.[24]

If a writer of such thoroughgoing scholarship, penetrating insight and implacable hostility to the mainstream view of Lenin as Harding could have made such a shift in his sympathies and analysis, then it is not surprising that most "social historians" of the Russian revolutionary experience in general should have made a comparable shift.[25] There is little evidence that such writers had ever definitively broken with the mainstream view of Lenin, and by the mid-1980s they were displaying a marked hostility in their judgement of Lenin's approach to party organisation, despite continuing criticism of the mainstream view of Russian history.[26] Thus the prominent historian

largely one of method, and hence the retreat from sympathy for Marxism by critical historians in the 1990s is not recognised. The growing relation between Soviet historians and their critical Western counterparts is touched on in this article. It is dealt with, from the Soviet and then Russian perspective, in the Introduction to Zelnick 1997, pp5-26.

20   Indeed the Marxist Mike Haynes describes this two-volume study as "two of the finest conventional attempts to understand Lenin's politics which he distilled with considerable sympathy" ("Social History...", in Rees (ed.) 1998, p63).

21   Harding 1996, pp6-7.

22   Most particularly in Harding 1996, p278.

23   Harding 1996, pp35-6, Harding 1999, pp89-106.

24   Harding outlines his position on the relation between Hegel, Marx and Lenin in the chapter "A Philosophy of Certainty: Dialectical Materialism", in Harding 1996, pp219-42.

25   It should be noted that the critical or "social" historians largely ignore the role of leadership and politics at the national level, writing what Haynes calls a "one legged history" ("Social History..." in Rees (ed.) 1998, p60) and hence consider leading figures, and Lenin in particular, only in passing. As a result, despite their similar assumptions and process of development, "social history" of the revolution and the critical re-examination of Lenin's role has occurred largely independently.

26   Perhaps clearest at the conclusion of a review and defence of "social history" by the leading figure Ronald Grigor Suny when he wrote: "Without forgetting the authoritarian traits in Lenin, Trotsky, and other Bolshevik leaders or the power of the image of the party outlined in *Chto delat'?*, we can move on to a new paradigm for understanding 1917 that reduces the former reliance on party organisation or personal political skills so central to older explanations". (Suny

Robert Service, author of a highly regarded study of the transformation of the Bolsheviks after 1917,[27] concluded the Introduction to the first volume of a new biography of Lenin by rejecting him as a model for contemporary political practice.[28] And perhaps the most prominent "social historian" in Britain, Steve Smith, equated Lenin's views on worker consciousness with an abbreviated outline of the position in *WITBD* in his widely lauded study of workers' control in the St. Petersburg metal industry over 1917.[29] Given these positions it is not surprising that Service should be associated with a mainstream stand by the late 1990s,[30] or that in 1994 Smith should have explicitly accepted a section of postmodern assumptions in a major article on future research into Russian history.[31]

Yet the radical turn in the social sciences was never wholly, and certainly could not have remained wholly, academic in its base and approach. This was perhaps most of all the case for those seeking to re-interpret Lenin's writings. Thus, in striking contrast to the wholly academic literature in the social sciences, a small number of critics, writing at least partially for a politically aligned audience, hardened their critique of the mainstream. These writers responded to the receding struggle after 1975 by examining more closely and sympathetically Lenin's interventionist approach to Marxism. Perhaps the most striking example of this trend is Tony Cliff. His major biography of Lenin could be considered a response to the failure of the first wave of protests in the late 1960s, while his subsequent biography of Trotsky could be seen as deepening this shift.[32] The major studies by John Molyneux and Paul Le

---

1983, pp31-52). Thus the revolution became a determined event implicitly occurring despite the malign influence of Lenin and other leaders, indeed implicitly without the role of leadership. Such a view is contrary to the method of this thesis which argues a central role for leaders and on that point accepts the mainstream critique of "social history". (See for example Pipes 1990, Introduction, ppxxi-iv.) Thus I accept Pipes' view that the revolution cannot be approached dispassionately or without value judgements (ppxxiii-iv), but I think it will become clear that my own judgements and purposes in relation to the revolution, as well as my view of the *way* in which leadership was central, are not the same as his.

27   Service 1979.

28   Service 1985, p10. Service contributed chapters on "Lenin" and "The Bolshevik Party" to Acton et al. 1997 (pp150-60, 231-44) suggesting that he was regarded as, and wished to remain being seen as, a critic of the mainstream.

29   Smith 1983, pp2-3, 140.

30   Haynes, "Social History…" in Rees (ed.) 1998, p64.

31   Smith 1994.

32   Cliff, 1989-99. The shift in emphasis within Cliff's position over time is evident by comparing the first volume of this collection, especially pp77-9, and his earlier writings as they relate to class consciousness and workers' reality. For an example of Cliff's earlier emphasis see "Trotsky on substitutionism", in Callinicos 1996, especially p74. This article was originally published in 1960.

Blanc could also be considered attempts, by writers at least partially orienting to an politically aligned audience, to understand the evident failure of the determinist expectations of the 1960s upsurge to be fulfilled. This thesis could be considered a further step in that developing process of understanding.

The mainstream: Alfred G. Meyer and the view of Lenin within a determinist interpretation of Marx

Arguably the seminal figure in the development of the postwar mainstream understanding of Lenin on party organisation was the American academic Alfred G. Meyer. He should be regarded as holding this position, and is worthy of detailed analysis from a Marxist viewpoint, because of the systematic and detailed way he argued the central points taken up by almost all mainstream writers. As such, Meyer synthesises the position of such writers, whether they adopted a thematic or the more common biographical approach. Further, contrasting with the approach that was taken by most mainstream writers, and in particular by the biographers, Meyer made a systematic attempt to analyse these ideas as part of the development of the Marxist tradition which Lenin himself purported to uphold.[33]

Meyer attempted to take an interested though detached approach to Lenin's writing which: "contains many an apt observation as well as much that is unrealistic; it combines bold new visions with stubborn old fashioned nonsense".[34] In taking this approach, he claimed to distance his own concern with the content of Leninism from those who sought only to understand how anyone could become a Leninist. Yet Meyer, in terms of his theoretical position, must be seen as part of the mainstream as this position fundamentally shaped the framework with which he approached Lenin's views on party organisation. This was made clear when he opened his study with an overview which concluded that Lenin's political interventionism made him "a pioneer of the totalitarianism of our age".[35] In common with most mainstream writers, Meyer analysed Lenin's ideas with very little historical context. Like them, his method was to construct an analysis based on limited passages extracted from unspecified circumstances. From this he purported to show that, despite pride in its tactical abilities, Lenin's party was characterised by "a spectacular lack of flexibility" related to "the totalitarian character of Leninist thought and action".[36]

---

33 Meyer 1972, pp7-8.

34 ibid., p3.

35 ibid., p4.

36 ibid., p20.

Meyer's outline of Lenin's ideas on party organisation is divided into five elements. Of these, the most significant for the issue of the role of understanding in workers' struggle are his discussion of Lenin's views on consciousness as well as the consequent organisational principle of "democratic centralism". In these discussions Meyer did not recognise any relation between shifts in Lenin's organisational proposals and changes in the nature of the struggle between classes. Indeed he explicitly rejects any connection between the direction of Lenin's comments and the context in which they were made. Thus anyone who had hoped that such a connection might have emerged with the introduction of a limited amount of democracy after 1905 was "sorely disappointed" as "they had not understood the premises on which his ideas were based".[37]

For Meyer, Lenin encapsulated the substitutionist and elitist voluntarism that was essential to the tradition of terrorism in the Russian empire. In his conspiratorial methods, fixation with dogma, and tactical flexibility Lenin, like other revolutionaries, made a particular response to the repression of the tsarist regime and the terrorist tradition of those opposing it.[38] In making this response Meyer saw Lenin standing opposed to two supposedly basic principles of the Marxism that he purported to uphold. The first and most fundamental of these was the primary role of the working class in overthrowing capitalism, while the second was the derivative role of consciousness in the making of history.[39]

Meyer supported his characterisation of Lenin's interventionism as a break from Marxism by giving an extended interpretation of Marx's theory of revolution. The core of this interpretation was a determinist account of Marx's understanding of history which almost completely echoes the position predominating in the Second International. In his opening comments, Meyer did recognise a "curious synthesis of determinism and voluntarism"[40] in Marx. Yet he subsequently interpreted Marx's most famous quote on historical transition[41] as suggesting there was no role for workers' consciousness in the making of history "as circumstances, particularly his position in the social structure, *force him to make it*"[42]. [my emphasis] So Meyer offered no

---

37   ibid., p103.

38   For comparable conclusions within a biographical approach see Conquest 1972, p19 or Ulam 1965, p54, Shub 1976, pp17-32, Tucker 1975, Introduction, ppxxvi-xxxiii.

39   Meyer 1972, pp20-1.

40   ibid., p21.

41   From Marx, Preface to *A Contribution to the Critique of Political Economy*, beginning "In the social production…" as cited in Burns 1982.

42   Meyer 1972, p21.

independent role for the class struggle, and in particular the necessity for such struggle in the transformation of workers' consciousness. As a result Meyer, like Bernstein, returns to idealism in his interpretation of Marx, who is now regarded as seeing the proletariat as the "Chosen People" and socialism as the "Promised Land".[43]

It follows that he saw the rise of reformism among workers as proving that Marxism was utopian.[44] For Meyer, Lenin now appeared as someone attempting to maintain Marx's radical vision of the working class, when the reality of that class's own consciousness proved that vision to be a utopia. It was for this reason that Meyer suggests Lenin saw class consciousness being generated among bourgeois intellectuals,[45] while workers themselves "can develop only trade union consciousness".[46] Consistent with this view on the source of consciousness, Meyer sees a counterposition in Lenin between "spontaneity" (among workers) and "consciousness" (among bourgeois intellectuals). The organisational consequence of this view is that for Lenin the party must remain a narrow contained and small group of intellectuals whatever the context.[47]

In Meyer's account, Lenin's conception of the party as a deliberately intervening leadership could only be a formula for an intelligentsia elite organised outside the working class. Hence it followed that the relationship between the party and the rest of the class could only be a titular no matter how intense the struggle between the classes. Thus while Marx "maintained that the spontaneous unfolding of events produces progress", Leninism "is more pessimistic and therefore became a manipulative theory of history".[48]

As workers could not become self-conscious, their support could only be sought with "irrational incentives, such as coercion and propaganda to make the proletariat submit to the conscious elite".[49] Because Meyer did not recognise Marxism as a scientific generalisation this propaganda could only be "a form of manipulation...the influencing of minds by non-rational messages of communication".[50]

------

43   ibid., p23.

44   ibid., p27.

45   ibid., p31.

46   ibid., p29.

47   For a comparable argument within a biographical approach see Conquest 1972, pp35, 39. For a somewhat different model of the party as a meritocracy see Ulam 1965, pp176, 181.

48   Meyer 1972, p41.

49   ibid., p47.

50   ibid., p49. This notion of manipulation is also used by Ulam 1965, p207 when discussing how Lenin's party reacted to the upsurge of 1905. He is one of the few mainstream writers to

Foreshadowing the approach of the critics, Meyer does on rare occasions acknowledge comments which stand at odds to his model of Lenin as a conspiratorial authoritarian. He also relates these formulations to periods of revolutionary turbulence, concluding at one point:

> Lenin was thus torn between two judgements about the working class. In tracing the ups and downs of proletarian rationality, we find that his opinion becomes optimistic as soon as the mass begin to engage in spontaneous revolutionary action.[51]

Such an analysis points to a "two Lenins" model which, as will be outlined below, was at least partly adopted by almost all the critical writers. Yet because he does not have any conception of class consciousness emerging in struggle, or the role of conscious intervention in catalysing that rise, Meyer dismissed such episodes as insignificant aberrations irrelevant to his overall interpretation of Lenin.

Consistent with his static interpretation of Lenin's views on consciousness, Meyer argues that party structure for Lenin was a rigid and unchanging framework, with the overwhelming emphasis on centralised control. This was despite the well-known label associated with that structure: "democratic centralism". For Meyer this label was: "but a crude and weak formula that did not enable Lenin to establish workable decision-making structures."[52] Meyer's focus on supposedly fixed and formal decision making arrangements does not allow him to understand how party organisation could shift dramatically with changes in the class struggle, or how in practice the conflicting demands of discussion and action could be reconciled. This leads him to see the notion of party infallibility, long identified particularly with Stalin, as germinating in Lenin.[53]

Between the mid-1950s and the appearance of Marcel Liebman's critical response in 1975, Meyer's interpretation was the most substantial and theoretical attempt to analyse Lenin's ideas on party organisation. Consequently within Meyer's study the weakness of the mainstream for Marxists are clearest. This weakness flowed from Meyer's determinist understanding of Marxism. As outlined in the Introduction, such an interpretation leads to the omitting of the role of consciousness from the conduct of class struggle. Yet the result of class struggle on worker consciousness was basic to Marx's case for the

recognise the role of such struggle.

51   ibid., p45.

52   ibid., p103.

53   ibid., p97.

possibility of socialist revolution, and was also at the heart of Lenin's writing on party organisation. Thus Meyer mentions the 1848 revolutions, where the working class as an independent actor played little conscious role, as well as the role of reformism, which could appear to deny the revolutionary potential of the class. Yet he makes no mention of events like the Paris Commune where the Marxist view of the potential of the working class was powerfully vindicated, while at the same time the efforts of the "superstructure" to crush that potential were clearly evident.

This omission of the role of class struggle explains Meyer's confusion over the apparently contradictory statements by Marx on worker consciousness, and hence to see Marxism as utopian. In the case of Lenin, for whom the class struggle and its results in worker consciousness were even more immediate, Meyer's inconsistency could be even greater. As a result there are points at which he was forced to abandon his attempt to analyse Lenin within a Marxist framework and revert to a liberal or even a conservative framework. Thus he is moved to explain Lenin's apparently contradictory shifts between periods of high and low class struggle:

> Similarly all ideas of democracy collapse once the faith in the common man's rationality is abandoned. Yet we are even less sure of it than was Lenin, whose lack of faith was based only on political horse sense, whereas ours is intensified by the incontrovertible findings of psychology and anthropology.[54]

The critics and the break with determinism

Over the early period of the Cold War a mainstream consensus deepened the view that Lenin was a conspiratorial authoritarian. The mainstream could arrive at this conclusion because they viewed his formation solely in relation to the repressive element of tsarist Russia as well as the tradition of terrorist opposition to that regime. In doing so they largely ignored the role of Lenin's interaction with the workers' movement and the Marxist tradition that opposed Tsarism. To the limited extent that they did consider Lenin in relation to the Marxist tradition they identified him as the logical outcome of an authoritarianism inherent in Marx's own conceptions of class and struggle between the classes. This conclusion was based on a very limited and thoroughly determinist understanding of Marxism by mainstream authors – an understanding that left little if any role for the conscious intervention that was at the centre of Lenin's political practice as a Marxist.

---

54 ibid., p44.

This led to an abstract approach to analysing Lenin's comments on party organisation. Thus their syntheses of his views were drawn from a limited number of passages, which were examined in isolation from the disputes within which they occurred. Indeed the overwhelming bulk of mainstream analysis is focused on several citations from the polemic *WITBD*. These passages alone are considered sufficient to prove the case for a model of party organisation characterised by conspiracy in method and elitism in purpose.

If the mainstream authors may be seen as reflecting the depths of working class passivity and international polarity of the early Cold War, then their critics must be seen as inspired by the period of agitation between 1968 and 1974, and in particular the events of May 1968 in Paris. The breadth and depth of struggle at this time fundamentally challenged the view of Marxism, and in particular its determinism, that was held by scholars both in the mainstream and the Eastern Bloc.[55] The defeat of the struggle, despite its intensity, raised the role of conscious intervention in a way that it had not been for many decades. These events inspired a new interest in Marxism, and resulted in a number of substantial critical reconsiderations of Lenin's ideas in the mid to late 1970s. The most substantial of these reconsiderations, by the authors Neil Harding,[56] Tony Cliff,[57] and Marcel Liebman,[58] must be considered the foundation of the critical view, and a discussion of their argument forms the largest part of this review.

Consistent with the era that inspired them, the critics regarded the Marxist tradition as embodying the aspiration to human liberation. Further, their work embodied an analysis of Lenin's ideas as a step in the development of the role of conscious intervention in achieving that aspiration, rather than the necessarily idealist culmination of a determinist and authoritarian doctrine. Thus in contrast to the narrow and abstract focus of the mainstream, they sought to encompass Lenin's views across the whole of his political activity. To the limited extent they were able, given their paucity of sources, the critics also outlined the audience to which his comments were addressed, as well the wider context of struggle in which they occurred. As a result they came to counterpose a political activist of great tactical flexibility, but also firm underlying principle, to the authoritarian conspirator portrayed by the mainstream.

Yet despite this overall judgement, there was a marked ambivalence by the

---

55   The symmetrical abstraction, and particularly the idealism, in method with which Lenin is approached both in Eastern Bloc and Western mainstream writings is noted but not developed by Liebman 1975, pp19-20.

56   Harding 1977-81.

57   Cliff 1975-79.

58   Liebman 1975.

early critics towards Lenin's comments on organisation prior to 1905, and this ambivalence has not been completely dispelled by the later more specialised writings within the critic's approach.[59] For if the mainstream base their case almost entirely on certain passages from *WITBD*, the critics also, though to a far lesser extent, tend to regard these passages as being inconsistent with Lenin's broader views, as well as Marx's fundamental purpose. As a result the critics retreated from a full break with the mainstream and pose an inconsistency, albeit only temporary and later resolved, in Lenin's thought. In this thesis it will be argued that if Lenin's comments are viewed in context they can be seen as flowing from Marx's own contradictory understanding of consciousness. While there were shifts within Lenin's tactical proposals, there was also a fundamental continuity in the role of conscious intervention across the dramatically changing junctures that he addressed. Thus in positing a break in Lenin's comments, the critics develop an understanding of Marxism which has not completely broken from the determinism in relation to the advance of class consciousness of the left wing within the Second International.

Marcel Liebman: A failure to break with determinism

One of the earliest critics, and perhaps the one who conceded most to the determinism of the mainstream, was the French writer Marcel Liebman. Thus Liebman's discussion of *WITBD* strongly echoes the central points of that framework. His analysis is strongly alluded to in the title of this discussion: "the *elitist* conception of the party: the proletarian *vanguard*".[60] [my emphasis] Substantially echoing the mainstream position that on organisational questions Lenin was essentially a Narodnik, he remarks about the book:

> Although, as a convinced Marxist, Lenin was opposed to the old revolutionary organisations of Russia, *he had in many respects taken over their heritage.*[61] [my emphasis]

Certainly Liebman discusses at some length an apparently basic concern in Lenin to give a conscious lead to workers.[62] And he appears to contradict his own general argument when he asserts that: "actually there was nothing

---

59   Here I am referring in particular to the book-length studies on the party question, John Molyneux, and Paul Le Blanc, and in particular their critical considerations of *WITBD*: Molyneux 1978, pp41-50, Le Blanc 1990, pp58-68.

60   Liebman 1975, p29.

61   ibid., p35.

62   ibid., p32.

Blanquist about Lenin"[63] due to his concern to maintain contact with workers. Yet Liebman also reproduced without critical comment attacks on Lenin's critique of "spontaneity" by Trotsky, Luxemburg and Plekhanov.[64] And he concludes his discussion of Lenin's organisational position up to 1905 on a note of ambivalence: "as for Leninism its future remained open".[65]

If, on the nature of Lenin's initial formulations, Liebman concedes much to the mainstream, then on the significance of his arguments during the First Russian Revolution he breaks sharply with the omissions or misinterpretations of that position. If writers within the mainstream here recognised any change at all, they dismissed it as at most a tactical shift by Lenin to incorporate a burgeoning movement within the titular framework of the party. Liebman, by contrast, sees here a break of great content and significance resulting largely, if not entirely, from the pressure of the mass movement.

This conception of a break in Lenin's views is very much related to Liebman's own understanding of the First Russian Revolution. That uprising definitively disproves what he regards as the essence of Lenin's critique of "spontaneity" in *WITBD*. Thus, Liebman sums up the lesson of the revolution: "Could this mean anything else but *the substitution of the masses for the party in one of its central functions – in a sense, a rehabilitation of proletarian spontaneity*".[66] [my emphasis]

For Liebman, Lenin is accepting this lesson in his well-known exhortations to open the party to workers due to the rapid change in mass consciousness. Thus the shift he made in 1905 was a passive, perhaps even a reluctant, response to mass pressure for change.

Consequently Liebman concludes his discussion of Lenin's organisational position during the turbulence of 1905:

> A few months later, having *submitted* himself to learning from the experience of the revolution, and after the revolution *itself* had taken huge steps forward, he *acknowledged* the merits, occasional but fundamental, of proletarian spontaneity and initiative.[67] [my emphasis]

Liebman's argument for such a large and significant break, indeed implicitly a return to the basic purpose of Marx, must be seen as a misinterpretation of

---

63 ibid., p36.

64 ibid., p42.

65 ibid., p42.

66 ibid., p49.

67 ibid., p49.

his limited sources. This misinterpretation occurred within a framework still at least partially influenced by determinism. Drawing on the nature of the labour movement, as well as the role of Marxists within it, a basic continuity can be shown in Lenin's comments from before and during 1905. This can be seen when Lenin's comments are viewed as the developing conception of party organisation as the means for conscious intervention within the class struggle. The extent to which, as well as the means through which, this intervention could be made changed with shifts in that struggle, but not the necessary catalytic role of the intervention as such.

A major point in Liebman's argument, indeed in that of almost all the critics, is to seek responsibility for the conduct of the Bolsheviks in 1905 within Lenin's own earlier comments on party organisation. He cites the widely held, though not entirely correct, view that Lenin's supporters were indifferent, if not actively hostile, to the various forms of the movement in 1905. Liebman cites approvingly Lenin's opposition to this tendency, and appears to regard this as further evidence of an alleged break in principle. Yet here also an ongoing feature of his writing can be shown in Lenin's advocacy of the role of conscious intervention in generalising understanding by workers, and hence his concern that the labour movement should go beyond the "spontaneous" forms of generalised struggle resulting from the ideological domination of the ruling class.

Prior to 1905 this concern took the form of a campaign to maintain the political independence of the fragile and weak labour leadership against the organisational and political encroachment of the tsarist state. In 1905, by contrast, this same concern took the form of a campaign for greater organisational and tactical daring by revolutionaries in order to lead the advancing labour movement beyond a radical reformism and definitively smash the weakened tsarist state. Thus party openness, the question over which Lenin clashed most heatedly with his supporters in mid-1905, was not a basic issue for Lenin either before or during 1905, as Liebman implicitly concludes. Rather Lenin judged all organisational forms according to their utility in carrying out the tasks of conscious intervention within each particular context of class struggle.

Lenin's contrasting approach to the role of conscious intervention reflected the contradictory understanding of worker consciousness within Marxism that was outlined in the Introduction. Liebman does not recognise this contradictory understanding, indeed he undertakes no specific consideration of the question of consciousness at all. It is this omission, which he shares with the determinism of the Second International as well as the mainstream, that leads Liebman to suggest an inconsistency in Lenin's views. Associated with this absence of a discussion of consciousness, Liebman appears to share the Second International view that the party, not the class, takes power in the process of transition to socialism.[68] This is evident in the way he appears to see "spontaneous" struggle alone as the means through which the working class takes power. In doing so Liebman echoes the critics of Lenin on the left wing of the Second International, particularly Trotsky and Luxemburg. It is this conception of the party taking power that leads Liebman to view Lenin's formulations programmatically rather than tactically, and hence give them a general significance that was not intended.

Thus Liebman's overwhelming focus on formal organisational structures prevented him from making a comprehensive critique of the mainstream. For such a focus does not encompass the transformation of worker consciousness in struggle that was central to Lenin's understanding of the advance to power by the working class. Without incorporating a critique of the mainstream non-Marxist view that such self-consciousness was impossible, Liebman was hindered in opposing the model of Lenin as an authoritarian.

Tony Cliff: An incomplete break with determinism

Marcel Liebman interpreted Lenin as breaking from an element of elitism in *WITBD* to espousing a consistently Marxist view in 1905, while the British academic Neil Harding argued that Lenin's formulations could be shown to be consistent with Marxism throughout. Between these two positions could be found a range of authors who, while in general regarding Lenin's position as within the Marxist tradition, still had some reservations about the certain well known passages in *WITBD*. Perhaps the most substantial example of such a position is the thematic biography by Tony Cliff, in which the centre of the author's attention is Lenin's role as the leading party organiser.

For Cliff, *WITBD*, taken as a whole, is clearly consistent with Marx's original purpose. Thus in his extended discussion of the book[69] he recounts without critical comment Lenin's position on taking up all issues of oppression, the need for organisational centralism, and the role of the revolutionary newspaper.[70] For Cliff, Lenin's well known modesty was not confusing, as it was for the mainstream, but definitively rebuts their argument that he viewed history as being made by "great individuals".[71] And in discussing Lenin's apparent rejection of many of his earlier themes in 1905, Cliff's conclusion is

---

68   This fundamental point is touched on by Chris Harman in the section "The social democratic view of the relation of party and class", pp16-8 in Callinicos 1996. First published in *International Socialism*, series 1, no. 35, Winter 1968-69.

69   Chapter four, "*What is to be done?*", in Cliff 1975-78, vol. 1, pp79-98.

70   ibid., pp82-90.

71   ibid., pp93-5.

sharply counterposed to that of Liebman:

> This does not mean that Lenin had been wrong in *What is to be Done?*. In 1900-03 his emphasis on the need for an organisation of professional revolutionaries *was perfectly justified*.[72] [my emphasis]

Despite this overall endorsement, Cliff is still critical of the well-known formulations on consciousness in *WITBD*. He particularly cites a passage not usually considered the most extreme:

> "Class political consciousness can be brought to the workers *only from without*, that is, only from outside the economic, from outside the sphere of relations between workers and employers. The sphere from which alone it is possible to obtain this knowledge is the sphere of the relationships of *all* classes and strata to the state and the government, the sphere of interrelations between *all* classes."[73] [italics in original]

For Cliff:

> There is no doubt that this formulation *overemphasised the difference between spontaneity and consciousness*. For in fact the complete separation of spontaneity from consciousness is mechanical and non-dialectical.[74] [my emphasis]

This conclusion partially echoes Liebman's critique of Lenin's views on "spontaneity" and could be subject to the same critique within a non-determinist Marxism. In particular it ignores the element of contradiction in Marx's own views on consciousness, and hence the need to examine any position taken on the question within the context of a particular balance in the struggle between classes. Indeed in concluding his discussion of 1905, Cliff implicitly contradicts this earlier comment when he writes about organisation, an issue which for Lenin was always closely connected to consciousness:

> Lenin's attitude to organisational forms was always historically concrete, hence its strength. He was never taken in by abstract, dogmatic schemes of organisation, but was always ready to change the organisational structure of the party to reflect the development of the class struggle.[75]

---

72   ibid., p176.

73   Lenin, *CW*, vol. 5, p422, cited in Cliff 1975-78, vol. 1, p80.

74   Lenin, *CW*, vol. 5, p80.

75   ibid., p182.

In a similar vein he concludes his discussion of consciousness in *WITBD* by positing that Lenin's "bending of the stick" was "quite useful operationally".[76]

Cliff, like Liebman, does not explicitly acknowledge Lenin's role for the party in leading the class in a struggle to impose its own state power, rather than inheriting the existing state power in the wake of struggle by the class. Certainly Cliff devotes a major discussion, linked to the 1905 revolution, to the development of Lenin's ideas on armed insurrection. Indeed Cliff goes so far as to comment:

> The armed uprising was central to all the resolutions of the Third Congress [held in May 1905]. Every item on the agenda was debated and decided in the light of it.[77]

Yet neither in this discussion, nor in that of Lenin's conception of the "dictatorship of the proletariat", is any direct relation shown between his conception of the working class in power and the role of conscious intervention in the seizure of that power.

This omission of a non-determinist role for conscious intervention is also evident in Cliff's discussion of Lenin's conflicts with his own supporters over organisation in 1905. Like Liebman, Cliff begins his discussion by seeing a cause of "committeemen" conservatism in comments within *WITBD*.[78] However Cliff is more balanced in his discussion of the committee-people than Liebman, being particularly positive about their qualities as individuals as well as their role in maintaining the party during periods of relative passivity.[79] Yet he acknowledges only in passing the role of state repression in the conservatism of the committee-people, and appears unaware of the extent to which they supported in principle, as well as hesitantly carried out, organisational change over 1905.[80] In his lengthy discussion of the conflict over openness at the Third Congress, Cliff does not relate the issue to that over armed insurrection which conditioned it, nor incorporate the changed circumstances which underlay Lenin's demands for organisational opening.[81]

---

76   ibid., p82.

77   ibid., p185.

78   ibid., p168.

79   ibid., pp168-71.

80   ibid., p169.

81   ibid., pp172-8.

John Molyneux: A greater break with determinism

There are a number of critical studies more sympathetic to Lenin's pre-1905 position on party organisation than Cliff's, though still to some extent ambivalent about the controversial sections of *WITBD*. Probably the most substantial of these is by John Molyneux, who discusses the development of Lenin's ideas as part of a wider consideration of the leading Marxist writers on the question of the party around the turn of the century. Like most of the critics, Molyneux rejects the notion that Lenin was essentially a Narodnik in his ideas on organisation. But he does note a number of features, supposedly unique to the Russian empire, which accentuated the development of Lenin's organisational exclusiveness and centralism. Firstly the repressiveness of the Russian context demanded that the party be limited in size.[82] Secondly the nascent nature of capitalism in the Empire made the anti-tsarist movement broader in its class base than a comparable movement would have been in the West, and this accentuated the need for careful selection of membership for the party.[83] However in making these comments Molyneux does not acknowledge that the empire marked the extreme point of a continuity with, rather than a break from, the other imperialist powers of the time.[84] Through this implicit acceptance of their characterisation of the Russian empire, Molyneux appears to give some ground to the case of the mainstream that Lenin's ideas reflected a fundamentally unique context and hence were of limited general relevance.

Molyneux's discussion of *WITBD* differs from that of Cliff on several significant points. Firstly the polemic is set clearly in its general political context – as the culmination of a struggle against the "Economists" who challenged the hegemonic role of the working class in the revolutionary movement.[85] Secondly, Molyneux recognises that for Lenin "consciousness" was not counterposed to "spontaneity" as a whole, but rather resulted from the deliberate intervention of Marxists within the existing anti-tsarist movement. This leads Molyneux, in contrast to Cliff, to explicitly accept as consistent with Marxism the comment that:

> Class political consciousness can be bought to the workers only
> from without, that is only from *outside the economic struggle*, from

---

82   Molyneux 1978, p39.

83   ibid., p40.

84   As argued earlier in chapter one.

85   Molyneux 1978, pp41-2.

outside *the sphere of relations between workers and employers.*[86]
[my emphasis]

Molyneux accepts as Marxist this limited declaration of the opposition to "spontaneism" that Lenin argued in *WITBD*. Yet he rejects its better known and more general formulation:

> We have said that there could not have been social democratic consciousness among the workers. It would have to be brought to them from without. The history of all countries shows that the working class, exclusively by its own effort, is able to develop only trade union consciousness i.e. the conviction that it is necessary to combine in unions, fight the employers, and strive to compel the government to pass necessary, labour legislation etc. *The theory of socialism, however, grew out of the philosophic, historical and economic theories elaborated by educated representatives of the propertied classes, by intellectuals.* By their social status, the founders of modern scientific socialism, Marx and Engels, themselves belonged to the bourgeois intelligentsia. In the very same way in Russia, the theoretical doctrine of social democracy arose altogether separately from the spontaneous growth of the working class movement; *it arose as a natural and inevitable outcome of the development of thought among the revolutionary socialist intelligentsia.*[87] [my emphasis]

For Molyneux there is a "clear distinction" between this formulation and its less general variant cited earlier. For him the latter variant of "from without" means from "outside the working class, specifically from the bourgeois intelligentsia".[88] If this were to be accepted, then "precious little is left of Marx's fundamental dictum that "the emancipation of the working class is *the act of the working class itself*". [89] [my emphasis] As a result, the revolutionary class would now become discontented intellectuals, the division of material and mental labour in capitalist society would be "sanctified in the revolutionary party",[90] and science would be seen as developing in isolation from workers' struggle.

---

86   Lenin, *WITBD*, p78, cited in ibid., p45.

87   Lenin, *WITBD*, pp31-2, cited in ibid., p47.

88   ibid., p47.

89   ibid., p48.

90   ibid.

68

These are substantial claims, and cannot be supported even by the passages from *WITBD* that Molyneux has cited, let alone the book as a whole or the polemic against the Economists of which it was the culmination. In reacting against what might be taken – indeed what almost universally has been taken – as a statement of the idealist elitism in Lenin's conception of the party, Molyneux has himself incorporated an element of determinism into his understanding of the growth of the labour movement and revolutionary consciousness.

Molyneux's critique of Lenin commences at the point where the elitist consequences flowing from the idealism of the mainstream misinterpretation are greatest. Thus for Molyneux it is because the ultimate agent of socialist revolution is supposedly no longer the proletariat itself, but rather discontented intellectuals, that little is left of the Marxist perspective of proletarian self-emancipation. This, of course, is the consequence of the passage for the mainstream, but it is not the only possible interpretation of the cited passage. For Lenin is not here talking about the ultimate overthrow of capitalism, nor even about the organisation of a revolutionary party, but only about the initial germs of theory around which that party may subsequently be organised – on the condition, however, that workers themselves take the initiative to do so. Thus Lenin here is not talking about a movement verging on power, but rather the "theory of socialism", that in its very earliest stages has been "elaborated by educated representatives of the propertied classes, by intellectuals". However widely elitist intentions may have been attributed to him, Lenin himself is not here explicitly suggesting that the theory, or the representatives, could substitute for a movement of workers that critically appropriates the theory and self-consciously struggles to make it a reality.

It might be concluded, indeed implicitly has been concluded within the mainstream, that by "intellectuals" Lenin was referring to the whole educated elite or at least a substantial section of it. In fact his citation of particular individuals, namely Marx and Engels as well as the founders of the Russian Marxist movement, suggests that Lenin was only referring to a politically defined scattering of theorists who, for particular personal reasons, had transferred their class loyalty from the ruling to the working class.[91] Indeed Cliff himself noted that for ten years the Russian "socialist movement" was in fact only five former Narodniks who were exiled in Geneva and confined to

91   The role of bourgeois intellectuals in the advance of the party, as well as the role of workers as intellectuals within the party, which is central to the interpretation of Lenin's ideas on party organisation before 1905 in this thesis, was developed by the Marxist theorist Gramsci in the notion of the "organic intellectual" (Sassoon 1987, p149). See also Molyneux in his discussion of Gramsci's ideas, in Molyneux 1978, pp153-4, "The Intellectuals", Introduction and selected texts by Gramsci, in Hoare and Smith 1971, pp3-23.

making a critique of the movement from which they came.[92]

If the mainstream view was correct and Lenin's intention was that the revolutionary agent was the intelligentsia, then it would also be true, as Molyneux claims, that the working class would be reduced to impotence and manipulated passivity. Yet this view is countered by Lenin's comments here and in other passages from the polemic against the Economists. Thus the theoretical incapacity of the working class at this point is conditioned by the clause "exclusively by its own effort". The implication is that workers could in fact become socialist theorists themselves – as long as revolutionary intellectuals did not adopt a determinist passivity in relation to this possibility. Indeed in a footnote shortly after the more general "from without" comment Lenin explicitly proposes that workers could become such intellectuals:

> This does not mean *of course, that workers have no part in creating such an ideology*. They take part however, not as workers *but as socialist theoreticians*, as Proudhons and Weitlings; in other words they take part only when they are able, and to the extent that they are able, more or less, to acquire the knowledge of their age and develop that knowledge.[93] [my emphasis]

Continuing this footnote, Lenin makes it clear that workers are hindered in becoming theorists, not by their own inadequacies, but precisely by the inadequacies of those intellectuals who claim that they are unable do so:

> But in order that working men *may succeed in this more often*, every effort must be made to raise the level of consciousness of the workers in general; it is necessary that the workers do not confine themselves to the *artificially restricted* limits of "literature for workers" but that they learn to an increasing degree to master *general literature*. It

---

92 Cliff 1975-78, vol. 1, p30.

93 Lenin, *WITBD*, *CW*, vol. 5, p385. It is significant that this citation has only recently been raised in the literature on Lenin, in the sympathetic discussion of his views on party organisation by Paul Le Blanc, Le Blanc 1990, p65. Le Blanc touches on many of the points developed in this thesis (most notably the worker intelligentsia and the erroneousness of the "good and bad Lenin" view) but he does not develop them systematically in the way that they are here. This no doubt flows from the nature of his book as a review of English language (and a very small number of French language and Russian in translation) sources. He is therefore not able to set Lenin's views in context to the extent that they are here despite his assertion that such a method is necessary. As a result, while Le Blanc is clearly inclined to the view of the "critics" argued here, with the exception of judgements of Marcel Liebman, he does not directly and sharply arrive at this view, and he does seem to slide into a programmatical rather than contextual reading of Lenin. See especially the conclusion to his discussion of *WITBD*, pp67-8.

would be even truer to say *"are not confined"*, instead of *"do not confine themselves"* because the workers themselves wish to read and do read all that is written for the intelligentsia, and only a few (bad) intellectuals believe that it is enough "for workers" to be told a few things about factory conditions and to have repeated to them over and over again what has long been known. [my emphasis]

This concern to facilitate, rather than eliminate, the role of workers as socialist theorists and leaders of the revolutionary movement was central to Lenin's whole campaign against the Economists, despite the widely accepted mainstream argument to the contrary. This concern was perhaps most forcefully put in an unpublished declaration drafted early in that campaign:

At a time when educated society is losing interest in honest, illegal literature, *an impassioned desire for knowledge and for socialism is growing amongst the workers*, real heroes are coming to the fore from amongst the workers, who, despite their wretched living conditions, despite the stultifying penal servitude of factory labour, possess so much character and will power that they study, study, study, and turn themselves into conscious social democrats – "the working class intelligentsia". *This "working class intelligentsia" already exists in Russia*, and we must make every effort to ensure that its ranks are regularly reinforced, that its lofty mental requirements are met *and that leaders of the Russian Social-Democratic Labour Party come from its ranks*.[94] [my emphasis]

This reference to a "worker intelligentsia" was one of many by Lenin and other leading Marxists prior to 1905. They were referring to a self-educated layer of some thousands of workers from among the metal worker "elite" who attended Sunday-Evening Schools that were established by factory owners and usually staffed by anti-tsarist teachers. In the 1890s the Social Democratic movement grew as these dissident teachers recruited their students to Marxist study circles led by Lenin and other Marxists. The political development of this layer, as well as the intervention of revolutionary intellectuals within that development, provides a strong argument in support of Lenin's critique of "spontaneity" and will be a major theme in this thesis.

His overwhelming concern to counter the idealist mainstream interpretation of *WITBD*, as well as an apparently limited knowledge of the struggle against the Economists, leads Molyneux to a determinist

---

94   Lenin, *CW*, vol. 4, "A Retrograde Trend in Russian Social-Democracy", pp280-1.

leaning in relation to this critique of "spontaneity". Such a leaning is most evident when he equates Lenin's position on party organisation prior to 1905 with the clear idealism of Kautsky's formulations.[95] Yet as was clear from earlier quotes, as well as a considerable quantity of further writing, there were subtle though very significant differences between the two, despite Lenin's repeated and fulsome endorsement of Kautsky's authority in general.[96] On this point Molyneux cites Marx against the Utopians who shared the supposed idealism of both Lenin and Kautsky. Yet the passage cited itself begins: "Just as the economists are the *scientific representatives* of the bourgeoisie, so the *socialists and communists* are the theorists of the proletariat".[97] [my emphasis] This passage goes on to suggest that these theorists can only generalise from the actual class struggle. However to suggest that such generalisation can only ultimately occur from concrete sources does not necessarily counter Lenin's emphasis, in the context of only limited concrete struggles prior to 1905, on the role of theorists and generalisation as such.

The final major point of Molyneux's critique of Lenin's more general version of consciousness "from without" is to cite a series of generalised struggles in which workers supposedly "spontaneously" rose above "trade unionist consciousness". The examples cited certainly appear to show the possibility of worker consciousness without conscious socialist intervention. But, as will be demonstrated for the case of the First Russian Revolution, all these "spontaneous" struggles required some form, albeit not necessarily fully Marxist, of conscious intervention to catalyse and concentrate widespread worker disquiet into a focused struggle. In each case the fact that this intervention was not fully Marxist, or that the Marxist element within it was not sufficiently effective, meant that the ruling class was able to seriously set back the workers' movement after it had failed to establish its own monopoly of power. Indeed Molyneux appears to partially acknowledge this argument when he recognises that even in the deepest struggle the radicalisation that occurs among workers is still uneven.[98]

The citation of such examples suggests that Molyneux, like most other critics, is still inclined to regard *WITBD* programmatically rather than tactically, despite disclaimers to the contrary. The result is that Molyneux, despite some distance from Liebman and Cliff, still does not consistently regard Lenin's

95   Molyneux 1978, p49.

96   These differences are outlined in part in Rees 1998, pp171-3.

97   Karl Marx from T.B. Bottomore and M. Rubel (eds.), *Selected Writings on Sociology and Social Philosophy*, London, 1963, pp80-1, cited in Molyneux 1978, p49.

98   ibid., p50.

comments on party organisation as arguing the role of conscious intervention within the class struggle, rather than reflecting a new state form resulting from that struggle. For Lenin in *WITBD* was addressing the role of conscious intervention in the weak and spasmodically organised labour movement prior to 1905. In the very different circumstances from early 1905 on, Lenin still argued a pivotal role for conscious intervention, but now by a large number of leading activists seeking to mobilise the mass of the class, and hence demanding very different structures of party organisation. Consequently the examples of apparently spontaneous uprisings cited by Molyneux do not rebut Lenin's position on worker consciousness prior to 1905 as they do not relate to his position at that time. Indeed they could be seen as fully consistent with his approach in the very different context from early 1905.

Thus the view, very prevalent among the critics, that there are two separate conceptions of the party in Lenin, one of which is more consistent with Marxism, is clearly a misinterpretation arising from an element of determinism in relation to the rise of the revolutionary consciousness and organisation. Such a view is very clear in Molyneux when he concludes his discussion of Lenin's ideas on the party in 1905:

> The party remains a vanguard, distinct from the class as a whole,
> but now it is a party of the advanced workers – *a part of the class, not
> the party of the declassed intelligentsia introducing socialism "from
> without".*[99] [my emphasis]

In fact, as outlined earlier, the possibilities for conscious intervention grew as the labour leadership was transformed from a tiny layer of isolated "intelligents" to a broad layer of "activists" leading a mass of workers. In these new circumstances Lenin was able to tactically transform the tasks and structures of the party only because he had earlier established the principle of the party as the vehicle of conscious intervention. This is implicitly recognised by Molyneux when he apparently contradicts himself on the relation between Lenin's two supposedly distinct conceptions of the party:

> The open-ended expansion envisaged by Lenin *in the revolutionary
> period* was possible *only* on the basis of the solid preparation of the
> party beforehand.[100] [italics in original]

---

99   ibid., p63.
100 ibid., p62.

Neil Harding: A break with determinism through relating consciousness to struggle

Neil Harding's thematic study of Lenin's ideas can well be seen as a critique of the mainstream view – indeed he goes further than other critical writers to argue that Lenin remained consistent with Marxism throughout his writing – and in particular within the controversial passages of *WITBD*. The critical writers regard Lenin as generally consistent with Marxism, which they view as a theory of human emancipation. Yet most are ambivalent in their view of Lenin's "from without" passages in *WITBD*, which they regard as at least a partial break with Marxism. Harding's declared aim was to wholly rebut the mainstream view of Lenin, including its interpretation of the argument in *WITBD*.

In making his case, Harding cited Lenin more extensively than other critics in order to establish the most comprehensive view possible of his ideas. In addition, Harding went to considerable lengths to set Lenin's ideas in context – by which he meant the revolutionary émigré milieu. For Harding, the Marxism with which Lenin remained consistent was the "orthodoxy" developed by the leading figures of that milieu, notably Gregorii Plekhanov and Pavel Axelrod.[101] Yet to define Marxism in this way gives no response to several contentious issues. In particular, Harding offered no reply to most other critical writers for whom this "orthodoxy" marked at least in part a break from Marx's basic purpose of workers' self-consciousness seizure of power. Thus while acknowledging that the "from without" passages in *WITBD* are very controversial,[102] Harding sees no need to directly reply to the arguments of other critical writers.

In a literature review published prior to his study,[103] Harding points to a method for providing such a reply which has much in common with the approach taken in this thesis. Here he condemned the whole corpus of studies on Lenin for failing to provide a context for Lenin's work. For Harding, this included the intellectual milieu in which he mixed which is provided in his study together with a compilation of readings,[104] as well as the labour movement into which he sought to intervene which is not. A discussion of Lenin's own intervention among his supporters, set within the context of the conscious intervention by those activists within the labour movement, would allow a judgement to be made about Lenin's adherence to Marxism in a way

---

101 A point returned to again and again; see for example Harding 1977-81, vol. 1, p188.

102 ibid., p168.

103 Harding 1976, p382.

104 Harding (ed.) 1983.

that a measure of conformity to the orthodoxy of an emigre milieu could not.

To the extent that he is able to set Lenin's comments in context, Harding is distinctive for the consistency of his critique of the mainstream. This is clearest in the case of *WITBD*. As outlined, most of the critics regard this polemic as containing some element of elitist idealism because of an apparent limit it placed on the development of consciousness among workers. Yet Harding argues correctly that Lenin was not so much interested in setting such a limit as overcoming the limit imposed on the development of worker consciousness by the inadequacies of revolutionary intellectuals.[105] Indeed Harding argues that Lenin goes beyond Marx in concretely conceiving of the working class as its own liberator.[106] Harding is also distinct among the critics in linking the shift in Lenin's comments from early 1905 to the task he saw immediately confronting the party – that of organising the insurrection. Thus for this period of general upsurge in struggle he develops at length the relation between the shift in workers' political consciousness and that in the tasks and structure of Social Democratic organisation.[107]

Harding's greatest and most significant difference with the mainstream lies in the direct relation established here between Lenin's proposals on party organisation and his assessment of the intensity of workers' struggle. Harding shows that for Lenin, during periods of relative passivity consciousness was limited to a small number of self-educated workers who were known at the time as "worker intelligents". In periods of greater struggle however this consciousness was accessible far more broadly,[108] and in particular to a large layer of "activists" leading the mass of workers in struggle. In this thesis an empirical study of the labour movement will be made to show how Lenin's conceptions were consistent with the actual reality of workers' struggle and consciousness.

---

105 Harding 1977-81, vol. 1, pp151-8.

106 ibid., p104.

107 In what is probably the clearest exposition of the relation between consciousness and organisation for Lenin, ibid., pp226-37, "The Organisation of Revolutionary Force and the Reorganisation of the Party", pp238-44, "Class Formation and Class Consciousness", and pp245-8, "The Realisation of Theory through Practice".

108 See in particular ibid., pp242, 244-5.

Conclusion: The break from determinism in the literature on Lenin

The determinist understanding of Marxism, so hegemonic in the Second International and subsequently so prevalent among those regarding themselves as Marxists, has deeply marked the understanding of Lenin by all commentators, whether supporting or opposing Marx's political aims. For those in the mainstream, such an understanding flows from their argument that Marxism is essentially a mechanical and authoritarian doctrine. Within such an approach, a model of Lenin as a conspiratorial and manipulative authoritarian is the logical consequence of the lack of conscious activity by the mass of the population.

From this elitist conception of society and historical development it follows that the mainstream approaches Lenin's ideas on party organisation through an abstracted discussion of particular isolated passages that are interpreted as the formula for a new ruling order. Following from such an approach there could be no purpose in relating these passages to any context, be it the class struggle at the time or the rise of revolutionary consciousness within that struggle. Intervention in this class struggle may arguably have always been Lenin's motive, but this is not recognised by the mainstream and hence such struggle is treated only in passing, if at all.

Inspired by the upsurge of 1968-75, a critical re-examination of Lenin sought to reject the economic determinism and consequent elitist idealism of the mainstream interpretation. To do so, the critics made a more comprehensive examination of Lenin's comments on organisation, and thereby noted sharp contrasts in his formulations, in contrast to the mainstream that could find only a consistent elitism. Further they were able to make some, if still only limited, efforts to locate these comments within the workers' struggle they addressed.

Yet the very emphasis the critics placed on rejecting the crude economic determinism of the mainstream led them to into an element of determinism in relation to the development of the labour movement and rise of revolutionary consciousness within it. Thus if the mainstream had strong echoes of the broad economic determinism of the revisionists and centrists in the Second International, then the critics at least partially echoed the determinism in relation to the class struggle of the revolutionary left within that movement. In particular, most critics at least partially rejected Lenin's critique of "spontaneity" and the consequent necessary role he gave to conscious intervention in the development of workers' struggle. This led them to see the First Russian Revolution as rebutting Lenin's views on worker consciousness and struggle, and to see an apparent reversal of Lenin's views on party tasks and structure at this time as a recognition of his former error.

As outlined in the final section of the Introduction, this thesis seeks to make a critique of this determinism in relation to the class struggle, and hence make a broader reply to the mainstream than was achieved by the critics. In the next two chapters, I will show how the supposedly "spontaneous" advance of the labour movement in St. Petersburg, both before and after Bloody Sunday, was always the result of conscious leadership by identifiable leaders. Certainly this leadership was not always, indeed was usually not, fully Marxist in its views. As a result, after rising to a certain point against the state, the movement was set back. Within this process of advance and retreat by the labour movement, the advance of a Marxist current, just as much among the large layer of "activist" leaders as among the earlier tiny circles of "intelligent" theorists, can also be seen as the result of identifiable conscious intervention and was also subject to setbacks due to errors and vacillation. Finally, Lenin's ideas on party organisation can be shown to be a conscious intervention aimed at enabling the Marxists to effectively intervene in these very different phases of the class struggle. Viewed in this way, rather than as a model for a new state form, Lenin's views on party organisation can be seen as consistent throughout, as well as compatible with the basic Marxist aspiration to working class self-emancipation.

Chapter 3

ST. PETERSBURG 1861–1905: FORMATION, EMERGENCE AND CONTAINMENT OF A "WORKER INTELLIGENTSIA"

Introduction

This chapter will demonstrate how the experience of St. Petersburg between 1861 and 1905 demonstrates the role of conscious intervention in the formation and advance of the labour movement in a period of rising though still relatively confined struggle by workers. Contrary to the expectation of a determinist framework, it will be shown how the development of productive forces proved a necessary, though still very far from sufficient, condition for the rise of workers' resistance to the ruling order of the Russian empire. Indeed the rise of that resistance involved a conscious intervention of increasing generality to articulate the growing contradictions of the tsarist system. This intervention was provided by the leading element of a "worker intelligentsia" formed through the initiative of aggrieved workers who sought education and political guidance from the general anti-tsarist intelligentsia.

The first two phases, from 1860 to 1885 as well as from 1885 to 1895, were dominated by the initial emergence of the material prerequisites for workers' struggle. The period 1895-1900 was one of full blown economic boom, with the consequent outburst of workers' struggle followed by the repression of the workers' movement. The final phase, from 1900 to 1905, was one of economic crisis with a consequently lesser though more embittered workers' struggle.

1860–1885: First workers' protests, and the emergence of a worker intelligentsia in St. Petersburg

Lenin came to be perhaps the most consistent Marxist in recognising the incompleteness of the determinist view. Yet prior to the emergence of Economism, Lenin, and indeed all Marxists of the time, were influenced by the evidence of an apparently inexorable rise of the labour movement associated with the growth of industry across the Russian empire. This rise culminated in the impressive spectacle of the accelerated industrial expansion and explosive industrial struggle between 1895 and 1900 in St. Petersburg.

Yet the basis for that growth, laid between 1860 and 1885, as well as the consequent foundation of the labour movement, was by contrast gradual and hesitant.[1] Thus, in this early phase of industrial development in St. Petersburg, the possibilities for conscious intervention by worker leaders were closely constrained by the limited economic advance of the time. Resulting from the tentative and vulnerable position of industry the issues which usually provoked disputes were poor or unpaid wages. Due to the insecurity of the workers' position, their protests tended to take the form of spontaneous outbursts such as demonstrations and riots, rather than deliberate actions such as strikes. It is indicative that the word "strike" was not used by the press to describe a protest in St. Petersburg until 1870.[2]

The immature material circumstances, as well as the consequently instinctive nature of protest, is evident in a study of five disputes just prior to Emancipation. Two of these disputes did not actually involve any stoppage of work at all, while the remainder were of a very short duration. Four of the five disputes were over poor wages, while the other was over non-payment of wages for work on a Sunday. For the remainder of the 1860s there is little evidence of disputes of any kind, and this led to the view that the Russian empire was immune to deliberate forms of workers struggle.[3]

Following the first strike in St. Petersburg in 1870 this form of action became both more frequent as well as more imposing over the decade.[4] Indeed a veritable strike "wave" occurred in 1878-95.[5] That embryonic prefiguring of later generalised struggle was a response to widespread sackings and reductions in conditions following the onset of economic crisis.[6] The deepening of this economic decline into the early 1880s led to a lesser though still significant number of disputes over the course of several years.[7]

Confirming the as yet immature material conditions, no ongoing labour organisation emerged from these initial spasms of protest. The earliest protests

---

1   For my periodisation of the labour movement I have largely drawn on P.V. Volobuev et al. "O periodizatsii Rabochego dvizheniia v Rossii", in Ivanov 1966, pp5-57.

2   Zelnik 1971, p163, Zelnik 1965a, p509. For some details of this protest see Venturi 1966, p509. For a summary of the limited labour protests over the 1860s in the Russian empire as a whole see pp507-9.

3   Zelnik 1971, p341.

4   See in particular the discussion of the Semiannikov strike, Diakin et al. 1972, pp150-1 and Kochakov (ed.) 1956, pp326-7.

5   About 30 disputes occurred in this two-year period (Diakin et al. 1972, p158).

6   For an assessment of the spread of disputes over the decade see Diakin et al. 1972, pp70-80, 90, 149, and Kochakov (ed.) 1956, p303, footnote 1.

7   For figures see Diakin et al. 1972, pp166-7, Kochakov (ed.) 1956, pp366-7.

around 1860 were inaugurated by individual activists – usually with the assistance of a relatively educated figure "from outside".[8] When these activists were apprehended their lack of consciousness and steadfastness was such that they typically lost their nerve entirely and were even prepared to inform on their associates.[9] The formation of St. Petersburg's first labour organisation, the Northern Union, did not in fact occur until the strike wave of 1878-79,[10] and followed the emergence of the first acknowledged labour leaders in the city, Stepan Nikolaevich Khalturin[11] and Viktor Pavlovich Obnorskii.[12]

Reflecting the still limited growth of industry this advance proved to be short lived. The Northern Union incorporated some 200 members and perhaps as many supporters with 15 centres, eight in metal factories and four in textiles.[13] In early 1879 it issued a political program,[14] and in early 1880 a paper. Venturi goes so far as to describe this period as "the golden age of the Northern Union".[15] However, shortly after these first significant steps, the Northern Union collapsed when its leadership embarked on a series of terrorist ventures. Obnorski, together with most other leaders of the Northern Union, was arrested in 1879 as a result of police infiltration. Khalturin escaped and played a prominent role in subsequent attempts on the tsar's life.[16] There can be little doubt that, owing to inexperience, they adopted such a course when mass protests declined after the strike wave of 1878-79.[17]

Thus at this point the labour movement, or rather lack thereof, reflected above all the immature material conditions within St. Petersburg. Yet for even a spasmodic movement to have emerged, these conditions must, to a limited extent, have prefigured those underlying the more grandiose events occurring later. Thus even at this stage the main centre of the movement was the Nevskii district, the oldest and most concentrated centre of industry in the city, and the area that would be the centre of the labour movement in the period covered by

---

8   Zelnik 1971, p350, Zelnik 1965a, pp516-8.

9   Zelnik 1965a, pp516-7.

10   Information about the Northern Union is contained in Kochakov (ed.) 1956, pp346-9.

11   Biographical information in ibid., p330 and Diakin et al. 1972, p160.

12   Biographical information in Kochakov (ed.) 1956, pp300, 327-8, and Diakin et al. 1972, pp160-1.

13   Kochakov (ed.) 1956, p351.

14   The program was issued on 12 January 1879. Details are given in Kochakov (ed.) 1956, pp346-7. An English translation is located in Harding (ed.) 1983, pp41-3.

15   Kochakov (ed.) 1956, pp351-2, Venturi 1966, p556.

16   Kochakov (ed.) 1956, p356, Diakin et al. 1972, p160. See for example his attempt to assassinate the tsar within the Winter Palace itself (Venturi 1966, p686).

17   Kochakov (ed.) 1956, pp359, 363, Diakin et al. 1972, p166.

this thesis.[18] Strikes and disturbances in St. Petersburg, when they did occur, tended to do so in the most modern and concentrated industry. Thus over the 1870s strikes in the Russian empire as a whole broke out predominantly in the longer standing textile industry, whereas in St. Petersburg they occurred predominantly among metal workers.[19]

Yet even at this point, when the determinist assertion of the complete predominance of material factors in the development of the labour movement has most legitimacy, a detailed understanding of the way disputes developed points to the role of conscious intervention in focussing worker grievances into struggle. And a consistent examination of the source of this consciousness shows that it was precisely "from outside", not only of the workplace but the working class as a whole. Reginald Zelnik, the major Western historian of this early labour movement, has concluded that there was negligible contact between worker leaders and the dissident intelligentsia up to 1870.[20] Even so it would seem not coincidental that the beginning of "real strikes" in the city occurred at the same time as worker leaders began sustained contact with the radical intelligentsia. These worker leaders acquired "outside" assistance, from local figures educated through experience in the church and army, to articulate their grievances. Further the final form of protest by these workers reflected the obsequious attitude to tsarism held by these relatively educated figures. Thus Zelnik points out that Khalturin, the principal leader of the Northern Union, worked in the Aleksandrovskii plant in the 1870s when, as in the 1860s, it was a major focus of worker discontent.[21] But Khalturin was also well acquainted with the radical intelligentsia of the time; and most of the other leaders of the Northern Union had also been involved with the Populist movement[22] and the program of the Northern Union reflected their position.[23] Indeed that program was first exposed in the liberal press and then discussed in the Populist press.[24]

In fact almost all the worker leaders of the 1870s were involved with the

---

18   Zelnik 1965a, p508; tables for number of factories by district in Zelnik 1971, pp217, 233.

19   Kochakov (ed.) 1956, p303.

20   Zelnik 1965a, p509.

21   ibid., p520.

22   Diakin et al. 1972, p153. For his contact with various populist elements see Venturi 1966, pp542-3, 551. Indeed in an approach more in sympathy with that taken in this thesis than by the "social historians", Venturi analyses the Northern Union as part of the history of that movement. (For the case of Khalturin as a worker leader as well as part of the Populist movement see p543.)

23   Kochakov (ed.) 1956, p347. Venturi 1966, pp552-4, reproduces a large section of the program.

24   Kochakov (ed.) 1956, p347, Diakin et al. 1972, p161, Venturi 1966, pp554-5.

liberal intelligentsia, and in particular its most radical element, the Populists.[25] Zelnik points to evidence that the earliest disputes around 1860 were the tip of a large iceberg of dissatisfaction[26] – yet it was only when a worker leader within a factory intersected with an educated figure capable of assisting in the articulation of a grievance that dissatisfaction coalesced into conflict.

As workers who sought to generalise from their own experience to an understanding of society in general, these early leaders could be regarded as the pioneers of what would come to be known as the "worker intelligentsia". It is noteworthy that one of Khalturin's main concerns was the establishment and maintenance of a library which was used by those outside the Northern Union as well as those within its organisation.[27] Thus the decline in workers' struggle in the early 1880s was almost certainly deepened by the repression of the general radical intelligentsia when Alexander II was assassinated in 1882.[28] With this intelligentsia "outside" the class now suppressed it would have been difficult for these initial "worker intelligents" to maintain and develop their own views. The failure of these early protests to produce even the embryo of an ongoing labour organisation, despite some advance in the economic conditions necessary for such a movement, was above all due to the failure of the early labour leaders to maintain such an intelligentsia.

Thus the point that most critics draw from the massive struggles of 1905 – that workers themselves develop a political consciousness in order to lead struggles, is seen embryonically in the very earliest and most limited struggles in St. Petersburg. The fact remains however that worker leaders developed this consciousness in relation to influence "from outside" the class, in both these early disputes as well as later in much more generalised struggles. The critics' point, correct as it is, supports rather than detracts from Lenin's polemic in *WITBD*.

In this embryonic period of the labour movement, the role of a more general consciousness in worker leadership was clear. Yet also exposed at this time was the basic concern of the state in preventing workers who sought the means of developing a critical understanding of tsarism from in fact doing so. As a result, tsarism's pervading repression was applied in a two-pronged approach to the tentatively emerging labour movement. Firstly, in every case

---

25   Harding (ed.) 1983, p2, Diakin et al. 1972, pp1524, 165, Kochakov (ed.) 1956, pp319-25, 330-1, Zelnik 1971, p373. For an account which argues the central role of the Populists in the political formation of the early labour leadership, and consequently stands somewhat in contrast to Zelnik's approach, see Venturi 1966, pp507-57 and especially pp512-5.

26   Zelnik 1971, p161.

27   Venturi 1966, p556.

28   Kochakov (ed.) 1956, p360.

of disputation the state was primarily concerned to identify and remove the "instigators" – those individuals who articulated the grievances felt by the mass of workers around them.[29] Secondly, the state was concerned to maintain the separation between these "instigators" and those dissident intellectuals "outside" the class who sought to provide them with the means to articulate the grievances of their fellow workers.

Thus the close supervision of all workers, as well as the overwhelming suppression of the radical intelligentsia, was not merely the reflection of an overriding concern with dissidence. It also reflected a particular concern to maintain the atomisation and lack of consciousness among the industrial workforce.[30] In order to maintain this worker passivity, the state complemented repression of broadening sweep[31] with increasing pressure on employers to improve conditions in response to symptoms of dispute and tension.[32] This pressure prefigured the later advent of what might be termed "police unionism", and was above all aimed at preventing workers from understanding the connection between improvements in their conditions and the struggle they waged against employers.[33]

At this early stage of the workers' movement, the political views of its "intelligents" were decidedly constrained by their own inexperience, the limited development of industry in the city, and the as yet limited development of the St. Petersburg's general anti-tsarist intelligentsia. Thus workers initially sought to understand tsarism within the framework propagated by radical liberal sources. However over the period as a whole a marked shift occurred towards the first adoption of Marxism. This shift may be taken to support a determinist view of a correspondence between consciousness and reality, but to do so ignores the active role played by these "worker intelligents" in their own development, as well as the complicated and uneven course of that development.

Up until the mid-1870s, workers' demands were formulated by educated figures "outside" the class with a political purpose limited to the liberalisation of tsarism.[34] From the mid-1870s this passive and loyal liberalism shifted toward its far more radical and active variant of Populism, and this shift

---

29 Zelnik 1965a, pp509-10, 512.

30 Zelnik 1971, p375, Diakin et al. 1972, p150.

31 See for example Trepov's demand of repression of the Nevskii strikers in 1870, reproduced in Zelnik 1971, pp352-5. He was appealing against light sentences imposed by the judiciary. (Diakin et al. 1972, p150, Kochakov (ed.) 1956, p303.)

32 Zelnik 1971, pp165, 320.

33 Zelnik's conclusion, argued in some detail, in Zelnik 1965a, pp510-1, 518, 520.

34 Zelnik 1965a, pp514-5.

culminated in the formation of the Northern Union.[35] In the late 1870s and early 1880s, Populism fragmented, and the Northern Union collapsed in the repression following the assassination of Alexander II. In the context of this failure of populism small numbers of workers became attracted to circles propagating Marxism.[36] Despite this trend, the workers' movement, like the anti-tsarist movement in general, still remained dominated by liberalism in some variant, reflecting the as yet limited material presence and apparent political power of the working class.[37]

Thus the early political development of labour in St. Petersburg could be drawn on to support Lenin's argument on worker consciousness against the determinist position of the Economists, as well as the critics' more muted determinism in relation to the rise of class consciousness among workers. The development of capitalism did indeed provide the material base to enable workers to resist exploitation and produced leaders who could articulate their grievances. Yet this articulation itself was a subjective process enabled by the critique of tsarism developed "outside" the workplace, indeed initially "outside" the working class as a whole. That critique was first made by dissident liberals, then Populists and finally by those moving towards a Marxist position.[38]

Yet if this role of those "outside" the class was the entirety of Lenin's argument, then the view of Lenin as at least in part an authoritarian would indeed be valid, for the basic initiative in the development of class consciousness would lie outside the class, and workers could be seen as the object rather than the subject of history. However, just as Lenin posed the reality of a "worker intelligentsia" throughout his polemic against the Economists, so even in these earliest interactions it is clear that worker leaders were active and critical in their acquisition of a critique of tsarism "from outside", rather than passive

---

35   Kochakov (ed.) 1956, p319; see also on the interaction between Narodniks and workers Diakin et al. 1972, pp152-6.

36   An account of the early Marxist groups in St. Petersburg is given in Diakin et al. 1972, pp150 (the "Black Earth" group), pp169-70 (the Blagoev group – Blagoev was the first major Marxist circle leader) and pp170-1 (the Tochiiskii group).

37   For an account of the political development of the anti-tsarist movement at this time see Kochakov (ed.) 1956, pp233-71. For the role of students in particular see pp251-9, 304.

38   In a recent article dealing with the early interaction of Populist intelligents and workers, Zelnik, now a leading "social historian", offers evidence that supports this position. Thus he particularly focuses on the development of one of the founders of the Northern Union, Obnorski, who in the early 1870s became the treasurer of a workers' library set up by the Populists (pp474-5). Zelnik comments that this experience with the Populists "paradoxically" allowed him to become their leader in the late 1870s, despite initially drawing him away from workers (p484). It was Obnorski's influence that led Khalturin to take up directorship of a new library (p487). All page references from Redzhinal'd Zel'nik (sic), "Rabochie in inelligentsiia v 1870-kh gg.", in Potolov (ed.) 1997, pp464-97.

84

and uncritical in the sense that is usually taken from Lenin's polemic.

Thus even at this initial stage workers appropriated the view of tsarism presented to them critically, and themselves became "intellectuals". The main base for doing this was the voluntary and legal educational movement known as the "Evening-Sunday Schools".[39] In later periods it would be a section of those workers given a basic education by this movement that would join the underground study circles and become the Marxist worker leaders of the class. As such the role of the Evening-Sunday Schools is important in understanding the rise of the labour movement, as well as removing a possible element of elitism in the understanding of Lenin's views on the development of worker consciousness.

The need for a skilled workforce, which underlay tsarist tolerance of as well as industrialist support for the Evening-Sunday Schools, encapsulated the dilemma of industrialisation and the consequent "labour question" for the tsarist ruling class. As such, this need and the steps taken to meet it vindicate the thesis common to both a determinist and an interventionist interpretation of Marx that the capitalists themselves prepare the material base for their own overthrow.

For without raising the skill of their workforces, industrialists could not utilise the most modern machinery to produce the arms that were necessary to defend the tsarist state from foreign threats.[40] Yet in raising this skill level industrialists could not help, despite their best efforts to do so, but facilitate an understanding through which leaders among their workforces could organise struggle against them, and indeed ultimately exercise hegemony within the general anti-tsarist movement. The Evening-Sunday School movement was very much the result of the need for skilled labour, and as such the attitude of the ruling class towards it very much reflected their attitude to industrialisation in general. The education provided by the schools could enable workers to understand the social world and articulate grievances, and for this reason they were always the subject of deep suspicion by the tsarist state and especially its security agencies.

Initially, as industry advanced and the contradictions of that advance were limited, the industrialists and tsarist security agencies were able to contain the course content and revolutionary impact of the schools. Thus while almost all workers who participated in the revolutionary movement passed through the schools, they still formed only a small though growing proportion of total student numbers. Workers who had raised their skill and cultural level

---

39   Usually referred to as "Sunday Schools" in the 1860s, and "Evening-Sunday Schools" from the 1870s.

40   Diakin et al. 1972, p145.

were always faced with the choice of whether to utilise these gains to their own immediate benefit within the existing order,[41] or to embark on the far more difficult course of struggling against that order.

As in all other aspects of the development of the labour movement, the activity of the Evening-Sunday Schools in this early period was constrained by the wavering commitment of the tsarist state to industrialisation.[42] Thus between 1858 and 1861 the movement blossomed[43] to very substantial proportions. This was part of a broader wave of liberal activity that was associated with the Emancipation,[44] and hence supported by industrialists and modernisers in the Court.[45] However, soon after this hopeful start, conditions turned against the movement. Within a short period of their foundation, enthusiasm among students and teachers at the schools waned,[46] as hostility and constraints on the part of the nobility and more archaic employers grew. The security organs placed the schools under close scrutiny,[47] but it is probably indicative of the as yet immature economic conditions that they found only a tiny amount of evidence of propaganda by the teachers and radicalisation among students.[48] Finally in early 1862 the schools were banned as part of a general shift away from industrialisation by the nobility.[49]

The ongoing difficulties of industrialisation meant that the schools failed to re-emerge and grow until the late 1870s, although they were formally legalised some 16 years earlier.[50] After a decade of limited though growing workers' struggle, educational activity by intellectuals in worker circles,[51] and the consolidation of industry, the base had been laid for the permanent re-

---

41 Zelnik notes that in the early days of the Evening-Sunday Schools workers asked for more workplace skills to be included in the curriculum and thought of themselves as entering a "higher world" through education (Zelnik 1965b, pp156, 168, Zelnik 1971, p183).

42 T.M. Kitanina, "'Shestidesiatniki' i dvizheniie za voskresnye shkoly dlia rabochikh. 1859-1869 gg", in Potolov (ed.) 1994, pp17-29.

43 For details see Zelnik 1965b, p152, Kitanina in Potolov (ed.) 1994, p23.

44 Kitanina in Potolov (ed.) 1994, pp17-18, 22, Zelnik 1971, p174, *IRL*.

45 Zelnik 1971, pp177, 183, 317.

46 Zelnik 1965b, pp154-63, Zelnik 1971, pp179-81.

47 Zelnik 1965b, p157.

48 Zelnik 1971, pp190-4; Zelnik 1965b, pp160-3, 169.

49 Zelnik 1971, pp187-9. For a discussion of the harassment and exile of Platon V. Pavlov, considered the founder of the schools, see Zelnik 1965b, pp152-4, 158-9, Kochakov (ed.) 1956, pp271-2, 260-1, 266, 274, Kitanina in Potolov (ed.) 1994, p28.

50 Zelnik 1965b, p170, Kochakov (ed.) 1956, p675. See Abramov 1900, p96 for a table of students by year in St. Petersburg proper (the Nevskii region referred to below not being regarded as part of the city).

51 Zelnik 1972, pp251-99, Diakin et al. 1972, pp152-6, Kochakov (ed.) 1956, pp323-4.

establishment of the schools. The reborn movement had its strongest centre in the Nevskii district – the strategic centre of industry, and hence the metal worker "elite" in this period and for some time into the future. The Kornilov school, historically the most significant of them (where Krupskaia and others taught), was founded in the Nevskii district in 1883.[52]

1885–1895: First traces of a mass workers' movement, with the consolidation of the worker intelligentsia

The advance of production in the Russian empire between 1883 and 1900 is a celebrated case of industrialisation in association with the state, and was marked above all by the transformation of St. Petersburg.[53] In all respects, though most notably in the growing proportion of workers in the population, the size and concentration of industrial plant,[54] and the modernisation of that plant, the advance was so great that an historical break could have been expected to follow – as indeed it did.

Overall figures for change do not capture the full significance of these developments. For while the number of workers grew overall, this growth was most marked in Nevskii – the main centre of workers' struggle.[55] This region experienced the second greatest growth of population in general, falling shortly behind the Vyborg district, a newly arising area that would also be profoundly significant in the subsequent revolutionary history of the city. Further, while the proportion of industrial workers grew, this growth was greatest for skilled workers, as well as workers in plants utilising advanced technology.[56]

This profound economic advance of St. Petersburg could be taken as evidence for the determinist expectation of consistent historical progress. Yet even the most superficial examination of the period reveals the deeply contradictory, uneven and as yet limited nature of this advance. Thus while both finance ministers Witte from 1891 and Vyshnegradskii from 1883 were associated with pro-industrialisation policies, sustained expansion only occurred from 1891, with the economy experiencing a slump in 1885-88 and

---

52   Gurevich 1939, pp38-40, Abramov 1900, pp100-3 including a chart of the growth of pupils in the Nevskii region. It is indicative that while 36 Evening-Sunday Schools had been established by the mid-1890s it is only the Nevskii school that received any particular discussion in Kochakov (ed.) 1956, pp677-8.

53   See for example the growth in the number of new plants (Kochakov (ed.) 1956, p79).

54   Diakin et al. 1972, p128.

55   Kochakov (ed.) 1956, p176.

56   Reflected in a much faster growth of heavy rather than light industry (Diakin et al. 1972, p183) and among metal workers (Kochakov (ed.) 1956, p184).

depression in 1890-91. Indeed the proportion of workers in the population in 1889 was slightly less than a decade earlier.[57] The more advanced metal industry certainly boomed, but until the mid-1890s it could be argued that the more backward textile industry was not displaced from its predominant place in industry overall.[58] Thus industry modernised, but only in sections and to a limited extent – archaic organisation of labour and machinery continued to predominate overall.[59]

The rise of industry did not lead to an associated rise in the living conditions and social role of the growing number of workers. Indeed living conditions overall declined, with working hours markedly increasing in the textile industry.[60] At the same time wages across industry as a whole did not rise as much as the cost of accommodation and subsistence.[61] This inflation flowed from the fact that, in the outlying working class districts of the city, population increase far outstripped growth in the provision of services.[62] The contradictory nature of the period was perhaps most evident in the contrast between the high level of literacy and culture of the impoverished working class and the continued restriction of the press as well as other avenues of political discussion.

Labour protest reflected the uneven and contradictory nature of this economic advance. Thus strikes and disturbances combined features of the earlier nascent period of the movement with glimpses of later mass protests. The issues provoking dispute still reflected the fragility of industry, and these would continue to be prominent well into the next century: cancelled or delayed wages, non-payment for religious holidays, reduction in working hours and increases in rates of payment.

While the subject of grievances reflected the continuing vulnerability of industrialists to economic crisis, the way in which disputes were fought reflected a growth of consciousness and stability among workers. Perhaps the most notable aspect of this emerging sophistication was the publicising of worker demands though the print media as well as the seeking of support in other factories.[63] Facilitating this sophistication was a growing involvement by the worker "intelligents" with the general anti-tsarist intelligentsia, and the consequent consideration of disputes within that milieu. This process

---

57 Diakin et al. 1972, p127.

58 ibid., p125, compare with pp127-8, and chart in Kochakov (ed.) 1956, pp83-4.

59 Kochakov (ed.) 1956, p93.

60 ibid., pp134-5, chart, p198.

61 ibid., p137.

62 ibid., pp202-10.

63 In particular during the dispute at the Morozov factory, see Diakin et al. 1972, p167.

did not proceed smoothly or without interruption however. The tsarist state effectively hindered the advance of revolutionary consciousness through the use of spies, jailings and exile to repeatedly break up worker and intellectual organisations, as well as to sever the links between them.[64]

It is indicative of the advancing though still limited consciousness and organisation among workers that protest activity in this period was largely a defensive response to the impact of economic slumps. Thus, perhaps the most significant strike of the period, in 1885, was a response to the illegal levying of fines and also sought a reduction in working hours.[65] Echoing the earlier period, the strikers' demands were formulated "from outside" by a Narodnik, and 200 workers demonstrated to present their demands beginning their manifesto to the tsar with the words: "We address you as children to a father." A number of further strikes occurred around this time, the most notable being in the Nevskii district, where workers at the Palia plant protested over declining wages. In a significant precursor to later events they were joined by other local plants[66] in demonstrations which were only dispersed with the intervention of Cossacks.[67]

In the first half of the 1890s, workers' protest continued to be mainly provoked by the effects of economic downturn. Thus a wave of defensive strikes occurred at the time of the 1890-91 depression and famine,[68] whereas between the end of 1893 and mid-1895 only three strikes occurred as the economy recovered while the anti-tsarist intelligentsia and workers' movement were suppressed. From mid-1895, the tempo of strikes began to rise again as revolutionaries reorganised and conditions matured toward the textile strike of early 1896.

Up to the mid-1890s workers' material weight in society, their role in production, and consequently their potential political role could still not be clear to the mass of workers. As a consequence their consciousness remained loyal to tsarism, despite the often explosive forms of the spasmodic protests of the time. However, even as most workers remained loyal to tsarism, the worker intelligentsia, which had adopted a critical view of tsarism, grew from a few scattered individuals to a layer of organised worker leaders.

Thus in the first half of the 1890s this tiny layer of radicalising workers

---

64   ibid., pp175-8.

65   Harding (ed.) 1983, pp72-3, Diakin et al. 1972, p158.

66   In fact the Morozov strike mentioned above drew an "all-Russian echo" (Volobuev 1996, p21).

67   Diakin et al. 1972, p167, Kochakov (ed.) 1956, p367.

68   See for example the case of the Thornton strike in Share 1987, p224. In fact there were 12 cases of worker protest between 1890 and 1893 (Diakin et al. 1972, p177).

cohered through a series of political events. The first such event occurred on 24 April 1891 with the funeral of the famous Populist writer [N.V.] Shelgunov. This was the first public demonstration in the city since 1876 and about 10 percent of the 1,000 or so people who participated were workers. They were mobilised by the Central Workers' Circle, the first city-wide workers' organisation since the Northern Union of 1879-1880. This intervention was significant because it showed a desire by the worker leaders to project an independent class presence, albeit still within the general framework of populism. Thus a delegation from the Central Workers' Circle visited Shelgunov shortly before his death, addressed him with the term "Dear Teacher", and made a speech of appreciation for the work he had done in researching the conditions of the working class. When Shelgunov died soon after, the funeral procession was led by workers bearing a wreath and banner.[69] Shortly thereafter, on Sunday 19 May, somewhere between 60 and 200 workers gathered to mark Russia's first May Day celebration with a picnic in a secret location and four speeches.[70] A year later, in rather less favourable circumstances, a similar event was held with eight speeches being given.[71]

It is generally argued in the mainstream Western literature that these events were the beginnings of an independent workers' movement that was subverted and displaced by radical intelligents – in particular the Marxist predecessors of the RSDLP. Yet such an argument ignores the considerable evidence that dissident intellectuals "from outside" were instrumental in the formation of worker leaders from the very first acts of worker protest. Thus Shelgunov was only the latest in a long series of populist figures whose works were important in inspiring a broad range of anti-tsarist leaders, while the May Day gatherings were held in direct response to a call from the First International.

The leadership of the Central Workers' Circle that organised the visit to Shelgunov came from within a layer of some 1,000 self-educated workers which could now be regarded as the core of the worker intelligentsia.[72] This layer had cohered around study circles, initially lead by anti-tsarist intellectuals, that

---

69   Share 1987, Kochakov (ed.) 1956, pp390-1, Diakin et al. 1972, pp174-5.

70   Share 1987, pp247-70, Kochakov (ed.) 1956, pp394-5, Diakin et al. 1972, pp176-7. It is indicative that these speeches were turned over to a Narodnik group for publication (Share 1987, p269).

71   Share 1987, pp291-300, Kochakov (ed.) 1956, pp395-6, Diakin et al. 1972, pp176-7.

72   Share defines this term as those involved in illegal study circles and suggests around one thousand workers out of a 77,000 or 100,000 total (1987, pp35, 128). He uses the term "worker elite" to encompass all those involved in self education. I regard his terminology as too narrow and will use "intelligentsia" to mean those involved in self-education and "elite" or "cadre" for skilled workers as a whole. Kochakov (ed.) 1956, pp382-4 comments on a "new type" of worker emerging in the late 1880s and Blagoev commented on the intellectual nature of the workers he met (Diakin et al. 1972, p169).

drew on the large pool of workers within the Evening-Sunday Schools. It was three workers from such a study group, led by Pavel Varfolomeivich Tochiiskii,[73] who in late 1889 convened the first city-wide workers' organisation, said to have at least 38 members, and which "encompassed most of the worker intelligentsia".[74] That these founders of the exclusively worker Central Workers' Circle should have come from the circle led by Tochiiskii is not surprising. He was distinguished by his strong opposition to populism, which led to a downplaying of the role of intellectuals within the workers' movement, as well as his stand that workers should act alone in the formation and leadership of their own organisations.

Yet, despite these origins, the organisation, methods and views of the Central Workers' Circle were determined above all by the repressive context in which it sought to organise.[75] Thus in its actual structure of organisation, the Circle adopted the hierarchical framework characteristic of all anti-tsarist groupings. Indeed, stymied by waves of arrests, the Circle came more and more to seek the involvement of dissident intellectuals in the conduct of its propaganda. In turn it sought to intervene within the disputes that divided these dissident students and professionals – in particular between the traditional oppositional ideology of populism and the more recent Marxism. More and more, the Circle leaders aligned themselves with the Marxist students[76] organised within the Central Students' Circle,[77] whose main leader was Mikhail Ivanovich Brusnev.[78] It is significant that both the Central Students' Circle and the Central Workers' Circle were formed at the same time and in the wake of student protests.[79]

This step towards an integrated workers political party was aborted by state intervention. The meetings to resolve the dispute between Populism and Marxism exposed the leaders of both the Central Students' and Central Workers' Circles to police spies, and both were crushed by arrests. Only the

---

73   On Tochiiskii see Kochakov (ed.) 1956, pp377-9, Diakin et al. 1972, pp170-1, Share 1987, pp68-72. On the activity of the Tochiiski group see Share 1987, pp72-83.

74   Share 1987, p84. In footnote 2, p129, Share gives a list of 38 members of the Circle. On the launching of the Circle see also Kochakov (ed.) 1956, p386.

75   For the methods and activity of the Circle see Share 1987, pp212-7, on the aborted launching of a paper, pp218-9. For the structure of the Circle see Share 1987, pp174-8.

76   For some details of the discussions see Share 1987, pp317, 335-41, Diakin et al. 1972, p192. Volobuev 1996, p22 cites Leonine as identifying the merging of Marxism and the workers' movement at this time.

77   For more on the Central Students' Circle, see Diakin et al. 1972, pp172-3, Kochakov (ed.) 1956, pp385-6, Share 1987, pp185-8.

78   For background on Brusnev, see Share 1987, pp87-90.

79   Share 1987, pp189-94, Kochakov (ed.) 1956, p387.

most outstanding figures remained at large when Lenin began his activity in 1893, and his initial development was influenced by the remnants of both these milieux. Thus Lenin joined a circle led by Stepan Ivanovich Radchenko,[80] the most outstanding conspiracist and propagandist follower of Brusnev. Yet he also sought to lead worker study circles, largely in the decisive Nevskii district. He was able to do this through the connections of the most vehement self-activist of the Central Workers' Circle, Vasilii Andreevich Shelgunov.[81] Thus the initial influences on Lenin were not one-sidedly conspiratorial as is usually suggested. Rather, Lenin sought influence from, and combined in his own activity, contrasting influences from both student and worker intellectual milieux.

The Central Workers' Circle, as well as independent circles, organised perhaps some one to two thousand workers. Yet this was only the peak of a far larger and more diffuse pyramid of workers who were to some degree critical of tsarism. The main organisational focus for this pyramid was still the Evening-Sunday Schools, which by 1895 had grown to a very substantial size. Thus the most important school, located in the Nevskii district, grew from 304 pupils in 1884 to 691 pupils ten years later. In the first ten years of its existence, some 7,293 workers attended its classes.[82]

The Evening-Sunday Schools were to grow even further in later years.[83] Yet it was in this period that their role in the formation of an intelligentsia, and the Marxist element within that intelligentsia in particular, was arguably most critical, due to the absence of any party organisation or press, or for that matter cultural outlets of any type.[84] Within the classes at these schools dissident teachers and workers could identify potential Circle recruits from the response of class members to leading questions and comments.

---

80   On Radchenko see Share 1987, pp328-31, Kochakov (ed.) 1956, p397. Mel'nikov 1975 is a full-length biography devoted to this significant though relatively ignored figure.

81   On Shelgunov see Share 1987, pp113-4, 133-4, 92-3, 303-7, 315. On his collaboration with Leonine see Kochakov (ed.) 1957, pp160-3, Diakin et al. 1972, p191. Shelgunov became a major figure in the Bolsheviks and the Soviet state (refuting Share's thesis that the worker intelligentsia faded with the rise of organised Marxism). There is a large amount of Soviet-era literature on him – perhaps the most significant being the biography by Rozanov (Rozanov 1976).

82   Abramov 1900, pp103-4. Some discussion also in Diakin et al. 1972, p147.

83   For an outline of numbers by class in 1911-12 at the Nevskii school (known more commonly by its name Smolenskii) see O.E. Belomshchkaia, "Vospominaniia o rabote prepodavatelei Smolenskikh vecherne-voskresnykh klassov v 1900-1905 gg. Fond 4000, opis" 5, dela 177, Central State Archive of Historico-Political Documents of St. Petersburg, p2.

84   Share 1987, p91. See also comments by V.S. Tsytsarin, "Vospominaniia o zaniatiiakh v Smolenskikh vecherne-voskresnykh klassakh v 1898-1905 gg. Fond 4000, opis" 5, delo 138, Central State Archive of Historico-Political Documents of St. Petersburg, p1.

Shelgunov actually went from class to class listening to responses.[85] At the largest and most significant school in Nevskii a significant number of the teachers were women gymnasium graduates.[86] Embittered by the sexist and repressive nature of the empire, they taught classes of mainly male workers whose initial stimulus for dissidence was usually also personal.[87] It was through this process that the core of the first Marxist city-wide organisation was formed over 1894-95.[88]

However, the overall result of this educational activity was rather different from that hoped for by the teachers, or indeed what may have been expected within a determinist understanding of advancing class consciousness. In the absence of widespread class struggle, or a large and clearly visible revolutionary lead, only a small minority of students adopted a fully revolutionary view of tsarism. When "worker intelligents" adopted a critical attitude to tsarism, they often did so in an abstract way that permitted an accommodation with the status quo in practice. This meant that of the very few that appropriated Marxism most did so in a very passive way.[89] Indeed most pupils used the schools as a means of escaping the drudgery of their workday existence[90] and some even utilised their education to rise within the factory hierarchy.[91]

At this stage the "worker intelligents" generally exhibited a markedly elitist attitude to the mass of workers, and this view was shared by those within the student-led anti-tsarist study circles. Thus a significant part of the appeal of Marxism over Populism was the gradualist, perhaps even passive, political practice that could be drawn from it. In addition Marxism appeared a far more elegant world view than the radical liberalism of Populism. Indeed "worker intelligents" went so far as to distance themselves from strike activity, ignore grievances in their own workplace, and condemn the often destructive forms of protest that were adopted by striking workers.

---

85   Kudelli 1939, p35.

86   Many went to the same women's higher education school (Rubanov 1982, picture p29).

87   Share 1987, pp133-5, 144.

88   Lenin made a report to a group of teachers on making propaganda in the schools (Kreidlina 1970, pp75-83).

89   Wildman 1967, pp36-7.

90   Harding (ed.) 1983, p18, Kochakov (ed.) 1956, p283, Wildman 1967, pp34-5.

91   In Vilna workers set up their own firms in their own turn (Wildman 1967, p42, Share 1987, pp41, 63).

1895–1900: Mass struggle followed by repression and demoralisation among the "worker intelligents"

The period between the first textile strike in 1896 and the onset of economic crisis in early 1900 forms a distinct phase in the history of the Russian imperial economy and labour movement due to the sustained boom over this time. The period from 1861, and especially from 1883, has usually been analysed as a case of accelerated industrial expansion under state sponsorship. Yet it was only from 1895 that industry grew full-bloodedly and without interruption due to economic crisis or political anxiety. Such conditions had not occurred before, nor would they do so again until 1909.

The results of this unique context were dramatic. The productive forces of St. Petersburg palpably advanced from the significant base that had already been established by 1895. Indeed, after only a further five years, industrial production, enterprise concentration and workforce numbers had nearly doubled. This dynamism had significant consequences for the composition of the city's industrial workforce, for it was at this time that the metal worker "elite" gained predominance. And the enrolments in the Sunday-Evening schools, legal base for the worker intelligentsia, doubled between 1893-94 and 1897-98. More than these particular indicators, the city's industry gave an impression of enormous power and dynamism, as well as enormous oppression. This accorded strongly with Marx's view of the basic contradiction of capitalism, and made a profound impact on the development of workers' struggle and the political views of the worker intelligentsia.

In this unique context of vigorous growth in both industrial production and workers' struggle, the determinist expectation of a labour movement spawned by and encroaching upon capital could have appeared valid. Thus, this period witnessed the first cases of widespread and sustained strike activity, but it also saw the rise of Economism, a political perspective for the labour movement based on the determinist assumptions predominant in the Second International and explicitly championed by its revisionist wing.

The two main attempts to analyse the rise of Economism both one-sidedly overemphasise only one of a pair of conditions necessary for its flourishing. Thus in the Soviet literature almost all attention is given to the repression of avowed revolutionaries as a causal factor, while the development of "worker-intelligents" as reformists within the localised struggles of a booming economy is ignored.[92] The mainstream Western literature generally viewed this limited struggle as the legitimate form of the labour movement, and consequently

---

92   See for example Diakin et al. 1972, pp216-31.

did not consider the role of tsarist repression in the inception and influence of Economism. Both these attempts to analyse Economism have limitations which flow from their view of the labour movement in general. Thus the Soviet view ignores the role of class struggle, however limited, in developing workers' consciousness in a way that mirrored the determinism and idealism of most mainstream Western studies of Lenin. The Western mainstream view ignored the limited scope for local struggles in a system subject to periodic crisis that became deeper and more general in character over time.[93]

The course of labour struggle over the period resulted from the conflicting influences of economic boom on the one hand and state repression on the other. Thus, early in the period there was a surge of strike activity that was the culmination of the previous history of the labour movement. This wave is usually equated with the textile strike of May 1896, due to its size, the involvement of a whole industry, and the intervention of Social Democrats. Yet this struggle and its successor in 1897 were only part of a generally higher level of strike activity over the whole period, albeit with a marked decline from early 1898.

In their scale and intensity the textile strikes marked a break from the past; yet they also contain elements in common with the struggle of earlier periods. Thus the focus of activity remained the older, more stable and harsher textile industry, while the metal industry, more dynamic and with improving conditions, experienced only faint echoes of the main protests. Further the struggle continued to be based in the traditional working class districts, with the Nevskii district in particular being the main centre of the more general actions.[94]

Undoubtedly the most significant aspect of the class struggle in this period was the generalised nature of the textile strikes, as well as the consequent advance of consciousness among the worker leaders involved.[95] As such, this historical experience could appear to support a determinist expectation of unimpeded worker advance, and it is not surprising that a political view based on this model could subsequently gain support in all sections of the anti-tsarist intelligentsia. The first strike was provoked by a traditional and basic grievance – non-payment for working days spent celebrating the ascension of the tsar. While beginning in several private factories, the strike quickly encompassed the whole industry and was able to adopt the single demand for a shorter working day, despite an apparent

93 See for example the analysis in Wildman 1967, pp89-151.

94 Diakin et al. 1972, pp187, 205, 216, 222, Kochakov (ed.) 1957, p144.

95 Keep 1963, p41, Kochakov (ed.) 1957, p147, Volobuev 1996, p29.

absence of industry-wide organisation.[96]

The adoption of the demand for a working day equivalent to that in the metal industry might suggest a worker leadership formed without the intervention of the general anti-tsarist intelligentsia. It has been suggested that such a leadership could have inspired workers to fight through agitation about conditions across the industry in which they are employed. This position influences most mainstream Western studies of the period and is put with particular force in the work of Richard Pipes.[97] Yet such an analysis ignores the earlier work of Social Democrats in the development of a layer of "worker intelligents" in both the metal and textile industries from the early 1880s, and especially over the 1890s.[98] In particular it ignores the role of addresses by Social Democrats at May Day events. The principle demand of May Day, that for an eight-hour working day, subsequently also became the main demand of the textile strike.[99] Further, Social Democrats were active in strikes leading up to the textile strike, and issued a number of May Day leaflets in 1896. These leaflets were cited by the police as being instrumental in precipitating the strike.[100]

In addition to its general demands and industry-wide character, the textile strike also marked an advance from earlier struggles in the forms through which workers conducted the strike. Thus whereas earlier struggles had been characterised by street disturbances, the textile strike witnessed calm in the working class districts,[101] the election of responsible delegates, and centralised control of the dispute by meetings of these delegates.[102] This growing cohesion and consciousness was also evident in a further unprecedented development six months after the initial strike – a new strike called for the same demands

96   Pipes 1963, p102, Diakin et al. 1972, pp205-6, Kochakov (ed.) 1957, pp182-3.

97   Pipes 1963, pp99-100.

98   For a sceptical commentary in relation to Pipes' claims *vis-à-vis* the late 1880s see Offord 1986, pp157-8. Offord critically discusses Pipes' use of a citation from the "worker intelligent" V.A. Shelgunov. In addition to Offord's comments about the limitations of this citation it should be noted that Shelgunov, perhaps the best known "intelligent", became one of Lenin's closest and longest standing collaborators and a prominent figure in the Bolshevik faction. As such he constitutes a powerful argument against the case of Pipes and Share for a complete differentiation and antagonism between Social Democracy and the worker intelligentsia.

99   The meeting place for the strikes was the traditional May Day venue (Diakin et al. 1972, p208).

100 Diakin et al. 1972, pp200-1, 206, Kochakov (ed.) 1957, pp171-2, Harding (ed.) 1983, pp142, 146-9.

101 Kochakov (ed.) 1957, p184.

102 Wildman 1967, Pipes 1963, pp103, 108, Keep 1963, p41, Harding (ed.) 1983, pp209-10.

that had still not been met.[103] While the textile strike of January 1897 was not as large as its predecessor, it was of perhaps even greater significance due to the obvious element of planning in its execution, after much of the student and worker intelligentsia had been arrested.[104] It is therefore not surprising that this strike induced the first general labour reform from tsarism.[105]

The textile strikes of 1896-97 marked the high points of struggle in this period although a further peak of struggle occurred in May 1898.[106] The political initiative in the launching of this latter wave of strikes was clear from its timing around May Day, as well as its demand for the eight-hour day.[107] Yet after receiving these initial blows tsarism was able to rapidly and substantially reaffirm its control through mass arrests that coincided with an economic boom. The arrests removed the most steadfast worker leaders who were moving toward cohesive political organisation. At the same time the boom offered the possibility of economic reforms through limited collective struggle, as well as opportunities for advancement on an individual basis, to many aggrieved workers who had as yet not become deeply involved in political activism. The base was thereby laid for the last two and a half years before 1900 to be relatively quiescent due to a decline in the class consciousness of workers.[108]

If this period was one in which the struggle of workers made a qualitative advance, then it was also one in which the repressive response of tsarism to that struggle also reached an unprecedented breadth, intensity and sophistication. And it was probably in this period that this repressive response made its greatest impact on the still inexperienced and weakly organised opposition to tsarist rule. The result was an unprecedented degree of organisational fragmentation and political demoralisation reflected in the rise and dominance of Economism among the worker intelligentsia.

As such the period cannot be analysed as vindicating the determinist interpretation of history as the Economists argued. Rather it can only provide a vindication of Lenin's polemical counterposition to the views of these Economists on the question of worker consciousness. For it can readily be shown that the dominance of this reformist political view was the product not of the rise of workers' struggle, but rather the repression of that struggle and the subsequent demoralisation of the "worker intelligents".

Determinism assumed the passivity of the ruling order in the face of

---

103 Wildman 1967, p77, Kochakov (ed.) 1957, p191.

104 Diakin et al. 1972, p212.

105 Pipes 1963, p112, Diakin et al. 1972, pp187, 212.

106 Diakin et al. 1972, pp216-7.

107 ibid., pp222-3.

108 Keep1963, p41, Diakin et al. 1972, p228.

encroachment on its power by the working class. Both mainstream Western and Soviet labour history implicitly accepted determinism in analysing workers' advance as a linear process rather than as a see-sawing dialectic of conflict between surging struggle and crushing repression. Thus tsarism's response to the textile strike was an escalation of its earlier policy of combining concessions to ameliorate the grievances that provoked the mass of workers, while at the same time removing as far as possible those student and "worker intelligents" who articulated those grievances. In the period leading up to the textile strike the authorities, anticipating a major outburst of struggle, removed virtually the entire leadership of the dissident intelligentsia in two sweeps.[109] Over the course of the strike itself, the most widespread arrests to that time occurred. Some 1,000 workers were taken, a figure roughly equivalent to the entire politicised peak of the worker intelligentsia, and some 56 were expelled from the city.[110]

Arrests on a large scale continued for the rest of the decade.[111] Thus little credence has been given to the fact that *Rabochaia Mysl'*, supposedly the expression of workers' self-activity, was broken up by arrests after its second issue.[112] Attempts by workers to hold May Day celebrations, the traditional mainstay of the workers' movement, were broken up by arrests in 1897 and subsequent years.[113] In fact repression was so complete after the textile strikes that worker organisation in the second half of the decade was less than in the first.[114]

The widely known, though relatively ignored[115] attempt by the tsarist security forces to launch a loyalist labour movement was motivated by the same considerations as this vastly increased level of repression. For the Ministry of the Interior, directly responsible for politically containing the labour movement, came to the view after the textile strikes that massive repression alone was insufficient to contain the revolutionary threat. The Ministry argued that, together with concessions, pro-tsarist imitations of Evening-Sunday Schools, agitational literature, and indeed unions, were necessary to keep workers as a whole separate from that section of the worker intelligentsia adhering to a

---

109 Pipes 1963, p95, Kochakov (ed.) 1957, p175, Wildman 1967, p64, Keep 1963, p47.

110 Diakin et al. 1972, pp210-1.

111 ibid., pp213-4.

112 ibid., p218.

113 Diakin et al. 1972, p215, Wildman 1967, p78.

114 Wildman 1967, p112, Pipes 1963, pp69, 79, 80, 86-7 makes mention of a "Central Workers' Group" in the latter part of 1895 but no comment about its activities after the textile strike.

115 The only book-length study in English being Schneiderman 1976.

revolutionary consciousness.[116]

The essence of the initiative which flowed from this approach was to establish a political rival to social democracy within the worker intelligentsia.[117] Thus Sergei Zubatov, the Moscow security chief most associated with these efforts, sought to win over arrested activists using personal persuasion and materials from reformist currents in Western Europe.[118] Certainly, the Interior Ministry's initiative to co-opt labour led to a growing conflict with more conservative elements around the tsar, in particular the powerful minister of finance Sergei Witte.[119] Yet the intention remained throughout to reinforce tsarism by competing with those undermining its ideological domination of workers.

The force of the textile strike shifted tsarism from a policy of pure repression of labour toward one involving a limited attempt at co-option and granting of concessions. At the same time, the force of repression in the wake of the textile strike shifted the balance within the worker intelligentsia and dissident movement away from a revolutionary attitude toward a more gradualist and reformist approach to tsarism. This shift has usually been analysed within the Western literature as a revolt by workers and particularly the worker intelligentsia against the non-worker intelligents leading the labour movement. The points cited to support this view are the ongoing struggles after the textile strike, albeit of a more limited and localised character, the continuing efforts to hold traditional political events such as May Day, and above all the launching of the supposedly "worker" paper *Rabochaia Mysl'*.

It is certainly true that the initial convenors of *Rabochaia Mysl'* were based in the traditional labour stronghold of Nevskii as well as the nearby township of Kolpinskii. Here vigorous attempts were made to celebrate May Day in the years following the textile strike.[120] Further, the dominance of the radical intelligentsia by Economist views reflected the emergence of a new layer of leaders after the removal of the traditional defenders of the former predominating Marxist position. The rhetoric of these new leaders placed great emphasis on a worker self-activity supposedly independent of intellectual involvement. However several features of the Economist trend contradict its own self-definition as a movement for workers' self-activity against a substitutionist elitism within the interpretation of Marxism predominating at this time. These features suggest

---

116 Schneiderman 1976, pp33-4, 39-47, 63.

117 This led him to be particularly concerned with eliminating leaders of the movement (ibid., pp54, 58).

118 ibid., pp29, 78-80.

119 ibid., pp31, 35-9.

120 Diakin et al. 1972, p225, Wildman 1967, p120.

a more accurate characterisation of Economism would be an elitist retreat to a determinist interpretation of Marxism that sought to justify a reformist political practice.

Thus, despite its rhetoric about "worker self-activity",[121] as well as its supposed worker composition, the leadership of the Economist trend actually comprised both students and "worker intellectuals" who were united by the view that workers' struggle should be limited to immediate economic questions.[122] The founders of *Rabochaia Mysl'* were a worker leader from Kolpinskii and a teacher from the Kornilovskii Sunday-Evening School,[123] while the leading article in the first issue was written by a doctor.[124] The best known figure among those who assumed control of the Marxist movement during the ascendancy of Economism was K.M. Takhtarev, a medical gymnasium student.[125] Just as student intellectuals were prominent in the Economist trend, so worker intellectuals and plant-based worker circles were prominent in opposing Economism and promoting the traditional interpretation of Marxism – the best known being the circle of workers around M.I. Kalinin at the Putilov plant.[126]

Following from their rhetoric about workers' self-activity, the Economists placed great emphasis in their literature on organisational openness and direct democracy.[127] Yet it is revealing that when the Economists gained control of the main centre of the anti-tsarist movement they did nothing to change its structure or involve workers within it. Indeed after he had been exiled from Russia, Takhtarev, without any consultation with its worker contributors, offered the editorship of *Rabochaia Mysl'* to Plekhanov.[128]

This gap between rhetoric and practice reflects an elitist assumption basic to Economism. For the activity and openness promoted in Economism's rhetoric are couched in a framework within which it was implicitly assumed that workers could not, or should not, challenge for state power. Associated with this limitation, the barrier between "worker" and "intellectual" was implicitly

---

121 See for example Wildman 1967, pp101, 123, Akimov cited in Diakin et al. 1972, p. 224, Pipes 1963, p108.

122 Wildman 1967, pp118, 133, 137-9, K.M. Takhtarev, "Our Reality" (1899): extracts in Harding (ed.) 1983, pp242-50.

123 Diakin et al. 1972, p217, Wildman 1967, p 119.

124 Diakin et al. 1972, p217.

125 Wildman 1967, pp112, 127.

126 Diakin et al. 1972, pp218, 222, 226, Wildman 1967, pp126, 135-6.

127 Pipes 1963, pp111-2.

128 Wildman 1967, p132.

seen as impenetrable.[129] Consequently, the notion of the "worker intellectual", often cited by Axelrod, the main strategist of party development from the early 1880s, and central to the conception of the party as the leadership of the working class in a struggle for power, became a contradiction in terms.

The elitist nature of Economism is also clear from its political development and the response of key state figures to it. Thus Zubatov, at that time attempting to launch a loyalist labour movement, welcomed its development as complementing his own efforts.[130] *Rabochaia Mysl'* included a theoretical supplement in its seventh issue with the explicit aim of clarifying its own political strategy.[131] This supplement included an article by Bernstein, by now clearly seen as the leading theorist of revisionism, which argued very sharply for a political perspective based on determinist assumptions.[132]

No doubt related to Economism's indifference to the question of state power and consequently illegal organisation, it was unable to cohere around itself any significant labour movement in the repressive conditions of the time. Rather, a series of localised groupings were quickly broken up by arrests.[133] Economism is important, however, as the form which the demoralisation of both the student and worker intelligentsia took in the face of apparently crippling repression and irrepressible economic growth in the late 1890s.

1900–1905: New revolt, again followed by repression and containment of the worker intelligentsia

In the latter part of the 1890s, circumstances were particularly conducive for the domination of a variant of capitalist ideas within the working class. The fundamental base for this domination was an economic boom which provided the means for the granting of concessions to less politically radical workers on an individual and group basis. Indeed the expansion of production in the empire at that time was the greatest in the world. As the industrial and political heart of the empire, the city of St. Petersburg particularly felt the stimulus of this growth. Consequently there were readily available channels for individual advancement open to the large and growing layer of skilled and educated "worker intelligents" concentrated particularly in the defence related metal industry.

---

129 See for example the position of Pipes 1963, p11.

130 Schneiderman 1976, p80.

131 Wildman 1967, p131.

132 See Wildman 1967, pp146-7 for the relation of Bernstein and the Economists to the Marxist tradition. See p141 for a very clear quote from Bernstein's article in *Rabochaia Mysl'*, no. 7.

133 Kochakov (ed.) 1957, pp196-7, Wildman 1967, p144.

Additionally necessary for its ideological domination, tsarism was particularly effective in suppressing those among the student and worker "intelligents" who sought to politically organise against it. Indeed, alongside the greatest economic expansion in the world stood the greatest police state. At this stage those elements opposing tsarism were still small, weakly organised and inexperienced in conspiracy. These conditions provided the basis for the dominance of Economism, a reformist political strategy based on determinist assumptions, among almost all the elements that made up the anti-tsarist intelligentsia of the time.

In the determinist interpretation of Marxism the contradictions of the system are ignored or denied. Yet from mid-1899 the economy of the Russian empire, formerly the fastest growing in the world, was the worst affected by a new crisis in the world economy.[134] This economic crisis underlay a new historical phase leading up to the first political crisis of tsarism beginning on Bloody Sunday, 9 January 1905.

The central political feature of this period was tsarism's increasingly drastic initiatives to restore its position among the working and middle classes of St. Petersburg. Whatever the initial success of these measures the underlying crisis of the economy ensured their ultimate failure, with the subsequent reversion to repression further undermining the legitimacy of the regime. Thus in mid-1903, Sergei Witte, minister of finance associated with policies that resulted in the boom of the 1890s, but also the slump and famine of the 1900s, was removed, and in early 1904 the Russo-Japanese War was launched.[135] In mid-1904 when the notoriously repressive minister of the interior Pleve was assassinated, he was replaced by a liberal.[136] Yet the removal of Witte did not lead to an improvement in the economy, the war proved a humiliating catastrophe,[137] and the flowering of discussion allowed by the new minister of the interior led to a deepening wave of protest which could only be curbed by a new policy of suppression.[138] Among workers, tsarism's more liberal approach led to the granting of a limited legality for worker delegates in 1903 as well as the permitting of a worker organisation formally independent of, though still closely supervised by, the police in 1904. It would be precisely this organisation, the inheritor of Zubatov's attempt to separate the mass of

---

134 Kochakov (ed.) 1957, p199, Diakin et al. 1972, pp231-2. From the end of 1902 a further deepening of the crisis occurred (Diakin et al. 1972, p258).

135 Kochakov (ed.) 1957, pp224-5.

136 Surh 1989, p100.

137 Most notably with the fall of Port Arthur; see among many commentaries Kochakov (ed.) 1957, pp225-6.

138 Sablinsky 1976, p141.

workers from revolutionaries, that became the vehicle for the most serious threat to tsarism.

The most significant result of the post-1900 economic crisis was the transformation in the circumstances of the metal worker "elite" and hence the worker intelligentsia. There was also a marked deterioration in the circumstances of textile workers.[139] The onset of the crisis led to a wave of sackings and an increase in the working day across all industries.[140] A further decline in conditions occurred, despite an easing of the crisis overall, with the onset of war in 1904.[141] Skilled metal workers who had earlier enjoyed a position of relative dignity, opportunity and privilege[142] were now subject to personal stagnation, deterioration in conditions and humiliation in the workplace.[143] The resentment generated by these changes provided the ground for a marked radicalisation in the variants of Economism, as well as a vigorous and persistent effort to form organisations based on the formerly predominant interventionist interpretation of Marxism.

Flowing from the transformed economic context there was a shift in the nature of workers' struggle from the turn of the century. This can be seen from the data for workers' protest activity. Reflecting the straitened circumstances of workers, as well as the more limited possibility for the granting of concessions by industrialists, the figures for the number of strikes and days on strike both fell by about one third in 1900-05 compared to 1895-1900. More dramatic than this overall decline in strikes was the shift in their balance towards the now disgruntled metal workers. Thus the percentage of strikes involving metal plants rose from 15 to 27 percent, while the percentage of metal workers among those on strike rose by far more – from 17.5 to 48.5 percent.[144] This is not to say that the period represented a complete break with the past – the textile workers predominant in strike activity earlier remained important, with 50 percent of strikes and 38 percent of strikers. And the regions of Vyborg and Nevskii, which had been the centres of struggle in the earlier period, remained so.

---

139 Kochakov (ed.) 1957, p200.

140 ibid., pp199-200.

141 Surh 1989, pp26-7, Heather Hogan, "Scientific Management and the changing nature of work in the St. Petersburg metalworking industry, 1900-1914", in Haimson and Tilly (eds.) 1989, p362, Leopold H. Haimson, "Structural processes of change and changing patterns of labour unrest: the case of the metal-processing industry in Imperial Russia, 1890-1914", in ibid., p384, Kochakov (ed.) 1957, pp228-9.

142 Hogan in Haimson and Tilly (eds.) 1989, p357, Haimson in ibid., p380-4.

143 Haimson in ibid., pp388-90, Surh 1989, pp65-7. Hogan in Haimson and Tilly (eds.) 1989, p362.

144 Diakin et al. 1972, pp231, 248, Haimson in Haimson and Tilly (eds.) 1989, p385.

Yet such figures still reveal a significant shift between the strikes of the mid-1890s and those of the 1900s. For if the earlier strikes were largely the response of textile workers to the failure of their conditions to improve as the economy boomed, then the latter were largely the protest of both metal and textile workers to a deterioration in conditions as the economy slumped. Consequently while in the earlier strikes the intervention of the anti-tsarist intelligentsia was still relatively indirect and peripheral to the development of protest, in the latter it was far more central to the course of the strikes.

Thus the strikes, as well as other forms of protest in the 1900s, represented much more a general political protest against tsarism than had earlier been the case, and were very much more related to the fortunes of the failing system. Thus the overwhelming bulk of strikes occurred in two waves associated with troughs in the economy in early 1900 and 1903 and were associated with the powerful class symbol of May Day.[145] The year 1904 by contrast saw very few strikes,[146] as an element of patriotism associated with war fever pervaded the early part of the year, and liberal protest dominated in the second half.

These features of the period are particularly evident in its main outburst of protest – a march, strike and uprising which became known as the "Obukhov Defence". As May Day 1901 approached the anti-tsarist intelligentsia was divided between those of more Economist persuasion who sought to organise a march in the city centre, and those of adhering to an interventionist interpretation of Marxism who preferred to organise strikes in the working class districts.[147] While the initial view prevailed among the anti-tsarist intelligentsia the march could not in fact be initiated, and in early May a strike wave, culminating in street fighting, occurred in Vyborg.[148]

This action was echoed at the Obukhov plant, one of the largest arms-producing metal plants in the Nevskii district, which until this point did not have a record of workers' struggle. The strike was joined by a number of other large plants in the district, and a prolonged battle was waged in the nearby streets after the armed forces were sent in to quell the disturbance. Of even greater significance than the size and radicalism of this action was the large number of attempts from outside the district to render support to the insurgents.[149] Reflecting the extent and radicalism of the insurgency the repression with which it was met was ferocious – surpassing even that used to put down the textile strikes. Further, while major concessions were granted

---

145 Diakin et al. 1972, p232.

146 ibid., p260.

147 Diakin et al. 1972, p239, Kochakov (ed.) 1957, p208, Surh 1989, p89.

148 Diakin et al. 1972, pp239-40.

149 ibid., pp241-6, Kochakov (ed.) 1957, pp208-10, Surh 1989, pp95-7.

initially, they were quickly withdrawn, and a repeat strike failed.

Thus it was clear that the onset of economic crisis had removed only one of the conditions for the dominance of the anti-tsarist intelligentsia by Economism. Other conditions hindering the development of workers' consciousness, such as the spasmodic nature of the class struggle and the pervading pressure of repression, continued as before – indeed their role was now probably greater. The result of this pressure meant that Economism, albeit of growing radicalism, continued to dominate all sections of the anti-tsarist intelligentsia, while only state-sponsored workers' organisations could continue to exist, albeit with growing independence.

At the turn of the century the St. Petersburg Union of Struggle for the Liberation of the Working Class, the organisation formed in late 1895 to centralise the efforts of Marxists, was still the main body of Social Democrats in the city. It was now dominated by Economism after the decimation of the movement following the abortive first Congress of the Russian Social Democratic Labor Party in 1898. Consistent with these Economist views, workers sympathetic to Social Democracy formed an organisationally independent Workers' Organisation whose structure and function was more of a trade union or cooperative than a political party.[150] Prior to the Obukhov Defence, the Workers' Organisation was a substantial organisation with some 300-500 members located mainly in the large factories of the traditional worker strongholds of Nevskii and Vyborg.[151] Yet the very success of the organisation in the Obukhov Defence exposed it to repression, which it predictably proved unable to resist. The result was that although the Workers' Organisation continued to exist until 1903, for the last two years of its existence it was an ineffective force.

If the Economists proved incapable of resisting repression, then the supporters of traditional interventionist Marxism were also effectively curtailed. Thus, as will be outlined in Chapter five,[152] *Iskra*'s influence within the St. Petersburg Union grew until early 1901, but was then broken by arrests in the period leading up to May Day. Despite the repeated arrest of organisers, support again built up until the St. Petersburg Union committed itself to *Iskra* in early 1902. However this victory proved to be shortlived, as a substantial group sympathetic to Economism split in the second half of the year. This split allied itself with St. Petersburg's newly formed Socialist Revolutionary organisation to publish the last issue of *Rabochaia Mysl'*. The split among

---

150 Gerald Surh, "Rabochaia demokratiia i khimera 'Ekonomizma': Peterburgskaia rabochaia organizatsiia, 1900-1903 gg." in Potolov (ed.) 1997, pp508-29, p510.

151 ibid., p510. Here the Nevskii district is termed the "Obukhov" district.

152 See the section "The build-up to the Second Congress of the RSDLP".

Social Democrats at the second Congress of the RSDLP was particularly felt in St. Petersburg, where the organisation was crippled in the first half of 1904, and most of the outlying district organisations aligned themselves with the Mensheviks towards the end of the year.

Thus, tsarism was able to effectively repress the revolutionary threat after the Obukhov Defence, just as it had been able to do so after the textile strikes. Yet it was undermined by an economic crisis after the latter struggle in a way that it was not after the former. This led it into more and more adventurous external initiatives to bolster its prestige, as well as experiments in worker co-option to bolster its standing among the increasingly aggrieved working class. While tsarism was seeking channels to co-opt workers a number of long term Social Democratic "worker intelligents" were, although pressured into Economism by tsarist repression, still actively seeking any channel through which to organise workers against their conditions.[153] When Economism as a state attempt at co-option was fused with this latter Economism as a dissident accedence to state repression, a vehicle for a qualitatively greater new threat to tsarism was conceived.

If worker Economism had faded in the early 1900s, then Economism openly associated with the state had also initially found barren soil in St. Petersburg. Zubatov's attempt to replicate his Moscow movement foundered in the face of hostility from the press, liberals and a worker intelligentsia profoundly suspicious of police involvement in the labour movement.[154] His failure and the subsequent demise allowed the priest-philanthropist Sergei Gapon[155] to successfully demand autonomy and immunity for his Assembly of Russian Factory Workers when it was founded in 1903.[156]

In early 1904 the historical turning point for the Assembly came when Gapon formed an alliance with the Economist leaders. Just as the Russo-Japanese War was being launched and the Assembly was being legally registered,[157] the two forces adopted a "secret program", amounting to Western trade unionism, which was to be campaigned for covertly.[158] In the second half

---

153 For background on these figures and their early involvement with Gapon see Sablinsky 1976, pp75-6, 99-100, 106-7, Surh 1989, pp116-9.

154 Diakin et al. 1972, p257. As well as continuing antagonism from the Ministry of Finance, Sablinsky 1976, pp66-9.

155 For Gapon's background see Sablinsky 1976, pp34-55, Ascher 1988, pp76-9.

156 Kochakov (ed.) 1957, pp237-9, Surh 1989, pp107, 110-1, Diakin et al. 1972, p260, Sablinsky 1976, pp81-97.

157 At a ceremony on 11 April 1904 at which 150 members attended and 73 new members joined (Sablinsky 1976, p106).

158 With the formation of a "secret committee" to organise for the "secret program", see Sablinsky 1976, pp102-4; program reproduced p103; Surh 1989, pp120-5.

of 1904, with the war being lost and liberal society in uproar, the Economists, through the Assembly, were able to organise a mass movement in preparation for launching the program. By the end of the year, the Assembly had grown to some 20,000 members in eleven branches.[159]

Yet despite the growing threat that the Assembly now posed to tsarism, the consciousness of its leaders and members remained reformist. Thus when Gapon considered launching his "secret program" as a direct challenge to the tsar, he sought the counsel and support of the leading theorists of Economism.[160] Gapon and his allies maintained their hostility and exclusion of orthodox Marxists[161] to the very brink of open confrontation with the state at the end of December, while continuing to entreat state officials. Within the framework of the Assembly, the Opposition, as the Economists became known,[162] confined their criticisms to the tactics for building the movement and did not challenge Gapon's ultimate acceptance of the tsarist state.[163]

Conclusion: St. Petersburg 1860–1905 – emergence, rise and containment of the worker intelligentsia

In St. Petersburg, as would have been foreseen by both determinist and interventionist interpretations of Marx, a massive rise in the productive forces did indeed lead to the growth of a labour movement with the latent potential to take power. The advance of this labour movement was not uninterrupted, nor did it develop without the intervention of conscious leadership. Thus the advance of productive forces was hindered by a ruling class equally fearful of internal dissent as of foreign threats, as well as by periodic shortages of capital arising from crises of world capitalism. From the Northern Union to the Gapon Assembly, the emergence of worker organisations required conscious leaders who critically appropriated elements of an ideology developed "outside" the class to articulate worker grievances. Such leaders could develop because industrialists themselves required an educated workforce and so facilitated the development of a self-educated worker intelligentsia within the metal worker "elite" of the arms factories. To contain these consciously led movements tsarism responded with a strategy of concessions to the base of

---

159 Sablinsky 1976, pp109, 122, 129, Diakin et al. 1972, p262. Figures vary for membership, for example 6,000 in Kochakov (ed.) 1957, p238.

160 The authors of the "Credo", the publication of which launched Lenin into his anti-economist campaign, Sablinsky 1976, p133, Surh 1989, pp140-2.

161 Expressed in the usual code of a hostility to the intelligentsia, Sablinsky 1976, pp125-6.

162 ibid., pp100, 119.

163 See for example ibid., pp102-5.

the movement and repression of its leaders, that grew in sophistication and scale with the growth of the movement.

As a result of the conflict between factors promoting and hindering the rise of productive forces, as well as the consequent labour revolt, the course of that revolt took the form of a dialectic of waves followed by troughs. The waves certainly grew in scope, reaching their highest peak in the mid-1890s. Yet following each peak came a trough caused by economic depression and state repression, in which a substantial portion of the earlier advance in workers' conditions and organisation was wiped out. This retreat was reflected not only in the fragmentation of any organisation that may have been established, but also by the political adaptation of its leaders to the status quo. Thus Economism was a political adaptation among leading workers to the realities of state repression following the highest peak of the mid-1890s.

Up to 1900, tsarism had been able to contain workers' revolt with relative ease, as the system maintained some advance overall, and consequently its contradictions were relatively mild. Certainly the peaks of struggle became higher as worker numbers, concentration, and experience grew. But with the industrial base of the system still advancing overall, tsarism had the means to contain the labour movement. This occurred both organisationally, through increasing repression of its leadership and limited concessions to the base, as well as ideologically, through the sponsorship of State Economism. Consequently the conscious labour leadership adapted to tsarism and was confined within the isolated "intelligentsia" of self-educated workers with at least some critical understanding of tsarism.

In the next chapter it will be shown how this situation was transformed in the political crisis of tsarism after Bloody Sunday. In this new context, the formerly isolated "intelligents" were able to lead the class as a whole through the medium of a large layer of worker activists seeking to foment struggles against tsarism. In subsequent chapters it will be shown how the Marxists formed a faction among the "intelligents" before 1905 and subsequently a militant section of the activists in 1905-07. In the final two chapters Lenin's ideas on party organisation will be discussed as a response to difficulties in cohering these contrasting forms of interventionist Marxist leadership.

Chapter 4

ST. PETERSBURG 9 JANUARY 1905–3 JUNE 1907: FORMATION, RISE AND CONTAINMENT OF A LAYER OF "WORKER ACTIVISTS"

Introduction: 1905–1907 – a context of escalated workers' struggle

The First Russian Revolution, often referred to as the 1905 revolution in Western literature, was an upsurge in struggle which gripped the Russian empire for fully two and a half years – from 9 January 1905 to 3 July 1907. The persistence of this break with the relative stability of the past reflected the depth of the contradictions created by the empire's participation in the emerging imperialist system. The revolution encompassed a revolt by all classes except the nobility against the economic distress and political authoritarianism of modernising tsarism; and the protests of capitalists, workers and peasants combined to threaten tsarism's grip on power.

The scale of the revolt reflected the fact that the economic prerequisites necessary for the overthrow of tsarism by workers had been achieved. Yet workers in fact failed to do so despite a gigantic advance in their organisation and consciousness. In addition to the material prerequisites for historical transition there was an essential role for fully class conscious intervention if the possibilities for labour advance were to be realised.

The break from relative passivity to agitation among the population as a whole was nowhere more marked than among workers. This could be seen in the figures for strike action, the most basic form of working class struggle, which became the hallmark of the revolution. Whereas previously such protests had been the exception and order the norm, now strike action, or the expectation of such activity, became the norm, and periods of undisturbed work were seen as times of respite and preparation. Thus, even between the peaks of struggle, figures for the number of strikes as well as the number of days on strike remained at tens of times those of the previous decades.

Strikes changed not only in quantity, but perhaps of even greater significance for worker organisation and consciousness, in quality. In the relatively limited crisis of earlier periods, they were usually confined to a particular plant with occasional district or industry-wide protests. In the current deep political impasse of the tsarist state, the expectation became that strikes would sweep across the whole of St. Petersburg in inexorable waves. In these struggles the potential of the working class as a political force could be directly seen by all, not least by the mass of workers directly involved in these generalised protests. The Marxist conception of the class, and hence Lenin's points in his polemic against the Economists, could now be clear not merely to a politicised element of the "worker intelligentsia", but also to a section of a much larger layer of leaders emerging in the struggle – a layer that could well be termed the "worker activists".

Formed in the mass struggles of 1905, and particular their high point over October and November of that year, the "worker activists" composed a layer of perhaps 10,000 workers. They embodied elements of both continuity and discontinuity with the "worker intelligentsia", around which they cohered, and it is the relation of these elements that will later be shown to explain what changed, as well as what did not change, in Lenin's comments on worker consciousness and party organisation after Bloody Sunday. Thus the "activists" marked an advance on, not a break from, earlier attempts at conscious intervention by worker leaders. As such they were also centred on the former strongpoints of the "intelligentsia" in the Nevskii district, as well as to a lesser extent in the newer centres of worker struggle in the Vyborg and Narva districts. Indeed the activists were cohered through the transformation of the centres of organisation, most notably the Evening-Sunday Schools, which had earlier been the centres of the "intelligentsia". Yet the intelligentsia were largely required to generalise from personal experience to a critical understanding of tsarism through abstract study, usually commenced at the Evening-Sunday Schools and then continued in secret study circles conducted by political dissidents. The activists, on the other hand, could make this generalisation far more directly through reflecting on their immediate experience of leading ongoing mass struggles. These mass struggles confronted the power and consequently exposed the nature of the capitalist class and tsarist state.

Particularly over the initial rise of the revolution, the activists were led by the Evening-Sunday School teachers and clandestine circle leaders who had earlier propagandised among the intelligentsia. However these leaders were now able to openly agitate among a vastly increased audience engaged in direct struggle. Thus, whereas the tiny intelligentsia had learnt by studying how others made history, the mass of activists learnt by actually making, or failing to make, history themselves. This meant that the theoretical disputes that had earlier fractured the intelligentsia persisted to divide the activists – but they did so in the form of divisions over tactics to be adopted in the mass struggle, rather than general questions of principle.

As a result of this ongoing reality or prospect of generalised struggle, much broader and more stable forms of class organisation arose and persisted among workers. Prior to 1905, organisation did not go beyond factory delegates, with city-wide gatherings only in exceptional circumstances, such as during the textile strikes. Generally these bodies only functioned during the course of strikes and were dispersed by the state shortly thereafter. In the new circumstances, worker representatives convened in ongoing city-wide organisations of struggle by the whole class. The most potent of these, the first Soviet, was associated with the height of the revolution in late 1905. As the revolution declined such city-wide class organisation was re-established in a less definite and direct way – initially through bodies such as trade unions and unemployed associations, and later through the assembled worker representatives in the First and Second Dumas.

The existence of these class-wide organisations could raise the Marxist vision of workers' power for a large mass of workers, and in particular a section of the "worker activists". Earlier this possibility had been limited to those "worker intelligents" associated with the Marxist section of the anti-tsarist intelligentsia. Now the greater base for this awareness meant that it was possible for the Marxist intelligentsia to initiate a formal relation with the working class as a whole through the party supporting delegates to the Soviet and subsequent representative bodies. In the limited struggles before 1905 this relation to the mass of workers could only be informal and diffuse through the medium of leaflets scattered as the opportunity arose.

The radicalisation of these worker organisations reflected what was probably the most significant feature of the revolution – and that with the greatest significance for Lenin's comments on party organisation. This was the dramatic shift in worker consciousness over the course of the struggle and in particular the shift among the leadership of those workers. In earlier periods spasms of struggle had punctuated a general flow of passivity. Consequently the consciousness of the mass of workers involved in these struggles had quickly resumed a practical submission to the status quo, while that of most politicised "worker intelligents" retreated to a radical reformism. Now, with an ongoing expectation of struggle and change, repressive attempts to crush the labour movement induced only greater indignation and radicalisation among workers. Among the emerging layer of activists this was eventually reflected in a growing membership of anti-tsarist parties, and ultimately their most radical fringe in the Bolsheviks.

This evident growth of class consciousness underlay the well-known shift of Lenin's comments over party organisation. For now the forces going into struggle, as well as the way in which they did so, were vastly greater than before, and posed very different demands on those deliberately intervening to lead that struggle. Even so, Lenin's basic concern continued as before – cohering an interventionist leadership to centralise the working class for a decisive struggle. For while the tactics open to Marxists in leading the working class had changed, the implacable hostility of its class enemy continued as before.

The four phases of the revolution

While the revolution witnessed a dramatic growth in the organisation and consciousness of the working class as a whole, this in itself was not sufficient to displace the tsarist state. Rather, while at times that regime was severely constrained, it still proved capable of re-establishing its power using the earlier combination of concession and repression, though now with both on a far greater scale to meet the far greater threat. With the conscious intervention of Marxists as yet limited by inexperience, weakness and division, the rising workers' organisations could not respond to repression by the state with decisive acts of their own. Consequently, after peaking at the end of 1905, the workers' movement was slowly but steadily driven back.

The interaction between the rising revolt of workers on the one hand, and the impact of tsarist initiatives to curtail that revolt on the other, resulted in the course of the revolution comprising four phases. In the period between the massacre on 9 January 1905 and the granting of limited democratic concessions on 17 October of that year, the pent-up bitterness of workers was expressed in a series of strike waves that drove back tsarism and secured significant democratic concessions. Between 18 October and the arrest of the Soviet on 3 December, the workers exercised the prerogatives they had won within a *de facto* democracy, while the tsarist state steadily prepared the ground to reassert its authority.

From 4 December 1905 and the dissolution of the First Duma on 9 July 1906 this restoration was commenced, but then set back due to resistance from a resurgent workers' movement. This was followed by the period from 10 July 1906 to the dissolution of the Second Duma on 3 June 1907, when the restoration was carried out more wholeheartedly, the workers' movement, despite some politicised protest, was forced into full scale retreat and the ground was laid for the complete reassertion of tsarist power. This advance and retreat by the labour movement provided the context for the advance and retreat of the Bolshevik faction and consequently for the shifts in Lenin's comments on party organisation that will be dealt with in following chapters.

9 January–17 October 1905: Emergence of the "worker activists"

As is the case for all aspects of the revolutionary history of the Russian empire, the interpretation of the rising labour activism in St. Petersburg between January and October 1905 reflects a general understanding of class struggle. Such a general understanding also conditions the way Lenin's comments on party organisation and the shift in these comments over 1905 are analysed. For even the mainstream, who attempt to consider Lenin's comments in abstract, must give some credence to the anti-tsarist struggle as part of the general historical background to Lenin's ideas. The critics who seek to set Lenin within his historical context see the workers' struggle as the basic element of that context.

The course of the labour movement between January and October 1905 has been referred to a great deal by the critics, as well as to a limited extent by the mainstream, because here occurs an apparently fundamental change in Lenin's views on party organisation, associated with a dramatic shift in the class struggle. The mainstream, leaning to the view of Lenin as a complete and consistent authoritarian, view this period within their general framework of labour protest as an enraged and unconscious delinquency prone to manipulation by a malign influence. The critics, leaning to the view that Lenin responded to pressure by shifting towards a less rigorously interventionist position at this time, view this movement as the outstanding example of a spontaneous outburst, and in doing so implicitly regard it as undifferentiated as well as advancing without either stimulus or setbacks from tsarism.[1] What these apparently antagonistic positions have in common is a limitation on, if not a denial of, the role of conscious intervention by worker leaders, as well as the stimulus and response of the tsarist state, in determining the course of the struggle.

The actual experience of struggle between January and October stands utterly against the unconscious delinquency at the centre of the mainstream model of worker protest, but also undermines what may be termed a

---

1   For a schematic summary of the evolution of these two positions as they relate to the history of Russia in general see Edward Acton "The Revolution and its Historians: the *Critical Companion* in Context" in Acton et. al. 1997, pp3-17. The critics' view is probably expressed most clearly by Marcel Liebman at the conclusion to the section "From the elite party to the mass party": "A few months later, having submitted himself to learning from the experience of the revolution, and after the revolution had taken huge steps forward, he [Lenin] acknowledged the merits, occasional but fundamental, of proletarian spontaneity and initiative." (Liebman 1975, p49.)

"spontaneist" model adopted by the critics within which the role of conscious leadership is limited or denied. Thus, conflicting directly with the instinctive delinquency of the mainstream view, the rising workers' struggle took the form of a series of deliberate actions by a growing body of workers. Further, over the course of their struggle, these workers concurrently established responsible delegate institutions to exercise collective control of their activity. Yet conflicting also with the unconsciousness of the critics' "spontaneist" view, these actions were launched through channels created by tsarism itself in an attempt to stabilise its weakening popular base. Rather than making a complete break with historical experience, the rising struggle was strongly conditioned by the earlier development of industry, leadership in earlier industrial struggles, and the prior growth of the worker intelligentsia. And while the immediate reaction of most workers to the initial momentous and traumatic events of the revolution was one of deep political questioning and tactical militancy, this did not lead most to directly join political parties concretely preparing insurrection.

Reflecting the prevailing models of the labour movement, the rising struggle of 1905 is usually treated as a single undifferentiated episode in most Western studies of Lenin. In fact the period comprised two peaks of turbulence around general strikes at the beginning and end of the year, with a relative hiatus of struggle through the mid-year months. This mid-year hiatus was partly broken by a lesser burst of struggle.[2] Usually seen as spreading in an arbitrary manner from an accidental stimulus, the general strikes were actually launched by the action of the best organised sections of the working class (the Putilov plant in January and the printing[3] and railway workers[4] in September). This lead was able to be given because tsarism allowed organisations of a trade union type (Gapon's Assembly early in the year and the printing and railway unions later) to function, indeed to openly prepare workers' struggle. It is significant to note in all the detailed analysis of the week leading up to Bloody Sunday no mention is made of state efforts to abort the obviously threatening movement.[5]

The general strikes did not spread evenly; rather, their success was determined by the action of the decisive section of the city's workers in the Nevskii district, and in particular the three "leading" plants of that district –

---

2   Among many sources in support of this overall analysis see the table of strike figures by month in Surh 1989, p260. See also his comment, p259, where he notes the relative fall in strike figures, but not their cause in the success of employers in stemming the "spontaneous" factory level struggle.

3   Surh 1989, pp277, 311-2, Shuster 1976, p142.

4   Surh 1989, pp320-1, Shuster 1976, p144, Kochakov (ed.) 1957, p314.

5   See for example Kochakov (ed.) 1957, pp154-200. In fact the Petersburg Governor rejected a proposal to arrest Gapon (Kochakov (ed.) 1957, p245).

Obukhov, Aleksandrovskii and Nevskii Iron and Steel. The October strike was prefigured by a strike in the Nevskii district from 4-6 October with demands being issued by a "Workers Strike Committee beyond the Nevskii Gate".[6] It was the action of these plants on 5 January,[7] as well as on 12 and 13 October, that escalated growing strike action to the point of a general strike.[8] Thus the decisive events of 1905 were centred precisely on that district with the longest tradition of struggle and the most extensive development of a leading worker intelligentsia. Indeed, it was the long term seat of that intelligentsia, the Kornilov Evening-Sunday School, which became one of their principle organising centres.[9] It seems clear that while the supposedly "spontaneous" upsurge did in fact involve vastly greater numbers in a far greater struggle than ever before, it was nevertheless still led by conscious "worker intelligents" who cohered around themselves an embryonic layer of activists seeking to fight tsarism.

The two peaks of the rising revolution were not the culmination of a rising tide of economic struggle as a "spontaneist" view might suggest. Indeed both peaks were preceded by a pause in strike activity.[10] Rather, the conditions for these generalised outbursts were created by a deep political crisis following catastrophe in war. In both cases, workers' activity followed in the wake of a general disquiet in society focused particularly on agitation by the liberal professions. Thus the January strike followed the fall of Port Arthur and the suppression of a very lively campaign of banquets by professionals, while the October strike followed the sinking of the Russian navy in the Straits of Tsushima and a deep disquiet over the proposed "Bulygin Duma".[11] Central to the mid-year rise in protest were military setbacks leading to a proposed draft of factory workers.[12]

Strike activity within particular factories and industries certainly continued at a far higher level between the two general strikes than it had before 1905.[13]

---

6   Surh 1989, pp313-4. See also Shuster 1976, pp142-3, 145-7 and Kochakov (ed.) 1957, p284, pp312-3 and p315.

7   On 4 January when disappointingly few factories went out, most of these were on the Nevskii side (Shuster 1976, p73).

8   Surh 1989, p324.

9   V.S. Tsytsarin in "Kornilovskaia Shkola" (Central State Archive of Historico-Political Documents of Saint Petersburg, fond 4000, opis' 5 delo 138, list 5) comments that "in fact the school became a party club in 1905".

10   See the case of September, Kochakov (ed.) 1957, p309.

11   See Shuster 1976, p139 about meetings over the Bulygin Duma.

12   Surh 1989, p270, Shuster 1976, pp131-3, Kochakov (ed.) 1957, p302, Diakin et al. 1972, p282.

13   Surh 1989, p259.

Such activity was particularly great among the workers of St. Petersburg's major plants over January[14] and February.[15] Following the pattern from the turn of the century, metal workers played the dominant role in these strikes with textile workers playing a major though subordinate role.[16] At this time a large number of workers who had limited experience in struggle caught a glimpse of their potential power through expressing indignation over the events of Bloody Sunday.[17] In the state sector, and particularly within the Nevskii district, this led to the widespread granting of the nine-hour day.[18]

Yet very quickly after Bloody Sunday private employers united to resist economic demands,[19] and from the end of February made effective use of the lockout to cow their workforces. This occurred with the most demonstrative effect over summer at the Putilov plant, where the factory was closed for a long period, and some 3,000 workers were not re-employed when it re-opened.[20] These lockouts, together with the onset of economic crisis, further embittered the radicalising worker activists and meant that the large factories were initially reluctant to join the October strike due to the limitation of its demands to economic issues. When these factories did in fact join the action they did so on the basis of demands that were more generally political.[21]

If the uneven course and deliberate leadership of the struggle in 1905 undermines a "spontaneist" model of the labour movement, then the growth of responsible class-wide organisation through that struggle definitively rebuts the mainstream model of protest. Over the course of the year, despite repeated waves of repression, a growing number of worker delegates proved capable of uniting in increasingly stable structures of representation. The celebrated Soviet, often regarded as rising without precedent and in a vacuum, was in fact the result of nine months of deepening organisation, particularly within the strategic Nevskii district. In fact it was the bastion of the worker intelligentsia, the metal workers of the Nevskii district (especially the Semiannikov and

14   For the continuation of the general strike after Bloody Sunday see Kochakov (ed.) 1957, p270, Diakin et al. 1972, pp271-2.

15   Particularly at the time of the convening and dissolution of the Shidlovskii Commission; see Kochakov (ed.) 1957, p277.

16   Kochakov (ed.) 1957, p288.

17   For some discussion of the second wave of strike activity in February see Surh 1989,   pp194-9. For a discussion of the immediate aftermath of Bloody Sunday see Shuster 1976, pp96-100.

18   Shuster 1976, pp100-1, Kochakov (ed.) 1957, p289.

19   Surh 1989, pp188-91, Kochakov (ed.) 1957, pp284-7.

20   Surh 1989, p292, Kochakov (ed.) 1957, pp302-3.

21   Surh 1989, p324. See for example the case of Obukhov on 4-5 October in Shuster 1976. For the demands of the Obukhov plant on 13 October see Kochakov (ed.) 1957, p316.

Obukhov factories) as well as workers from the Vyborg district who were the core of the meeting at the foundation of the Soviet on 13 October.[22]

The historical roots of the Soviet should be traced back to Gapon's Assembly at least. Perhaps influenced by high Soviet stereotypes, the consequences of this movement are usually thought to have ended with Bloody Sunday. Yet as a locally based organisation of between 11,000 and 20,000 members, and recognised by the state as a representative of the working class, the Assembly prefigured later labour organisation and involved many activists who went on to become workplace delegates and founders of trade unions. The importance of the Assembly was evident in the frequency of the demand for the freeing of its arrested activists and the re-establishment of its branches during the campaign around the Shidlovskii Commission. This Commission was decreed on 18 February to placate the still burning indignation felt by workers after the events of Bloody Sunday.[23] Yet following the pattern of so many tsarist attempts at co-option around this time, the ongoing bitterness of workers meant that, instead, the Commission became a vehicle for the re-establishment of workplace organisation and one of the precedents for the Soviet.

The Commission was intended as a board of inquiry with members to be delegated from a body of representatives elected by the city's workers. Yet despite a restricted franchise in the elections many of these representatives were former Assembly activists,[24] and they boycotted the Commission when its appointed head refused to adopt a broad scope for the inquiry. The basis for the election of delegates to the Commission, one to every 500 workers, was later adopted by the Soviet and one of the chairs of the assembled electors, the lawyer Nosar, later became the Soviet's founding chair.[25]

The period between the dissolution of the Shidlovskii Commission in February and the formation of the Soviet in October was one in which worker organisation was on the defensive in the face of employer victimisation and state repression of activists.[26] As a result workplace organisation was weakened if not eliminated altogether outside the large plants. Yet from the middle of the year there were a number of organisational developments that were significant for the subsequent development of worker struggle. Thus several

22   Kochakov (ed.) 1957, p318.

23   ibid., p275.

24   Between January and March many factory managements were forced to recognise delegates (ibid., p290).

25   On Nosar see Surh 1989, pp233-8.

26   Surh 1989, pp221-2. Trepov was appointed governor of St Petersburg with dictatorial powers following Bloody Sunday. He immediately arrested 688 people, which included all Bolsheviks active in the Assembly (Kochakov (ed.) 1957, p274).

unions that would play a leading role in the struggles at the end of the year were established, among them the printers and railway workers. And in the stronghold of the Nevskii district, workplace delegates not only persisted but were able to organise councils within their factories as well as a coordinating body between the three main factories of the district.[27] In an action that prefigured the later broad concerns of the Soviet, the council successfully organised a boycott of rent rises across the district in the middle of the year.[28] In October this body became the initial core of the Soviet.[29]

The rise of struggle and organisation in 1905 reflected and promoted the most significant feature of the period for students of Lenin's ideas on the party – the rise in class consciousness among the mass of workers. Well documented is a dramatic shift from the predominance of loyalty to tsarism to a stand at least passively sympathetic to the insurrectionary overthrow of that regime. For those who analyse the workers' movement within a "spontaneist" framework this shift is closely related to that occurring in Lenin's ideas on party organisation – with the pressure of the former leading directly to the latter.

There can be no doubt that over the course of the year's struggle an enormous shift occurred in the views of all sections of the working class. But it is also clear that this shift did not occur solely through experience in struggle, that the extent of radicalisation was not even within the class or across districts, and that the relation between this shift and that in Lenin's ideas was very far from being one of simple pressure. For contrary to what might have been expected from a "spontaneist" view, this radicalisation was associated with an explosion of intellectual activity by workers, along with a deepening political differentiation across St. Petersburg's districts as well as between the occupational sectors of the working class. Thus, at the opening of the year's struggle, the consciousness of Assembly members, let alone workers as a whole, very much reflected the hegemony of ruling class ideas in the former period of relatively unbroken passivity. This is clear from the celebrated symbols of the march to the tsar on Bloody Sunday – the obsequiousness of the wording of the petition, the icons carried on the march, and the excited and humble expectation of the marchers.[30] It is equally clear from the disconcerted horror and disarray of the marchers when they were confronted with volleys of fire. At this stage the anti-tsarist intelligentsia as a whole was still a tiny

---

27   Shuster 1976, p117 and Diakin et al. 1972, p279, which also lists other plants where delegates were established. (I am taking Nevskii Iron and Steel and Semiannikov as alternative names for the same plant.)

28   Surh 1989, pp267-8; Diakin et al. 1972, p280.

29   See Shuster 1976, pp152-3, on the foundation and early functioning of the Soviet.

30   Kochakov (ed.) 1957, pp256-7.

group marginalised from the mass of workers.[31]

Yet even at this initial stage of protest the movement against tsarism was not undifferentiated. The celebrated symbolism of the day is drawn most of all from the largest of a number of marches – by the Narva district of the Assembly which left from the Putilov plant under the leadership of Gapon himself. In the Narva district the development of the worker intelligentsia had been weaker than in Nevskii, the movement was consequently more limited in its understanding of tsarism, and Social Democratic speakers received a more hostile reception in the week before Bloody Sunday.[32] Yet there were also marches from four other districts on that day, and here the workers proved to be less naive and easily disoriented than in the Narva district.[33] Thus in the Vyborg district marchers fought a street battle with the armed forces while on the Vasilevskii Island they erected barricades and fought for some days.[34] This may have been due to the proximity to the university – certainly it was a Bolshevik student who led the arming.[35] In Nevskii, with its long tradition of struggle and large "worker intelligentsia", the attitude to the march was sober and Social Democratic speakers received a more sympathetic hearing than in Narva.[36] Rather than collapse in disarray the march from Nevskii dispersed and regrouped to reach the centre of the city when met with volleys of fire.

For two months following Bloody Sunday St. Petersburg was gripped by indignation over the traumatic events of the day. This period did indeed witness the greatest shift of consciousness among workers to that time. However this shift could not be limited to a new understanding of their immediate circumstances but also involved a reconsideration of the world in general. Thus radical "intelligents" in the factories who had earlier been marginalised were now received with a new receptiveness.[37] Beyond the

---

31 For example ibid., p252 cites a figure of 300-400 for the number of the Bolsheviks in the city.

32 Shuster 1976, p76. He claims (p75) that local Social Democrats were instrumental in winning the district to the strike although Nevskii supported the march uncritically (p74). See also Kochakov (ed.) 1957, pp246-7, 251. Gapon was extremely alarmed by the distribution of a Bolshevik leaflet on 5 January (Kochakov (ed.) 1957, p245); p249 claims that the idea of the petition came from "Gapon and the Narva district". Diakin et al. 1972, pp267-8, claims that the reception for the Bolsheviks in the Nevskii and Vasilevskii Islands was quite friendly, citing a number of speakers, in particular the long term "worker intelligent" and collaborator of Lenin, Shelgunov.

33 For a discussion of the marches see Shuster 1976, pp89-90.

34 For coverage of events in other districts see Kochakov (ed.) 1957, pp258-67.

35 Diakin et al. 1972, pp269-70.

36 Shuster 1976, pp87-8. Some Obukhov workers even stood on the side of the march as it passed, urging workers not to participate. See also Kochakov (ed.) 1957, p258.

37 See for example Surh 1989, pp227-9.

factories there was an enormous growth in general education of the type that had earlier been the preserve of the Evening-Sunday Schools. Workers sought this education through the most varied and widespread channels – one case is known of a group of workers hiring a student to teach them. The process of the establishment and growth of the worker intelligentsia in the early 1890s was repeated, but now on a vastly greater scale, among the layer of worker activists engaged in leading struggles. With society now in turmoil and the possibility of deep social change, the earlier deradicalisation of the mass of workers, associated with a declining interest in broader education, was being reversed.[38]

A qualitative leap in this radicalisation of workers, in association with anti-tsarist dissidents "outside" the class, occurred with the granting of autonomy to the universities as they re-opened in mid-September. With tsarism now in peril, and the potential power of workers palpably evident, the universities provided a forum for avowed revolutionaries to lead tens of thousands of workers in continuous and concentrated discussion.[39] It is indicative of the advance in consciousness that workers who merely recounted the horrors of the factories, as mainly occurred in the Assembly in January, were now told to sit down in favour of those "who knew more". If the turmoil of January and February reproduced the experience of the Evening-Sunday Schools on a mass scale, then that in September-October did the same for the former clandestine Marxist circles of "worker intelligents".[40]

Owing to the newly formed and fluid nature of institutions established by workers, it is difficult to quantify the radicalisation that occurred in this initial rise of the revolution. Yet the evidence suggests that the general view of the mass of activists leading the movement shifted from one of hopeful expectation of reform within tsarism to a passive sympathy for armed insurrection against that system. This transition was marked by the support for Social Democrats in the Shidlovskii Commission,[41] the large and militant protests on the six month anniversary of Bloody Sunday,[42] and the emerging predominance of Menshevism in the leadership of the Soviet.[43]

---

38   Points made by Surh 1989, pp238-41, although Surh does not relate the change to a rise in the class struggle. He also does not make the vital distinction between "socialist intelligents" and others. For a discussion of this reopening and its consequences for the revolutionary movement across the Russian empire see Ascher 1988, vol. 1, pp196-206.

39   Surh 1989, pp295-9.

40   Shuster 1976, pp148-50. On the role of the universities and students in centralising the working class in the October strike, see Surh 1989 and Kochakov (ed.) 1957, p310.

41   Surh 1989, pp223, 225, cites a study suggesting that 20 percent of Shidlovskii electors were Social Democrat supporters while 65-75 percent were Assembly supporters.

42   Surh 1989, p272, Shuster 1976, pp133-5, Kochakov (ed.) 1957, p304.

43   See Kochakov (ed.) 1957, p318, for the initial composition of the Executive Committee of the

Yet while the worker base of the activists moved to a position of sympathy for extreme action against tsarism, at this stage they were not yet prepared to be directly involved in such action and the parties of the far left did not grow substantially within the general movement.[44] Thus after the universal support for the position of the Social Democrats in the Shidlovskii Commission in late February, participation in May Day events was a crushing disappointment.[45] And while the Soviet in principle supported armed struggle only a few hundred turned out to confront tsarism's closure of the university, its principle centre of organisation, on 15 October.

18 October–3 December 1905: The worker activists confront tsarism in a situation of dual power

The period between the granting of limited democratic liberties on 17 October and the arrest of the Soviet on 3 December marks the plateau of the revolution. This was a short-lived period of comparatively unrestrained initiative that workers had won by their struggle in the previous phase of the revolution's rise. In general the period was one in which workers sought to challenge and ultimately liquidate tsarism through daring mobilisation. Within this characterisation of the period overall, two phases are clear. Thus workers' strength and confidence initially grew until their defeat in what became known as the "November General Strike". This peak was followed by a clear decline as the labour movement failed to make an effective response to the combined offensive by the tsarist state and industrial capitalists.

The period of the revolution's rise showed above all the potential of workers to mobilise themselves and lead all classes in a struggle to constrain tsarism. This potential was manifest despite the fact that the class as a whole shifted in consciousness to at most a radical liberalism – indeed despite that fact that it was members of the radical middle class that led workers in struggle. Yet the "Days of Freedom", as they were called, also showed the limits placed on workers in pursuing their own immediate interests, as well as waging a revolutionary struggle against tsarism, when they had not broken from liberalism, however radical.

The concessions of 17 October reflected the pressure of a mobilisation that

---

Soviet. Diakin et al. 1972, p287.

44   Among others who comment on this, Surh 1989, p261.

45   Surh 1989, pp263-5. For a less jaundiced view of the day see Shuster 1976, pp122-6. Also less jaundiced, and emphasising police repression (with 743 arrests) see Kochakov (ed.) 1957, pp296-8. Note especially the prominent role played by the Nevskii region in the protests. Diakin et al. 1972, p281 emphasises the split between Bolsheviks and Mensheviks.

was centred on the workers' general strike, but which rallied at least passive and often active sympathy from all classes, including industrial capitalists. The success of the October general strike, and the consequent isolation of the tsar, consolidated support for a radical liberalism among the mass of workers. This view underlay the adventurous tactics adopted during the Days of Freedom to secure a number of traditional democratic demands – most notably freedom of the press and the right to organise. Yet this radical approach proved insufficient to gain victory in the central struggle over the Days of Freedom – that for the eight-hour day. For while workers regarded this measure as a basic democratic demand, capitalists strongly felt the threat to their economic position posed by its adoption. They responded to workers' attempts to establish de facto the eight-hour day with a widespread lockout, and then supported the consolidation of tsarist power flowing from the defeat in that struggle. In the wake of this sharp assertion of class reality, some workers, particularly from the traditional stronghold of class consciousness in the Nevksii district, began to turn away from radical liberalism and make preparations for military confrontation with tsarism. Yet by the time of the arrest of the Soviet in December, these preparations were still only beginning, and consequently no effective reply could be made to the blow from the state.

The labour movement during the Days of Freedom has been relatively ignored by students of Lenin. This is perhaps because the difference in response to the class struggle between Lenin and the other Bolsheviks has not been regarded as being as great as that earlier in the year. Nor has Lenin's break with his pre-1905 formulations on worker consciousness been seen as so dramatic as that in the immediate wake of Bloody Sunday. Nevertheless the Days of Freedom posed a radically new and challenging context for Lenin, as for all revolutionaries – that of a burgeoning adventurist mass movement within an unstable but very real semi-legality. Lenin's articles and speeches at this time in fact continued the main themes from the period of the rising revolution. Yet, as will be shown in later chapters, the context of a legal labour movement, as well as the impending showdown with tsarism, led him to labour the role of deliberate intervention by Marxists with at least equal intensity to that earlier. Thus the demands on his still relatively reticent supporters for openness in party affairs, as well as aggression in public external intervention, were a response to the enormous potential of the workers' movement outlined in this chapter.

Undoubtedly, the most significant development of the Days of Freedom was the organisation of the Soviet, which gave a concrete form to the Marxist position that the working class is able to rule society and remake it in its own image. Flowing from the significance of its activity, the Soviet was a central focus for all political actors at the time. For state and capitalist representatives the containment and destruction of this "dual power" was the central priority. For revolutionaries, and Lenin in particular, understanding the nature and potential of this unprecedented form of workers' organisation became the key to advancing the revolution. Thus the role of the Soviet as a revolutionary government, and the consequent tactics of revolutionaries within it, now became the central point of his critique of the Mensheviks. In making his assessment of its potential, Lenin clashed sharply with many of his own supporters, who adopted a dismissive attitude to the Soviet. This flowed from their view that Soviet-led struggles could not go beyond a capitalist framework. As will be argued later, Lenin's supposed libertarianism in these debates flowed from his perception of the Soviet as embodying the Marxist potential of the working class in power.

Undoubtedly, these discussions were deeply marked by the very embryonic nature of the Soviet as a representative organ of workers' power. Thus the call for a "workers' committee" was issued by the Mensheviks in the name of a group of activists on 14 October.[46] By 29 October, when the eight-hour campaign was launched, some 281 delegates were attending meetings, and this grew to some 562 in mid-November.[47] Yet the Soviet was still a body based in the traditional strongholds of the "worker elite". Thus the overwhelming proportion of delegates were metal workers, while textile workers were very poorly represented – even from factories with a history of struggle.[48] The largest single contingent came from the Printers Union, a traditional source of self-educated workers,[49] and another very large contingent came from the Railway Workers.[50] The largest number of factory delegates came from the two leading Nevskii plants, Semiannikov and Obukhov,[51] as well as the Putilov plant in the Narva district.[52] The Executive of the Soviet comprised two and later four representatives of the city's districts, together[53] with six representatives of the two factions of Social Democracy and

---

46   A copy of the leaflet with this call can be viewed at the Museum of the Political History of Russia (St. Petersburg), Fond 2, Inventory Number 337.

47   Surh 1989, p352.

48   In perhaps the only collated list of delegates of the Soviet, located at the Central State Archive of the city of St. Petersburg, Fond 9618, Opis', 1, Ed. Khr. 2, only one delegate is listed from the Cheshire Factory (sheet 24). [This source is hereafter referred to as Fond 9618.]

49   This contingent is listed in ibid. as comprising 22 members including Khrustalev-Nosar, the first chair of the Soviet (sheet 6).

50   Sixteen members of this contingent are listed on sheet 2. Their importance is suggested by their placement immediately following "representatives of parties" on sheet 1.

51   The contingent from Semiannikov comprised eight and another possible eight (sheet 9). The contingent from Obukhov comprised 14 and another possible two (sheet 10).

52   ibid. lists 24 members of the Putilov contingent on sheet 11.

53   Shuster 1976, p153, Kochakov (ed.) 1957, p355.

three representatives from the Socialist Revolutionaries.[54] The Soviet was thus potentially an organ of power, but one that was only beginning to emerge from earlier traditions of struggle by the working class.

The organisational activity of the Soviet very much reflected its embryonic character. Meetings of the Executive as well as full Soviet sessions were held on an ad-hoc basis as the struggle demanded.[55] The Soviet's paper was issued spasmodically through "expropriations" of commercial printeries.[56] And although they were not allowed to affiliate, liberal unions and professional associations provided most of the Soviet's budget. The Soviet was thus a still imperfect representative institution of the whole working class – but an institution developing with dramatic rapidity in the intense class struggle of the Days of Freedom. For instance, the Soviet even set up its own militia, which began to contest the authority of the police.[57]

The October Manifesto to the eight-hour day campaign: The workers rise

The actual course of the class struggle during the Days of Freedom, as in the case of the revolution's rise, confounded the mainstream model of the labour movement as an instinctive delinquency, but also the spontaneist expectation of a relatively irresistible, straightforward and uninterrupted rise in consciousness and organisation. Indeed the very intensity of events in this period accentuates the limitations of these frameworks which underlie the position taken on Lenin's organisational ideas.

In the wake of the October strike, inspired by what they thought had been a decisive victory and the consequent expectation of easy advance, workers made a qualitative leap in their political intervention within society in general, as well as in the improvement of their own conditions. Yet in making this very advance the still uneven and limited nature of workers' organisation and consciousness was sharply exposed by the hesitation and retreat of the movement in the face of the state's obvious preparation for repression. Lenin's argument for conscious intervention and hence centralised leadership if workers were to achieve the necessity of armed insurrection was starkly evident. However, by the end of the Days of Freedom, his position was clearly not accepted by the mass of workers or their activist leaders.

54   A list of these is given Fond 9618, sheet 1.

55   Thus there was no meeting between 22 and 29 October (Surh 1989, p350).

56   On the paper and its printing see Shuster 1976, p178, Kochakov (ed.) 1957, p332, Surh 1989, p346, Ascher 1986, p221.

57   Ascher 1986, pp277-8.

The contradictions of the context was evident in the first flush of victory between 18 and 29 October. Thus on 17 October, the tsar conceded his Manifesto in the face of complete popular isolation. Yet at the same time workers were prevented from meeting in the universities by martial law, and there was an atmosphere of extreme anxiety in the face of anticipated civil war. In these circumstances, the workers' movement continued to be organised through two very large mass meetings in the traditional "fortresses" of the Nevskii side. For example, very large and long meetings of some 7,000 were held in the Nevskii Iron and Steel Plant and 10,000 in the Obukhov Plant.[58] On 18 October the Manifesto was greeted by a wave of jubilant demonstrations throughout the city, although these were dominated by a feeling of relief rather than combativity.[59] Although clashes did occur, reported deaths were few.

Meeting the day after the tsar issued his Manifesto, the Soviet understandably rejected the limited concessions offered, and after calling for the strike to continue, adjourned to lead a demonstration demanding freedom for political prisoners.[60] Yet even though the strike continued to grow over the next few days, the Soviet leadership of this demonstration felt constrained to avoid direct clashes with the police,[61] and no significant attempts were made to call further street protests.[62] Although nothing further was conceded, the Soviet resolved on 19 October to make a demonstratively united return to work at midday two days later.[63]

It seems clear that the great majority of the worker base of the Soviet believed that the decisive battle had been won and could now be consolidated by struggle at the factory level.

It was in the crucial battle for the eight-hour day that this limited consciousness was dashed against the ongoing reality of tsarist power in the state and capitalist power in the factories. In this struggle the Nevskii district continued its leading role, and between 24 and 27 October, the workers of most factories there took the impudent measure of simply stopping work after eight hours.[64] On 29 October the Soviet endorsed this step, and called all workers to

---

58   Diakin et al. 1972, p285.

59   See discussion in Surh 1989, p337, Shuster 1976, p155.

60   Kochakov (ed.) 1957, p325.

61   ibid., pp325-6.

62   For considerations over this period see Surh 1989, p345, Kochakov (ed.) 1957, p330, Diakin et al. 1972, p289.

63   Shuster 1976, p156.

64   Surh 1989, p347, Kochakov (ed.) 1957, pp336-7, Shuster 1976, p160.

similar action on 31 October.[65] This call was taken up in a very combative spirit[66] and a new general strike resulted after the introduction of martial law in Poland and the repression of sailors at the Kronstadt naval base on 1 November.[67]

Yet the adventurous tactics which had proved so successful when capitalists were passively or even actively sympathetic to workers' demands proved inadequate in a struggle in which their vital interests were threatened. These capitalists responded to the eight-hour campaign with a growing lockout to which the Soviet, still dominated by a radical liberal consciousness, had no effective reply. They then followed this attack up with very widespread victimisation of activists as workers were forced back to work under the old conditions.[68] On 7 November, after hesitation and bitter acrimony, the General Strike was called off,[69] as was the campaign for the eight-hour day on 13 November.[70]

The end of the eight-hour campaign to the dissolution of the Soviet

The consciousness that predominated among the activists might be described as a type of syndicalism, a militant reformism or "adventurous spontaneism". But however described, these ideas had now led the workers' movement to an impasse. Following the defeat of the eight-hour day campaign, the capitalists aligned themselves with the tsar, and a combined campaign of repression at the factory and state level built up against the Soviet. Thus, on 10 November, the Soviet was actually prevented from meeting, although this action was not repeated. In the factories, employers more and more refused to recognise representatives of the Soviet. Finally on 26 November Nosar, the chair of the Soviet, was arrested, and on 3 December the Soviet was taken into custody as its Executive was meeting.[71]

Contrary to what might have been suggested by a "spontaneist" view, the impasse confronting the Soviet did not lead to the immediate and complete transformation of the views of its base or representatives. Rather, flying with greater and greater force against the evident reality of retreat, the Soviet leadership continued to pursue a decentralised strategy aimed at undermining

---

65   Shuster 1976, p160.

66   Kochakov (ed.) 1957, p337.

67   For details, including numbers on strike, see Shuster 1976, pp162-4.

68   Diakin et al. 1972, pp292, 300, suggests that 20 percent of workforces were victimised.

69   Surh 1989, p367.

70   ibid., pp372, 374.

71   Shuster 1976, Surh 1989, pp398-9, Kochakov (ed.) 1957, p355.

the tsarist state by indirect means. Thus, from mid-November, a wine and vodka boycott was initiated to deprive the state of taxation revenue;[72] and then on 2 December, an attempt was made to escalate this action to a general financial boycott.[73]

The radicalisation consequent on Bloody Sunday demonstrated the general Marxist conception that workers' consciousness is transformed in struggle. The defeat of the workers in the Days of Freedom supported the premise of an interventionist Marxism that this transformation, even while it continues or accelerates, is not immediate, complete or even across the class as a whole. Thus the mass of mobilised workers, and particularly their leadership, the worker activists, moved from a position of at most critical loyalism to tsarism on Bloody Sunday to one of implacable confrontation for democratic reform by the October general strike. By the end of the Days of Freedom the predominant view had shifted again to support for the abolition of tsarism – though as yet this abolition was still to be achieved through indirect and decentralised tactics. The most convincing evidence for this shift was the growing dominance of the reformist leaning though very radical Menshevik faction within the Soviet. Thus the previously liberal chair Nosar declared his allegiance to the faction, and on his arrest the three-person body elected to replace him were all Mensheviks. They included the Mensheviks' most voluble spokesperson, and editor of the faction's paper, Trotsky.[74] The Mensheviks also dominated the contingents from the three main plants in the Nevskii district that were the initial core of the Soviet and had been the traditional heart of the activists.[75]

While the predominant view within the leading worker activists did not go beyond a militant reformism, there is evidence that some, though a relatively insignificant minority, began to break from this position in the face of events. These worker activists, moving towards centralism and insurrectionism, were particularly found in those areas where the struggle had been deepest. Thus the Nevskii district, although generally dominated by the Mensheviks, still witnessed the growth of a militia to some 6,000 members as well as nightly patrols of between eight and ten workers to challenge police and members

---

72 Surh 1989, p374, Shuster 1976, p194.

73 Kochakov (ed.) 1957, p355, Surh 1989, pp398-405, Shuster 1976, pp198-9.

74 To label Trotsky over this period as a Menshevik is a controversial statement but one I think convincingly supported by his inclusion on the Executive of the Soviet as a representative of the faction (Fond 9618, sheet 1), his editorship of the paper *Nachalo*, his continuing publication in the Menshevik *Iskra*, even after he had been removed from the editorial board, and his alignment with the faction at the Fourth Congress of the RSDLP.

75 The membership of contingents cited in Fond 9618 above includes factional affiliation where known. Other secondary and primary sources can be drawn in support.

of right wing organisations.[76] Following the defeat of the eight-hour day campaign, the Menshevik leadership of the Obukhov factory were subject to bitter criticism and loss of support. And the contingent from the Putilov factory, the subject of a prolonged lockout at mid-year, always included an unusually high proportion of Bolsheviks.[77] Even so, despite these beginnings of support for a revolutionary position, wholehearted preparations for armed struggle never occurred, nor did the majority of activists join parties clearly identified with insurrection.

From the arrest of the Soviet (3 December 1905) to the dissolution of the First Duma (9 July 1906): Revival of the labour movement around the worker activists

In the months following the arrest of the Soviet, workers in general were cowed, while the activists began to show the tendencies toward sectionalism and tactical adventurism seen in earlier periods of disarray. This disorientation reflected the pressure of tsarist repression. Thus the activists were in retreat following the dispersal of the Soviet, which was accompanied by the sacking and expulsion from the city of many of the prominent members of its activist base. At the same time a deepening economic recession, leading to widespread fear of unemployment, intimidated the mass of workers.

Yet by April 1906 this retreat was giving way to a new class-wide mobilisation based on organisation of the unemployed as well as shop committees and trade unions. And by May, a new wave of economic struggle was rising in the factories as the newly elected Duma proved to be an extraordinarily powerful stimulus for political interest and protest. The expectations awakened over 1905, and particularly on 17 October, had not been met, and on 3 July 1906 the tsarist regime was forced to deliver a further repressive blow in an attempt to defuse the movement rising to realise them.

Thus the course of the labour movement over the seven-month period between the arrest of the Soviet on 3 December 1905 and the dissolution of the First Duma on 3 July 1906 can well be divided into three phases of roughly equivalent length. The first period, over December and January when the state pursued a policy of unrelenting repression, was one of disorderly decline and disruption. The second period, roughly over February and March 1906, when the tsarist state eased repression and allowed some independent political activity, was one of recovery and re-establishment of the labour movement.

---

76 Shuster 1976, p173.

77 See Fond 9618, sheet 11.

128

The third period, roughly from April to June, when the state was thrown somewhat onto the defensive in the face of a growing storm in the Duma, was one in which the labour movement resumed the offensive in a series of political and industrial campaigns.

December 1905–January 1906: Disarray

The period following the dissolution of the Soviet included protests that were symptomatic of an ongoing bitterness among workers. Thus it opened with an impressive protest strike against the arrest of the Soviet,[78] and included a significant strike on the anniversary of Bloody Sunday.[79] Yet within these protests, forceful though they were, limitations were clearly evident. Thus the protest over the arrest of the Soviet became a virtual general strike after only a few days – but it then collapsed just as quickly.[80] Of most significance, it did not incorporate the railway workers,[81] and this failure permitted troops for the crushing of the Moscow uprising to be transported there. And of almost equal importance it did not invigorate a newly established Soviet – which was never viable and was arrested on 2 January.[82] Despite the significance of the day, only about half those who had struck in December came out on the anniversary of Bloody Sunday. Political meetings were held on this occasion, but they were small and had to be organised in a clandestine manner.[83]

These weaknesses reflected the impact of a relentless ruling class offensive against a labour movement dominated by a liberal "spontaneism" that left it unprepared for such intense repression. Many of the larger factories, and in particular the bastions of the activists in the Nevskii district were closed for much of this period,[84] and when they re-opened a substantial proportion of the activists were excluded from the new workforce. Further, many workers who eventually returned to work in January were required to sign pledges of obedience to the management.[85] The state reinforced this intimidation with very widespread arrests, searches and expulsions.

78   Surh 1989, p402, Diakin et al. 1972, p301, Kochakov (ed.) 1957, pp359-60, Shuster 1976, pp200-1.

79   Some 64,000 struck in virtual police state conditions. See Kochakov (ed.) 1957, p368, Diakin et al. 1972, p304, Shuster 1976, p211.

80   Surh 1989, p404, Kochakov (ed.) 1957, p361, Shuster 1976, pp203-4.

81   Surh 1989, p403, Kochakov (ed.) 1957, p361, Shuster 1976, pp201-2.

82   Kochakov (ed.) 1957, p357.

83   Shuster 1976, p209, Diakin et al. 1972, p304.

84   Kochakov (ed.) 1957, pp364, 367, Shuster 1976, p206.

85   Kochakov (ed.) 1957, p368, Shuster 1976, pp193, 205, 207-8, Diakin et al. 1972, p303.

By the end of January 1906, it could well have appeared that the worker intelligentsia had been eliminated entirely, while the activists had been rendered impotent. Strike activity had been halted, unions had virtually ceased to exist, and political parties had been forced to return underground. The intelligentsia seemed to have been eliminated through the arrest of the Soviet, the banning of the press and the expulsion of 1,700 leading figures from the city, while the activists were largely isolated from their audience through the sacking of 20,000 workers on a political basis.[86]

February–March 1906: Consolidation

The immediate repressive response of tsarism to the upsurge in 1905 had been a predictable repeat of its reaction to all earlier generalised threats. As such, the Court no doubt hoped, and almost certainly expected, that the impact of this repression would be similar to that against earlier revolts, most notably that of the mid-1890s. As recounted earlier, the embryonic layer of activists of that time had been intimidated into inactivity, while most of the intelligentsia had adopted a sectional view which opened the way for tsarist attempts at labour co-option in the 1900s. No doubt in anticipation of this possibility, the repression of December and January was followed in February and March by a limited legal opening and toleration for the labour and anti-tsarist movements.

Thus over these two months a number of concessions were made which, limited though they were, opened the way for a later significant labour mobilisation. In February, a limited right of political association was granted, which permitted the formation and growth of the unemployed movement as well as assisting the semi-legal re-emergence of avowedly Marxist organisation. Then, on 4 March, the government announced a limited legalisation of trade unions.[87] These initiatives, obviously aimed at creating a co-opted labour and popular movement within a constrained democracy, allowed the activists to reorganise and begin contesting control of the workplace and state.

The principal vehicle through which this reorganisation took place was the Council of the Unemployed – an organisation that occupied a central place in enabling the activists to lead the labour movement, much as the Soviet had during the Days of Freedom.[88] The Council did this through its delegate structure, which incorporated not only organisations of unemployed such as

---

86   For figures on the level of "political" unemployment see Kochakov (ed.) 1957, p369, Mikhailov 1995, p17.

87   Bonnell 1983, p194.

88   Parallel drawn by Shuster 1976, p223. See also Mikhailov 1995, p17.

soup kitchens, but also employed workers on a similar basis to that formerly adopted by the Soviet. Founded in March by a meeting of some 30 activists, by the end of May the Council had between 300 and 400 delegates representing between 90,000 and 100,000 workers, both employed and unemployed.[89]

Associated with this growth in size was a growth in the scope and radicalism of the Council's activities. Initially organised around soup kitchens, as well as other forms of individual assistance to the unemployed, the Council went on to demand and receive a grant from the city Duma for publicly funded works carried out by the unemployed under their own control.[90] Of more profound significance, the Council undertook to support the wave of strikes building up towards the middle of the year, including the collection of strike funds,[91] and its existence prevented the unemployed being used as strike breakers.[92]

In the wake of the unemployed movement, as well as the growing interest in politics generated by the Duma sessions, a range of other labour organisations emerged and grew. The most notable of these were the trade unions which first emerged in mid-1905, were crushed at the end of that year, and then began to re-emerge in March and April 1906.[93] At the time of the Duma sessions in May and June, the number of unions and union members grew dramatically, most notably among the printers, a traditional centre of the intelligentsia, and most significantly in the activist strongholds of the Nevskii district.[94] As during the Days of Freedom, unionisation was particularly marked among artisans and workers in small to medium workplaces, who were only loosely linked to the main vehicle of class organisation in the Council of the Unemployed.[95]

April–May 1906: A new upsurge

By the summer of 1906 it was clear that any prospect of establishing a contained labour movement through a strategy of limited opening following on repression had failed. On the contrary, the first half of 1906 had only reproduced, at a very accelerated pace, the process of the late 1890s and early 1900s, when the limits of State Economism had earlier been burst by worker resentment. As in that period, the very success of vehicles established to co-opt the labour movement contributed to the potency of the threat to tsarism

---

89   Mikhailov 1995, p17.

90   Kochakov (ed.) 1957, p370. Shuster 1976, pp224-5.

91   Mikhailov 1995, p20.

92   ibid., p6.

93   Kochakov (ed.) 1957, p372.

94   See charts in Hogan 1993, pp129-30.

95   Shuster 1976, p250.

that subsequently emerged.

Thus the foundation of the trade unions certainly marked a profound retreat for the workers' movement. Accepting, despite misgivings and protest, very restricted functions and close supervision, and led by moderate socialists and liberals, the unions at first appeared to strongly echo the earlier "police unionism" of Zubatov and Gapon.[96] As such they may reasonably have been expected to repeat the initial success of co-option carried out in the early years of the century. Further, from the outset the organisational growth of the unions was hindered by sectionalism and localism, not only in small and medium-sized industrial establishments, but even among the metal worker strongholds of the Nevskii district.[97] However, by June the unions would become the vehicle for a very widespread and significant economic struggle by the "second line" of workers such as bakers[98] and shoe makers. As such they followed a similar pattern of advance to the unemployed movement, which had grown to great size and effectiveness by June, after being initially subject to anarchist political influence and a leaning toward excessive militancy and individualism in tactics.[99]

Perhaps the greatest and most perilous miscarriage of tsarism's limited liberalisation was the conduct of the First Duma. Heavily weighted towards the upper classes, the elections to this body were expected to produce a loyal buttress to the regime. Yet among those elected over the empire were a discomforting number of radically democratic Cadets and Trudoviks. And in St. Petersburg, the outcome of the election was particularly menacing. There, an almost complete boycott of the election by workers demonstrated a deep alienation from tsarism.[100] The contingent eventually elected from the other classes of the city was made up entirely of Cadets – indicating the expectation of further democratisation by the middle and upper classes. These results suggested that tsarism was still very vulnerable, and indeed as the Cadets, Trudoviks and a small contingent of Social Democrats generated a greater and greater storm within the Duma, they drew greater and greater interest and

96   See for example the comments by a capitalist that the unions should hinder the workers' "unity with politics", Shuster 1976, p249, Diakin et al. 1972, p317. This parallel became even more marked later when police agents, most notably Malinovski, played a leading role in organising the unions.

97   See early Economist influence in the unions, Kochakov (ed.) 1957, p370, and the formation of "apolitical", "local" unions, Diakin et al. 1972, p317. On the attitudes in Nevskii see Hogan 1993, pp129-30.

98   See for example Shuster 1976, p251, on the bread workers.

99   Diakin et al. 1972, p317.

100 On the elections and the boycott see Kochakov (ed.) 1957, p372, Shuster 1976, pp218-20, Diakin et al. 1972, p307.

support from workers outside. Ultimately, the general political atmosphere in St. Petersburg reached a pitch comparable to that during the Days of Freedom, with some 315 rallies and 34 demonstrations between April and June 1906.[101]

By time of the dissolution of the First Duma, it was clear that the layer of worker activists that had emerged in the period up to the arrest of the Soviet had remained stable or grown in number, while shifting to a clearer and more radical political consciousness. However, it is much harder to chart the change in views of these activists than it is for the much smaller and clearly defined intelligentsia that anteceded it. This continued to be so in 1906, even as ongoing repression was forcing most activists to define more clearly their strategy, although less so than in 1905 when many were engaging in struggle for the first time.

Yet it seems clear that the centre of influence within the activists shifted sharply to the left after the repression of December 1905 and January 1906, and that the Bolsheviks in particular grew in prominence. Most indicative is that while Mensheviks led the First and Second Soviets, the initiators of the Council of the Unemployed were largely Bolsheviks.[102] Further, among the Social Democrats within the city, now a substantial force of 2-3,000 members, the Bolsheviks had the support of a majority, though very far from an overwhelming one.[103]

However it would be utterly false to claim, as was the practice in Soviet literature and might have been expected within a "spontaneist" framework, that the Bolsheviks provided exclusively, or nearly exclusively, the leadership of the workers' movement. Clearly there was substantial support among the activists for the Mensheviks, most notably among those organising the trade union movement. There is also evidence of significant support for the Socialist Revolutionaries and even the Cadets and individual liberals. Such heterogeneity of political views must be expected given the still very turbulent nature of the political period, as well as the large numbers of workers who continued to be drawn into political activism.

---

101 An estimate by Mikhailov 1995, p21.

102 ibid., p17.

103 Taken from support for the position of "active boycott" of the Duma within the party.

From the dissolution of the First Duma (9 July 1906) to the dissolution of the Second (3 June 1907): A weakened revival by the worker activists in a period of further retreat and radicalisation

The period between the arrest of the Soviet and the dispersal of the First Duma can be seen as one of disorderly retreat followed by recovery and a new offensive by the workers' movement. The next eleven months to the dissolution of the Second Duma can be seen as repeating this dynamic – though on a markedly reduced scale and in a complex and contradictory way. This decline and contradiction reflected the unequal clash between the ongoing, perhaps even growing, bitterness and combativity among workers in St. Petersburg, and the consolidating tsarist power across the Russian empire as a whole. With the activity of the labour movement being increasingly constrained within ever more adverse conditions, those consciously intervening to lead it began to move back from being activists engaged in open mass struggle to again becoming "worker intelligents" engaged in clandestine activities of propaganda.

An indication of the nature of the period overall is again evident in the most basic measure of the class struggle – strike statistics. Strike days for the empire as a whole fell substantially between 1905 and 1906, and even more so in 1907.[104] Yet in St. Petersburg, while strike days in 1906 were only a third of the year before, in 1907 they rose sharply to half those of 1905.[105] However, this figure does not reflect an economic offensive by workers, but rather a growth in bitter though passive political radicalism. Thus the spring strike wave for improvements in conditions in 1907 was considerably weaker than its predecessor the year before, while most of the strike days over the year were accounted for by a small number of very large actions of political protest. Indeed a near general strike on May Day, the long term rallying point for the labour movement, accounted for one third of the year's strike activity.

A further indication of the political balance shifting against the labour movement was the relative decline of strike activity among metal workers, the "worker elite" bastion of both the intelligentsia and then the activists. Thus while strike days among textile workers were two-thirds those of metal workers in 1905 and 1906, they surpassed them in 1907. There can be little doubt that this relative decline reflected the cumulative impact of waves of victimisation that had decimated the activists, as well as the immediate impact of a serious

---

104 Kochakov (ed.) 1957, p366.

105 ibid., p405.

economic downturn in intimidating the mass of metal workers.

Over the second half of 1906, and especially the first half of 1907, state repression and economic depression resulted in a growing defensiveness in workers' struggle that was associated with a marked shift in the nature of workers' organisation and consciousness. The latter half of 1905 and early 1906 had seen a consolidation of sectional organisation and reformist consciousness – most clearly evident in the growth of the trade unions and influence of the Menshevik faction of the RSDLP. This trend was severely set back in 1907. The membership of unions and co-operatives stagnated, while activity by the Council of Unemployed was at first constrained and then the movement virtually collapsed. On the other hand party organisation, reflecting greater firmness and consciousness, and hence more capable of withstanding the adverse circumstances, grew substantially.

The containment of struggle and organisation limited the numerical growth of the activists, while also leading this layer to a deeper political generalisation and extremism. This shift was associated with a massive increase in education of the type earlier associated with the intelligentsia. Thus the principal activity of the trade unions became propaganda, conducted through their press, as well activities like the presentation of lectures and the opening of libraries. The radicalisation of the activists could be seen most clearly in the shifting balance between the two factions of the RSDLP. Up to the dissolution of the First Duma the Mensheviks dominated district organisation in the activist strongholds of Nevksii and Vyborg, yet in the elections to the Second Duma these districts supported Bolshevik or Socialist Revolutionary candidates. And the overwhelming bulk of the very substantial recruitment to the party over the campaign for the Second Duma aligned itself with the Bolshevik faction.[106]

In the first half of 1906, Lenin sought to orient his supporters as the labour movement recovered, and most revolutionaries expected a new political crisis of the tsarist state in the short term. On the question of the Duma, which quickly became the central focus of political life in the empire, this led him to shift his position from one of militant abstention to intense interest and daily comment. Following the dissolution of the First Duma, Lenin had to adjust to a context in which the revolutionary crisis was at least delayed, although a deep bitterness and combativity continued among workers. These circumstances led him to campaign in the second half of 1906 for participation in the elections to the Second Duma, a position adopted by the Bolsheviks with little apparent opposition.

However while both factions of the RSDLP accepted the necessity of

---

106 These developments will be discussed in detail in chapter six.

participation, they differed radically about the attitude to be adopted to the other parties participating in the election. Consistent with a deepening shift towards reformism, the St. Petersburg Mensheviks adopted a strategy of forming a bloc with the Cadets, and in early 1907 split from the formally united RSDLP to pursue this course. As will be detailed in the final chapter, the result was that almost every written intervention Lenin made in the first half of 1907 was devoted to attacking the Mensheviks' course, while defending the Bolshevik position of independence from the Cadets and seeking a bloc with the Trudoviks. In doing so, it is clear he made a comparable shift to that of the labour leadership as a whole, and began to see himself once again as defending Marxist principles among an intelligentsia in circumstances of workers' retreat, rather than formulating tactics through which activists could pursue an advance.

The class struggle in the period between the dissolution of the First and Second Dumas was dominated by the decline in confidence and aggression of workers and the converse gain of these qualities in the tsarist state and capitalist class. This was immediately evident in the weak response to the dissolution of the First Duma in June 1906. In contrast to the arrest of the Soviet seven months earlier, there was not a swift reaction by workers,[107] but rather a limited wave of strikes some eleven days later in the wake of two mutinies.[108] This strike wave involved few workers outside the bastions of the Nevskii district and other factories of the Navy Ministry[109] – in particular it did not involve the textile workers.[110] Its impact was also undermined by a sharp split in the RSDLP over the aim and conduct of the strike. The action thus represented neither a wholehearted attempt to reverse a state action, nor an industrial struggle for improved conditions. Rather it was an expression of embittered sentiment as well as an implicit threat from that section of the working class still able to support the activists.[111] As such it launched the predominating pattern of workers' struggle for the next eleven months.

The fading of worker aggression was evident in the months following the dissolution of the First Duma. Very quickly the industrial action that had been building up over the spring of 1906 ceased,[112] and the now illegal Metal Workers' Union resolved to support only a limited range of disputes about which it had been informed in advance. Widespread sackings over the winter

---

107 Tiutiukin 1991, p77.

108 On the mutinies see Kochakov (ed.) 1957, pp389-90.

109 Kochakov (ed.) 1957, p390, Shuster 1976, p244, Tiutiukin 1991, p178.

110 Shuster 1976, p244.

111 See for example the conclusions drawn by Shuster 1976, p245, Diakin et al. 1972, p318.

112 Kochakov (ed.) 1957, p384.

of 1906-07 were hardly resisted outside the bastions of worker strength,[113] in marked contrast to the general solidarity and confrontation of the year before. Repeating the pattern of that earlier period, a wave of struggles over conditions spread through medium-sized plants outside the metal industry in the spring of 1907.[114] Yet this offensive was weaker than its predecessor and much less successful in the face of determined lockouts by employers. In the starkest defeat the bakers, who a year earlier had won significant concessions, were now defeated after a seven week lockout.[115]

Corresponding with this decline in industrial aggression by workers was the growing confidence of capitalists and the state. Thus following the failure of the protest over the dissolution of the First Duma, the Metal Workers' Union, the largest and most significant union in St. Petersburg, was banned. In fact 28 unions were banned on 29 July 1907.[116] At the same time, employers began refusing to recognise union representatives.[117] During the period of the election campaign for the Second Duma the union movement as a whole was banned,[118] and the day of the election was characterised by harassment and obstruction of worker voters by employers.[119] From 1 March 1907 the state attempted to ban the formerly ubiquitous factory meetings and stationed military detachments in many factories to enforce this.[120] At the same time, employers took the opportunity of an economic downturn from the beginning of the year to carry out a further "filter" of activists.[121] The plight of these and other unemployed deteriorated when in September 1906 the City Duma refused further funds for work projects carried out by the unemployed and later for dining halls despite a petition of some 26,000 workers.[122]

The impact of this offensive was to intimidate workers, but not to reconcile them to tsarism. Indeed the repression of the activists, as well as the defeat of the struggle for improved conditions, only broadened and deepened disenchantment. This sentiment found expression in growing support for

---

113 Diakin et al. 1972, p320.

114 Kochakov (ed.) 1957, pp399-400, Diakin et al. 1972, p329.

115 Kochakov (ed.) 1957, p399.

116 Kochakov (ed.) 1957, p391, Shuster 1976, p252, Diakin et al. 1972, p319.

117 Shuster 1976, p253.

118 Bonnell 1983, p280.

119 Shuster 1976, p263.

120 ibid., p268.

121 Diakin et al. 1972, pp320, 329.

122 Shuster 1976, p256, Diakin et al. 1972, p323. On further failed efforts see Mikhailov 195, p26, Kochakov (ed.) 1957, p398.

political protests with a symbolic focus. Thus apart from May Day there were significant protests on the anniversary of Bloody Sunday[123] and the trial of the Soviet. The attitude of most workers to tsarist attempts at co-option shifted from one of disdain to active hostility. Thus, while workers had continued working during the opening of the First Duma despite an attempt to declare a public holiday, the opening of the Second Duma was greeted with a street demonstration and clashes with police.[124]

The upsurge in 1905 found expression in a class-wide organisation of activists, the Soviet. The retreat and then advance of the labour movement up to the dissolution of the First Duma found an organisational expression in the Council of Unemployed – an organisation less directly linked to the mass of workers and in which conscious intervention played a greater role than in the Soviet. In the even more unfavourable context prior to the dissolution of the Second Duma, this trend for general class organisation to be more politically aligned, and less directly responsible to the class as a whole, went a step further. For now the assertion of class identity was limited to the vote in the worker curia of the Second Duma. This made the representatives of the worker curia, almost entirely Social Democrats, a very limited and indirect focus for class organisation. They exercised this role through the presentation of petitions as well as speeches in the well-publicised sessions of the Duma, but above all through reports to local assemblies of workers – most notably in the Nevskii district, the bastion of the activists.[125]

Broader industrial and social organisations of workers certainly continued to exist. Yet they were limited by their small size, weak traditions, and circumstances very hostile to the germs of mass organisation. As a result these organisations were restricted to making propaganda for the role of solidarity, rather than actually delivering it. Their principle initiators were thus "intelligents" from the RSDLP, almost always supporting the Menshevik faction, as well as radical liberals. Over the sessions of the Second Duma there was a burst of union registrations as had occurred the year before during the First Duma.[126] However these new unions were also small (by the spring of 1907, 37 unions were registered in the city, of which 22 were "small")[127] and a city-wide Central Bureau of Trade Unions was very limited in its activities due to lack of funds and recognition. With living conditions

---

123 Kochakov (ed.) 1957, p399, Shuster 1976, p267. A major collection for striking workers in Lodz (Shuster 1976, pp269-70) could be considered a similar sort of action.

124 Kochakov (ed.) 1957, p396, Shuster 1976, p266.

125 Shuster 1976, p266, Diakin et al. 1972, p327.

126 See chart in Bonnell 1983, p204.

127 Shuster 1976, p271.

deteriorating over 1907, there was a rise in cooperatives which campaigned for the regulation of food prices.[128] However these cooperatives usually failed due to the inexperience of their managers as well as the competition from commercial retail outlets.[129]

By crushing class-wide organisation as well as repressing open political activity the tsarist state no doubt hoped to again intimidate workers in general, drive activists into apathy, and pressure "intelligents" into Economism under some guise. The immediate impact of its actions however was rather different. With revolutionary parties again the main available means of worker organisation, a significant section of the activists now joined or associated themselves with them. With the possibilities for militant struggle for reforms again limited, the activists sought to educate themselves, and the process of worker education which had formerly been largely concentrated in the Nevskii district spread through the city as a whole. In 1906 10,329 and 23,367 in 1907 attended lectures of the People's Universities. Although certainly a section of the worker students in this process would have reformist or career aims given the context, it would seem reasonable that most saw themselves as "arming against the boss".[130] As a result of these developments the shift to the left in the working class that had been seen in the first half of 1906 hardened in the first half of 1907. In the first half of 1906 the political and organisational core of the class, the unemployed metal worker activists accepted the lead of Bolsheviks in the Council of Unemployed. A year later a significant section of these activists appeared to be actually joining or aligning themselves with the faction.[131]

There was also a marked shift towards an insurrectionary political perspective among the worker base of these activists. Thus in the former Menshevik strongholds of the Nevskii and Vyborg districts, factory workers voted Socialist Revolutionary and Bolshevik in the elections for the Second Duma, rather than endorse a bloc with the Cadets who were shifting toward a relatively conciliatory attitude to tsarism. By the time of the dissolution of the Second Duma, the ground had been laid for a much larger leading worker intelligentsia to emerge from the activists of the First Russian Revolution. It was the most political section of these "intelligents" that would maintain the Bolsheviks during the downturn and then implement Lenin's conception of the workers' paper and party after 1912. Note that

---

128 Hogan 1993, p151. Unions also began to carry out mutual aid from mid-1906 (Bonnell1983, p256).

129 Diakin et al. 1972, p331.

130 Shuster 1976, p273-4.

131 Details of the growth of the faction will be outlined in chapter 6.

Lenin commented about a worker intelligentsia taking over the party after the former students had deserted.[132]

Conclusion

Contrary to the view of a "spontaneous" advance, a detailed analysis of the First Russian Revolution demonstrates that conscious leadership is both a requirement for as well as a result of workers' struggle. Thus the revolution marked a sharp break in the relative stability of tsarism, but a break that resulted from the earlier development of protest led by a tiny intelligentsia of labour leaders. The main form of struggle was strike action by workers but, contrary to a "spontaneist" view of ever-advancing economic struggle, the revolution emerged from a political crisis consequent on defeat in the Russo-Japanese War. Contrary to both the mainstream and critical view of labour protest, the waves of strike action that characterised the revolution involved deliberate leadership by identifiable figures within opportunities created by this political crisis of tsarism.

The essential feature of the revolution was the generalisation of previously limited outbursts of protest and radicalisation to produce a qualitatively new context of ongoing and generalised struggle. Yet without a sufficiently large and effective intervention by consistent Marxists, this generalised struggle still proved to be insufficiently focussed to topple the tsarist regime, despite the evident possibility of doing so. The predominantly non-Marxist consciousness, or the determinist Marxism, of those who led the movement meant that after advancing for ten months the workers were steadily driven back for 18 months as the tsarist state re-established its power.

The relatively high level of struggle throughout the two and a half years of the revolution reflected the fact that the inadequate development of productive forces was no longer a significant factor in containing struggle. Rather the principal limitation was now the lack of consciousness and experience among the many workers emerging as leaders in the anti-tsarist struggle. Thus although general organisations which united this leadership were repeatedly created, most notably the Soviet in October 1905, these organisations could not become a vehicle for workers' power because most of their members were not concretely prepared to mount an insurrection against the tsarist state.

The layer of newly emerging leaders that united to form these class-wide organisations might well be termed the "worker activists". In contrast to the confinement and abstraction of the earlier tiny circles of "intelligents"

---

132 Cited in Diakin et al. 1972, p340.

the activists were a large group that could base their critical understanding of tsarism on engagement in large scale conflict. The activists emerged and radicalised to the point of an adventurous liberalism between January and October 1905. Constrained in numbers, and waging a bitter defensive struggle with tsarism over the next 18 months, many activists hardened in their politics toward support for the revolutionary parties, and in particular the Bolsheviks. It was they who formed a new and much larger layer of "intelligents" over the slump in struggle between 1907 and 1912.

Based on this shift, the Marxists were also able make the transition from an intelligentsia to a layer of activists, as will be outlined in the following two chapters. The contrasting though related sources of class consciousness for the activists relative to the "intelligents" can explain the contrasting structures and tasks of the Marxists before and after 1905. This change in the source of class consciousness also explains the shift in Lenin's comments on party organisation before and after 1905. Before 1905 Lenin was attempting to maintain a faction based on Marxist principle within a relatively small workers' intelligentsia. In 1905-07 he was attempting to lead the Bolsheviks in a struggle for the adoption of a revolutionary strategy by a large layer of worker activists. Lenin's consequent tactical shifts, within an ongoing role for conscious intervention, will be outlined in the seventh and eighth chapters.

Chapter 5

ST. PETERSBURG 1861–1905: FORMATION, EMERGENCE AND CONTAINMENT OF MARXISM AS THE MOST CLASS CONSCIOUS SECTION OF THE WORKER INTELLIGENTSIA

Introduction

The protests during the years 1861 to 1905 did not occur spontaneously. Rather they required the conscious intervention of identifiable leaders who articulated grievances through a framework developed "outside" the working class by the anti-tsarist intelligentsia. Apart from particular spasmodic protests the state was able to organisationally and ideologically curb these leading "worker intelligents", and the labour movement they aspired to lead was usually confined to isolated circles.

If conscious intervention was necessary for the articulation of labour grievances and the formation of an embryonic labour movement, then it was even more necessary for the formation of a Marxist current within that movement. For the advance of such a current required an even broader understanding than for the formation of a labour leadership, and was subject to even more pervasive repression than this leadership. Consequently such an understanding came almost entirely from "outside" the direct experience of the working class, and Marxists were confined within an "intelligentsia" even more than the general labour leadership.

Hence in the earliest years of the anti-tsarist and labour movements, Marxism was a theory conceived "outside" the empire as a whole, by exiles who made a critique of the predominating radical liberalism of the early democratic opposition to tsarism. These exiles were able to develop at most a tenuous relation with workers through the medium of occasional student correspondents who were conducting study circles of "worker intelligents". From the mid-1880s to the mid-1890s Marxism made perhaps its greatest advance in St. Petersburg, coalescing from a layer of circles and individuals engaged in independent and isolated study to a centralised city-wide movement intervening directly in workers' struggles. This advance was associated with perhaps the only major involvement of "worker intelligents" in the central leadership of the movement.

Yet, even more than for the labour movement in general, the period from the mid-1890s to 1905 was a one of retreat and disorientation for Marxists, with a defensive struggle being maintained by a group of exiles in Geneva. In these circumstances Lenin and his fellow exiles sought to maintain the interventionist nature of the Marxist current within the St. Petersburg worker intelligentsia, but their efforts were repeatedly set back by the direct and indirect consequences of state repression.

1861–1885: The emergence of Marxism as a current within the embryonic worker intelligentsia of St. Petersburg

The period between 1861 and 1885 was one in which the first short lived germs of a workers' intelligentsia emerged. It did so as a result of the initial hesitant industrialisation and spasmodic labour protests associated with tsarist Russia's entry into the imperialist world system. Associated with these material developments was the emergence of Marxism from a subsidiary element of the democratic critique of tsarism to a distinct general understanding of social development within the Russian empire. This occurred as Marxism organisationally coalesced from a foreign system of ideas viewed with sympathy but detachment by many radical democrats, to a circle of theorists in exile linked to a small layer of "worker intelligents" in St. Petersburg.

Given the very limited development of the labour movement in St. Petersburg, this process of theoretical development could reflect workers' experience only in the most indirect way. Indeed Marxism initially coalesced through the critique of ideas predominating within a critical literary and student layer that had mobilised for a democratic constitution in the Russian empire. This layer initially blossomed in the wake of the Crimean defeat but was then suppressed shortly after the Emancipation in 1861. Re-emerging during the surge of turbulence in the 1870s, these radical democrats embarked on a number of strategies aimed at gaining a mass base for democracy in order to overcome tsarism. The first Marxists formed a separate organisation as the majority of these democrats turned to a strategy of terrorism. Reacting against the voluntarism of this approach, the initial appropriation of Marx by the exiles from St. Petersburg was markedly deterministic.

Workers were almost certainly involved in this movement for democracy, perhaps in significant numbers. For throughout the period democratic activists sought to gain support among the urban poor through such means as lectures, the first Evening-Sunday Schools, clubs and ultimately political study circles. But for most of this period, and especially in its initial stages, the involvement of workers was as individuals separated from the collective identity of factory and district life. It was only late in the period that democrats organised circles specifically for workers within the industrial districts, and these did not go beyond general education.

Thus the emergence of Marxism in St. Petersburg between 1855 and 1885 can be analysed in three phases. The first of these, roughly from 1855 to 1865, was a period when Marxism exerted a limited influence within the rise and decline of a movement which saw the literary and professional intelligentsia, supported by the peasantry, as the vehicle for radical democratic reform. The second phase, roughly from the late 1860s to the late 1870s, was one in which Marxism had a more concrete influence due to the translation and publication of *Capital*, as well as the inspiration of workers' revolts in Western Europe. In the third phase, roughly from the late 1870s to the mid-1880s, a particular Marxist perspective for the Russian empire was developed by ex-student dissidents in exile – and these exiles gained support from a small layer of "worker intelligents" in St. Petersburg.

1855–1865

The democratic agitation between 1855 and 1865 was centred on a layer of literary critics who, in the disquiet and uncertainty following the Crimean defeat,[1] became increasingly direct and general in their criticism of tsarism. With the established order in some disarray, and a major change expected in the status of the peasantry,[2] this criticism grew in stridence up to 1861. This growing stridence struck an echo among broader elements of the intelligentsia – particularly the students of the expanding St. Petersburg University.[3] The height of protest, culminating in overt political mobilisation, was reached from late 1861 to mid-1862 as tsarism attempted to re-establish its former unchallenged domination. By the end of 1865 this outburst of political activity had been suppressed and order re-imposed through the use of censorship, jailings and expulsions from the city.

The main vehicle for the rising democratic movement of the late 1850s was the literary journal *Sovremennik*,[4] particularly articles written by Nikolai Gavrilovich Chernyshevskii,[5] the principal public figure of the movement.

---

1   See for example Kochakov (ed.) 1956, pp20, 25, 32.

2   ibid., p44.

3   ibid., p35.

4   On *Sovremennik* and its role see ibid., pp27-30.

5   On Chernyshevskii and his role see ibid., pp22-4. Venturi describes Chernyshevskii as the "politician of populism" who "not only gave it ideas but inspired its main course of action" (Venturi 1966, p129). He devotes a chapter to Chernyshevskii's role in the development of Populism (pp129-86). On the development of Chernyshevskii's writing in *Sovremennik* see ibid., pp145-74.

144

Chernyshevskii was a student at St. Petersburg University, where his thesis became the subject of bitter dispute.[6] Like a significant number of radical intellectuals of the time he was aware of and respected Marx's writings.[7] Yet like most dissidents for some time to come, Chernyshevskii felt that these writings related mainly to a foreign context, and as such were not directly relevant to the Russian empire.[8] In contrast to Marx's focus on the historical role of the working class, Chernyshevskii concerned himself mainly with criticising the limited emancipation of the peasantry then being discussed in tsarist circles.[9] Associated with this critique of the central point of the proposed reform of tsarism was a protest at the limited political liberalisation of the regime. In particular Chernyshevskii came to the defence of the growing student body chafing under the legal restraints of the time.[10]

The rising literary criticism reached the point of political mobilisation at the turn of the 1860s. This occurred when tsarism, having settled on the form of peasant emancipation, sought to definitively re-establish its control of the university and restrain the oppositional intelligentsia.[11] Its first measures to do so provoked an outburst of student protest from the start of the 1861 academic year, and this in turn was met with mass arrests and the closure of the university.[12] In the heightened political atmosphere created by these events a committee of students conducted a "free" university in the early months of 1862,[13] a centre for political discussion was opened under the guise of a chess club,[14] and the first anti-tsarist political organisation, "Land and Freedom" was founded.[15] This politicisation reached its peak on 2 March 1862 with a rally at which the main public figures of the movement, Chernyshevskii, N.A. Nekrasov (an editor of *Sovremennik*), and Platon Pavlov, the founder of the Evening-Sunday Schools, gave academic speeches indirectly critical of tsarism.[16]

---

6   Kochakov (ed.) 1956, pp39-40.

7   ibid., p295. For a discussion of Chernyshevskii's early intellectual development and his relation to Hegel and the utopian socialists see Venturi 1966, pp134-42.

8   For a summary of early Populist reactions to Marx and Engels see Offord 1986, pp117-20.

9   Kochakov (ed.) 1956, pp55-7.

10   ibid., pp255-6.

11   These attempts corresponded with a return to passivity and tsarist control in the countryside after a period of protest (Venturi 1966, pp208-19).

12   Kochakov (ed.) 1956, pp247-51, Venturi 1966, pp225-31.

13   Kochakov (ed.) 1956, p260.

14   ibid., p258.

15   ibid., p257.

16   ibid., p260.

Despite the impressive scope of the movement, as well as the promising beginnings of political organisation, these advances were still very tentative. Organisationally, the movement was diffuse and focused on a series of prominent individuals. Theoretically, guidance was given by a series of unrelated manifestos characterised by a general anti-authoritarianism.[17] The movement involved a large number of St. Petersburg's poor, including workers, but this involvement was as yet diffuse, spasmodic and passive.

These tentative germs of political organisation could not survive the onslaught of full-scale tsarist repression from mid-1862. The Free University, Chess Club and Evening-Sunday Schools were quickly closed, and some time later a number of important critical journals were suppressed.[18] Of most significance, Chernyshevskii was held for two years prior to trial and then sentenced to seven years in exile.[19] By the mid-1860s, criticism of tsarism had again reverted to indirect artistic and literary commentary confined to academic journals.[20] Epitomising this confined though continuing defiance, Chernyshevskii wrote the seminal literary classic *What is to be done?* which would prove to be an inspiration to many subsequent revolutionaries.

The theory of the radical literary critics from the 1850s and early 1860s did not go beyond an extreme democracy. Yet in making the first generalised critical understanding of tsarism these litterateurs laid the base for the subsequent development of Marxism. Ex-student intelligents "outside" the working class critically extended the work of the democrats to develop a Marxist perspective for the Russian empire, and the worker intelligentsia critically appropriated this perspective to cohere workers as a political force. For this reason, a wide range of commentators, including Lenin, were correct to see Chernyshevskii and his associates as the antecedents of Russian social democracy.[21]

1865–1879

Over the second half of the 1860s, the anti-tsarist intelligentsia was again restricted to a tiny layer of democrats engaged in wholly literary criticism. Yet through the 1870s this intelligentsia blossomed in a new wave of political uncertainty following economic crisis from 1873, the Russo-Turkish War, and

17   See for example ibid., pp238-9.

18   ibid., pp266, 270-1, 290-1.

19   ibid., pp276-7.

20   ibid., p287.

21   On Lenin's ongoing interest in and veneration of Chernyshevskii, and the novel *What is to be done?* in particular, see Offord 1986, pp150-1.

then a surge of workers' struggle and organisation.[22] This new resurgence built on earlier experience, with theoretical positions being developed in a more systematic way, and Marx's views being more clearly and concretely posed within this process of clarification.

Thus the 1870s was a decade in which theoretical clarification flowed from the testing in practice of strategic conceptions. Over the first half of the decade, avenues were sought to engage in educational activity as a means of mobilising for democracy. This trend culminated in the "going to the people" movement of mid-1874.[23] The failure of this movement opened a discussion in which the majority of radical democrats turned to a strategy of terrorism. In their rejection of this strategy, the future Marxists shifted from being radical democrats with a tactical orientation to propaganda among urban workers to constituting a separate current with a distinct conception of the working class as the leader of the democratic revolution in the Russian empire.

The movement from 1869 to 1874 advanced from the foundation laid in the late 1850s. Thus its main base was among the students of the higher education sector – though now in the Medical and Technical Institutes rather than the State University.[24] The movement continued to be loosely organised around a series of prominent individuals and these figures tended to align themselves with the anarchist wing of the First International.[25] However, while the movement continued to be dominated by a radical democratic view, Marx's influence grew in both its theory and tactics. This influence was particularly facilitated in 1872 when *Capital* was published in Russian, and was subsequently the subject of widespread private and group study.[26] The impact of this publication was reinforced by news of the Paris Commune, which had for the first time raised in practice the historical role of workers.[27] Almost certainly stimulated by these developments, a number of students began establishing study groups for workers, and received a response from within the embryonic worker intelligentsia interested in education and Western ideas.[28] Up to this time, this intelligentsia had been limited to attending Evening-Sunday Schools, forming private libraries, funded by a 2

---

22 Kochakov (ed.) 1956, p295. For a discussion of nature and significance of strikes in the 1870s see pp301-3.

23 ibid., pp308-9. For the leadership and nature of this movement see Venturi 1966, pp469-506.

24 Kochakov (ed.) 1956, p304.

25 ibid., p306.

26 Kochakov (ed.) 1956, pp295-6, Zakharov (ed.) 1980, pp19, 24.

27 Kochakov (ed.) 1956, pp298-300, Zhuikov (ed.) 1977, p23.

28 Kochakov (ed.) 1956, pp319-23, Diakin et al. 1972, p153, Zakharov (ed.) 1980, p20, Zhuikov (ed.) 1977, p20, for a discussion of attempts by various individuals to establish groups.

percent levy on workers, and undertaking overseas travel in their pursuit of a critical understanding of tsarist society.[29]

The failure of the "going to the people" movement in mid-1874 precipitated a clarification that culminated in the emergence of Marxism as a theory applied to the Russian empire. At this point leading radical democrats reformed the political party Land and Freedom and commenced an intense discussion of a new strategic path.[30] At the same time, those democrats who had been conducting propaganda among urban workers redoubled their efforts following the failure of the attempt to mobilise the rural population.[31] This met with "unexpected success" according to Gregorii Plekhanov, a forestry student who is regarded as the founder of Russian Marxism. Plekhanov was an energetic worker propagandist and prominent figure in the democratic movement. In particular he was a speaker at what is considered the first political demonstration in Russia on 6 December 1876 at the Kazan Cathedral.[32] As Land and Freedom steadily moved to a strategy of terrorism over the late 1870s, Plekhanov became sharper in his hostility to this strategy and firmer in his support for continued propaganda among workers.[33] Finally in August 1879 he broke with Land and Freedom to form Black Repartition, an organisation committed to this propaganda.[34]

1879–1885

The period between the launching of Black Repartition in 1879 in St. Petersburg, and the founding of the Liberation of Labour group in 1883 in Geneva, was one of further faltering and gradual clarification in Plekhanov's conception of revolution in the Russian empire. Through this clarification Marxism was generalised from an element of the democratic critique of tsarism, strategically oriented to gaining support for democracy among urban workers, to a conception of the workers themselves as the leadership of the democratic

---

29   See Kochakov (ed.) 1956, pp323-4 for a discussion of these libraries as well as the growing assertiveness of workers. See also Diakin et al. 1972, p154. On the role of travel of workers see the example of the worker leader Obnorskii in Zhuikov (ed.) 1977, p23.

30   Kochakov (ed.) 1956, p332, Zhuikov 1975, pp20-3. On the course and significance of developments that led to the foundation of Land and Freedom see Venturi 1966, pp558-74; see pp73-4 for a section of a programmatic statement.

31   Kochakov (ed.) 1956, p333. On the pioneering work by the "Chaikovskist" populists among workers see Venturi 1966, pp507-57.

32   Kochakov (ed.) 1956, pp334-7, Diakin et al. 1972, p157.

33   For a short extract of some of his arguments see Venturi 1966, pp625-6.

34   Zhuikov 1975, p57. See Offord 1986, pp26-7. Venturi 1966, pp653-65 for the process of the split and the initial positions of Black Repartition.

revolution. As the initial and most abstracted phase of the development of Marxism in the Russian empire this clarification occurred more "outside" the working class than any subsequent advances. Indeed it involved the changing views of only a few individuals outside the empire entirely – principally Marx and Plekhanov. Even so this reflection and clarification ultimately drew on the experience of propaganda among workers in St. Petersburg, and very quickly found a response in the formation of study groups oriented to Marxism among the worker intelligentsia of the city.

In breaking from the strategy of terrorism, as well as fleeing from Russia, Plekhanov and his associates were initially confronted with isolation, indeed ostracism. Within St. Petersburg the great bulk of students and "worker intelligents", most notably the leaders of the Northern Union, continued to support terrorism.[35] Perhaps most disconcertingly, Marx himself disparaged the exiles, hailed terrorist attempts on the life of the tsar, and appears to have endorsed a strategy of terrorism in the case of the Russian empire.[36] Consequently he initially collaborated with the foreign representatives of Land and Freedom rather than Plekhanov.[37]

Over the first half of the 1880s, this isolation was overcome as Plekhanov developed and argued the concrete applicability of Marxism to the Russian empire. The centre of this development was the growth in the role of the working class from a support to the peasantry, to the principal leader of the democratic revolution. Associated with this growth was a more ambitious purpose for propaganda and organisation among workers – the task of study circles now broadened from general education to the formation of a political party. In developing these positions Plekhanov gained the support of Marx, launched the Liberation of Labour group in 1883, and outlined his position in several fundamental texts.[38] At the end of 1884 he launched the first of a series of publications in a Workers Library, aimed at winning support for Marxism among the worker intelligentsia.

As this breakthrough in the application of Marxism to the Russian empire was occurring in exile, the general sympathy for Marx's ideas continued to deepen in St. Petersburg. This was particularly the case at the State University,

---

35   Kochakov (ed.) 1956, p352, Diakin et al. 1972, p165. Offord 1986, pp51-6. Venturi 1966, pp700-8 gives an account of work by the terrorist-oriented People's Freedom among workers.

36   Perhaps most notably in his reply to a letter from Zasulich in 1881 (Zhuikov 1975, p79). For an English language discussion of Marx and Engels' views see Offord 1986, pp120-5.

37   Zhuikov 1975, pp63-79.

38   Principally in *Socialism and Political Struggle* (1883) and *Our Differences* (1885) which made a deep impression in St. Petersburg and which were not effectively replied to (Zakharov (ed.) 1980, pp27-8). On the development of Plekhanov's position see Offord 1986, pp125-31.

where his works were distributed,[39] a eulogy was published on the occasion of his death, and discussions were held with representatives of the First International. It was a student at the university, Dimitri Nikolaevich Blagoev, who led the workers' study circles which established the first formal contact with the Liberation of Labour group in 1885.

Blagoev attended the university from 1880 to 1883 and became a supporter of Marx through reading *Capital*. Over 1884 he was successful in propaganda activity among "worker intelligents" – establishing a number of groups in districts as well as publishing a paper reaching some 100 readers.[40] In discussions with Plekhanov from January 1885 the "intelligents" around Blagoev modified the reformist views they had adopted from the German Lassalle[41] and began formal literary collaboration.[42] The Blagoev group was eliminated by arrests in early 1886,[43] but in reaching a size of some 200 supporters it had pioneered the organisation of Marxists within the worker intelligentsia of St. Petersburg.[44]

1885–1895: Advance from abstract propaganda among the intelligentsia to concrete agitation among the mass of workers

Between 1885 and 1895 these initial germs of organisation made a qualitative advance. Thus while Marxist views gained the upper hand over Populism within the literary and intellectual milieu critical of tsarism, the organised presence of Marxism among the worker intelligentsia advanced from a number of isolated and scholarly study circles to a united organisation concretely intervening within workers' struggles. As a result the theoretical development of Marxism came to reflect workers' experience more directly, and a number of "worker intelligents" were centrally involved in that development.

The pivotal moment in this transformation was the economic crisis and

---

39   Kochakov (ed.) 1956, p377. In fact a significant quantity of material was despatched by German Social Democrats in early 1884 (Zhuikov 1975, p163).

40   Kochakov (ed.) 1956, p375, Diakin et al. 1972, p169.

41   For a discussion of the eclectic mix of views of the Blagoev group see Kochakov (ed.) 1956, p370, Diakin et al. 1972, p169, Zhuikov 1975, pp177, 181, Zakharov (ed.) 1980, pp31-2. Offord 1986, p133 suggests that their attraction to Marxism was associated with the electoral success of the German SPD. On the influence of Lassalle see pp133-5.

42   Zhuikov 1975, p173.

43   Zakharov (ed.) 1980, p34.

44   For a summary of the development and role of the Blagoev group see Offord 1986, pp131-8.

famine of 1891.[45] Like the earlier defeat in the Crimean War, as well as the later Russo-Japanese War, this trauma profoundly undermined the standing of tsarism among the urban population, and led to a political awakening[46] that had some parallels with those of the late 1850s and 1905. As outlined in chapter three this turmoil incorporated workers, for the first time identifying themselves as such, in general political protest and discussion, but of even greater significance in strike action.[47]

This burst of working class activism posed a profound challenge for all Marxists. The political crisis demanded a shift by the abstract theorists in Geneva, but the need for such a change in approach was felt most of all by the local propagandists among St. Petersburg's worker intelligentsia. In response, these circle leaders made the first attempts to lead workers as a mass in struggles for economic demands, and to facilitate this engagement began a process of consolidation that culminated in a city-wide organisation based on the industrial districts. This process in an embryonic way prefigured the advance of *Iskra* between 1901 and 1903, though perhaps far more the transformation of the two factions of the RSDLP in 1905.

Thus the famine of 1891 creates two phases within which the advance of Marxism among "worker intelligents" can be discussed. Yet the famine still marks a shift in emphasis rather than a complete break in the organisation and activity of Marxists. Further, owing to state repression, this shift from abstract study to concrete intervention could not be completed, and the movement ultimately retreated and fell into disarray following the waves of arrests from the end of 1895. Thus in the first half of the 1890s, just as in the latter half of the 1880s, the exiles, and particularly Plekhanov, continued to be the focus of the movement not only theoretically but also tactically. It was they who were to prepare the first all-empire publication that would have been the basic step in the transition from abstract propaganda to intervention. Further circle education, albeit now more concrete in its orientation, continued to be the basic activity of the movement, and the basis of this education continued to be material produced by the exiles.

---

45   A view also taken very commonly in the Soviet literature, probably following Lenin's own position. See for example Zhuikov 1975, pp146-7, and citing Lenin p231.

46   Dan 1964, pp192, 188-9, Kochakov (ed.) 1956, p395, Baron 1963, pp117, 128, 140, 142, Keep 1963, pp27-8.

47   Some sources suggest the context of the labour movement improving from 1887. See for example Kochakov (ed.) 1956, p379, Zhuikov 1975, p100.

The late 1880s

As outlined in chapter three, the second half of the 1880s saw tsarism surging in confidence, the anti-tsarist intelligentsia retreating into personal concerns, and the workers' movement dispersed. In these circumstances Marxists, both in exile as well as in St. Petersburg, continued and even deepened the abstraction of their propaganda. Consequently the direct role of worker experience in the development of that propaganda was even less than during the first half of the 1880s. Thus the attempt by the Blagoev group to maintain contact between Geneva and St. Petersburg, as well as to issue a paper to "worker intelligents", could not be sustained or repeated. Indeed for some ten years the Liberation of Labour group had no direct contact with St. Petersburg,[48] and could only continue to develop in abstract the application of Marx's ideas to the Russian empire. Within St. Petersburg those "intelligents" interested in this development became increasingly passive and scholastic as their isolation from the worker intelligentsia as a whole deepened.

In a faint echo of the comparison between the movement before and after Bloody Sunday, most Western and even Soviet writers view this period as largely negative in its consequences for the future of the Marxist movement. Their harrowing personal situation and political isolation[49] is thought to have marked the Geneva émigrés with features of elitism, insularity and personal irritability, which prevented them giving a lead to a new generation of local worker and student leaders emerging in the struggles of the 1890s. These weaknesses are also usually seen to a lesser extent within the Marxist "worker intelligents" of St. Petersburg who sank deeply into personal study and hesitated before, or even resisted, the turn to intervention after 1891.

However this overall characterisation one-sidedly overemphasises the negative features of this period of theoretical development. For however much they hesitated, a section of those "worker intelligents" who developed as Marxists abstractly in the 1880s provided the base for intervention within the workers' struggles of the 1890s. And the literary means for that development was supplied by the Geneva exiles, who translated and published the major works of Marx while also deepening their critique of Populism. It was these publications that made possible the growing influence of Marxism among "worker intelligents" in the late 1880s.[50] Conceived entirely "outside" the

---

48   Baron 1963, p127.

49   Probably most marked in the case of Plekhanov, see ibid., p131.

50   For comments on this largely unquantifiable, invisible though very significant phenomenon see Kochakov (ed.) 1956, pp384-5, Diakin et al. 1972, pp171-2, Zakharov (ed.) 1980, p35.

current experience of the working class, they cohered and gave confidence to those worker leaders who subsequently organised not only a Marxist faction but also the general workers' movement.

Plekhanov's first major step in his critique of Narodism, the book *Socialism and the Political Struggle*, can be considered the founding document of Marxism in the Russian empire. It was the first edition in a Library of Contemporary Socialism which would comprise ten publications. This body of theory was aimed at dealing with the strategic questions confronting the worker intelligentsia – an audience that Plekhanov explicitly identified and addressed as such.[51] In addition, the exiles published a Workers Library – a series of translations of the major theoretical works by Marx and Engels, with introductions relating these works to the Russian empire. The exiles attempted to launch a journal, but their lack of contacts and support confounded them; while three issues were produced in 1890, only one further issue subsequently appeared, in 1892.[52] These literary efforts made the Geneva Liberation of Labour group the focus for the growing number of those interested in Marxism in St. Petersburg as the 1880s came to an end.

Within St. Petersburg, the activity of Marxist students and "worker intelligents" became more and more insular and abstract in a way that mirrored the deepening abstraction of the exiles. Between the dispersal of the Blagoev group and the end of the decade there were a number of attempts to establish and co-ordinate study networks. Yet none achieved the stage of launching a publication or even establishing formal circles,[53] and therefore could not be considered heirs to the Blagoev organisation. The most substantial and best known of these networks was focused on the student Pavel Varfolomeevich Tochiiskii. Centred on a library of 700 books, of which 200 were illegal, the network conducted education from a range of sources, among which the works of Plekhanov were prominent.[54] However, after two years of existence this network was broken up in 1888 when Tochiiskii was arrested.[55]

Thus by 1889, despite its undoubted influence, the formally organised presence of Marxism in St. Petersburg was at its weakest ever. Yet at the same time widespread private reflection by students, former students and worker intellectuals was laying the basis for the most significant breakthrough in

---

51 Zhuikov 1975, pp192-3.

52 ibid., p141.

53 Thus the Tochiiskii "circle" never actually established study circles (Diakin et al. 1972, p171).

54 Zakharov (ed.) 1980, p34.

55 Kochakov (ed.) 1956, pp377-9. It is noteworthy that most of the contacts were in the Nevskii district. For a summary of the role of the Tochiiskii Group see Offord 1986, pp141-5.

such organisation.[56] This was the establishment of the first avowedly Social Democratic organisation[57] with a perspective of propaganda.[58] Centred at the Technological Institute and led by the students Mikhail Ivanovich Brusnev and Leonid Borisovich Krasin, this group sought to develop worker intellectuals as "Russian Bebels" through a three-tiered structure of study groups.[59]

The Brusnev group, as it has become known, was the culmination of the propagandism and circle mentality of the 1880s and was subsequently criticised by many of its members for academicism and insularity.[60] But the group could also be considered the culmination of the struggle to establish a Marxist framework in relation to the Russian empire. That struggle, which had begun with Plekhanov's tactical turn to workers in the mid-1870s, could now be considered completed. The Brusnev group was the base from which emerged the leadership that implemented the turn to concrete intervention in the 1890s.[61]

The early 1890s

The theoretical grounding gained through individual and circle study in the 1880s enabled Marxists to make a mass intervention, albeit in an incomplete and one-sided way, in the new and far more favourable circumstances of the 1890s that were outlined in chapter three. In two surges, broken by a crushing wave of arrests during which the authorities concentrated on the student core of the Brusnev group and largely ignored those workers involved,[62] this intervention advanced from the issuing of local leaflets based on limited local contact and information,[63] to the preparation of a city-wide workers' newspaper based on a network of contacts enabling the systematic collection

56 See for example Offord 1986, p156.

57 The opinion of Zhuikov 1975, p226.

58 Zakharov (ed.) 1980, p35.

59 Zhuikov (ed.) 1977, p35-6. See also a quote by Krupskaia in Mel'nikov 1975, p7.

60 See for example the later opinion of G.M. Krzhizhanovskii cited in Zhuikov (ed.) 1977, pp40-1.

61 For a useful memoir of the Brusnev group by Brusnev himself, which shows the change in structure and activity of the group from 1890, see Brusnev 1923, pp17-33. See also the memoirs of L.B. Krasin in Krasin 1923. For an overview of the group's development and intervention see Roslova 1956, pp88-95. For an overview of the movement at this transitional point see Offord 1986, pp155-60.

62 Kochakov (ed.) 1956, p392., Diakin et al. 1972, p175.

63 For a discussion of this early activity by the Brusnev group see Kochakov (ed.) 1956, pp389-92, Diakin et al. 1972, p175., Zakharov (ed.) 1980, p37, Zhuikov (ed.) 1977, p39.

of information about conditions in factories.[64]

Yet despite this turn to intervention, and the consequent establishment of city-wide organisation, Marxists at the time continued to be engaged in propaganda – albeit of a far more concrete type. This was despite the erroneous self-conceptions of almost all the leading figures at the time. Thus their activity continued to be education among circles of interested workers, though now more focused on current issues and grievances. The period culminated in the formation of a city-wide organisation based on districts, in which the traditional labour movement stronghold of Nevskii district was particularly prominent. Yet at the same time the core of this structure remained students and young professionals, despite the noticeable involvement of a number of locally based "worker intelligents".

The changes in the activity of Marxists in St. Petersburg over this period have usually been associated with the term "agitation" – taken to mean a sharp rejection of the earlier focus on theory as well as a turn to supporting workers' struggle for immediate economic demands. This turn was supposedly associated with a loosening and legalisation of organisational structures. The bearers of the new strategy have usually been seen to be a new set of locally based leaders who emerged with the failure of the Geneva exiles to provide a concrete lead in the changed circumstances after 1891. These widely held views on the nature and sources of agitation are not completely accurate. It is certainly true that the most generalised formulation of the strategy reflected the experience of two students active in the labour movement of the Jewish Pale.[65] Yet even in this formulation the role of general theory is still acknowledged[66] and in 1895, Martov, the better known author of this document, led his supporters into the newly centralised organisation of Social Democrats in St. Petersburg.

Contrary to the view that agitation was solely a local initiative, a strong argument could be made that the seminal formulation of the new strategy was made by Plekhanov in his "Tasks of the Social Democrats in the Struggle against the Famine in Russia". Here the advocate of the earlier strategy of creating a current within the worker intelligentsia[67] gave an outline of the relation between propaganda and agitation that has yet to be surpassed in

---

64   For the questionnaire through which this information was to be gained see V.I. Lenin, "Questionnaire on the Situation of Workers in Enterprises" (sic), in Harding (ed.) 1983, pp138-9.

65   For an English translation of the statement regarded as defining the strategy see A. Kremer and Yu. Martov, "On Agitation", ibid., pp192-205.

66   See for example ibid., p201.

67   For a statement of this strategy which in essence anticipates many themes developed by Lenin in the polemic against the Economists see G.V. Plekhanov and P. Akselrod, "From the Publishers of the 'Workers' Library'", ibid., pp68-72, especially p71.

Marxist literature.[68] Written in 1891, this piece by the established theorist of the movement must have been influential in the development of newly emerging local leaders like Lenin and Martov.[69] Yet despite the ongoing role of theory it remains true that in all the formulations of "agitation" there is still no discussion of the role of the state in suppressing class consciousness. Consequently there is no conception of propaganda and agitation as two forms of intervention necessary for the development of consciousness, but related to differing phases of the class struggle. Such omissions could subsequently allow the "tactic" of "agitation" to be generalised into the determinist strategy of Economism.

Like all substantial tactical shifts, that to "agitation" was hindered by pressures coming from both within and outside the Marxist movement. Those most active in implementing the new perspective were particularly exposed to surveillance, and in early 1892 as well as late 1895 mass arrests crippled promising beginnings that had been made in implementing the new strategy. Within the movement a significant section of prominent ex-students and worker intellectuals, with long experience in the narrowness of circle propaganda, were anxious and hesitant about an approach whose broadened scope they could not grasp. The first abortive attempt at "agitation" may be considered the support given to a number of strikes by the Brusnev group over 1890-91, as well as the group's subsequent involvement in the Shelgunov funeral. Yet shortly after this event, the group was broken up by arrests. This setback left the most insular conspirators and propagandists, Radchenko and Krasin, to recohere those careful enough to have evaded capture.[70] Among the city's Marxist "worker intelligents" the speeches at the first two May Days in 1891 and 1892 showed that a propagandist view continued to predominate.[71]

A more wholehearted and successful shift to agitation came with commencement of activity by Lenin in St. Petersburg and Martov in Vilno. Lenin recognised the central importance of the theoretical struggle against Narodism, and he made that struggle his main priority. Yet he was critical of the abstract and obscure way it was being waged at the time – most notably

---

68   For extracts in English, see G.V. Plekhanov, "The Tasks of the Social Democrats in the Struggle against the Famine in Russia" (extracts), ibid., pp100-7. For the definition see especially p104.

69   As suggested for Martov in Getzler 1967, p22.

70   For the impact of the arrests and the subsequent recovery see Kochakov (ed.) 1956, p397, Kochakov (ed.) 1957, p151, Diakin et al. 1972, p178, Zakharov (ed.) 1980, p38. On the character of Radchenko see Mel'nikov 1975, especially p9 and pp14-5.

71   See Diakin et al. 1972, p176 for quotes from the speeches in 1891. Zhuikov (ed.) 1977, pp39-40, Zakharov (ed.) 1980, p38, Kochakov (ed.) 1956, pp393, 396.

by the leading Social Democratic spokesperson at that time, Krasin.[72] With his more concrete approach Lenin immediately became the leading spokesperson for organised Social Democrats in St. Petersburg.[73] Flowing from his approach Lenin conducted a new type of study circle in which discussion of theoretical questions was combined with that of factory issues.[74]

On the basis of this approach to propaganda, Lenin formed a new city-wide leadership that omitted Radchenko and Krasin and based itself on the three main industrial districts of the city.[75] After quelling a revolt by the former leaders against the centralism of this new structure,[76] he was able to attract those around Martov as well as a number of groupings and printing presses leaning to Narodism to the new organisation.[77] The potential of the new approach, as well as the centralised organisation to implement it, was evident in the months leading up to the textile strikes. Thus in the last two months of 1895 eight leaflets were produced[78] as well as the draft of a city-wide newspaper.[79] Lenin would subsequently speak of there being "10-16 on committees, 20-30 workers' committees and 100 connections with factories" at the time of his arrest in early December 1895.[80]

---

72   In particular at a meeting in which Lenin criticised Krasin's approach to the problem of markets. For Lenin's position see "On the So-Called Market Question" in Lenin, *CW*, vol. 1, pp75-128.

73   Diakin et al. 1972, p191, Zakharov (ed.) 1980, p39, Mel'nikov 1975, p33.

74   Zhuikov (ed.) 1977, p47, Kochakov (ed.) 1957, p164, Diakin et al. 1972, p193, Zakharov (ed.) 1980, p41, Mel'nikov 1975, p24. The new three person "agitational" leadership adopted a new program of study for circles in 1895 (Mel'nikov 1975, p40).

75   The new structure was adopted at a meeting on 2 April 1895 and implemented over the autumn (Zakharov (ed.) 1980, p42, Diakin et al. 1972, p198, Kochakov (ed.) 1957, p172).

76   The adoption of "agitation" came after a long period of discussion and hesitation by the propagandists with the hardened conspiracists Radchenko and Krasin leading the final revolt against their marginalisation. For a discussion of the meeting they called and at which Lenin spoke and defeated them see: Mel'nikov 1975, p51.

77   These groupings came into the new structure in October 1895 leaving only the future Economist leaders I.V. Chernyshev and K.M. Takhtarev outside the organisation. (For a limited and clearly hostile discussion of these figures and those around them see Kochakov (ed.) 1957, p190.) On the Narodnik leaning groups see Diakin et al. 1972, pp197-8.

78   Zakharov (ed.) 1980, p42, Diakin et al. 1972, p200, Kochakov (ed.) 1957, p172. Over the whole of 1895 11 leaflets were produced.

79   The contents are discussed in Baron 1963, p158, Kochakov (ed.) 1957, p174.

80   Lenin cited in Kochakov (ed.) 1957, p169.

1895–1900: Advance of, but then setback for, Marxist organisation among the "worker intelligents" of St. Petersburg

Between the mid-1850s and late 1880s, Marxism in St. Petersburg emerged from within the radical democratic milieu to become a significant, though isolated and passive presence within the dissident student milieu and metal worker intelligentsia of the city. This advance required the conscious intervention of theoretical pioneers within a context of unsteady though substantial growth of industry and the spasmodic emergence of a labour movement. Over the first half of the 1890s this presence coalesced into an organisation of growing clarity and centralism, which was able to intervene with growing impact within political events and workers' struggles. That breakthrough was ultimately ground in the acceleration of industrialisation following a traumatic economic crisis and famine in 1891. Yet here too the intervention of local leaders like Lenin and Martov, as well as the continuing support of the theoretical pioneers in Geneva, was pivotal to realising a further organisational advance.

In 1896 these advances in Marxist organisation reached their peak in relation to the previously discussed textile strike – the first generalised labour protest in the Russian empire. For a short time, Marxist organisation and influence grew in a way that prefigured the general revolt of 1905-07. And as at that time, this growth raised questions of party structure and activity, and in particular the composition of leading bodies the methods of leadership and the role of external publications.

Yet if 1896 witnessed the greatest advance in Marxist organisation, then the years that followed saw that advance more than reversed. By the end of the decade, such organisation had been reduced to its level of some ten years earlier. The determinist interpretation of Marxism, clearly evident in the general view of how "agitation" should be carried out, left Marxists of the time with little understanding of the need for conspiracy in the face of state repression, or retreat in the face of a decline in workers' struggle. Persisting with an approach that was becoming less and less appropriate, most Marxists, and particularly the "worker intelligents", were arrested and sent into internal exile. Only the smallest fragments remained of a movement that had virtually collapsed as an organised force.

Retreating from the evident inadequacies of their approach these fragments diverged through generalising a particular aspect of "agitation", although all ultimately remained within the limitations of the determinist way in which this tactic had been generally interpreted. The predominant view – focusing entirely on immediate struggle and the prospect of legality – would subsequently become known as Economism. Reacting against this political liquidation, a number of study circles adopted a strategy of abstract propaganda which was reminiscent of the activity of Marxists in the late 1880s. Yet for all their purported consistency and firmness in principle, these groups were characterised by considerable wavering in their organisational structure and political positions. Both these reactions against the original conception of "agitation" involved a break with its essential conception of involvement in sectional struggles – but involvement to generalise these struggles through the formation of a city-wide political organisation.

This meant that, leading up to the turn of the century, Marxist leadership again came predominantly from "outside" the class – indeed outside St. Petersburg and the empire as a whole. On questions of general theory, the long-term exiles in Geneva continued to provide leadership through the publication and distribution of what had become a substantial amount of material. Such material propagated the implacable opposition of the exiles, and particularly Plekhanov, to German revisionism, though in relation to Economism their attitude was more conciliatory.

Among those exiled within the empire Lenin, who had played a pivotal role in the turn to "agitation", did not at first grasp the full significance of developments among St. Petersburg's Marxists organised in the Union of Struggle for the Liberation of the Working Class (hereafter referred to as the "Union of Struggle"). Thus, despite being confronted by the presence of nascent Economism just before going into exile, Lenin still devoted two years to an extended critique of Narodism, which he presumably still regarded as the principal threat to Marxism. It was only the publication of the "Credo", an explicitly theorised declaration of Economism, that impelled him to commence the polemic that would become a rallying point for supporters of an interventionist interpretation of Marxism in St. Petersburg, as well as throughout the empire.

The textile strikes

Between the arrest of most of its leaders on the night of 8-9 December 1895 and the start of the textile strike on 23 May 1896, the St. Petersburg Union of Struggle continued to demonstrate the potential of its recently established strategy and structure. Uniting some 200 members, more than half of whom were "worker intelligents" in the metal industry, the Union of Struggle had contact with some 70 factories, of which 39 were large. Utilising these contacts, the Union of Struggle distributed some 17 leaflets over the first four months of

1896.[81] Usually directed at a particular plant, the appearance of these leaflets was sometimes sufficient in itself to induce concessions from factory owners. On a number of occasions more general leaflets were issued. The most notable of these was on the anniversary of the Paris Commune,[82] while the most significant called for the celebration of May Day 1896. On that occasion some 2,000 leaflets were distributed to 40 factories and, as outlined earlier, these leaflets were considered by the police to be a catalyst in precipitating the textile strike.[83]

This sustained activity occurred despite the loss of four out of the five central leaders of the Union of Struggle, as well as the most prominent Marxist "worker intelligents" from the districts on 9 December 1895. Among the latter was the long term leader of Nevskii district, Shelgunov, as well as the most prominent figure in the Narva district, Boris Zinoviev.[84] In January the impact of this blow was reinforced when the remaining member of the central leadership was taken, as well as Ivan Vasil'evich Babushkin, perhaps the most prominent of Lenin's "worker intelligent" collaborators from the Nevskii district. Indeed it was Babushkin who had assumed responsibility for leaflet distribution following the earlier arrests and had written the declaration responding to them.[85]

While not immediately crippling the Union of Struggle this intervention by the state resulted in a shift that would later lead to political degeneration and organisational fragmentation. Thus the removal of the entire leadership associated with "agitation" opened the way for a return to prominence by the overwhelmingly conspiratorial Radchenko.[86] At the same time a group known as the "youngsters", who had initially refused to join the Union of Struggle, now began distributing leaflets and sought to associate themselves with the organisation.[87] With the tempo of labour struggle rising in early 1896, the consequences of these shifts were as yet muted. The new city-wide leadership included not only Radchenko but also Lenin's companion Nadezhda Konstantinova Krupskaia and M.A. Sil'vin, a prominent "worker intelligent" from the Nevskii district. Further, the former leadership was not

81   Diakin et al. 1972, p203. The leaflets are reprinted in *Listovki Peterburgskogo "Soiuza Bor'by za Osvobozhdenie Rabochego Klassa"*, 1895-97, Moscow, 1934, pp22-50.

82   Kochakov (ed.) 1957, p179.

83   Diakin et al. 1972, p205. See Harding (ed.) 1983, pp171-3 for the text of the leaflet.

84   Zakharov (ed.) 1980, p43. A list of those arrested is to be found in *Krasnyi Arkhiv*, no. 1, 1934, p95.

85   Kochakov (ed.) 1957, p179, Diakin et al. 1972, p203. Leaflet reproduced in Tovstukhi 1934, p20.

86   Diakin et al. 1972, p203.

87   ibid., p205, Mel'nikov 1975, p66.

immediately removed from the city – Lenin was able to intervene through some 100 letters as well as advice through his sister who was permitted personal contact with him.[88]

The organisational advance made by the St. Petersburg Social Democrats during the textile strike of 1896 was arguably the most significant advance for Marxism prior to the First Russian Revolution. As outlined in chapter three, the strike was an unprecedented culmination of earlier developments and united a whole industry of some 30,000 workers in deliberate action. The response of the Union of Struggle was a burst of activity with some 15 leaflets being produced over the 20 days of the strike. The focus of these leaflets advanced from announcing the strike and listing demands,[89] to attempting to maintain the strike and arguing against returning to work. Finally these leaflets sought to gain solidarity action from workers of the large metal plants.[90] This shift suggests that the Union of Struggle had begun to grasp how difficult it would be to win the strike as a result of employer and state resistance

This burst of activity led to a dramatic growth of the Union of Struggle. Its membership doubled to some 400, of whom a majority were workers. Given this small number, it could be presumed that the majority of new members were metal worker "intelligents" rather than textile strikers themselves. Responding to this growth and the changed circumstances, the Nevskii "worker intelligent" Sil'vin sought to open the organisation by including representatives from factories on the Union of Struggle's central coordinating committee as well as re-launching a city-wide publication. However these proposals were stymied by opposition from the more conspiratorial S.I. Radchenko in a debate that prefigured the conflict over openness in mid-1905.[91]

The end of the textile strike to 1900: Decline, degeneration and disintegration

While the effects of the arrest of the central leadership were not evident during the Union of Struggle's intervention into the textile strike, the waves of repression following that strike crippled its activity and led to political decline and fragmentation. On 9 August 1896 Krupskaia and Sil'vin were arrested, leaving Radchenko as the only member of the former centralist

---

88   ibid., p203.

89   Kochakov (ed.) 1957, pp183, 187, Diakin et al. 1972, pp206-7, Harding (ed.) 1983, p174.

90   Kochakov (ed.) 1957, p189. See Tovstukhi 1934, pp68-74 for these five leaflets published on 15 June, 17 June and 19 June 1896.

91   Mel'nikov 1975, pp68-9.

"oldster"[92] leadership still at large. Radchenko's role had grown during the strike, as his flat served as the base for the Union of Struggle's activity, and with the other "oldsters" now removed he became the predominant figure in the Union's leadership.[93] At the same time as these leaders were removed, some 80 "worker intelligents" were taken from the districts, and the strategic centres of the intelligentsia, the Kornilov and Glazov Evening-Sunday Schools, were closed.[94] The result of these blows was a dramatic decline in external intervention by the Union of Struggle – in the last five months of 1896 only eleven leaflets were produced.[95]

Compounding these pressures towards inactivity and conspiracy among the traditional "oldster" leaders of the Union of Struggle was the entry and growing prominence of those "youngsters" who had earlier opposed the formation of a centralised city-wide organisation.[96] Already the heat of the textile strike had produced a tendency to downplay politics within the weakened leadership of the Union. In some reminiscences Krupskaia later commented that Babushkin's response to the arrests in December 1895 was considered "too political" by the Union and was only published due to Babushkin's status as a worker.[97] Now the "youngsters" formulated and sought support for a position that organisational activity should be limited to the collection of strike funds, and political intervention limited to support of economic struggle.[98] Indeed the "youngsters" had already shown the logic of their view during the textile strike, when they issued leaflets calling for a support fund which did not incorporate any organisational identification.[99]

If over 1896 the organisation of Marxists in St. Petersburg advanced to a peak, despite the incipient potential for decline and fragmentation resulting from state repression, then over the years 1897 to 1900 that repression definitively crushed the movement, and the potential for decline was fully

---

92   A term for the generation of leaders that had formed the Union of Struggle and were identified with the former implicitly interventionist interpretation of Marxism.

93   Mel'nikov 1975, p70.

94   Zakharov (ed.) 1980, p50.

95   Kochakov (ed.) 1957, p190, Diakin et al. 1972, p211. The leaflets are reproduced in Tovstukhi 1934, pp91-116.

96   Diakin et al. 1972, p211, Kochakov (ed.) 1957, p190.

97   See for example the comments of Krupskaia and Sil'vin cited in Kochakov (ed.) 1957, p189. Krupskaia's memoir, Central State Archive of Historico-Political Documents of Saint Petersburg, fond 4000, opis' 5, delo, 58, list 15.

98   Diakin et al. 1972, p214, Zakharov (ed.) 1980, p50. Compare this basis for distinguishing between "oldtimers" and "youngsters" with Keep 1963, p48, who concerns himself solely with the issue of structure.

99   Kochakov (ed.) 1957, p190.

realised. In a period characterised by tentative initiatives which were met with a crushing response, supporters of an interventionist Marxism were broken up into small circles and individuals engaged in the most abstract propaganda. As a result the Union of Struggle shifted steadily to a wholeheartedly Economist position in a way comparable to the previously outlined demoralisation of St. Petersburg's worker intelligentsia as a whole.

This meant that the presence of Marxism in the city was again based on smuggled propaganda rather than workers' struggle – in particular the publications of Plekhanov and the Liberation of Labour group. As in the late 1880s, this material sustained a series of propagandist groups as well as a burgeoning general interest in Marxism. Towards the end of this period, several of Lenin's polemics against Economism were circulated, but there is no evidence that these made a significant impact.

The weakening of the Union of Struggle was evident in its response to the second textile strike in January 1897. Only four leaflets were issued over the week of the strike,[100] and these did not have the distribution or influence of those in the first strike.[101] At this time, a city-wide publication, the "Petersburg Workers' Leaflet" was launched,[102] but a second issue could only be produced from exile in September. The decline and isolation of the Union of Struggle could be seen in the abstract content of their leaflets[103] as well as the reason cited for the defeat of the strike in one such leaflet – "an inability to discuss and develop a plan of action".[104]

In February 1897 a special meeting of the Union of Struggle was held just prior to the "oldtimer" leadership going into exile. Here the clarity and influence of the "youngsters" was evident, although the "oldtimers" prevailed and a new leadership around S.I. Radchenko was elected.[105] While Lenin was concerned at the political leaning of the "youngsters'" position,[106] it seems clear that he had as yet a determinist complacency about the development of the Union of Struggle, and lacked the concern with organisational detail that would later become his hallmark. For the next two years he devoted little attention to organisation, devoting himself instead to the critique of Narodism.

Between the departure of the "oldtimer" leadership in February 1897 and the First Congress of the RSDLP in March 1898, the "oldtimers" maintained

---

100 ibid., p192, Diakin et al. 1972, p213. Reproduced Tovstukhi 1934, pp121-31.

101 Kochakov (ed.) 1957, p192.

102 ibid., p191, Diakin et al. 1972, p212.

103 See for example Harding (ed.) 1983, pp219-20.

104 Cited in Kochakov (ed.) 1957, p192.

105 Zakharov (ed.) 1980, p51.

106 As outlined among other places in Kochakov (ed.) 1957, p193.

their dominance of the St. Petersburg Union of Struggle. However this dominance was largely formal and reflected the disorganisation and vulnerability to police suppression of their "youngster" opponents. On the occasion of May Day 1897, the Union of Struggle issued an official leaflet with a markedly more sober tone than those of the textile strikes,[107] and this provoked a crippling wave of arrests over the course of May.[108] The first issue of *Workers' Thought* was issued by the "youngsters" late in 1897, but they too were broken up by arrests early in 1898.[109] By 1898 the Union of Struggle was no longer able to intervene in strikes,[110] and it is indicative of its weakness that the delegate to the Founding Congress of the RSDLP was selected through a private discussion of the four-person "oldtimer" leadership.[111] It seems clear that in the unfavourable circumstances prevailing at the time, the formally interventionist Marxist dominance of the Union of Struggle resulted entirely from the conspiratorial and manipulative abilities of Radchenko.[112]

Between the First Party Congress in March and the end of 1898 this formal dominance of the Union of Struggle by "oldtimers" was broken, to be replaced by a predominant Economism, together with a series of small propagandist circles that had broken from the organisation. Soon after the Congress Radchenko was left isolated in the city-wide leadership,[113] and the Congress manifesto received only limited circulation due to opposition from the "youngsters". The fragmentation of the Union of Struggle was evident on May Day 1899 when three separate leaflets were produced – one from the weakened "oldsters", one from a propagandist split, and one from a localised circle.[114] Arrests followed the distribution of these leaflets, with the publishing houses of the latter two being suppressed, while the strength of the "youngsters" grew within the Union of Struggle.[115] In autumn 1898 the propagandists, going under the title "Workers' Flame", reformed for a second time and established a number of circles within significant factories, most of which were located in the Nevskii district. Their activity contributed to a major strike and rising known as the Maxwell Defence, yet for all their clandestinity and propagandism "Workers' Flame" was again crushed by

---

107 Text in Harding (ed.) 1983, pp210-5.

108 Mel'nikov 1975, pp94-5, Diakin et al. 1972, p214.

109 Diakin et al. 1972, p218.

110 ibid., p219.

111 Kochakov (ed.) 1957, p194.

112 Mel'nikov 1975, pp87-8.

113 ibid., p111.

114 Diakin et al. 1972, p220, Zhuikov (ed.) 1977, pp90, 93-4.

115 Diakin et al. 1972, p221, Zhuikov (ed.) 1977, pp94-5.

arrests shortly after this uprising.[116] At the end of 1898 came the definitive triumph of Economism within the Union of Struggle, as it formally merged with the *Workers' Thought* paper.[117]

The years 1899-1900 were a period of Economist domination within the Union of Struggle, as among almost all those "worker intelligents" sympathetic to Marxism. In turn, their interventionist opponents were fragmented, isolated and propagandist. This Economist dominance was evident early in 1899 when the Union of Struggle issued a three-stage "Program of Self-Education" developed from "the realities of life",[118] as well as put forward local leaflets as the means to mobilise a general strike. In May 1899 the Union of Struggle changed what was seen as the political demand for the eight-hour day to the economic concession of a reduction in daily working hours to ten.[119] At this time they also issued a May Day leaflet calling for a general strike around solely economic issues.[120] These trends culminated in the split of the Union of Struggle between a circle of intellectual "advisers" and a "Workers' Organisation" of some 300-500 "worker intelligents".[121] This split was associated with the adoption of a decentralised organisational structure in which leadership bodies could not act without prior sanction of their constituents.[122] The Economist-inspired shift to moderation in program, as well as localism in organisation, did not halt the weakening of the Union of Struggle, and in April 1899 the organisation was crushed by a large number of arrests.[123] Following the adoption of the decentralised structure in mid-1900, most local groups were inactive, and only four out of six district organisations proved to be viable.[124]

With the labour movement now in retreat, most Marxist students and "worker intelligents" who had looked to the Union of Struggle accommodated themselves in practice to tsarism through adopting an Economist view. Reacting against this accommodation, an array of individuals and circles sought to maintain the former revolutionary tradition of the Union. In attempting to do this, they could draw on a very substantial volume of literature being smuggled into St. Petersburg from the Liberation of Labour

---

116 Diakin et al. 1972, p222, Zhuikov (ed.) 1977, pp104-5.

117 Diakin et al. 1972, p223, Zakharov (ed.) 1980, p54.

118 Zhuikov (ed.) 1977, p95.

119 Diakin et al. 1972, p225.

120 ibid., p229, Zhuikov (ed.) 1977, p111.

121 Diakin et al. 1972, p230.

122 ibid., pp229-30.

123 ibid., p225.

124 ibid., p230.

group in Geneva,[125] a burgeoning "legal Marxist" literature within the city, and the writings of exiles such as Lenin within Russia. Yet the very pressures that led to Economist accommodation also led to this formally interventionist Marxism being maintained as an academic abstraction divorced from the limited though still real possibilities for workers' struggle at the time.

The most prominent and enduring current that attempted to preserve the interventionist tradition of Marxism was the "Workers' Flame" group. Breaking from the Union of Struggle in 1897, even as the "oldtimers" were still formally dominant,[126] this group was twice crushed by arrests and revived. The group issued leaflets with an extremely propagandistic tone – most notably on the occasion of May Day between 1898 to 1900.[127] It also published three issues of a newsletter, maintained contact with Plekhanov, and at the height of its activity incorporated some 25 members and 18 circles.[128] Yet the "Workers' Flame" group was hindered in gaining influence by its abstentionism in relation to struggles as well as academicism in relation to theory. Thus it renounced strikes, while being unclear in its concrete political program and consequently inconsistent in its organisational relations with other groupings.[129]

By 1900, there was a range of propagandist groupings which shared the limitations of "Workers' Flame". Their small size and abstract approach are indicated by names like the "Group of 20" and "Social Democratic Workers' Library".[130] Echoing the practice of the late 1880s in their closed structures and abstracted approach to propaganda, these students and "worker intelligents" of the late 1890s provided a base for Lenin's projected new paper when he again began making contacts in the city in February 1900.[131]

1900–1905: The struggle to re-establish an interventionist Marxist current within the worker intelligentsia of St. Petersburg

Emerging from the setbacks of the late 1890s, the period 1900-1905 was one of dogged struggle to re-establish a Marxist current intervening concretely within workers' struggle. In this new period of spasmodic and largely limited worker protest, as well as unrelenting state pressure, such an endeavour was

---

125 Zhuikov 1975, p280, Zhuikov (ed.) 1977, p100.

126 Zhuikov (ed.) 1977, pp88, 90-2.

127 Diakin et al. 1972, p227.

128 Zakharov (ed.) 1980, p55, Bondarevskaia et al. 1982, p83, Zhuikov (ed.) 1977, p109.

129 Zhuikov (ed.) 1977, p103.

130 Zakharov (ed.) 1980, p56, Zhuikov (ed.) 1977, p108, Bondarevskaia et al. 1982, pp75, 83-4.

131 Diakin et al. 1972, p228, Zakharov (ed.) 1980, pp56-7.

and could only have been a series of hesitant advances followed by severe setbacks. Thus in St. Petersburg the intervention of exiles, as well as the efforts of local supporters, led to the formation of a pro-*Iskra* "Petersburg Committee" in mid-1902. As a result, for the first time since the mid-1890s, most Social Democrats in the city were organised in a single organisation. Yet this breakthrough was almost immediately followed by a new split and further dissidence which weakened the Committee, and ultimately led to the sending of two competing delegations to the Second Party Congress in mid-1903. This Congress was expected to be a breakthrough in party development, yet it culminated in the well-known emergence of Bolsheviks and Mensheviks.

Following this division among the exiles, the Petersburg Committee at first appeared cohesive in supporting the Bolsheviks. But support for the Mensheviks quickly emerged, and this support grew stronger as the Committee was weakened by arrests. Despite the efforts of Lenin, the local Bolsheviks showed a marked tendency to conciliate the Mensheviks and mask the political differences that divided the two factions. Finally the Committee broke in two at the end of 1904, after a controversial and unsuccessful student demonstration, and most of the local organisations within the industrial districts went over to the Mensheviks. Thus, on the eve of the First Russian Revolution, the core of the Marxist movement within St. Petersburg, as well as in exile, was far more sharply defined and experienced than it had been ten years earlier. Yet it seems clear that despite this crystallisation, the organised base of this leadership was not substantially larger in 1905 than it had been in 1895.

The class struggle in its advanced stages takes the form of a struggle between masses of workers to a greater or lesser extent influenced by capitalist ideas. In periods of relative stability this struggle takes the form of a battle over theoretical positions within an "intelligentsia" drawn from a range of class positions. Prior to 1900, this intelligentsia in St. Petersburg was formed through the propaganda of dissident students and young professionals among a layer of "worker intelligents". In the re-formation of an orthodox movement after 1900 the central role of such elements was even more pronounced than it had been earlier. Thus Social Democratic organisation was centred on a number of prominent higher educational institutions, the secretary of the Petersburg Committee became the focus of student activity, and general political activity reflected the cycle of the student year. With class struggle and opportunities for concrete intervention limited, students predominated within the Social Democratic movement and "worker intelligents" were yet again relatively peripheral.

In this difficult period, Lenin grew from being a prominent, though still apparently subordinate, defender of the traditional view of Marxism prior to the Second Congress, to become the overwhelming focus of this position following the split at the Congress itself. In his writing and organisational activity at this time, Lenin formulated the positions that most came to be identified as a purported "Leninist" position on party organisation. This is usually taken to be based upon conspiratorial, elitist and manipulative methods in gaining control of local party committees.

This predominant view of Lenin's role involves a considerable distortion or ignorance of the historical evidence. For the correspondence between Lenin and his supporters in St. Petersburg shows a dogged struggle by Lenin for openly declared and clear political leads, consistent organisational arrangements, and the maximum involvement of workers in organisational leadership. These demands were met with hesitation or outright opposition on the part of his correspondents within the city, who responded to state pressure as well as the strength of their political opponents by adopting a more conspiratorial approach than Lenin wished. Thus it was precisely Lenin who waged a persistent, if not entirely successful, campaign against the organisational methods that have been attributed to him.

The build-up to the Second Congress of the RSDLP

From early 1900 the short period of relatively favourable circumstances allowed a series of energetic *Iskra* agents to build up support in the city to the point of launching an official Party Committee. As outlined earlier, the economic crisis at the turn of the century led to a short upsurge in political activism embodied in the Obukhov Defence, as well as a series of student demonstrations in St. Petersburg and other cities.[132] The limited response of the Economist-influenced Union of Struggle to these events undermined the standing of Economism and precipitated the formation of a pro-*Iskra* left wing within the Union of Struggle.[133] At the same time as this differentiation was occurring, intellectuals directly linked to *Iskra* were independently building up support in the city. In early 1900, as Lenin passed into exile, he established contact with a number of long term supporters in the city, most notably the perennial conspiracist Radchenko, who was still at large and actively organising.[134] Although formally still a member of the Union of Struggle, Radchenko collaborated with the remnants of the propagandist groups to

---

132 This context is outlined in chapter 3 of this thesis and also in Kochakov (ed.) 1957, pp199-200, Diakin et al. 1972, pp231, Zakharov (ed.) 1980, p58, and Zhuikov (ed.) 1977, pp116, 118.

133 Diakin et al. 1972, pp244, 234, Zakharov (ed.) 1980, p58, Zhuikov (ed.) 1977, pp121, 128, on the response of the Union of Struggle. Zhuikov (ed.) 1977, p132, Diakin et al. 1972, p253, on the development of its left wing.

134 Kochakov (ed.) 1957, pp202-3, Zakharov (ed.) 1980, pp56-7, Zhuikov (ed.) 1977, p123, Bondarevskaia et al. 1982, p86, Mel'nikov 1975, pp115-6.

distribute a growing number of the newly published *Iskra*.[135]

The considerable impact of *Iskra* in opposing Economism was reinforced by Lenin's pamphlets and books – most notably *WITBD*, which arrived in the city in early 1902.[136] Although Radchenko, Lenin's original agent, was arrested, he was succeeded by a series of less conspiratorial figures who continued to build up support for *Iskra* despite crippling waves of arrests against the paper's promoters.[137] Their efforts culminated in a meeting on 14 July 1902 between representatives of the Union of Struggle and the city's "*Iskra* organisation" which resolved to form an *Iskra*-aligned official "Petersburg Committee". The new Committee counted on the support of some 70 members.[138]

While Lenin lauded this advance, there were still differences of emphasis between his own approach to the formation and conduct of the Committee, and that of his local collaborators in St. Petersburg. These differences were to lead to serious tensions later as the political heterogeneity and fragility of the new body became clear. The local *Iskra* agents were concerned primarily with a formal organisational commitment from the former Union of Struggle leadership, and the subsequent development of organisational collaboration with this leadership. Lenin on the other hand was concerned above all with an open political victory over the Economist ideas that had predominated within the Union of Struggle. He therefore sought, without success, a public self-criticism by the former Union leaders of their previous position. For Lenin, this self-criticism would facilitate the integration and confidence of the worker supporters of the Union – a greater concern to him than the working arrangements between the two former leaderships.[139]

---

135 One estimate is that out of 1,000 printed some 200 were sent to St. Petersburg (Zakharov (ed.) 1980, p58). Another is that 140 copies of the first issue and 300 copies of the second were sent to St. Petersburg (Zhuikov (ed.) 1977, p124). On propagandist groups as suppliers see Diakin et al. 1972, p235. In late 1900 most anti-Economist groups came together in "Workers' Flame" (Zakharov (ed.) 1980, p56).

136 On the impact of *Iskra* see Diakin et al. 1972, p235. The Okhrana regarded the *Iskra* network as the "most dangerous threat" (Zhuikov (ed.) 1977, p125). On the publication and impact of *WITBD* see Kochakov (ed.) 1957, pp213-6, Zakharov (ed.) 1980, pp66-7, Zhuikov (ed.) 1977, pp134-6.

137 Radchenko together with V.P. Nogin was arrested on 2 October 1901 (Mel'nikov 1975, pp124-5). By the end of the year only about four or five supporters of the paper were left free (Zakharov (ed.) 1980, p65, Zhuikov (ed.) 1977, p133). These blows came after a formal *Iskra* centre was established by Nogin in September 1901 (Zakharov (ed.) 1980, p64).

138 The most useful report on this meeting would be "1 Sobranie predstavitelei peterburgskoi gruppy 'Iskry' i peterburgskogo 'Soiuza Bor'by za Osvobozhdenie Rabochego Klassa'" in Bondarevskaia et al. 1986, pp12-5. Some discussion also in Kochakov (ed.) 1957, p216 and Diakin et al. 1972, p254.

139 On Lenin's approach to the unification, see Volin et al. 1969-70, vol. 2, letters from V.I. Lenin

The formation of the Petersburg Committee was a significant advance, but over the second half of 1902 a lack of firmness within its leadership, as well as a lack of clarity among its supporters, led to its effective dissolution. It is indicative of the central role of students in the movement that the crisis commenced when a former Union of Struggle leader returned from holidays in September, and challenged the legitimacy of the Committee at one of its meetings. Rather than dismiss this initiative out of hand, the Committee adjourned without considering any further business – effectively dissolving itself.[140]

Lenin was indignant at this dramatic and early setback, yet despite a strong protest from himself and Martov, the pro-*Iskra* elements of the Committee were not prepared to wage an open and unremitting political campaign against "Bouncer", as the former leader was known.[141] Within a short time some half of the Committee,[142] as well as three-quarters of its worker supporters,[143] had gone over to the position of Bouncer which amounted to a re-assertion of Economism, despite the efforts of the outstanding worker intellectuals Babushkin and I.I. Egorov, sent by Lenin to bolster support work in the districts.[144] As usually occurred in such splits, organisation was set back, with money not being collected, leaflets not being issued, and perhaps most seriously of all a series of arrests which removed leading figures.[145]

By the end of the year it was clear that the Committee had been still-born, and Lenin was still unable to get even his closest supporters to resolutely adopt an implacable stand against Bouncer.[146] However several of his correspondents

to I.I. Radchenko in St. Petersburg, 25 July (7 August) 1902, pp122-5, 9 (22) July 1902, pp84-6, 3 (16) July 1902, pp71-5. Note that I.I. (Ivan Ivanovich) Radchenko was the brother of Stepan Ivanovich Radchenko.

140 For an account of this meeting see the letter from A.A. Shneerson to *Iskra* reproduced as "5. Rasshirennoe zasedanie Peterburgskogo Komiteta RSDRP" in Bondarevskaia et al. 1986, pp20-2. See also Letter from V.N. Shaposhnikova in St. Petersburg to the editor of *Iskra*, 7 (20) September 1902, Volin et al. 1969-70, vol. 2, pp256-8.

141 Not surprisingly given its general approach this (or any) defeat for Lenin is hardly dealt with in the Soviet literature. For a recent recognition see Zhuikov (ed.) 1977, p140.

142 See letter from A.A. Shneerson to the editorial board of *Iskra*, 12 (25) October 1902, Volin et al. 1969-70, vol. 2, pp368-9.

143 Letter from V.N. Shaposhnikova to the editorial board of *Iskra*, 30 October (12 November) 1902, Volin et al. 1969-70, vol. 2, p428.

144 Despite this "matters were still difficult" (Zhuikov (ed.) 1977, p142).

145 As recounted by Stasova in a series of letters to the editorial board of *Iskra*, Volin et al. 1969-70, vol. 2, pp445-6, 6 (19) November 1902.

146 See for example his letter to Babushkin, 6 January 1903 in response to an earlier defensive reply, Volin et al. 1969-70, vol. 3, pp21-2.

were prepared to make an analysis of the support for this figure as a resurgence of Economism among the worker base of the Committee.[147] Such a resurgence could have been expected, given the arrests that had weakened *Iskra*'s base,[148] as well as the return to industrial passivity following the Obukhov Defence.

If the general passivity of the second half of 1902 was associated with the dissolution of the Petersburg Committee, then a limited resurgence of workers' struggle in the first half of 1903,[149] together with the prospect of the Second Congress, lead to a burst of activity and collaboration between the three fragments now claiming its mantle. The year started inauspiciously. Relations between Lenin and Yelena Dimitrievna Stasova,[150] now the secretary of the Committee, were almost broken off amidst recrimination and allegations[151] over the split with Bouncer, and then a new split of "litterateurs" occurred over the organisational arrangements of the Committee.[152] Yet shortly after this new fracture, all the fragments of the former Committee began a period of collaboration to intervene in several workers' struggles,[153] and even more significantly issued a joint call for strike actions and celebrations on May Day 1903.[154] All three fragments sought representation at the Second Congress based on their organisational strength, with Stasova seeking sole representation on the part of the official Committee.[155]

It is significant to note in the light of later characterisations of Lenin as an inflexible centralist, formalist and conspirator, that he and Krupskaia did

147 See for example the letter from V.N. Shaposhnikova to the editorial board of *Iskra*, 22 September (5 October) 1902, Volin et al. 1969-70, vol. 2, pp307-10 and another letter on 30 October (12 November) 1902, pp423-9.

148 Thus on 7 January 1903 three of the most significant organisers for *Iskra* in the city, I. Babushkin, V.P. Krasnukha and I.I. Radchenko, were arrested (Kochakov (ed.) 1957, p218, Diakin et al. 1972, p257.)

149 As outlined in chapter 1 of this thesis; see in particular Diakin et al. 1972, p258, Zakharov (ed.) 1980, p76.

150 One of the most prominent of Lenin's collaborators and later a long term Soviet functionary. A considerable Soviet literature exists on her exploits – see for example Gil'gulin 1957.

151 See for example the letter from Lenin and Krupskaia to Stasova in St. Petersburg, 15 (28) January 1903 in Volin et al. 1969-70, vol. 3, pp79-80.

152 As conceded by Stasova in a letter to the editorial board of *Iskra*, 9 (22) January 1903, Volin et al. 1969-70, vol. 3, p70.

153 In fact 43 leaflets were published by the Petersburg Committee in the first half of 1903 (Kochakov (ed.) 1957, p220).

154 Kochakov (ed.) 1957, p220, Diakin et al. 1972, p258. For the meeting discussing the intervention on May Day see Bondarevskaia et al. 1986, pp24-5, report of a meeting of the Petersburg Committee, April, before the 14th (27th), 1903.

155 Thus Stasova's outline of the strength of the "official" Committee is given in footnote 5, Bondarevskaia et al. 1986, p24.

not accede to this demand. To the chagrin of Stasova, they held discussions with the "literary opposition",[156] as they were known, declared the matters in dispute to be tactical rather than principled,[157] and could not prevent a quantity of *Iskra* material returning to Russia in the hands of the "litterateurs". While making clear their continued support for as well as recognition of the Committee, Lenin and Krupskaia showed considerable allowance for the "literary opposition", which extended to them being represented at the Congress despite their obvious Economist leanings.

The Second Congress and after

The Second Congress of the RSDLP was expected to definitively end the struggle against Economism, firmly establish the party's organisational and political basis, and lead to new growth among the worker intelligentsia evident in the Russia empire, and especially St. Petersburg. The disputes, losses and chronic factionalism that had so plagued the core of student and ex-student intellectuals and their thin layer of worker intellectual supporters that comprised the Social Democratic movement, were now to be put in the past and a new beginning made around a concretely intervening workers' paper.

The course and consequences of the Congress dramatically differed from expectations. Rather than establishing a definite unity against Economism, the Congress culminated in a new split, with strong echoes of the struggle it was supposed to have terminated. This division was all the more startling because it cut across the tensions existing within the former exile leaders of Social Democracy. Thus the main contenders were Martov and Lenin, the two figures who were arguably the principal leaders of the "agitation" phase in St. Petersburg. Yet prior to the Congress they had together clashed repeatedly with the more abstractly propagandist Plekhanov. Confronted with this unexpected turn of events, Lenin was initially disoriented and conciliatory. Over the final months of 1903 he was steadily isolated among the exiles in the face of Menshevik intransigence, while his supporters within the empire were either confused or hoped that the split would be transitory and resolved through ongoing work.

By the turn of 1904, Lenin's position had clarified and hardened in the face of the intransigence of his opponents. As a result he embarked on a course

---

156 Letter from Krupskaia to E.D. Stasova in St. Petersburg, 28 March (10 April) 1903, Volin et al. 1969-70, vol. 3, pp285-6.

157 In fact in a familiar theme Krupskaia was angry with the Committee for conducting the dispute with the "litteratteurs" away from the gaze of the worker supporters of the Committee (letter from N.K. Krupskaia to E.D. Stasova in St. Petersburg, 2 (15) March 1903, Volin et al. 1969-70, vol. 3, pp219-20).

that in many ways repeated the struggle that had culminated in the Second Congress. Thus in May 1904 he published the aptly titled *One Step Forward, Two Steps Back* (hereafter *One Step*), which reworked and refined many of the arguments made earlier in *WITBD* but now against Menshevik rather than Economist opponents. Rallying his undoubted support from the Committees within the Russian empire, he built up endorsements for a new party Congress, launched a factional leadership in August, and began preparing a factional paper at the end of 1904.

The Petersburg Committee has gained something of an iconic status as a supporter of Lenin in this factional struggle following the Second Congress.[158] Indeed this position is hardly surprising given its "purified" nature prior to that Congress, and is supported by the records that it left. Thus the Committee adopted a pro-Bolshevik position immediately after the Congress,[159] bluntly spurning an attempt by the Kiev Committee to gain support for the Mensheviks.[160] From mid-1904 it explicitly supported Lenin's position in *One Step*, as well as his call for a new Congress.[161] In the immediate aftermath of the Second Congress, the Committee called for recognition of, as well as loyalty to, the existing party centres as these reflected the Bolshevik majority in the Congress.[162] As these bodies defected to or conciliated the Mensheviks, the Committee became more conditional in its support, and clearly identified itself as a Bolshevik factional centre.[163]

Yet, as in the period before the Second Congress, there was a tendency for Lenin's local collaborators to be wholly focused on formal organisational positions, as well as unclear in their understanding of the issues at the centre of the split. In an echo of the struggle prior to the Second Congress, Lenin was confounded as the Committee politically and organisationally conciliated the Mensheviks while paying scant attention to the clarity and support of those

---

158 See for example Kochakov (ed.) 1957, p221.

159 Zakharov (ed.) 1980, p77, Zhuikov (ed.) 1977, p153. For an extremely short report see Bondarevskaia et al. 1986, pp26-7.

160 Details of the meeting and replies in Bondarevskaia et al. 1986, pp34-6, "From a 'Short Outline of the activity of the PK'" over November-December 1903, between 20 and 26 November 1903, "From a 'Short report of the activity of the PK'", mid-December, 1903.

161 Bondarevskaia et al. 1986, pp49-51, "Resolution on the book by V.I. Lenin 'One Step Forward, Two Steps Back' and the necessity of the convening of the Third Congress of the Party", adopted unanimously at a meeting of the Committee on 23 June (6 July) 1904.

162 Bondarevskaia et al. 1986, pp33-4 "Resolution of the Petersburg Committee in support of the central institutions of the party with censure of the disorganising activity of the minority", end of October, not later than 2 (15) November, 1903.

163 See for example Bondarevskaia et al. 1986, p121, "Resolution of the Petersburg Committee of the RSDRP in response to the questionnaire from the CC", 26 December 1904.

workers looking to the factions for leadership. In the latter part of 1903, the Committee refused to send representatives to Geneva to resolve the split at the Second Congress,[164] and Stasova analysed it as merely a personal clash between the leading figures in exile.[165] Undermined by arrests and disorientated by the defection of prominent exiles, most notably Plekhanov, the Committee intervened weakly in the turmoil around the start of the Russo- Japanese War in early 1904,[166] and corresponded very little with Lenin and Krupskaia over the first half of that year.

The Committee sought to ignore the Mensheviks in the city, despite their growing presence in the anti-war turmoil rising through 1904. Even in late 1903 when the Committee was formally unanimous in supporting Bolshevism there were differences within it – with one member clearly leaning towards the Mensheviks.[167] By October 1904 the growth of Menshevik support had reached the point where the Bolsheviks felt the factional alignment of the Committee was in peril, and desperate demands were made on Lenin to send organisers to bolster their position.[168]

Much to the chagrin of Lenin and Krupskaia, the Committee did not respond to this growing Menshevik strength with a political defence of the traditional Marxist positions on which Bolshevism was based, but rather co-opted Menshevik-leaning members.[169] This political wavering led to a dramatic setback in late November 1904. A student demonstration called against the war with the expectation of worker support, failed after the Committee withdrew endorsement temporarily and leaflets publicising the event were burnt.[170] This occurred despite the clear Bolshevik majority on the Committee.

---

164 Volin et al. 1974-77, vol. 1, pp154-5, letter from E.D. Stasova in St. Petersburg to the Editorial Board of *Iskra,* 24 September (7 October) 1903.

165 ibid., pp364-5, letter from E.D. Stasova to the Overseas Section of the CC of the RSDLP, 26 November (9 December) 1903, pp389-90, Letter from E.D. Stasova in St. Petersburg to the Overseas Section of the CC of the RSDLP, 7 (20) December, 1903.

166 The Committee met 16 times in the first half of the year (Bondarevskaia et al. 1986, pp37-51) and issued eleven leaflets (*Listovki Peterburgskikh Bolshevikov 1902-1917,* Index p556). Up to spring that year more than 50 meetings were held against the war but it is not clear what the nature of these gatherings were or how large the audience (Diakin et al. 1972, p260).

167 Volin et al. 1974-77, vol. 1, pp389-90, letter from E.D. Stasova in St. Petersburg to the Overseas Section of the CC of the RSDLP, 7 (20) December 1903.

168 Volin et al. 1974-77, vol. 3, pp31-3, letter from N.K. Krupskaia to M.I. Ul'ianova and P.I. Kuliabko in St. Petersburg, 23 September (6 October) 1904, pp130-1, letter from N.K. Krupskaia to M.I. Ul'ianova in St. Petersburg, before 19 October (1 November) 1904.

169 Volin et al. 1974-77, vol. 3, pp151-4, letter from. N.K. Krupskaia to P.I. Kuliabko in St. Petersburg, 28 October (10 November) 1904.

170 This demonstration became a notorious episode in the history of Social Democracy. One of

Perhaps the most significant feature of these events was that none of Lenin's correspondents were subsequently prepared to provide a frank explanation of the political causes for this dramatic failure of leadership.[171]

This failure led to the biggest setback for the Committee since the "Bouncer" split in mid-1902. While the Mensheviks themselves had opposed the demonstration, they used its outcome to discredit the Committee among many "worker intelligent" supporters, and gained control of all the main working class district organisations except Vyborg.[172] Based on this support, they set up their own leadership body in the city, the "Petersburg Group", and this body was recognised by the Menshevik-conciliating Central Committee.[173] The "official" Committee was reduced to a core of student and ex-student intellectuals in the centre of the city and a minority of the Social Democratic "worker intelligents" in some of the industrial districts.[174]

The Petersburg Committee thus confronted the movement rising toward Bloody Sunday with a weakened "worker intelligent" base as well as a growing political rival of at least equal strength.[175] The organisational opportunism in relation to Mensheviks, which had contributed to its weakness, was now combined with a formalism and abstraction in relation to the evidently rising workers' struggle.[176] This contributed to the Bolsheviks' difficulty in gaining

---

the few accounts sent to Geneva from St. Petersburg (Volin et al. 1974-77, vol. 3, pp290-2, letter from V.V. Lipshitz from St. Petersburg to I.D. Mordkovich in Geneva, 8 (21), December 1904) became the basis for Lenin's article "Time to call a halt", *CW*, vol. 8, pp35-9.)

171 For Krupskaia's letters with demands for information see Volin et al. 1974-77, pp296-7 (letter from N.K Krupskaia to R.S. Zemliachka, V.V. Lipshitsy, P.I. Kuliabko and members of the Petersburg Committee, dated 5 (12) December 1904) and pp301-2 (letter from N.K. Krupskaia to V.V. Lipshitsy in St. Petersburg, 12 (25) December 1904). An account sympathetic to the Mensheviks which makes clear the Bolsheviks' weakness is given in Schwarz 1967, pp255-6 ("Appendix 2: The Demonstration of November 28, 1904, in Petersburg").

172 Gavrilov 1933, p26, "Doklad Peterburgskogo Komiteta RSDRP k III Partiinomy S'ezdy" in *Tretii S'ezd RSDRP...*, 1959, p544.

173 Kochakov (ed.) 1957, p235. For a useful and detailed account of these events and their consequences for Social Democratic organisation from a Menshevik view, see "The Social-Democratic Organisations on the Eve of the First Russian Revolution", in Schwarz 1967, pp51-8.

174 See table, Bondarevskaia 1975, pp292-3.

175 A figure of 300 to 400 factory supporters is given for the Petersburg Committee in Kochakov (ed.) 1957, p252. Most other commentators give the Petersburg Group at least equal forces. Perhaps the most authoritative estimate of the faction's strengths is by Bondarevskaia 1975, pp75-6. She gives the Bolsheviks "300-400 members" and a third grouping 100 members out of "roughly 800" Social Democrats in the city on the eve of Bloody Sunday.

176 Thus Kochakov (ed.) 1957, p252 describes the Committee's leaflets against the Bloody Sunday march as "highly polemical". Schwarz 1967, pp58-74, describes a fairly comparable approach by both factions, and is particularly hostile in relation to the Bolsheviks. His survey is,

a hearing within Gapon's Assembly as the St. Petersburg workers rose in support of the Putilov strike.

Yet for all these limitations, the Committee responded to the rising movement with an energy and enthusiasm that would allow it to advance and transform itself over the course of the next two years. Thus a significant lead was given by the long-term "worker intelligent" and labour movement leader, Shelgunov, at a joint meeting of Putilov and Semiannikov workers on 2 January.[177] Over the week leading up to Bloody Sunday, the Committee issued eight leaflets,[178] and on the eve of that day, despite its opposition to the tactics of Gapon's Assembly, instructed its supporters to be at the convening points the next day at 6am and take part in the proposed marches to the Winter Palace.[179]

Conclusion

For a wholly or "absolutely" determinist understanding of Marxism, the rise of class consciousness among workers is the inevitable and uninterrupted consequence of the rise of their struggle and the labour movement. That struggle and movement in turn results directly from the advance of productive forces within capitalism. The experience of the labour movement in St. Petersburg between 1861 and 1905 clearly stood against this model of uninterrupted and direct advance in consciousness. Thus the productive advance, basic to the whole process, was subject to stagnation owing to political vacillation, as well as setback due to economic crisis. Further class struggle and the formation of a labour movement required the conscious intervention of definite leaders, rather than being merely the unconscious or "spontaneous" process suggested by a determinist framework. Consequently the movement, after making dramatic advances, was repeatedly set back by state pressure, and confined to isolated circles of leaders within a workers' intelligentsia.

In these defensive circumstances Marxism, both as a theory and an organised current, was generally isolated "outside" a working class subject to the pervasive and overwhelming ideological domination of the ruling class. Indeed this marginalisation was even more severe for the Marxist current, which embodied a broader generalisation in consciousness, than for the labour movement as a whole. Thus Marxism in its application to the Russian empire

---

however, limited in scope.

177 Kochakov (ed.) 1957, p244, Diakin et al. 1972, p264, Zakharov (ed.) 1980, p86.

178 *Listovki Peterburgskikh Bolshevikov 1902-1917*, Index, p557.

179 See Bondarevskaia et al. 1986, pp124-7 for the details of the meeting on the eve of Bloody Sunday. Zakharov (ed.) 1980, p88.

was formulated and initially propagated by ex-Narodnik exiles in Geneva. It could only grow within St. Petersburg as a series of deeply clandestine and isolated study circles over the 1880s, and these circles were led by a series of ex-student dissidents. Only in the early- to mid-1890s did the current cohere and begin to intervene within the growing workers' struggles of the time. As a result, for the first and only time prior to 1905, organised Marxists gained some audience among mobilised workers and "worker intelligents" took leading roles within the current. Yet Marxism was again marginalised "outside" the class with the restabilisation of tsarism from the late 1890s to 1905. In these circumstances the St. Petersburg Marxists were once again led by exiles, who waged a difficult defensive struggle for an interventionist Marxism within a deeply clandestine and isolated movement.

Thus the struggle by Lenin, first against the Economists and then the Mensheviks, marked the culmination of a long process of theoretical clarification by identifiable exile leaders "outside" the working class. Given the circumstances of relatively shallow political and economic crises within the empire, as well as the relative effectiveness of tsarism in containing worker protest, the base did not as yet exist for a further advance of Marxism to become a current with a significant influence "within" the mass of workers in St. Petersburg. In these circumstances the struggle for Marxism could only take the form of an abstract defence of ideas among an "intelligentsia". The struggle for Marxism as a strategy adopted by the mass of workers could only come with the generalised crisis of tsarism and ongoing mobilisation of the mass of workers consequent on the massacre of Bloody Sunday. In the subsequent growth of Marxism from a small number of isolated "intelligents" to a significant layer of leading "activists", outlined in the next chapter, this defensive struggle by the exile leaders was vindicated.

Chapter 6

ST. PETERSBURG 9 JANUARY 1905–3 JUNE 1907: FORMATION, RISE AND CONTAINMENT OF THE BOLSHEVIKS AS THE MOST CLASS CONSCIOUS ELEMENT OF THE "WORKER ACTIVISTS"

Introduction

In the generalised workers' mobilisation following Bloody Sunday the advance of the Marxist current both contributed to and resulted from the rise of the labour movement in general. That current is here identified with the interventionist Marxism of the Bolshevik faction that resulted from the long process of theoretical development outlined in the previous chapter. As a result Marxism could now be seen as "within" the class in the way that it had not been earlier, and in a complementary development "worker activists" now played a more direct role in the development of Marxist theory. The Bolshevik faction grew in the rising struggle of 1905, but not as far as the labour movement in general, nor in the straightforward way that would be suggested by the determinist inclination of most critics. In contrast, the decline of the class struggle, while initially impacting more severely on the Bolsheviks than the labour movement in general, ultimately led to their dramatic growth as the possibilities for activism based on radical liberalism were exhausted.

Thus the advance of the Bolsheviks was related to the generalising consciousness of the labour movement, but a determinist understanding of that advance is even more misplaced than for the labour movement as a whole. For the growth of the faction over 1905 was still hindered by the tactical conservatism, organisational defensiveness and a conciliationism in relation to the Mensheviks, that had hardened in the earlier defensive period. Then, in the revolution's decline from early 1906, the Bolsheviks at first failed to recognise the retreat of the class struggle, and consequently adopted a strategy that hindered their intervention in those opportunities for defensive struggle that still arose.

Over time these limitations were substantially overcome, but only through persistent intervention by Lenin and other central leaders. These former exiles often grasped the potential of each strategic juncture in a way that many leading local figures did not. The belated and incomplete success of these initiatives meant that the Bolsheviks were unable to decisively settle the course of the revolution. Yet the tactical flexibility within a principled Marxist framework that was embodied in this intervention became part of the collective tradition of the Bolshevik faction. The ground was thus laid for the Bolsheviks to become a mass party in 1917.

9 January–17 October 1905: Initial shift from "intelligents" towards "activists"

On the eve of Bloody Sunday, the St. Petersburg Bolsheviks were a relatively well-defined current of between 200 and 400 supporters within a layer of some 1,000 Social Democrats. That layer, in turn, was part of a larger movement of several thousand anti-tsarist "worker intelligents". The Bolsheviks could be considered the culmination of a process of differentiation from radical liberalism to Marxism within the anti-tsarist intelligentsia that had its genesis in the defeat of tsarism during the Crimean War. Within the confines of the limited and spasmodic labour protest prior to 1905, this development could only have resulted from a defensive struggle for an historically interventionist interpretation of Marxism against a determinist accommodation to the prevailing capitalist hegemony. Such hegemony limited the Marxists to a confined and isolated current within the anti-tsarist section of the worker intelligentsia, that was itself "outside" the working class as a whole.

As argued in chapter four, the period of the revolution's rise between Bloody Sunday on 9 January 1905 and the granting of significant democratic concessions on 17 October 1905 marked a qualitative break with the earlier pattern of class struggle. In this new context the leadership of the workers' movement began to grow from a small and marginalised group of "intelligents" "outside" the class to a broad and influential layer of "activists" "within" it. As part of this shift the Bolsheviks, representing a broader political radicalisation, also began a comparable process as they sought to intervene within the burgeoning labour movement. Grounded in the workers' struggle, the shift in the Bolsheviks did not occur evenly over the year but, as with the transformation of the labour leadership, was concentrated around its beginning and end. Thus for the Bolsheviks the most dramatic changes occurred in January and February in the wake of Bloody Sunday, as well as over September and October in the course of the Great October Strike. The mid-year period on the other hand was one of relatively limited change in the faction's size and organisational structure.

1905 witnessed substantial growth and organisational change in the Bolsheviks. Yet the nature and extent of these changes contradicts the "spontaneist" model of the labour movement, as well as the associated view of the rise of revolutionary consciousness, usually found in the critics.[1] Thus the new layer of leading "worker activists" in general cohered around, and at least partly reflected, the earlier history of the "worker intelligentsia". Yet the transformation of the Bolsheviks was limited by the caution of its "intelligent" core, as well as the as yet incomplete radicalisation of those "activists" moving towards it. These factors were accentuated by the presence and even greater growth of the Mensheviks, a generally more moderate pole of attraction for radicalising workers, yet one still claiming the mantle of Social Democracy.

The transformation of the Bolsheviks, as well as its limitations, are clearly revealed by the patterns of supporter growth and organisational change. Thus in the first quarter of 1905 the faction grew by four to five times. Yet this growth was proportionately far greater in the inner urban centres which almost certainly provided a base of support for the core of the worker intelligentsia, and also provided the residential centres for student dissidents. It was far less in the outer urban districts, most notably Nevskii and Vyborg, where the growth of the leading labour movement activists was centred.[2] Here the growth of the Bolsheviks was far more limited and Menshevik dominance deepened.[3] Over the year the organisational structure of the faction became far more decentralised and open. Yet this occurred only gradually and spasmodically, hindered by the ongoing caution and lack of vision shown by many local leaders of the faction.

For the seven years prior to Bloody Sunday, Lenin was consumed with the struggle to maintain an interventionist Marxism among the Social Democratic section of the anti-tsarist worker intelligentsia. From Bloody Sunday he was confronted with a new struggle – for the adoption of tactics flowing from such an interventionist Marxism by the emerging layer of leading labour activists. In this initial period of the revolution the controversy between Lenin and leading St. Petersburg Bolsheviks over the organisational measures necessary to wage this struggle could be particularly heated. The depth of these disagreements flowed from the unexpected and radical break in the context, as well as the impact on the leading local Bolsheviks of the earlier bitter struggle. Thus

---

1   Models have been outlined in chapter two.

2   See table in Bondarevskaia 1975, p79, for the four main districts of the city. Overall membership grew from 145 to 732 (5.04 times). Growth in the City district was 40 to 325 (8.13 times) and Peterburgskii district was 15 to 128 (8.53 times, while growth in Nevskii was 50 to 150 (3 times) and Vyborgskii 40 to 129 (3.23 times).

3   In the St. Petersburg report to the Third Congress the Nevskii district is clearly the largest centre of heavy industry with factories totalling 37,000 workers plus a further 60,000 workers in the satellite of Kolpino (p538). Bolshevik strength is given as 150 in 20 circles but Menshevik strength "a great deal more – perhaps 60 circles" (*Tretii S'ezd RSDRP...*, 1959, p550).

180

Lenin's shift of focus following Bloody Sunday cannot be seen as a renunciation of his earlier positions. Rather, as the firmest defender of interventionism in principle earlier, it is not surprising that Lenin should become the most far-reaching in promoting what he saw as the tactical application of that interventionism now that the context made it possible to do so.[4]

The essence of Lenin's intervention among the leading St. Petersburg Bolsheviks was the need to provide a concrete lead to large numbers of agitated workers now that insurrection was an evident possibility. This need underlies Lenin's comments over 1905 on party openness, the radicalisation and consequent recruitment of workers to the party, and the role of these newly recruited workers as Committee members and faction leaders. In making his arguments, Lenin usually found initial acceptance, indeed enthusiasm, from his principal collaborators in the Petersburg Committee. However as the practical demands and difficulties of fully implementing these positions became clear, this initial acceptance gave way to growing misgivings. Many leading St. Petersburg Bolsheviks had earlier been unclear and reluctant in their break with Menshevism, when the potential and nature of workers' radicalisation was contested in theoretical debate. Now they only partially and hesitatingly adopted the practical measures flowing from Lenin's recognition of that radicalisation in reality.

January–February 1905

The shift in the character of the Petersburg Committee, as well as the limits to that shift, was evident in the initial wave of the revolution over January and February 1905. Contrary to the conclusion drawn by many of those who argue for a significant break in Lenin's views on Bloody Sunday,[5] the Committee intervened with great energy and sacrifice in the key events of this period. Thus a number of Bolsheviks were killed marching on Bloody Sunday,[6] while others played a leading role in what must be regarded as the most radical point of the day's struggle – the building of barricades on Vasilevskii Island.[7] Indeed over February the Committee gained an exaggerated view of its influence when it was able to convene meetings

---

4   This point will be argued at length in chapter 8.

5   In the most extreme case of the critics' erroneous judgement flowing from their determinist leaning, Liebman describes the Bolsheviks as "reticent and hesitant in the face of some of the most striking aspects of this agitation" (Liebman 1975, p43).

6   Bondarevskaia 1975, p63.

7   Diakin et al. 1972, p269, Bondarevskaia 1975, p73. "Letter from S.I. Gusev from St. Petersburg to the Urals Committee of the RSDLP in Ekaterinburg, 23 (10) January 1905", reproduced in Antoniuk et al. 1979-91, vol. 1, book 1, pp35-6.

of workplace delegates that intervened successfully within the Shidlovskii Commission.[8]

These particular interventions by the Petersburg Committee were based on a dramatic overall rise in activity by its supporters. Thus in the three months leading up to Bloody Sunday, only 15 leaflets were produced by the Committee, with seven of these produced in the week prior to the day itself.[9] By comparison, in the week following Bloody Sunday some 20 leaflets were produced, and over January as a whole 44 leaflets were produced with 113,600 copies.[10] This massive increase in publication was made possible through a printing organisation that grew to some 95 people and 60 clandestine organising centres.[11]

Such a rise in activity resulted in the growth, diversification and opening of the Committee's organisation. Thus by the beginning of March the supporters of the Committee had more than doubled to between 1,000 and 1,200,[12] of which some 60 were full-time agitators.[13] Responding to this growth the Committee began meeting on a weekly basis,[14] districts were divided into subdistricts,[15] and after some discussion a decision was taken to include all district organisers on the city-wide body.[16] Over this time the regularity and frequency of correspondence by Committee members with the still exiled Lenin dramatically increased – particularly from the secretary Gusev.[17] Of the eleven full-time organisers that Lenin sent to Russia five went to St. Petersburg.[18]

Over the first months of 1905 the Petersburg Bolsheviks commenced a process of organisational transformation, but their leadership was still marked by the earlier unfavourable circumstances. Thus, even as the Bolsheviks doubled in size, their radically democratic-leaning Menshevik

8   Bondarevskaia 1975, p73, Kochakov (ed.) 1957, p278, Diakin et al. 1972, p275, Schwarz 1967, pp95-12 [sic].

9   *Listovki Peterburgskikh Bolshevikov 1902-1917* (hereafter *Listovki Peterburgskikh…*), Index, p557.

10   Zhuikov (ed.) 1977, pp165-6.

11   ibid., p165.

12   Zakharov (ed.) 1980, p95, Keep 1963, p168.

13   Zakharov (ed.) 1980, p100, Bondarevskaia 1975, p73, Zhuikov (ed.) 1977, p164.

14   Records have been left of such regular meetings over February and March and more spasmodically over January and April (Bondarevskaia et al. 1986, pp123-60).

15   Zhuikov (ed.) 1977, p177.

16   Zakharov (ed.) 1980, p77.

17   Bondarevskaia et al.1982, p107.

18   ibid., p108. In contrast to this source Krupskaia informed Gusev that 30 organisers had been sent to Russia in a letter dated 17 (30) January 1905 (Antoniuk et al. 1979-91, vol. 1, book 1, p89).

rivals grew even more. This growth was particularly evident in the deepening Menshevik influence among the activists within the principal working class districts like Nevskii and Vyborg.[19] The limited gains of the Bolsheviks reflected not only the still incomplete radicalisation of the activists leading the emerging labour movement. Also hindering their growth was a wariness relative to the rising labour movement,[20] a narrow focus on organisational presence,[21] and a disdain for workers moving toward the faction,[22] that was shown by the leading local Bolsheviks as well as those secondary exile figures who had been sent to assist them. While their gains among the activists were limited, the Bolsheviks assumed complete control of the Social Democratic student organisation[23] – an attainment that must be seen as resulting from the deeper immediate radicalisation of the volatile student population at this initial point of the revolution. The importance of the student movement for the Committee as well as their role within it is clear from the number of documents included in the St. Petersburg report to the Third Congress. By comparison the report on the Vyborg and Petersburg districts comprises just over three pages, the Nevskii district two paragraphs and the city district just over two pages. The report begins by explaining a fall in activity in summer 1903 as due to the absence of students (some 20,000) over the vacation.[24]

By the start of March the Petersburg Committee had grown dramatically and had begun to transform its structure, but its essential character as a propaganda group of students and worker intellectuals remained as before. This could be seen most clearly in the limited role of leadership from within the industrial districts. Almost all the considerable number of leaflets issued over January and February were published centrally rather than by district

---

19   Zakharov (ed.) 1980, p95.

20   Evident in the danger of "democratism" and "spontaneism" seen by Gusev, the secretary of the Committee, in a letter written to Lenin and other members of the *Vpered* editorial board one week after Bloody Sunday (Antoniuk et al. 1979-91, vol. 1, book 1, pp83-4).

21   See for example ibid., p84, which significantly refers to comments made prior to Bloody Sunday.

22   See for example Gusev's comments in a letter to Lenin on 20 January (2 February), reproduced in Antoniuk et al. 1979-91, vol. 1, book 1, p113.

23   Zakharov (ed.) 1980, pp97, 101.

24   It includes a "Report on the United Social Democratic Organisation of Students of St. Petersburg" (pp557-64), a report on literature distributed (pp564-5), a "Plan of Organisation of Students" (pp566-71), "Rules of the United Social Democratic Organisation of Students of St. Petersburg" (pp571-4) and 'Topics for Agitation (Pamphlet Propaganda) amongst Students suggested by the 'Social Democratic Group of Students of St. Petersburg University'" (pp575-6). Reference to students on vacation (p539). All references from *Tretii S'ezd RSDRP...*, 1959.

sub-committees,[25] and while district organisers were formally included in the Committee, their role,[26] as well as that of the district organisation, remained limited. While many leaflets were produced, a city-wide political newspaper, which could have become the medium for organising activity at a district level, failed after its first issue.[27]

If the practice of the Petersburg Committee changed dramatically, then Lenin's views about the possibilities for intervention in the new context, and hence the demands placed on the Bolsheviks, changed even more. In a series of articles, letters and conversations that culminated in the position argued in "New Tasks and New Forces",[28] Lenin sought to deepen the shift toward intervention in struggle, as well as openness in organisational structure, that had been commenced by his supporters within the empire. In the immediate tumult of the revolution's opening, his views were formally accepted by his St. Petersburg collaborators. However they did not go as far as Lenin in their assessment of the movement's potential, and hence showed some hesitance concerning his organisational proposals.[29] Towards the middle of the year, as the initial agitation of the revolution subsided, these misgivings would deepen into overt opposition.

March–August 1905

In the circumstances of declining struggle and a relative stabilisation of the state between March and August the Petersburg Committee experienced a retreat from the massive growth in the first months of the year to a stagnation, perhaps even a decline, in the number of supporters. At the same time there was a consolidation rather than continuing transformation of organisational structures. City-wide activity was limited to involvement in two general protests around mid-year, as well as the preparation and consideration of

---

25 In fact only two leaflets were not published by the Committee: one by the Vyborg region after 20 January 1905 (no. 102 in *Listovki Peterburgskikh...*, p186), and one by "social democratic workers" (no. 97 in *Listovki Peterburgskikh...*, p180).

26 This measure was the subject of a characteristically long discussion at the Committee meeting of 23 February (8 March) 1905 (Bondarevskaia et al. 1986, pp143-6). Also characteristically this meeting began with a report about discussions with the Mensheviks over the Third Congress.

27 Kochakov (ed.) 1957, p292, Zhuikov (ed.) 1977, p167. (Some 1,500 copies were produced.)

28 Lenin, *CW*, vol. 8, "New Tasks and New Forces", pp211-20, published in *Vpered*, no. 9, 23 February (8 March) 1905.

29 See for example Gusev's opposition to opening the Petersburg Committee in a letter written to Lenin on 12 (25) February 1905 (Antoniuk et. al 1979-91, vol. 1 book 1, pp330-5).

the Third Party Congress.[30] In these circumstances of relative tranquillity, misgivings about Lenin's organisational proposals hardened.

Over January and February the intensity of tsarism's crisis had provided many opportunities for propaganda and agitation by the Petersburg Committee. Between March and August these opportunities occurred only spasmodically – principally the occasions of May Day, and the half-yearly anniversary of Bloody Sunday on 9 July. While the Committee was able to distribute considerable propaganda on both occasions there was a great disparity between the response to the strike call on May Day and that on the anniversary of Bloody Sunday. It is indicative of the defensive context that the Committee opposed a Menshevik proposal for "armed demonstrations" in favour of meetings on May Day. A figure of only 11,400 strikers in the strongholds of Nevskii and Vyborg on Monday 2 May 1905 "at the call of the Petersburg Committee"[31] is recorded, while 100,000 had demonstrated on the anniversary of Bloody Sunday. This suggests some hardening of the gap between that section of the activists influenced by revolutionaries and the mass of anti-tsarist workers. The former figure, as the audience for revolutionaries at this time, is reinforced by the distribution of the announcement for the Third Party Congress – some 9,000.[32]

This lack of city-wide struggle limited the general activity and propaganda of the Committee. Thus while some 44 leaflets were issued in January this declined to nine in March, five in April, three in May, six in June, and seven in July.[33] Meetings of the Committee were held weekly over January and February, but these became spasmodic over the spring and summer months apart from the two weeks prior to the Bloody Sunday anniversary.[34] By the end of February, district and even sub-district committees had been formally established. Yet with the relative stability over the middle of the year, these organisations could not flourish. Indeed repression in the period leading up to and following May Day broke up a number of important district organisations. In May, the City, Vasilevskii Island and Nevskii district committees were broken up.[35] Over

30 The Petersburg Committee did play a significant role in the preparation of the Congress see Zakharov (ed.) 1980, pp102-3, Kochakov (ed.) 1957, p292, Bondarevskaia et al.1982, pp109-10.

31 The figure for May Day comes from Kochakov (ed.) 1957, p298. For a discussion of the preparations and protest on 9 July 1905 see Bondarevskaia et al. 1986, pp117-9, Kochakov (ed.) 1957, p303, Diakin et al. 1972, p282.

32 Zakharov (ed.) 1980, p107.

33 *Listovki Peterburgskikh…*, Index, pp559-60.

34 I am taking this from the sparse records and memoirs for the summer months in Bondarevskaia et al. 1986, pp159-78.

35 Zakharov (ed.) 1980, p108.

April May and June, 140 active party workers were arrested, with more than 100 taken on the night of 4-5 April, so that of 51 circles less than ten remained, weakening the city-wide Committee itself. It is indicative of the continuing weight of repression that it was felt necessary to change the secretary of the Committee six times over 1905 in order to prevent arrest.[36]

In these relatively unfavourable circumstances Lenin sought to consolidate support for the position outlined in "New Forces and New Tasks". In his correspondence with St. Petersburg, Lenin particularly focused on the greater role of leading workers on Committees, as well as the role of the Third Congress in providing a political lead for the labour movement in Russia. In response Gusev, the Secretary of the Committee, expressed doubts about and even disparaged the new forces emerging in the struggle.[37] On the other hand a number of district organisers, closer to the radicalising "activist" labour leaders, were more receptive to Lenin's arguments. The misgivings among the leading St. Petersburg Bolsheviks were echoed across the empire and were evident at the Third Congress. Here, the initiative by Lenin and Bogdanov to have all Committees constituted on the basis of direct election from the membership was met with indignant opposition from the "committeemen" and defeated.[38]

On an issue related to that of opening the Committees, Lenin persisted with his campaign to have the St. Petersburg Bolsheviks break clearly and irrevocably with the Mensheviks. Yet throughout the year his supporters tended to seek an alliance with the Mensheviks at major eruptions in the class struggle. At the Third Congress, Lenin felt unable to move the expulsion of the Mensheviks from the RSDLP,[39] showing that this conciliationism was still a general feature of the faction. From early April to the end of June, Lenin's direct contact with St. Petersburg was limited as he focused on the preparation and conduct of the Third Congress, and subsequently the defence of the Congress decisions in his major publication for the year, *Two Tactics of Social Democracy in the Democratic Revolution.*[40]

36   Bondarevskaia et al. 1986, p4.

37   See for example his letter to Lenin 7 (20) March 1905, reproduced as Letter 364 in Antoniuk et al. 1979-91, vol. 1, book 2, pp158-60.

38   The vote was lost 12 to 9.5 (Keep 1963, p211). For a discussion of the challenges to the former regimes in both Bolsheviks and Mensheviks see Schwarz 1967, pp216-30.

39   Keep 1963, p213.

40   Lenin, *CW*, vol. 9, pp15-140.

August–October 1905

On 6 August the tsar made a further attempt to placate the demand for a new constitutional order. The support for this demand had grown with the recent defeat at Tsushima, and had earlier been clearly evident in the massive response to the half-yearly anniversary of Bloody Sunday. The minor concession to parliamentary rule that became known as the "Bulygin Duma" was so trivial that it only provoked a wave of struggle that rose over September and culminated in the October General Strike.

The Bolsheviks grew substantially over January and February, but they still remained essentially a group of students and "worker intelligents". In this new wave of protest they made the first major steps toward becoming a faction of "worker activists". This was achieved through their intervention within the rising tide of strike action, and was evident in the shift in the balance of the faction's activity towards the large factories of the industrial districts. Many of the organisational changes that Lenin had campaigned for earlier were now at least partially implemented. Yet even so the influence of the faction continued to be limited by a caution in the transformation of its organisational structure which was associated with an inclination to sectarianism in its approach to the growing struggle.[41]

It was the re-opening of the universities, freed of state supervision, that allowed the activity of the Petersburg Committee, together with the rest of the labour movement, to grow dramatically.[42] Thus a burst of protest meetings as well as other agitational activity swept through the working class districts, most notably the traditional strong points of Nevskii[43] and Vyborg, over September. Associated with this rise in activity was a shift in the weight of the faction toward the industrial districts. On 14 September 1905 a new district covering the far outer areas of the city was established and on 22 and 26 September reports were received on the armed organisation and in one of the major factories of the Vyborg district, the Metal factory, the number of Bolsheviks grew

---

41 In particular the opposition or wavering of the Petersburg Committee in relation to the general strike and formation of the Soviet. For some discussion of the complex question of the attitude of the Committee and its development see Diakin et al. 1972, p286, Zakharov (ed.) 1980, p118, Zhuikov (ed.) 1977, p192.

42 The universities were officially re-opened on 27 August 1905 under a "Provisional Law" (Kochakov (ed.) 1957, p311). On 13 September a student Congress decided to accept the opening in order to use the universities as a base to organise against the Bulygin Duma (Kochakov (ed.) 1957, p311).

43 See Kochakov (ed.) 1957, p311, on meetings in the Nevskii district and universities in which the Bolsheviks were able to intervene.

from between five and six to 70. In Vyborg some 14 new factory circles were established over September,[44] with district organisers again being included in the Committee. On 26 September the Committee discussed strengthening itself for the anticipated upsurge in struggle, members were forbidden to leave their place of work without permission, two organisers and two agitators were sent from Moscow,[45] and a plethora of letters were sent to Lenin by district organisers and activists.[46] A good example of the new prominence of activism and "activists" among Bolsheviks is that the printers' solidarity strike was led by a committee chaired by a Bolshevik from the Obukhov works.[47] The culmination of this trend toward open agitation in the industrial districts, as well as the consequent shift in Committee organisation, was the formation of a collective of agitators to intervene in the plethora of protest events now being organised.[48]

The "active boycott" position of the Bolsheviks in relation to the Bulygin Duma gave them an audience among the Menshevik worker activists of the peripheral districts, but this did not lead directly and immediately to a transfer of support to the faction. These activists had not had the concrete experience of an insurrection, and at this time the Bolsheviks were advocating insurrection directly,[49] and hence opposing the drift toward a general strike.[50] As a result most Menshevik-leaning activists appear to have supported formal organisational unification of the two factions rather than joining the Bolsheviks. Indeed this pressure appears to have been a major factor in the formation of a Federated Committee between the two factions in early September.

In the context of activist radicalisation and Committee development, many positions Lenin had campaigned for through the year, most notably the

---

44 Bondarevskaia 1975, pp128 and 202. In late September Krupskaia was moved to comment on the excellent organisation of the Petersburg Committee. The preparation of the armed organisation is also covered in Bondarevskaia et al.1982, pp115-6.

45 Zakharov (ed.) 1980, p115.

46 In fact 47 letters were sent between Geneva and St. Petersburg over the month of September 1905. The Index of Antoniuk et al. 1979-91, vol. 4, published in 1991, reproduces 30 letters that were sent from correspondents in St. Petersburg to Lenin or Krupskaia, and 17 letters that were sent to St. Petersburg. Bondarevskaia 1975, p260, contains a table for correspondence which gives figures that are somewhat lower than this, but shows clearly the peaks of correspondence during January-February and August-September, as well as the steady rise of correspondence from mid-year.

47 Bondarevskaia 1975, p126.

48 ibid., pp131, 133, Zhuikov (ed.) 1977, p183.

49 Bondarevskaia 1975, p127.

50 On the difficulties for the Bolsheviks as the strike built up see Schwarz 1967, p 139-40.

inclusion of workers in leading bodies, were to a substantial extent achieved. Yet even as alignment was being reached in practice on these organisational questions, a new dispute erupted over the attitude of the faction to the Bulygin Duma. Flowing from this difference arose a further conflict over the nature of relations with the Mensheviks. It seems clear that many St. Petersburg Bolsheviks were initially reluctant to advocate an active boycott against the Bulygin Duma – indeed at one point the St. Petersburg-based Central Committee threatened to cut off funds to *Proletarii*, through which Lenin was very actively promoting this position.[51] Associated with this wavering over strategy was an organisational leaning towards the Mensheviks.[52] It was only as the Mensheviks moved to a very conciliatory position in relation to the proposed Duma that the Petersburg and Central Committees shifted back towards Lenin and the "active boycott" position – a position that was being supported very strongly in the working class districts. Almost certainly reflecting his more immediate grasp of the circumstances, Lenin himself began to shift away from the direct insurrectionism of his district correspondents when he returned to St. Petersburg. As a result of this shift his position came closer to the more measured tactical approach of the Central Committee.[53]

18 October 1905–3 December 1905: Consolidation of a significant base among the "worker activists"

Between Bloody Sunday (9 January 1905) and the proclamation of the "October Manifesto" (17 October 1905), the Bolsheviks grew by some two to three times and took a major step towards becoming an interventionist and open party of worker activists. They did so in the context of a state power weakening under assault by intense labour unrest that was focused particularly on general strikes in January and October. As outlined in chapter four, the short period between 18 October and 3 December was one in which this weakening of state power and rising of workers' struggle equalised to create a

---

51   I am taking the evidence of this threat from the letter of V.I. Lenin in Geneva to the Bureau of the Central Committee of the RSDLP in St. Petersburg, 2 (15) September 1905, reproduced as Letter 134 in Antoniuk et al. 1979-91, vol. 4, pp257-61.

52   Letter from the Bureau of the Central Committee of the RSDLP in St. Petersburg to V.I. Lenin in Geneva, 24 August (6 September) 1905, reproduced as Letter 53 in ibid., pp117-9. Letter from N.V. Doroshenko in St. Petersburg to N.K. Krupskaia in Geneva, 20 August (2 September) 1905, reproduced as Letter 12 in ibid., pp45-7. Letter from P.A. Krasikov in St. Petersburg to V.I. Lenin and N. K. Krupskaia in Geneva, 22 August (4 September) 1905, reproduced as Letter 24 in ibid., pp73-8.

53   The basic evidence of this shift being a letter from Lenin to M.M. Essen in St. Petersburg, 13 (26) October 1905. Reproduced as Letter 421 in ibid., p229.

balance of "dual power". The focus of this short plateau of the revolution was the Soviet, whose representatives formed a peak of activity and consciousness in a pyramid-of perhaps some 10,000 worker activists.

Over this period of ongoing mobilisation the Bolsheviks made a further advance toward becoming an "activist" party – growing to over 3,000 members by the beginning of December,[54] gaining control of a daily paper with a large circulation which rose to 80,000,[55] and firmly establishing a locality-based structure of organisation. Yet despite these dramatic advances the predominant view among the activists in general still remained a type of adventurist liberalism, and consequently the Soviet was unable to prevent the steady consolidation of state power after the defeat of the struggle for the eight-hour day. Consequently the Bolsheviks, together with the rest of the anti-tsarist movement, proved to be impotent when the Soviet was arrested on 3 December.[56]

The inability of the St. Petersburg Bolsheviks to influence the majority of worker activists at least partly flowed from their continuing failure to understand the potentially radicalising impact of non-party worker mobilisation in a period of generalised workers' struggle. Thus although leading Bolsheviks appear to have shifted on the questions of worker leadership and organisational openness within the faction, they do not appear to have generalised this shift to the relations between the faction and those activists moving towards it. Indeed some of those most in favour of party opening were also most defensive in relation to non-party organisation. The fateful result of this defensiveness was that the Bolsheviks were hardly represented within the Soviet – the vehicle through which the leading labour movement activists might have organised a challenge for state power.

As during the rise of the revolution, this defensiveness in relation to non-party organisation was combined with a tendency to organisational conciliation with the Mensheviks. Such a tendency reflected the continuing failure of many local leaders to understand the fundamental basis of the political divergence between the two emerging political tendencies. Such an

---

54   Bondarevskaia 1975, p202, claims 3,000 Bolsheviks "by the end of 1905".

55   The paper *Novaia Zhizn'*. Twenty-eight issues were published between 27 November and 3 December 1905 (Kochakov (ed.) 1957, p351, Zakharov (ed.) 1980, p162). The circulation of the illegal *Vpered* had been at most 10,000. The official newspaper of the Soviet, *Izvestia*, had a circulation of between 40,000 and 60,000.

56   On the day following the arrest a meeting of 30 leading members of the Bolsheviks, Mensheviks and members of the Soviet Executive was held for an hour but could not resolve on a course of action (Bondarevskaia et al. 1986, pp193-4, "Meeting of the Central and Petersburg Committees of the RSDRP and members of the Executive of the Petersburg Soviet of Workers Deputies", 3 (16) December 1905).

understanding was made particularly difficult in the last months of 1905 by a new leftism among the Mensheviks. At this initial stage of their separate existence the Mensheviks were still very sensitive to surges in workers' struggle and the faction was dominated by the left around Trotsky and Parvus. The shift to radicalism, indeed formal commitment to insurrection, shown by the bulk of Mensheviks, made the declared positions of the two factions of the RSDLP very similar.[57] Thus by late 1905 a Federated Committee had been established between the two factions, united action was being organised in many districts, and a wave of new supporters unfamiliar with the history of conflict between them was bolstering both organisations. This meant that the Bolshevik position, most notably on concrete preparations for insurrection, was neither clearly put nor sharply distinguished from that of the Mensheviks.

The struggle of workers over the Days of Freedom peaked with the "November Strike" from 31 October to 8 November. The highpoint of Soviet influence and organisation followed in the wake of this burst of struggle. For comparable reasons to the growth of the Soviet, it must be assumed that the main growth of support for the Bolsheviks among the worker activists also occurred in mid-to late November. At this time many activists radicalised by the struggles from September would have shifted toward revolutionary organisations. A substantial part of this wave could have been incorporated into the faction through the great variety of party organisations that had been established and linked by a large circulation daily paper. This incorporation would also have required a further opening of the Committee to those forces rapidly gathering around it. While there can be no doubt that there was great pressure for this opening from the activists themselves, an essential catalyst in its achievement was the struggle waged by Lenin and other exiled leaders who arrived in the city on the day after the end of the November Strike.[58]

The October Manifesto to the November Strike

The October Manifesto, like the massacre of Bloody Sunday, opened a period of escalated class struggle within which there were qualitatively greater opportunities for revolutionaries. Yet, as in that earlier outburst of protest, the members of the Petersburg Committee – inexperienced, harassed and hence narrow in their perspective – do not appear to have fully grasped the

---

57   See among other sources Getzler 1967, p111.

58   For a useful Menshevik-aligned summary of the transformation of both factions as well as Lenin's role, see Schwarz 1967, pp235-45, "The Party Organisations during the Days of Freedom". It is significant that Schwarz again returns to his "Two Lenins" theme in explaining Lenin's role at this time (p244).

scope of this break.[59] Consequently their immediate response was confined to maintaining the pattern of activity developed earlier. The Committee's meeting held the morning after the declaration of the Manifesto did not go beyond rejecting in principle the concessions offered, and little attention was paid to the implications of the Manifesto for worker confidence and struggle. To the extent that the Committee adopted a perspective, it merely restated the general line of the Third Congress concerning the need for insurrection to overthrow tsarism.[60] Such a general approach could suggest no particular lead, and the Committee was confined to endorsing a march to the jail holding political prisoners.[61]

This failure to provide its own lead must also have been related to the tactical collaboration that the Committee, as in earlier moments of escalating struggle, now sought with the Mensheviks. Thus on the most significant decision of the moment – when to end the general strike – it was the cross-factional Federated Committee which moved in the Soviet to resume work on 21 October.[62] Further, several Social Democratic leaflets calling for workers to arm were issued under the name of the Federated Committee rather than by the Petersburg Committee itself.

Over the three weeks or so between the ending of the October strike and the defeat of the November strike, the Committee and the bulk of its supporters appear to have been relatively passive in relation to the deepening tactical leftism of most activists. Certainly between September and December the monthly number of leaflets issued by the Committee rose from four to 17; yet this output pales against that of January and February.[63] The Committee supported in principle the eight-hour day campaign despite the opposition of the Putilov plant, the only substantial base of the Bolsheviks in the Soviet. Yet it is significant that the Committee did not issue its own leaflet about this decisive campaign. This suggests that these leading Bolsheviks, like the Mensheviks and Soviet leadership in general, were reluctantly following in the wake of the support growing behind the activists of the three "fortresses" in the Nevskii district.[64] Given this leaning to routinist passivity and abstention from struggle by their leaders, as well as their limited visibility within the Federated

---

59   I am drawing this absence of a discussion of perspectives from the memoirs of the meeting in Bondarevskaia et al. 1986, p186, "Meeting of the Petersburg Committee, 18 (31) October 1905".

60   Memoirs of Kanatchikov, cited in Bondarevskaia et al. 1986, p186.

61   Memoirs of M.M. Essen in ibid.

62   Kochakov (ed.) 1957, p326.

63   ibid.

64   Kochakov (ed.) 1957, p337. Compare this with Lenin's enthusiasm for the action.

Committee, it seems unlikely that Bolsheviks would have grown substantially among the overwhelmingly self-confident worker activists over the first half of the Days of Freedom.

Perhaps even more than was the case at the earlier turning point in the class struggle on Bloody Sunday, there is a striking gap between the excited response of Lenin to the Manifesto and the relative routinism of the Committee. In contrast to the Committee, Lenin clearly foresaw the opening of an unstable escalation of struggle leading to the decisive battles of the revolution. Over a series of articles, he developed the notion of an "equality of power" to describe the new balance between the organised workers and the tsarist state. This strategic analysis in turn led him to focus particularly on the nature and role of the Soviet or "strike committee" as he initially called it.[65] Thus Lenin's supposed "libertarianism" in relation to the Soviet reflected above all the role he saw it playing in this very particular context of generalised struggle by the working class.

In contrast to Lenin's position, the Petersburg Committee's disinterest and defensiveness in relation to the Soviet is well known.[66] That attitude was the culmination of their limited grasp of the context and its consequent potential. Reflecting the Committee's initial wariness of the October strike, as well as its long-standing suspicion of non-party organisation, only three Bolsheviks were present at the meeting of 35-40 labour movement activists which convened the Soviet. Perhaps the only significant Bolshevik figure present, the local Vyborg leader N.M. Nemtsov,[67] was almost certainly responding to the pressure of Menshevik predominance in his district.

The Soviet grew to some 562 delegates, yet the Bolshevik representation grew to just 40, of which 10 were from the Putilov plant and five were delegated from the faction itself to the Executive Committee.[68] This severe under-representation,[69] particularly among the metal-worker activists who comprised 350 delegates, must to a substantial extent have reflected the disinterest shown by the Committee and its supporters. It meant that Bolshevik positions, most notably on concrete preparation for armed insurrection, could

---

65   See for example "The First Victory of the Revolution", Lenin, *CW*, vol. 9, pp427-34.

66   See for example the relatively well-documented commentary by Schwarz 1967, pp178-89.

67   Bondarevskaia 1975, p153.

68   For the Bolshevik representation on the Soviet see ibid., pp155-7. L.A. Fotieva, "Pamiatnye Dni (Iiul'-Dekabr' 1905 g.)" in Spirin (ed.) 1984, pp139-49.

69   Lenin in fact thought that Social Democrats should constitute 65 percent of the delegates (Avraham Yassour, "Modèles d'organisation révolutionnaire à Petersbourg en 1905", in Girault et al. 1974, p231).

not be put, or could receive only the most cursory consideration.[70]

The attitude of the Petersburg Committee to the Soviet did not reflect an authoritarianism or rigidity innate to Bolshevism as such. Rather it reflected the doggedly routinist conservatism of a particular local leadership who showed themselves incapable of grasping how dramatically workers' consciousness could be transformed in this revolutionary context. Probably the most significant of these leaders was the Petersburg Committee delegate to the Soviet Executive, Bogdan Minaevich Knuniants (also commonly referred to by his pseudonym Bogdan Radin).[71] He argued, echoing the Committee's earlier attitude to Gapon's Assembly, that a non-party organisation could only become anti-socialist and should therefore either merge with the RSDLP or confine itself to trade union matters.[72] Other leading Bolsheviks took a similar though less extreme position.[73] Thus a number of Lenin's allies on party openness, such as the district organisers N.V. Doroshenko and M.M. Essen, as well as the Central Committee member A.A. Bogdanov, sought to have the Soviet adopt the RSDLP program. Significantly for claims of Menshevik democratism, this position was adopted by the Federated Committee, although the Mensheviks subsequently refused to participate in the attempt to implement it.[74]

The position that the Petersburg Committee's attitude to the Soviet reflected an authoritarianism or conservatism inherent in Bolshevism is rebutted by the development of a position by Lenin that was almost the complete opposite to that taken by the local leadership. Lenin's approach was outlined most clearly in a proposed "Letter to the Editor" with the principal title "Our Tasks and the Soviet of Workers' Deputies". Here the culmination of Lenin's focus on the Soviet was to see it as the embryo of a "provisional revolutionary government" consequent on a successful insurrection. For Lenin the working class initiative shown in the Great October Strike, as well as the leadership given to that initiative by the Soviet, were the promise of revolution which the Bolsheviks must seek to realise – not the threat of an anti-socialist diversion from the

---

70   The proposal for preparation for armed struggle was raised by Bolshevik figures on at least three occasions – by Nemtsov on 29 November (the session that resolved to generalise the struggle for the eight-hour day), on 31 November (Diakin et al. 1972, p296), and by Radin and Krasikov as the culmination of a general strike at the last session of the Soviet Executive on 2 December (Kochakov (ed.) 1957, p357).

71   Radin gives something of an apologia for his position and role in B.M. Knuniants, "Pervyi Soviet Rabochikh Deputatov", in Spirin (ed.) 1984, pp150-222.

72   A.N. Kuraev, "Diskussiia o Sovietakh na Stranitsakh Gazety «Novaia Zhizn'» (1905 g.)", *Voprosy Istorii KPSS*, no. 8, 1991, pp71-82, Kochakov (ed.) 1957, p349; Avraham Yassour in Girault et al. 1974, pp223-4.

73   The question was discussed in issues 5 to 13 of *Novaia Zhizn'* (Kuraev, "Diskussiia…", p74).

74   ibid., p77.

party.[75] Given the conflict between this position and that of the Petersburg Committee, it is not surprising that Lenin showed an unusual reticence in arguing for it.[76] Nor is it surprising that his views made little immediate impact on the leading St. Petersburg Bolsheviks.[77]

End of the November strike to dispersal of the Soviet

The peak of Soviet organisation followed the defeat of the eight-hour day campaign. With capitalist and tsarist confidence resurgent, the worker base of the activists was locked out and sharply felt the need for class-wide organisation. Corresponding with this turn by their base was a deepening politicisation among the activists, which saw them deepen the shift towards the Social Democrats. This radicalisation, combined with the ongoing *de facto* legality of the Bolshevik faction, would have allowed for a massive expansion of the Bolsheviks between the end of the strike on 8 November and the arrest of the Soviet on 3 December.

A major catalyst for such an expansion was the arrival in St. Petersburg of Lenin, as well as a number of other significant exile Bolshevik leaders, the day after the end of the November strike. This no doubt assisted in converting *Novaia Zhizn'* into a wholly Bolshevik paper. Lenin was now in a position to respond directly and immediately to events, as well as to intervene and argue his positions personally through a mass circulation daily paper. This meant that he could press for his positions on involvement in struggles and non-party organisations, together with the transformation of the faction's structure, with much greater force than had earlier been the case. This lead, combined with the pressure from the radicalising activists, saw the faction grow and transform its organisational structure.[78]

Lenin was not firm enough in his own position on the Soviet to open a direct assault on that of the Petersburg Committee through articles in the faction press. Nor did he directly challenge the Committee over the associated question of involvement in limited economic struggles. Yet from his first day

---

75   Lenin, *CW*, vol. 10, pp17-28.

76   This reticence is seen in the article outlining his position taking the form of a "letter to the editor" of the faction paper and opening with the reservation that he was writing as an onlooker to events rather than as a participant (ibid., p19).

77   The development of Lenin's position will be outlined in detail in chapter 8 of this thesis. It is significant that Schwarz's account of Lenin's position and its reception amongst the Bolsheviks has the title "Two Lenins" (Schwarz 1967, pp189-95). Here his failure to set the development of Lenin's position in the context of the general class struggle and his ultimate Marxist aims lead him to see a contradiction through a method comparable to that of most critics.

78   Thus Fotieva, in Spirin (ed.) 1984, p147, talks about "great growth" in November 1905.

in the city he vehemently raised the question of the Soviet at meetings of the Committee[79] as well as with influential individuals.[80] And while not directly criticising the Committee, the role of the Soviet featured in almost all his articles written at this time. Further, Lenin gave a personal lead by attending his first session of the Soviet three days after returning to St. Petersburg, moving a major proposal to combat the lockout the following day,[81] and regularly attending meetings of the Soviet Executive.[82] In the face of this pressure the position of the core of the Petersburg Committee appears to have changed little. However those more peripheral to the city-wide Committee and hence closer to local activist radicalism, in particular the district organisers, were more receptive. Thus M.M. Essen, formerly critical of the Committee for its failure to take armed preparation seriously, now devoted daily attention to the Soviet[83] and together with several other district organisers convened an Unemployed Council in mid-November.[84]

Lenin's impact on the question of the Soviet was confined and limited. By contrast, the echo he found on the issue of structural change was profound and general. In three articles published soon after his arrival he argued for opening and diversifying party organisations, direct democracy in the convening of all leading bodies, and reunification with the Mensheviks as the basis for a new Party Congress.[85] Lenin had been making arguments in favour of the first two of these initiatives all year, but now the circumstances for their implementation were far more favourable than earlier. Indeed the speed and decisiveness with which the Committee responded to Lenin's proposals supports the evidence available that it was subject to overwhelming pressure and in some cases was endorsing a *de facto* reality. Thus, in the issue of the Bolshevik paper following Lenin's articles, the Committee published a resolution calling for the composition of all party bodies on the basis of election from the membership,

---

79   See the memoirs of this meeting in Bondarevskaia et al. 1986, pp188-9, "Broadened Meeting of the Petersburg Committee with the participation of V.I. Lenin, 8 (21) November 1905".

80   I am thinking in particular of Shelgunov, who mentioned Lenin's article "Our Tasks…" as late as 1938, although it was thought lost (Bondarevskaia et al. 1986, p190, footnote 2).

81   Reprinted in Lenin, *CW*, vol. 10, "Resolution of the Executive Committee of the St. Petersburg Soviet of Workers' Deputies on Measures for Counteracting the Lock-out. Adopted on November 14 (27), 1905", pp50-1.

82   Bondarevskaia 1975, pp162-3.

83   M.M. Essen, "V. 1905 gody. Iz zhizni Peterburgskogo Komiteta RSDRP", in Spirin (ed.) 1984, pp133-8.

84   The three organisers were M.M. Essen, A.M. Essen and B. Peres (Bondarevskaia et al. 1986, p174, Knuniants in Spirin (ed.) 1984, pp197-8).

85   Reprinted in Lenin, *CW*, vol. 10, "The reorganisation of the Party", pp29-39. This article will be discussed in detail in chapter 8.

the creation of a wide range of party organisations, and the uniting of these new bodies in a district structure.[86] In subsequent issues, announcements were published dealing with unity discussions with the Mensheviks as well as the voting procedures for a new Congress.[87]

By the end of November the St. Petersburg Bolsheviks could hardly have presented a greater contrast to the faction prior to Bloody Sunday. Many districts, notably the activist strongholds of Vyborg and Nevskii, had discussed the reorganisation in cross-factional mass meetings,[88] and were operating in an almost entirely open and legal manner.[89] A great variety of party forms, most notably local clubs and factory committees, had been established, while some districts had gone so far as to issue party tickets.[90] All levels of party organisation, including the Committee itself, were subject to election and readily recallable.[91]

4 December 1905–9 July 1906: Consolidation after a setback and a new offensive

By the time of the Soviet's arrest the Bolsheviks had grown to perhaps 4,000 worker activists. As such they had become a significant though not predominant section of the activist leadership of St. Petersburg's mobilised working class. Further they had re-established a loose and evolving organisational association with the Mensheviks, a faction of lesser though still substantial size and almost certainly greater influence among the activists. Now the size and composition of the Bolsheviks meant that their advance was more directly related to that of the labour movement than had been the case prior to 1905 or during the first period of the revolution. Thus, following the advance and retreat of the labour movement, the faction suffered a serious setback over December 1905 and January 1906,

---

86   Text reprinted in Bondarevskaia et al. 1986, p190, "Resolution on reorganisation", Meeting of the Petersburg Committee before 19 November (2 December) 1905.

87   The text of these announcements is reprinted in Bondarevskaia et al. 1986, pp191-3, Resolution "For the Unification of the Party", Meeting of the Petersburg Committee 22 November (5 December) 1905, Meeting of the Petersburg Committee together with the Petersburg Group of the CC RSDRP, 23 November (6 December) 1906, "Resolution on the elections to the Fourth Congress of the RSDRP", 30 November (13 December) 1905.

88   This occurred in the Vyborg, Vasilevskii Ostrov, Gorodskii, Universitet as well as the Semiannikov sub-district of the Nevskii district on 18 November (Zakharov (ed.) 1980, p126, Bondarevskaia 1975, p200).

89   Bondarevskaia 1975, p207.

90   Zakharov (ed.) 1980, p127.

91   For the case of the Petersburg Committee itself see Zakharov (ed.) 1980, p126.

a period of re-establishment and consolidation over February and March 1906, and then a rising burst of activity and influence through the middle of the year.

Yet as the most politicised section of the activists, the advance and retreat of the Bolsheviks could not be identical with that of the labour movement as a whole. As the particular target of state repression, they were especially set back by the end of January, and then found it unusually difficult to re-establish organisation. Despite the burst of class struggle over mid-1906, by early July the Bolsheviks were still confined to about 2,500 supporters, something over half their probable December 1905 peak. Overall they had been able to maintain the core of their membership in difficult circumstances but could not make a major advance.

The consolidation and recovery of the Bolsheviks was certainly limited by the repression to which they and the labour movement were subject. But, as following Bloody Sunday, as well as during the Days of Freedom, their gains were also limited by their own errors and mistaken perspectives. In October and November most leading Bolsheviks had failed to fully grasp the pivotal nature of the historical moment as well as the decisive role of the Soviet. As a result of this failure, they did not realise the extent of the setback that had been inflicted on the revolution through the dissolution of that body in early December. For the Bolsheviks, and particularly the local St. Petersburg leadership, this blow was seen as having only passing consequences, and hence a new insurrectionary upsurge was expected in the short term. Given this expectation the Petersburg Committee adopted the position of actively boycotting the First Duma – the convening and conduct of which became the central feature of political life in the city. It was through campaigning for this position that they distinguished themselves from the Menshevik faction as well as radical liberals. From such a position flowed a disdain for the partial struggles and organisations which more and more arose in the course of the rising defensive struggle against tsarism.

The general perspective of the Petersburg Committee was substantially mistaken. Yet that leadership was also prepared to make some adaptation to the struggle rising against tsarism, and this limited the gap opening between the nature of its intervention and the opportunities created by the now defensive workers' struggle. The Committee was compelled to return to co-option in leadership and propaganda in method as it re-established itself over February and March. Yet by the time of the surge of struggle in May and June it had adopted perhaps the greatest openness, interventionism and direct democracy up to that time. In doing so, it partially regained the membership and influence achieved in the second half of November 1905.

Lenin supported and promoted the mistaken expectation of imminent insurrection. During the periods of retreat and then consolidation he was a vociferous polemicist against the strategic pessimism of the Mensheviks within the newly reunified Social Democratic party. Yet he had always been distinguished by his concrete approach, which could be seen earlier when he had grasped the role of partial struggles and the Soviet in a way that most Bolsheviks did not. Thus as the defensive struggle against tsarism rose toward mid-year, Lenin paid attention to and promoted the role of the particular forms through which this struggle was being waged. Ultimately he devoted considerable attention to the RSDLP deputies in the Duma, as they became the main vehicle for generalising this defensive struggle. In doing so he shifted further and more systematically in his implicit perspectives than other Bolsheviks, and this shift culminated in his opposition to the formation of a new Soviet at the height of the mid-year upsurge of workers' struggle.[92]

December 1905–January 1906: Setback

In the month following the arrest of the Soviet, the Petersburg Committee experienced an especially severe setback as the whole labour movement was forced into retreat. While the Committee had generally been disdainful of the Soviet's role over November, the circumstances of retreat over December showed just how related the role of Soviet and Committee were. Thus despite its limited representation, the Soviet's arrest removed some of the most significant leaders and worker activists from the Committee – most notably B.M. Knuniants from the city-wide body, as well as the influential district leaders Nemtsov from the Vyborg district and Shelgunov from the Nevskii district.

With the Soviet repressed, those central political leaders remaining at large were denied the medium through which to mobilise the rest of the activists and hence workers in general. Thus although a meeting of leading Bolsheviks, Mensheviks, and members of the Executive of the Soviet convened the day after the arrest, this gathering broke up without issuing any call to action.[93] Three days later, on 6 December, another meeting did issue such a call,[94] but this must be seen as the belated response to pressure from the main activist

---

92 This shift and the conclusions Lenin drew for party organisation will be discussed in detail in chapter 8.

93 For memoirs of this meeting see Bondarevskaia et al. 1986, pp193-4, "Meeting of the Central and Petersburg Committees of the RSDRP and members of the Executive of the Petersburg Soviet of Workers Deputies, 3 (16) December 1905". It is noteworthy that no intervention by Lenin is recorded.

94 Diakin et al. 1972, p301.

centres in the Vyborg Narva and Nevskii districts.[95] As the strike was fading on 12 December, the Committee issued a call to continue, but this made little impact on the evident decline in support for the protest.[96]

With the strike wave precipitously declining from 12 December, the Bolsheviks were especially vulnerable to the repression of the labour movement activists in general, and their organisation was broken up. As early as 8 December, the legal and open forms of Bolshevik activity, notably the political clubs, were closed down. On 12 and 13 December a decisive blow was dealt when the Central Committee of the RSDLP, the Fighting Committee and the printing presses were seized. Altogether 122 arrests were made at this time and Lenin was forced to flee to Finland.[97] Over the remainder of December between 800[98] and 1,000[99] Bolsheviks were arrested, about one quarter of the faction's supporters.

Following the crippling blows of early December, with pressure continuing against the activists, Bolshevik organisation was almost non-existent until the end of January. Indeed the Petersburg Committee itself ceased to exist and an initiative to relaunch it resorted to co-option.[100] The one exception to this inactivity occurred at the start of the year, and was no doubt related to the deep feeling among workers over Bloody Sunday. At this time a meeting of the Federated Committee, together with worker representatives from the districts,[101] issued a call for a protest on the anniversary of that outrage. This call was spread through a number of leaflets issued by that leadership group.[102] It was also at this moment that the only article published by Lenin over January appeared – in a new journal that was suppressed after its first issue. From later figures it appears clear that Bolshevik strength continued to decline over January, though less dramatically than had been the case in December.

Contrasting sharply with the difficult context and limited activity of

---

95   Kochakov (ed.) 1957, p360, Zakharov (ed.) 1980, pp133-4; p133 refers to meetings in districts on 4 and 5 December to consider action which showed a "very combative spirit".

96   Kochakov (ed.) 1957, p361. For material on the Committee meeting which issued this call see Bondarevskaia et al. 1986, pp196-7, "Meeting of the Petersburg United Committee", 12 (25) December 1905.

97   Zakharov (ed.) 1980, p137, Bondarevskaia et al. 1982, p128. Kochakov (ed.) 1957, p363.

98   Figure from Zakharov (ed.) 1980, p137.

99   Figure "up to 1,000" taken from Bondarevskaia et al. 1982, p128.

100 See the resolution reproduced in Bondarevskaia et al. 1986, p199, "Resolution on the formation of a Committee", Meeting of the Petersburg Committee January 1906.

101 Material about this meeting is reproduced in Bondarevskaia et al. 1986, pp198-9, "Meeting of the Petersburg United Committee with participation of worker representatives from the districts 4 (17) January 1906".

102 See *Listovki Peterburgskikh...*, Leaflet no. 183, pp309-10, Leaflet no. 190, pp312-3.

the Bolsheviks was the combative tone of the small amount of propaganda they were able to distribute. It seems clear that the primary aim of these declarations was to prevent a precipitate demoralisation of the activists, and in particular those within and around the faction, rather than present a considered assessment of the immediate prospects. Thus Lenin in his January article "The Workers' Party and its Tasks in the Present Situation"[103] recognised that revolutionaries had to learn from the December defeat. Yet he also argued that this defeat was a step toward a new higher stage of revolt through the crushing of illusions as well as the involvement of the masses in an armed form of struggle.[104] The local St. Petersburg Bolsheviks went further and simply dismissed the consequences of the December defeat. In a leaflet produced from the January meeting of the Federated Committee it was claimed that the defeat "had not strengthened the government but rather given it a heavy blow".[105] Closely tied to these optimistic judgements was the earliest rejection of any involvement in the proposed First Duma.[106]

February–March 1906: Consolidation

As repression eased and the activists in general regrouped over February and March, the Bolsheviks re-established their organisation and resumed activity. The accelerated historical repetition, which saw the labour movement as a whole quickly break the bounds of legal co-option, had its parallel in the rapid re-emergence of the Bolshevik faction. Thus within a short period the Petersburg Committee shifted from an emphasis on education in activity and secretiveness in organisation to an approach that was far more open and interventionist. This process was associated with the sharp reassertion of the conflict with the Mensheviks, despite the formal reunification of the two factions. That polarisation recurred as the question of the Duma split the Social Democrats into sharp and recognised blocs at regularly held City Conferences. From the votes at these conferences, as well as other organisational indicators, it is evident that the Bolsheviks had come to enjoy

---

103 Lenin, *CW*, vol. 10, "The Workers' Party and its Tasks in the Present Situation", pp93-6.

104 ibid., pp93-4.

105 Bondarevskaia et al. 1986, p.198, "Meeting of the Petersburg United Committee with participation of worker representatives of the districts, 4 (17) January 1906".

106 Probably the first discussion of the issue in St Petersburg occurred at the meeting on 4 January (Bondarevskaia et al. 1986, p198, "Meeting of the Petersburg United Committee with participation of worker representatives of the districts, 4 (17) January 1906"). For Lenin's position see "Should We Boycott the State Duma (The Platform of the Majority)", Lenin, *CW*, vol. 10, pp97-100. This article was published as a leaflet by the CC and joint CC of the RSDLP in January 1906.

a clear though far from overwhelming majority among the Social Democrats of St. Petersburg.

The contradictory and uneven nature of the revolution's decline, as well as the Bolsheviks' response to that decline, was especially marked in this initial re-establishment of organisation over February 1906. Such a contradictory response was an initiative of the Petersburg Committee to re-establish circle education across the city. By early February such circles had largely disappeared from the industrial districts, and were concentrated around the traditional inner city and university centres of the intelligentsia. Over the phase of consolidation, despite growing prospects for activism, the concern with educational activity re-emerged in the industrial districts. As a result the Committee discussed a lack of student propagandists in March, and forbade their departure from the city without permission in April.[107] This interest in education, even as activism resumed, was indicative of an underlying retreat by the labour movement, with clear implications for the activity of the Bolsheviks. The deepening defensiveness of workers' struggle demanded a greater understanding from the Marxist worker activists seeking to lead those struggles, and this was reflected in the growing demand for education within the Bolshevik faction. As the revolution continued to decline, this shift to education in activity, although still within an overall framework of concrete leadership of mass struggles, became more marked.

Associated with the limited external activity of the months of consolidation was an internal focus on developing perspectives and reordering organisational structures. Thus several meetings of the Petersburg Committee were taken up with disputes and crisis in party units – particularly those focused on insurrection such as the "Fighting Groups".[108] On 7 February the first of two Social Democratic discussion bulletins was published[109] and included a major article by Lenin on perspectives and the Duma.[110] After a discussion organised around relatively small meetings and including only part of the membership, the city-wide Conference to deal with the issue of involvement in the elections to the First Duma was held on 21 and 22 February.[111] The voting at this meeting suggests that Bolshevik strength in St. Petersburg had fallen to about 2,000, or

---

107 Bondarevskaia et al. 1986, p221, Resolution "On the question of the departure of comrades", Meeting of the Petersburg Committee, April 1906.

108 Bondarevskaia et al. 1986, pp200-1, "Protocol of the Meeting of the Petersburg Committee, 10 (23) February 1906".

109 Andronov 1978, p55.

110 Lenin, *CW*, vol. 10, "The Present Situation in Russia and the Tactics of the Workers' Party", pp112-9.

111 For discussion of this conference see Bondarevskaia 1975, pp216-7, 220-1.

about 60 percent of the city's organised Social Democrats.[112]

Over February the city-wide Petersburg Committee re-established Bolshevism on an essentially propagandistic and defensive basis. Yet even at this early stage there was clear evidence of the reactivation of the leading labour movement activists within the working class districts, as well as Bolshevik involvement in this reactivation. Thus in Vyborg, now emerging as a leading industrial centre, the Bolsheviks issued two leaflets concerning the question of unemployment,[113] and the United Committee issued a further statement about the formation of party cells in non-party organisations.[114] At the beginning of March, the Petersburg Committee acceded to a request from the Vyborg district to include those organising protests around the issue of unemployment as Social Democrat members.[115]

Over March this tentative and defensive process of reactivation by the Bolsheviks deepened and generalised, although activity did not approach the levels of the previous November, nor was there a substantial increase in faction membership. The culmination of this reactivation was the Fourth Party Congress. In contrast to the February City Conference, the discussion for the Congress involved all Social Democrats who gathered in larger meetings than earlier. Lenin was able to intervene personally at ten of the 60 meetings which were held, each of between 50-60 members[116] although he could not return to permanent residence in the city. These interventions reinforced a major article on the current context and the intervention of Social Democrats into the forthcoming Duma elections that he wrote for the second issue of the internal party bulletin.[117] Drawing on the process of discussion Lenin subsequently drafted a platform for the Bolsheviks attending the Fourth Congress.[118] While the Committee could not yet publish a legal publication, an unusually large number of leaflets were distributed over March 1906,[119] and of these a significant proportion were produced by sub-committees in the industrial

112 My assessment, based on figures in Bondarevskaia 1975, pp214-5, 220.

113 *Listovki Peterburgskikh...*, Leaflets no. 199, p328, and 200, p329.

114 Bondarevskaia et al. 1986, pp199-200, "Resolution on the convening of party cells in non-party unions", Meeting of the United Petersburg Committee, January-February 1906. *Listovki Peterburgskikh...*, Leaflet no. 195, p325.

115 Bondarevskaia et al. 1986, p204, "Resolution on Unemployed", Meeting of the Petersburg Committee 9 (22) March 1906.

116 Zakharov (ed.) 1980, p142, Bondarevskaia et al. 1986, footnote 3, p206.

117 Lenin, *CW*, vol. 10, "The Russian Revolution and the Tasks of the Proletariat", pp135-45.

118 ibid., "A Tactical Platform for the Unity Congress of the RSDLP", pp147-63.

119 In all 17 leaflets are attributed to the Bolsheviks over the month. *Listovki Peterburgskikh...*, Index, p562.

districts.[120] It was activist representatives from these districts who demanded that the city-wide Committee take action to improve education at the meeting of 30 March.[121] By the end of March the Committee felt confident enough to issue a call for, as well as begin planning, a strike on the occasion of May Day. The organising meeting is significant because it marks the culmination of earlier developments. Of 15 attendees only two were Mensheviks, others being absent "for private reasons".[122]

April–June 1906: A new advance

As part of the rising labour movement over the second quarter of 1906, the Bolsheviks were able to move from consolidation to a restricted advance. In doing so they continued to gradually rebuild their strength and organisation in circumstances that weakly paralleled those from September to November 1905. Thus the number of Social Democrats represented at the Fourth Congress in the first half of April had been 3,500, of whom just over 2,000 were Bolsheviks.[123] By the time of the city Conference in early June, the number of Social Democrats had grown to about 4,000,[124] and Bolshevik support to about 2,500.

In April the phase of consolidation terminated with the successful convening of the Fourth Party Congress. Then the large response to May Day opened the new period of advance for the Bolsheviks. Thus on 9 May Lenin was able to present the Bolshevik perspective on the revolution at a major public forum,[125] and on the same day the first of a series of legal daily papers was launched.[126] Associated with this public re-emergence was a major effort to re-establish direct democracy in dealing with fundamental questions of perspectives. This was evident in the preparation for the second city-wide Conference in early June. Perhaps of even greater ongoing significance than these developments was the opening of a Bolshevik publishing house in St.

120 From the Vyborg district 1 leaflet (no. 203, pp340-1), from the Narva district one leaflet (no. 216, p358), from the Nevskii district three leaflets (nos. 208 p347, 215 p356-7, 219 p364). All references *Listovki Peterburgskikh…*.

121 Bondarevskaia et al. 1986, p208, "Protocol of the Meeting of the Petersburg Committee 30, March (12 April) 1906".

122 See material on the meeting, Bondarevskaia et al. 1986, pp207-9. In addition to discussing the questions of May Day and education the Committee elected a five-person executive.

123 See table in Bondarevskaia et al. 1986, pp292-3.

124 Comment by Lenin, *CW*, vol. 11, "Yes-Men of the Cadets", p64.

125 Zakharov (ed.) 1980, p143, Diakin et al. 1972, p308, Kochakov (ed.) 1957, pp378-80.

126 Andronov 1978, pp55-6, Kochakov (ed.) 1957, p385, Zhuikov (ed.) 1977, p168.

Petersburg.[127] This was part of a massive expansion in Marxist publishing[128] and, together with the earlier noted demand for education by the Bolshevik activists, could be seen as beginning the process of their conversion into a new far larger layer of "worker intelligents" that would be noted by Lenin in the wake of the revolution.[129]

Yet in the context of growing reaction over the empire as a whole, as well as a rise of workers' struggle in St. Petersburg that was still largely defensive, the possibility for the Bolsheviks to advance was limited. Thus while some 56 issues of various daily papers were produced before the dissolution of the First Duma, 30 of these were subject to some degree of seizure.[130] The June Conference, coming at the end of a discussion of the Duma question, was forced to relocate due to police pressure, and then several major leaders were arrested at its closing.[131] It is significant that while the struggle outside the Duma grew over May and June it was the reflection of that struggle within its proceedings that occupied the attention of the Petersburg Committee. Thus by the end of June the Committee was organising meetings between Social Democratic deputies and delegations of workers, opposing calls for a new Soviet, and arguing against a proposal for the Council of Unemployed to take the lead in economic struggles.[132]

The constrained improvement in the prospect for the Bolsheviks was reflected in Lenin's writings over the second quarter of 1906. Over April, Lenin was still required to write articles that were long, defensive and addressed largely to his fellow Bolsheviks. These responded to unexpected developments

---

127 Zhuikov (ed.) 1977, p172.

128 Kochakov (ed.) 1957, p386, Zhuikov (ed.) 1977, pp172-4.

129 While it is outside the scope of this thesis, the basic argument is supported by Lenin's return to the role of "worker intelligents" after 1907, in particular in the formation of the party press in 1914. This point is touched on by Evgenii Ol'khovskii as part of a general discussion of the "worker intelligentsia" and the attitude of Lenin and other leading Marxists to it (E.R. Ol'khovskii, "Formirovanie rabochei intelligentsii v Rossii v kontse XIX -nachale XX v." in Potolov (ed.) 1997, pp77-113, especially pp 78-9).

130 Kochakov (ed.) 1957, p385.

131 Bondarevskaia 1975, p222.

132 Bondarevskaia et al. 1986, pp234-9, "Resolution on the organisation of meetings between the Social Democratic fraction in the Duma with representatives of Petersburg workers", Meeting of the Petersburg Committee 17 (30) June 1906, "Resolution on the organisation of a meeting of the Social Democratic fraction of the First Duma with representatives of Petersburg workers", Meeting of the Petersburg Committee 21 June (4 July) 1906, "Resolution of the Executive Commission of the Petersburg Committee on links with the Duma fraction", Meeting of the Executive Commission of the Petersburg Committee 22 June (5 July) 1906, "'Resolution on the Soviet of workers deputies and the impending address of the State Duma to the people concerning the agrarian question", Meeting of the Petersburg Committee before 4 (17) July 1906.

– the return of a Duma with Cadet domination[133] as well as the majority gained by the Mensheviks at the Fourth Party Congress.[134] Yet from May there was both the possibility and necessity for Lenin to address a far larger audience through the daily Bolshevik press. Then over the two month period of the mid-year upsurge, his articles became more and more polemical and topical in relation to developments within the Duma, as well as the class interests these manoeuvres reflected.

Throughout this writing Lenin's principal target was the Cadets, who had become the main focus of the anti-tsarist movement following their success in the First Duma elections. Following from this polemic against the Cadets, he criticised the Mensheviks, who were tending to a parliamentarist focus on the Duma and hence to ally themselves with the Cadets. Yet implicit in much of his writing is also a criticism of an ongoing dogmatism in relation to the Duma, as well as of an abstention from partial struggles and organisations, among his fellow Bolsheviks. In this implicit criticism, the struggle between Lenin and other leading Petersburg Bolsheviks over 1905 continued, though now in a milder and more indirect form. Indicative of this continuing difference is that Lenin was the only leading Social Democrat in St. Petersburg to take an active interest in the unemployed movement, and it was he who made the crucial proposal to seek delegates from employed as well unemployed workers into its leading bodies.[135]

Lenin from the first recognised that the Cadet vote included a section of the population committed to an irreconcilable struggle against tsarism.[136] He also welcomed the election of Social Democrats to the Duma following the Fourth Congress,[137] and mentioned without critical comment the decision of that Congress to intervene within the elections. The now cross-factional Petersburg Committee, and its Bolshevik section in particular, took some time to recognise the popular sentiment reflected in the Duma composition, and sought to address that sentiment only after considerable discussion and hesitation.[138] By June, Lenin was commenting daily on the proceedings of

---

133 Lenin, *CW*, vol. 10, "The Victory of the Cadets and the Tasks of the Workers' Party", pp199-276.

134 "Report on the Unity Congress of the RSDLP", ibid., pp316-82.

135 Mikhailov 1995, p14.

136 Lenin, *CW*, vol. 10, "The Victory of the Cadets and the Tasks of the Workers' Party", p212.

137 ibid., "The Social-Democratic Election Victory in Tiflis", p423.

138 See for example the discussion reprinted in Bondarevskaia et al. 1986, pp213-6 (the protocol of the meeting on 19 April (2 May) 1906 of the Petersburg "United Committee of the RSDRP"). The protocol includes two resolutions (p214), one to reach an agreement with the Social Democratic deputies of the Duma so as to bring their activity under the control of the party, which received nine votes, and one not to reach any agreement, but campaign for a

206

the Duma.[139] Yet his personal lead appears to have made little impact on the Committee, which was still inclined to remain aloof from these events, and only organised meetings between Social Democratic members and worker delegates in order to forestall the Menshevik-dominated Central Committee from doing so.[140]

10 July 1906–3 June 1907: Dramatic growth of the Bolsheviks among the activists

The pattern of disarray followed by recovery was essentially repeated for both movement and faction between the dispersal of the First Duma in July 1906 and the suppression of the Second some eleven months later in June 1907.

However, if the advance of the faction had earlier been a weaker reflection of that by the activists in general, then now the growth of the Bolsheviks far outstripped the limited revival of struggle and the labour movement. Thus most general organisations of labour experienced at best a limited re-emergence over the latter half of 1906, but were then contained by defeats in struggle as well as legal restrictions over the first half of 1907. The Bolsheviks also stagnated in activity and contracted slightly in membership over the latter half of 1906 to have 2,100 supporters at the end of the year.

Constitutional Assembly, which received four votes. There is no indication of the factional alignment of these votes; pp219-20 a resolution adopted "15 against 15" at a meeting not later than 28 April concerning the attitude of the Committee to the Duma; pp223-5 a resolution passed not later than 19 May (1 June) 1906 by an "Expanded Meeting of the Petersburg Committee of the RSDRP"; pp226-7 a further resolution on the relation to the Duma Ministry passed 24 May(6 June) 1906; pp232-3 a resolution on the question of a Duma Ministry passed not later than 6 (19) June 1906; pp234-5 a resolution about the organisation of meetings between members of the Social Democratic Duma fraction and worker representatives from St. Petersburg passed on 17 (30) June 1906; pp235-6 a further resolution on this question passed 21 June (4 July) 1906.

139 See for example Lenin, *CW*, vol. 11, "The Parties in the Duma and the People", pp101-4; "A Bold Assault and a Timid-Defence", pp96-100; "The Bourgeoisie's Censures and the Proletariat's Call For Action", pp83-4; "The Cadet Duma Grants Money to the Pogrom-Mongers' Government", pp60-3; "Famine Relief and the Tactics of the Duma", pp43-7; "The Declaration of our Group in the Duma", pp32-7; "The Duma and the People", pp24-6; "Unity!", pp20-3.

140 Bondarevskaia et al. 1986, pp234-8, "Resolution on the organisation of meetings between the Social Democratic fraction of the Duma with representatives of Petersburg workers", Meeting of the Petersburg Committee 17 (30) June 1906, "Resolution on the organisation of a meeting between the Social Democratic fraction of the First Duma with representatives of Petersburg Workers", Meeting of the Petersburg Committee 21 June (4 July) 1906, "Resolution of the Executive Commission of the Petersburg Committee on links with the Duma fraction", Meeting of the Executive Commission of the Petersburg Committee 22 June (5 July) 1906.

Yet, through energetic and wholehearted participation in the Second Duma elections, they grew to 5,100 supporters in March 1907, and grew further to 5,991 supporters by May.[141]

The disproportionate growth of the Bolsheviks can be reflected the growth of inconsolable bitterness among the activists as the revolution declined. Such deep bitterness emerged to a relatively limited extent in the first half of 1906, as there could still appear to be the possibility of radical reform. Following the dissolution of the First Duma, with unemployment rising and repression growing, such a possibility was dramatically less evident for the most experienced and thoughtful section of the activists. Consequently, the number of those seeking a more general consciousness within which to understand the encroachment of tsarism, as well as a more combative and centralised organisation to respond to that encroachment, grew dramatically. This meant that a much larger audience for Bolshevism existed among the activists.

The Bolsheviks were able to address this audience effectively because they, like all political forces in St. Petersburg, had greatly increased their own understanding and flexibility over the course of the revolution. With a core of some 2,000 relatively experienced members, the faction proved capable of completing the shift to a locally based directly democratic structure through which all members were involved in deciding questions of general policy. They were able to do this over the second half of 1906 and early 1907 despite the continuing loss of leading members and the lack of a legal press. In contrast to early 1906, the faction now agreed to intervene within the election for the Second Duma with comparatively little hesitation and controversy. Thus, the struggles that Lenin had waged in 1905 and earlier for an open and flexible faction had by late 1906 to a significant extent been achieved.

Having consolidated their organisational structure, and adopted a very clear political profile independent of the Cadets, the Bolsheviks were able to take great advantage of the opportunity provided by the elections and proceedings of the Second Duma. In doing this, they made a stark contrast with their Menshevik rivals, who leaned towards supporting the Cadets and split from the Petersburg Committee in January 1907 to pursue this course. With their bitterness towards tsarism deepening, most labour movement "activists" were repulsed by the prevarication of the Cadets, and consequently support for the Menshevik faction did not grow.[142]

---

141 Figures taken from table in Bondarevskaia 1975, p293.

142 ibid.

July 1906–January 1907

Following the dissolution of the First Duma, the Petersburg Committee experienced a period of disarray, impotence and isolation, much as it had after the repression of the Soviet. Thus Committee support for a new Soviet[143] found little if any response, and no call was issued for generalised strike action, due to dissent from Menshevik members of the still joint body. However there could no doubt that some Bolsheviks also had misgivings about calling strike action. Yet such strike action did begin to break out from 21 July in response to a series of mutinies, but this occurred within the Menshevik-led district of Vyborg.[144]

The mutinies themselves occurred spontaneously, prematurely and independently of the Bolsheviks, despite the fact that the faction did have some contacts in the garrisons.[145] In perhaps the greatest blow to the Committee, 18 out of its 22 members were arrested on 23 July, when it attempted to meet and discuss the course of the growing strike.[146] Further to blows such as this directed specifically at its own organisation, the Bolsheviks were also constrained by the wave of repression against the labour movement in general. In particular its legal daily, together with the rest of the anti-tsarist press, was closed as the Duma was dispersed.

Yet if this initial disarray and impotence strongly echoed the experience of December 1905, then the far greater speed and effectiveness with which the Committee recovered showed the cohesion that had developed over the course of the revolution, and particularly over the first half of 1906. Thus just five days after the arrest of the Committee the core of a new body met to endorse ending the strike while still calling for a Soviet.[147] Over the rest of the year this new Committee met with growing regularity and accountability to consider a plethora of organisational issues relating to district organisation,

---

143 Bondarevskaia et al. 1986, p241, "Account of the meeting and resolution exposing the policy of the Menshevik-leaning CC and calling for the convening of a Soviet of workers deputies", Meeting of the Petersburg Committee 15 (28) July 1906.

144 This is the explanation given in Diakin et al. 1972, p318.

145 In fact the Petersburg Committee sent a delegation to Sveaborg on 18 July (Kochakov (ed.) 1957, p389). See also Bondarevskaia et al. 1986, pp242-4, "Resolution on the sending of a delegation to Sveaborg", Meeting of the Petersburg Committee 16 (29) July 1906, which makes rather incongruous the claim by Zakharov (ed.) 1980, p149, that the "revolts were led by the Bolsheviks".

146 Bondarevskaia et al. 1986, pp245-6, "Meeting of the Petersburg Committee, 23 July (5 August) 1906".

147 ibid., p249, "Account of the meeting of the Petersburg Committee, 28 July (10 August) 1906".

as well as the intervention of Social Democrats within the trade unions[148] and unemployed movements.[149] Underlying these particular issues were two ongoing concerns that were raised by the development of the faction since Bloody Sunday. These were the preparation of a fully "democratic centralist" structure of organisation[150] as well as a program of campaigning for the Second Duma elections.[151]

Associated with this accelerated organisational consolidation was the relaunching of a Committee publication. Thus after the faction's legal daily was suppressed on 7 July 1906,[152] a new underground publication was begun on 21 August in the name of the St. Petersburg and Moscow Committees. While having a lesser circulation and frequency than its legal predecessors, this paper still provided the means to re-orient and consolidate the Petersburg Bolsheviks over the second half of 1906. Thus the leading article in the first issue, "Before the Storm",[153] written by Lenin, once again argued the prospect of imminent insurrection, though now via a more difficult and protracted path. Two further articles by Lenin developed points flowing from this perspective – firstly "The Boycott",[154] arguing to other Bolsheviks the need to participate in the Second Duma elections, and secondly "The Political Crisis and the Bankruptcy of Opportunist Tactics",[155] making a polemic against the Mensheviks' approach to such participation. Through further articles and pamphlets Lenin and other Bolshevik writers developed these basic themes over the remainder of 1906.

This rapid re-cohering of the St. Petersburg Bolsheviks, in a context where the concrete class struggle was declining, and becoming more abstract and

---

148 ibid., p265, "Protocol of the meeting of the Petersburg Committee, 24 October (6 November) 1906", p273, "Account of the meeting of the Petersburg Committee, 30 October (12 November) 1906".

149 Zakharov (ed.) 1980, p140.

150 For discussions on the Committee of this process see Bondarevskaia et al. 1986, p249, "Account of the meeting of the Petersburg Committee, 28 July (10 August 1906)", p250, "Report of the meeting of the Petersburg Committee, 9 (22) August 1906)", p259, "Report of the meeting of the Petersburg Committee. 26 September (9 October) 1906)", pp262-3, "Protocol of the meeting of the Petersburg Committee, 1 (14) October 1906", p269, "Report of the meeting of the Petersburg Committee in October 1906".

151 For example at a meeting in October a special commission was formed to run the election campaign (ibid., p271, Inclusion 2, "Meeting of the Petersburg Committee in October 1906").

152 Kochakov (ed.) 1957, p386. In fact no legal publication could be produced for the rest of the year.

153 Lenin, *CW*, vol. 11, pp135-40.

154 ibid., pp141-9.

155 ibid., pp150-66.

ideological in form, led to a sharpening of the conflict with the Mensheviks. Earlier, when the revolution had been rising, differences in tactics had not been so sharp, or so closely connected to broader ideological issues. This trend had culminated in the formation of the joint Petersburg Federated Committee late in 1905, as well as some shifting between factions over particular questions by members of this joint leadership body. With the labour movement activists now very much on the defensive, tactical differences were clearly counterposed, leading to a new organisational polarisation and public disputation. The dispute over role of the Cadets generalised the tactical differences between Bolsheviks and Mensheviks, and this generalisation accentuated the trend of the two factions to once again become two currents within an "intelligentsia".

Thus the new organ of the St. Petersburg and Moscow Committees, *Proletarii* was clearly seen as a factional mouthpiece issued by the two bastions of Bolshevism.[156] On 9 August the Petersburg Committee resolved to issue a leaflet criticising the Menshevik-controlled Central Committee, which had earlier called for partial strikes in the wake of the dissolution of the First Duma as well as support for the Cadets in the Second Duma elections.[157] The Central Committee was also defied by the convening of a conference of Fighters and Soldiers' Organisations in November.[158] As before the Third and Fourth Congresses, the demand for a new Congress became a prominent theme in publications of the St. Petersburg Committee.

January–June 1907

As had earlier occurred in the second quarter of 1906, from January 1907 a period of consolidation was followed by one of supporter growth and organisational development for the Bolsheviks. Once again this was associated with a more agitated atmosphere created by the conduct of the Duma, as well as a weak revival in economic struggle. Yet while the overall pattern of the struggle between the classes was repeated, there was a significant shift in the intervention of the Bolsheviks, as well as in the results achieved by that

---

156 Certainly, this was the interpretation promoted in the Soviet literature – see for example Bondarevskaia 1975, p276, Zakharov (ed.) 1980, p143. For the vote and discussion to establish the organ see Bondarevskaia et al. 1986, p253, "Resolution on the necessity of a special Congress of the Party", passed: 15 votes for, 7 votes against, one abstention, at the meeting of the Petersburg Committee 15 (28) August 1906.

157 See Bondarevskaia et al. 1986, pp250-1, "Report on the meeting of the Petersburg Committee, 9 (22) August 1906".

158 On this Conference see Zakharov (ed.) 1980, p150. For the discussion on the Committee where the Mensheviks opposed the convening of this conference see Bondarevskaia et al. 1986, pp278-80, "Report of the meeting of the Petersburg Committee of the 6 (19) November 1906".

intervention, over the first half of 1907. For now the faction's perspective of using involvement in the elections to make propaganda allowed them to address effectively the intimidated though increasingly embittered workers of St. Petersburg. Consequently the faction grew by two and a half times between January and March – a growth that marked the greatest increase in support since the Days of Freedom. As a result of this advance, the process of democratisation and opening that Lenin had campaigned for since early 1905 could be substantially completed. At the same time, the differences between the two factions of Social Democracy were generalised in a way not seen since the height of polemics in 1904. The ground was thus laid for the emergence of two much expanded currents of "worker intelligents" following the definitive crushing of the revolution in early June 1907.

As in early 1906, the culmination of the process of consolidation was a major party meeting – in this case a city-wide Conference held in January 1907. As the issue to be resolved here was Social Democratic involvement in the Second Duma elections, discussion was held and delegates were selected on a clear factional basis. The result – 40 delegates representing 2,148 Bolsheviks and 31 delegates representing 1,733 Mensheviks – showed that both factions had contracted slightly over the second half of 1906, and that the Bolsheviks would predominate at the Conference.[159] By this time, factional tensions were so strong that, after a series of frustrated organisational manoeuvres by the Menshevik-leaning Central Committee, the Menshevik delegates walked out of the Conference prior to discussion.[160] They then proceeded to independently implement their strategy of providing electoral support for the Cadets.

It is indicative of the clarity and openness of the several thousand now relatively experienced activists of the Bolshevik faction that they almost unhesitatingly proceeded with their own strategy of a "left bloc", despite the opposition of the Central Committee as well as the Menshevik faction of the RSDLP.[161] Indeed, more than at any other time except January 1905, the activity of the Bolshevik faction appears to have been characterised by a high level of membership mobilisation. Thus over the period of the elections to the Second Duma, electoral committees were formed down to the street level and some 285,000 leaflets and 77,000 pamphlets were distributed.[162] Over the first months of 1907 the Bolsheviks succeeded in producing a series of legal

---

159 Kochakov (ed.) 1957, p392, Zakharov (ed.) 1980, p152.

160 Kochakov (ed.) 1957, p392, Zakharov (ed.) 1980, p152.

161 At a meeting 13 (26) February the Mensheviks left the Committee and a confrontation ensued with the Central Committee representatives (Bondarevskaia et al. 1986, pp291-9, "Full protocol of the meeting of the Petersburg Committee of 12 (26) February 1907").

162 Zakharov (ed.) 1980, p152, Zhuikov (ed.) 1977, p199.

papers for a short time before they had to be suspended. These initiatives laid the basis for a daily newspaper over the first week of the Duma proceedings. This paper and subsequent publications reached a circulation of 25,000[163] – a substantial figure, though much lower than that of the Bolsheviks' press during the Days of Freedom. Such legal daily publication allowed Lenin to make frequent polemical commentary on the Duma proceedings as he had done in the second quarter of 1906.

The gains of the Bolsheviks during the course of the Duma elections accentuated their earlier development towards sensitivity, directness and openness in organisational structure.

Thus, on 25 March, a further city-wide Conference was held at Lenin's refuge at which more than 80 percent of delegates were worker activists and between 80 and 90 percent of Social Democrats voted in the elections for representatives. It adopted the most systematic and detailed structure of organisation since the Days of Freedom.[164] The focus of this new structure was the city-wide Conference – a body to be re-elected twice a year by mass meetings of members and convened twice a month.[165] Answerable to this body were to be all those organs responsible for day to day activity, in particular the city-wide and local district Committees.[166] Complementing this openness and sensitivity, Lenin repeatedly called over the second quarter of 1907 for the widest possible discussion of basic issues confronting the RSDLP – in particular tactics to be followed in the Second Duma.

The Bolshevik success also led to a further deepening of the polarisation with their factional rivals. Despite their walkout at the January Conference, the Mensheviks participated in the March Conference, submitting an unsuccessful proposal for an organisational structure based on federalism.[167] Yet in spite of their formal unity, relations between the factions continued to deteriorate, as their day to day activity brought them increasingly into conflict. Thus Lenin's polemic against the Mensheviks became more and more sweeping over the course of 1907, and they in turn replied in an ever more bitter tone. This process of polarisation ended in Lenin's arraignment before a party tribunal on charges arising from his published assessment of the split at the January Conference.[168]

---

163 On the Bolshevik press over the first half of 1907 see Andronov 1978, p72, Kochakov (ed.) 1957, p400.

164 Zakharov (ed.) 1980, p154, Bondarevskaia 1975, p325.

165 Zakharov (ed.) 1980, p154.

166 The full structure is often reproduced in diagram form. See for example Bondarevskaia et al. 1986, p305.

167 Zakharov (ed.) 1980, p155.

168 For background on this charge and Lenin's reply see *CW*, vol. 12, "Report to the Fifth

Thus, by the time of the Fifth Congress in May, the last before 1917, the ground had been laid for a formal split and the formation of the RSDLP as a solely Bolshevik organisation in 1912.

Conclusion

The advance of the labour movement from a tiny "intelligentsia" to a relatively large layer of "activists" after Bloody Sunday can be shown to have been the result of conscious intervention within a severe crisis of the tsarist order. The corresponding transformation of the Bolsheviks required, perhaps even more than the labour movement, a deliberate intervention if the possibilities for the advance of revolutionary consciousness were to be realised.

Thus there were great opportunities over both the rise and fall of the revolution, and, through intervention, the Bolsheviks did make qualitative advances towards becoming a faction of worker activists. Yet the St. Petersburg Bolsheviks were also hindered by a leadership insufficiently able to adapt to the new context, and in particular not fully aware of the possibilities for worker class consciousness in the generalised struggle of the time. An earlier reluctance to break with the Economists and then the Mensheviks over the possibilities for worker consciousness in principle was now reflected in a limited ability to give a tactical and organisational lead in practice to masses of agitated and potentially conscious workers. This limitation in the local Bolshevik leadership resulted in a tactical conservatism and organisational defensiveness over the revolution's rise, a sectarian attitude to the Soviet during the Days of Freedom, and a failure to give sufficient attention to the limited defensive struggles occurring over the revolution's decline. The conscious intervention by Lenin, as well as other central leaders of the faction in exile, was earlier necessary to defend the possibility of workers' consciousness in principle; now their intervention was decisive in enabling the Bolsheviks to realise the material possibilities for that consciousness in a context of generalised struggle.

In making this intervention, Lenin received formal endorsement, but not thoroughgoing practical support, from the leading St. Petersburg Bolsheviks. Rather, over the initial phase of the revolution, he was frustrated by their conservatism, as well as by the limited challenge to this conservatism from the still insufficiently conscious labour activists around and within the faction. It was only over the plateau and decline of the revolution, as the inadequacy of a determinist historical model became increasingly evident to the most political section of the leading labour activists, and the need to transform the faction was

Congress of the R.S.D.L.P. on the St. Petersburg Split and the Institution of the Party Tribunal Ensuing Therefrom", pp419-36. These events will be discussed in detail in chapter eight.

concretely adopted by the local Bolshevik leadership, that Lenin's proposals for transformation of the Bolsheviks were substantially implemented.

Through making his interventions before and after Bloody Sunday, Lenin formulated the views on party organisation that are discussed in the next two chapters of this thesis. Drawing on his contact with the struggle between classes across the empire as a whole, and most particularly from that in St. Petersburg where he was directly involved, Lenin sought to defend the possibility of class consciousness in a defensive period, and then facilitate its complete and concrete adoption in one of offensive struggle. Thus his approach to organisational structure was always based on a particular assessment of the possibility for class consciousness, and the consequent tasks of Marxists in intervening to develop that consciousness. In doing so, he made an interventionist break with the determinism of the Second International that was both internally consistent, and compatible with Marx's own basic purpose.

Chapter 7

1893–1905: LENIN'S CONCEPTION OF THE PARTY AS A "WORKER INTELLIGENTSIA"

Introduction

Lenin's ideas on party organisation flowed from his intervention into the struggle for Marxist influence within St. Petersburg, as well as later contact with Social Democrats throughout the Russian empire. His political activity up to December 1895 was focused almost entirely on centralising the organisation of Marxists within St. Petersburg. Yet his writing at that time was largely concerned with countering the influence of liberal Narodism and dealt only peripherally with questions of organisation. To the extent that he did deal with such questions, Lenin appears to have closely followed the earlier pioneering work of Plekhanov and Axelrod. Lenin emerged as an empire-wide leader of Social Democracy through his campaign against Economism between 1898 and 1902. In some contrast to the approach of the founders of Russian Marxism, he did not confine this campaign to a literary polemic. Complementing these literary efforts, he also focused on the consolidation of organisational support within the Russian empire, and particularly in St. Petersburg, which he regarded as a decisive sphere of activity.

From early 1902 until the Second Congress, Economism appeared to be in terminal decline, and Lenin responded to requests from St. Petersburg by codifying his ideas on Committee structure in a very detailed and concrete way. Then between the end of the Second Congress in August 1903 and Bloody Sunday, Lenin focused on questions of organisation more than at any other time, and made the most extended and theoretical defence of the interventionist conclusions he saw as flowing from Marxism. He did so in response to the implicit break of most of his fellow exiles from the anti-Economist position they had earlier defended together. At this time, most of those active in Russia, particularly in the industrial belt encircling St. Petersburg and Moscow, remained firm in their support of the former exile position. Lenin's writings sought to harden this support, and then mobilise it for a new Congress through which to re-establish an interventionist party.

Thus the development of Lenin's ideas on party organisation must be seen as reflecting his own intervention within the Social Democratic movement. Prior to the end of the textile strikes in early 1897, Lenin was deeply involved in the concrete detail of political organisation, yet wrote little on the issue as such. The evidence available suggests that he saw himself developing and applying the lead set by others – most notably the notion of a current within the "worker intelligentsia" conceived by Plekhanov and Axelrod, as well as the strategy of "agitation" outlined by Plekhanov, Kremer and Martov. However in defending an interventionist interpretation of Marxism against liberal Narodniks as well as the nascent legal Marxism, and in particular through his concrete approach to that defence, Lenin foreshadowed the critique of determinism with which he would later be particularly identified.

It was in the polemic against the Economists from early 1898 to mid-1902, as well as in the consolidation of that polemic up to mid-1903, that Lenin generalised from his early organisational activity and ongoing contact with St. Petersburg to political practice over the Russian empire as a whole. It was in this polemic, which at the time he saw as relating only to Russian conditions and a temporary political threat, that Lenin for the first time explicitly linked the centralisation and consciousness of revolutionaries with maintaining the interventionist character of the Marxist movement. Despite the notoriety which it later gained, this polemic was not at the time regarded as substantially original or general. Indeed in making many of his points, Lenin continued to explicitly draw on the earlier work of Axelrod, and even as he defended his formulations he also conceded their one-sidedness.

Following the Second Congress of the RSDLP, Lenin was forced to further generalise his ideas on organisation from the level of practice in the Russian empire to the nature of the Marxist party as such. This flowed from the fact that the issue dividing the former *Iskra* editors was the full organisational implications of their earlier struggle against Economism. It is therefore justified to view this new polemic as a theorised restatement of his earlier more concrete critique of the Economists.

In particular, Lenin here explicitly defended and developed the consequences of the conception of Social Democracy as a class conscious minority deliberately intervening to oppose capitalist domination within the rest of the working class. He did so with a vehemence that reflected the adverse circumstances within the Russian empire and particularly in St. Petersburg, yet even here he foreshadowed transformed tasks and structures in more favourable circumstances.

Thus Lenin's views on organisation prior to 1905 developed in three cycles of broadening generalisation, and it is misleading to regard them as developing straightforwardly and abstracted from his own political activity. Yet such an approach has been generally pervasive in the mainstream and is also clearly influential amongst the critics. Such a method has led most writers to see Lenin proposing an elite that is abstracted from and substitutes for the working class. Lenin prior to Bloody Sunday did most certainly respond to the difficulties of a Marxist current in adverse circumstances by seeing Social Democrats as a cohesive political force intervening within the working class – an elite in terms of their social consciousness, organisational structure and general political tasks.

Indeed in each reworking he further generalised the interventionism, and hence accentuated the "elitism", of this conception. Yet it is clear that this "elitism" was precisely emphasised to enable the intervention of Social Democrats within the working class – which in turn was aimed at enabling that class to self-consciously seize state power.

St. Petersburg 1893–1897: The tasks of the "socialist intelligentsia"

Lenin's initial political activism, significant though it may have been for the cohesion of Marxists in St. Petersburg, is generally regarded as having limited importance for the overall development of his ideas on party organisation. Indeed, it may be argued that Lenin himself initially embraced the organisational determinism that he would later so unremittingly oppose. Such a view could draw on his wholehearted support for "agitation" as well as in his defeat of the former propagandist leadership of the city's Social Democrats. In addition Lenin's writings at this time were largely focused on a trenchant critique of the Narodniks, and made only limited and general comments about organisation until after the textile strikes of the mid-1890s.

It is certainly true that prior to the textile strike Lenin was absorbed with the struggle against what he termed "liberal Narodism", and in doing so he exhibited the characteristic method of narrowly focusing on his immediate opponent. In comparison, he devoted little attention in his writing to questions of organisation and strategy. This lack of focus on issues relating to organisation almost certainly flowed from the relative ease with which actual organisational advances were made in the early 1890s. Thus the tsarist state and capitalist class could have appeared relatively impotent against the workers' movement rising toward the textile strike, while the resistance to "agitation" and centralism among Social Democrats was overcome without a formal split. For the sharply focused Lenin there would have been little pressure to augment the seminal conceptions of Plekhanov, Axelrod, Kremer and Martov.

Yet it would still be wrong to see Lenin's early one-sided critique of "liberal Narodism" as standing in contrast to his later positions on party organisation. For even in these earliest anti-Narodnik polemics, Lenin already displayed the concern that would later also underlie his polemic against the Economists and Mensheviks. This was to concretely maintain the traditional Marxist role of the working class as the self-conscious subject of revolution. Resulting from this fundamental concern was a break with the determinism and idealism now coming to predominate in the Second International. Thus, almost from his first writing against the liberal Narodniks, Lenin also attacked the "objectivism" of his "legal Marxist" fellow critics of Narodism and in particular their most prominent figure Peter Struve.

The repression in St. Petersburg following the textile strikes, which dispersed the Marxists and demoralised the worker intelligentsia, marked a turning point in the balance of Lenin's interest. He continued to be mainly concerned with rebutting the arguments of the Narodniks. However, in contrast to the waning organisational vigour of most other leading activists, he responded to the adverse circumstances by focusing on how Marxists could advance in the pervading repression. The result of this turn was at first limited – a short pamphlet on the question of organisation in Russia, with a postscript containing concrete proposals addressed to the particular circumstances of St. Petersburg. Yet despite the modesty of this beginning, several points, basic to Lenin's subsequent writings on organisation, were introduced in this pamphlet. These were the connected concepts of what Lenin termed "advanced workers" as the base for party membership as well as the associated role of "consciousness", meaning an understanding of all conflicts and contradictions in society, as the base for the propaganda activity of the party. In being a section of workers that were implicitly defined by their openness to Marxist propaganda, the "advanced workers" could here be regarded as equivalent to the politically conscious section of the "worker intelligentsia" as used in this thesis. A number of concrete organisational points, which were later to take on far broader significance, were introduced in his appendix addressed specifically to the St. Petersburg movement. Of most importance it was here that Lenin introduced the central role of the "routine and unrecognised" activist, as well as the associated need for discipline and specialisation, in the advance of revolutionary organisation.

Lenin's early writing

The rigour and detail which were to become hallmarks of Lenin's later writings were amply evident in his initial polemics against the liberal Narodniks and "legal Marxists". While his first presentation to the St. Petersburg Marxists, "On the So-Called Market Question",[1] laid the basis to

---

1   Lenin, *CW*, vol. 1, pp75-125.

displace the propagandists Radchenko and Krasin from the local leadership of the current, this paper was largely a technical work and did not deal with issues of organisation as such.

It was in the longer polemical publications – "What the 'Friends of the People' are and how they Fight the Social Democrats"[2] (hereafter referred to as "What the Friends…"), as well as "The Economic Content of Narodism and the Criticism of it in Mr. Struve's book"[3] (hereafter referred to as "The Economic Content…") – that Lenin touched on issues related to party organisation for the first time.

Thus Lenin's first comments came at the conclusion of "What the Friends…" where he drew explicitly on Plekhanov's work in the 1870s and 1880s.[4] Lenin's basic concern here was to define the tasks and dangers before what he termed the "socialist intellectuals" – figures who could be seen as the socialist "worker intelligents" and non-worker intellectuals at the core of the party. Even at this initial point Lenin saw a major danger from pressures to liquidate Social Democracy into radical liberal democracy and against this threat cited Plekhanov on the role of industrial workers in leading the "whole working population".[5]

However, contrary to the way that his writing prior to Bloody Sunday has often been characterised by both the mainstream and critics,[6] Lenin was here also concerned with the dangers of isolation, sectarianism and elitism for the "socialist intellectuals". Thus while theory was important, it had to be linked to practice, and the immediate task of these "intellectuals" was to produce concrete economic analysis and exposures.[7] Indeed, contrary to the predominant role he supposedly vested in intellectuals, he here first raised a task for these educated figures that would be basic to his future organisational proposals: "to make special leaders from amongst the intelligentsia unnecessary".[8]

This conception of a "socialist intelligentsia", that maintains its revolutionary identity while also raising the political level of workers moving

---

2   ibid., pp129-332.

3   ibid., pp333-507.

4   ibid., pp290-8.

5   ibid., pp292-4, 298.

6   For the critics a position argued perhaps most clearly by Marcel Liebman. See for example a section entitled "Centralization and internal democracy" in Liebman 1975, pp37-42. For the development of Lenin's positions at this time and the associated organisational traits in Bolsheviks development from a mainstream biographical perspective see Shub 1966, pp72-90.

7   Lenin, *CW*, vol. 1, "What The Friends…", p296.

8   ibid., p298.

towards it, is also evident in Lenin's first use of the term "worker intellectual".[9] He did so at the end of "What the Friends...", when rejecting the limits placed on the propaganda of worker leaders or "intellectuals" if they were subordinated to a democratic movement led by right wing Narodniks. Thus from the way in which he used these terms it cannot be argued that Lenin conceived the "socialist intelligentsia" as comprising predominantly and permanently bourgeois dissidents. Rather, flowing from his own experience as a propagandist in the Nevskii district, it seems clear that he at least implicitly conceived the "socialists" as a current that was becoming part of the "worker intelligentsia".

In "What the Friends...", the role of a "socialist intelligentsia" is defined against the liberal idealism and passivity into which the leading Narodnik theorists had fallen by the early 1890s. At the same time Lenin was equally critical of the idealism and passivity which flowed from the determinism of the "legal Marxists", who at that time were emerging as the principal opponents of Narodism.

Thus "What the Friends..." concludes with an appendix[10] outlining and bemoaning the narrow, uncritical, abstract and nonrevolutionary way in which Marxist propaganda was evolving under the pressure of publication in the legal press. This approach to Marxism, as well as its implications for organisational practice, was subject to a full scale critique in "The Economic Content...". It is here that Peter Struve, the most prominent legal Marxist, was analysed as an "objectivist not a materialist",[11] as he viewed history as an abstract and determined process rather than as a struggle between concrete forces. For Lenin, the task of the "socialist intelligents" was to identify and expose the basic nature and dynamic of these forces.[12] As result of his determinism the force of the critique that Struve could make of the Narodniks was limited for Lenin. In particular, Struve's understanding of the division of the rural population into classes, a crucial element in the development of capitalism within the Russian empire, lacked concreteness. Overall, according to Lenin, the transformation of class relations was presented by Struve as an abstraction, just as it was for the liberal Narodniks.[13]

---

9   ibid., p331.

10   ibid., pp326-32.

11   ibid., "The Economic Content...", pp400, 499.

12   ibid., p401.

13   ibid., p468.

Leading up to and immediately following the textile strikes

The textile strikes, and the repression that followed them, provoked a turn in Lenin's focus that corresponded with a shift in the labour movement and the Marxist current within it. In the period leading up to the strikes and his arrest, Lenin had participated in the strategy of "agitation" through the political exposure "What are our Ministers thinking about",[14] as well as the pamphlets of concrete propaganda *To the Working Men and Women of the Thornton Factory*[15] and *Explanation of the Law on Fines Imposed on Factory Workers*.[16] Yet with his own imprisonment and subsequent exile Lenin was limited in his involvement in political struggle and forced to focus more on general issues.[17] It was at this point that he first concerned himself directly on the nature of party organisation. Thus he wrote the general "Draft and Explanation of a Programme for the Social Democratic Party"[18] (hereafter referred to as the "Draft and Explanation…") while still confined in St. Petersburg, and his initial modest organisational intervention *The Tasks of Russian Social* Democrats,[19] in his first year of exile.

From mid-1895 to his exile in February 1897 Lenin continued to refine his conception of a "socialist intelligentsia" that intervened concretely in the workers' movement. He did this as a supplementary aspect of the general propaganda that culminated in the "Draft and Explanation…" and clearly still saw himself as being based on the position set out by Marx and Plekhanov. Thus Lenin's review of Engels' life notes his materialism and activism and concludes by noting his suspicion of turning away from revolutionary struggle to focus solely on economic reforms.[20] In his discussion of the law on fines, he seeks to show how concessions are the result of workers' struggle,[21] while the Thornton pamphlet lauds the ability of workers to rise above their individual interest and wage a collective struggle.[22]

One of Lenin's first political exposures dealt with a Ministerial memorandum about the danger of propaganda by dissident professionals amongst the worker

---

14   ibid., vol. 2, pp87-92.

15   ibid., pp81-6.

16   ibid., pp29-72.

17   Resulting most notably in ibid., vol. 3, "The Development of Capitalism in Russia".

18   ibid., vol. 2, pp93-121.

19   ibid., pp323-54.

20   ibid., "Frederick Engels", pp19-27.

21   ibid., p39.

22   ibid., p81.

students of the Evening-Sunday Schools.[23] This no doubt reflected the role of the Schools in the formation of the "worker intelligentsia" and in particular its most conscious section, as well as Lenin's own activity among the students of the Nevskii district. The exposure is noteworthy, for it again shows that from these earliest writings Lenin did not conceive of the "socialist intelligentsia" as comprising solely or even largely of bourgeois dissidents. On the contrary, workers themselves could, and should, utilise every opportunity to develop their own class consciousness. Thus Lenin concludes with the declaration:

> Workers! You see how mortally horrified are our masters at the working people acquiring knowledge! Show everybody then, that no power will succeed in depriving the workers of class-consciousness! Without knowledge the workers are defenceless, with knowledge they are a force! [my emphasis][28]

The "Draft and Explanation…" may be considered the summation and culmination of Lenin's initial political activity in St. Petersburg. In the weight given to a defence of materialism as well as the historical role of the working class, this work reflects the still only tentative hegemony of Marxism within the formerly Narodnik-dominated revolutionary intelligentsia of the city. In its very concrete, detailed and extended demands, as well as the very limited discussion of organisation, the "Draft and Explanation…" reflected an apparent prospect of unhindered advance for the labour movement as well as the Social Democratic current within it. Thus the nature of class struggle as a generalised conflagration,[24] as well as the broad nature of Social Democratic consciousness,[25] are laboured. Yet at the same time the relation of revolutionaries to the rest of the class is only vaguely defined as "assisting the struggle"[26] and this, together with ill-defined formulations on the state,[27] could have allowed for a determinist perspective on the tasks of Social Democrats.

The fragmentation of the St. Petersburg Marxists and the demoralisation of the "workers' intelligentsia" coincided with Lenin's first years in exile and a new focus on party organisation in a section of his writing. Thus he continued his studies directed against the Narodniks and wrote his major pamphlet analysing the new labour law.[28] Yet at the same time he also wrote the modest pamphlet

---

23   ibid., "What are our Ministers Thinking About?", pp87-92.

24   ibid., p107.

25   ibid., pp96, 112.

26   ibid., pp96, 116.

27   ibid., pp108, 110, 113.

28   ibid., "The New Factory Law", pp267-315.

The Tasks of Russian Social Democrats (hereafter referred to as *The Tasks…*),[29] that drew on his experiences in St. Petersburg to outline the organisational tasks of Social Democrats with greater clarity than before. Appended to this pamphlet was the detailed proposal for an organisation capable of advancing in the wave of repression then sweeping the city. As such, this pamphlet and particularly its appendix mark the first independent contribution by Lenin on the question of social democratic organisation.

The main body of *The Tasks…* comprises a reworking of the traditional strategic conceptions of Social Democracy, but now with reference being made to the experience of the St. Petersburg Emancipation of Labour Group in the early to mid-1890s. Thus the role of industrial workers as the leader of the working population in general,[30] the nature of Social Democratic organisation as an "intelligentsia",[31] the associated role of consciousness in the activity of Social Democrats,[32] and the need for Social Democrats to provide a lead to all democratic struggles and to understand the role of other classes in these struggles, are all reworked with greater force and clarity than earlier, but without substantial originality. Yet in the appendix to *The Tasks…*, "To the Workers and Socialists of St. Petersburg from the League of Struggle",[33] Lenin felt able to make what should be regarded as his first original contribution on the issue of party organisation. Thus it is here that the conception of the party with a broad layer of sympathisers, but a tightly organised and clearly defined membership, was germinated. In particular Lenin laboured the need for differentiation, training, and above all specialisation, if the movement was to advance against police pressure. This led him to focus on the central role of the party supporter performing a limited task, a focus that when generalised to the Russian empire as a whole could be seen as basic to his later split with the other leading Social Democrats. Even in this initial outline the qualities of these supporters were the key to the movements' advance. Thus Lenin wrote:

> We know that specialisation of this kind is a *very difficult matter*, difficult because it demands of the individual the greatest endurance and selflessness, demands the giving of all one's strength to work that is *anonymous, monotonous*, that deprives one of contact with comrades *and subordinates the revolutionary's entire life to a grim and rigid routine*. But it was only in conditions such as these *that the greatest*

---

29 ibid., pp323-54.
30 ibid., pp330-1.
31 ibid., pp335-6.
32 ibid., pp334, 343.
33 ibid., pp348-51.

men of revolutionary practice in Russia succeeded in carrying out the boldest undertakings.[34] [my emphasis]

Mid-1899–early 1902: Four "links" in the organisation of the "socialist intelligentsia"

Up to mid-1899, Lenin had dealt with questions of organisation almost entirely in an indirect, brief and non-polemical way. This approach had persisted for some years despite the evident danger to the hegemony of an interventionist Marxism posed by the emergence of the "youngsters" in St. Petersburg. Such an approach was shattered by the emergence of Economism as an explicit ideological focus in exile, as well as the takeover of the St. Petersburg labour movement by its "youngster" sympathisers. While continuing to produce a considerable volume of material concerning the economic development of the empire, as well as a number of popular political exposures, Lenin now began to make the main focus of his attention the issue of revolutionary organisation and the associated question of worker consciousness.

The position Lenin eventually outlined on these issues was initially developed in a number of articles, largely unpublished, that were written while he was still in Russia in the last half of 1899. These articles were followed up by several more over 1900 as he prepared and negotiated the distribution of *Iskra*. Using the vehicle of *Iskra*, Lenin further developed and promoted his ideas through a series of articles which culminated in *What is to be Done?*. The launching of *Iskra* thus concluded an initial defensive reaction, when Lenin took a stand against the predominance of Economism in the context of organisational disarray among Social Democrats.[35] This was followed by an offensive period in which particular aspects of his position were developed in the context of a limited resurgence in the labour movement associated with a consolidation of support for the interventionist traditions of Marxism.[36]

---

34 ibid., p350.

35 The major documents of this initial period were "A Protest by Russian Social Democrats" (ibid., vol. 4, pp167-82), the only one of Lenin's earliest responses published, "A Retrograde Trend in Social Democracy" (ibid., pp255-85), and "Our Immediate Task" (ibid., pp215-20). Of lesser though still substantial significance are several articles intended for the publication in the first issue of an all-empire paper, *Rabochaia Gazeta*, "Our Programme" (ibid., pp210-4) and "An Urgent Question" (ibid., pp221-6), as well as a series of articles written in the period just prior to the launching of *Iskra*: "Draft Declaration of the Editorial Board of *Iskra*" (ibid., pp351-6), "Apropos (sic) of the *Profession de Foi*" (ibid., pp286-96), "Preface to the pamphlet May Days in Kharkov" (ibid., pp357-65).

36 The key documents in this later offensive period were the articles "The Urgent Tasks of Our Movement" (published in *Iskra* no. 1, December 1900, ibid., pp366-71), "Where to Begin" (published in *Iskra* no. 4, May 1901, ibid., vol. 5, pp13-24), "A Talk with Defenders of Economism"

For the mainstream, it is this polemic that outlined a view of organisation distinct to Lenin, and subsequently followed by him without essential change. According to this view Lenin here made the break with the claimed ideals of human emancipation in Marx and the Second International, and hence laid the basis for the future authoritarianism of the Bolsheviks and ultimately the Soviet state. Yet whatever conclusions may be drawn with historical hindsight, it seems clear that Lenin did not see himself as making a break from the apparent mainstream within Marxism at this time. For while generalising from his own experience in St. Petersburg, as well as later contact with the Russian empire as a whole, Lenin was only making explicit a model of organisation implicit in the initial conceptions of Plekhanov and Axelrod. Through such means as the Workers Library it was these pioneers who had first argued for the supposedly "Leninist" conceptions of the generalised nature of Social Democratic consciousness, the consequent nature of Social Democracy as a current within an "intelligentsia", and the role of Social Democracy as the leader of the democratic movement in general.

Lenin extended these basic positions into a concrete model of organisation oriented to the adverse circumstances within the empire as a whole, and particularly in St. Petersburg, prior to Bloody Sunday. Neither he nor anyone else at this time saw his concrete proposals as marking a break in principle from the interventionist Marxism to which the Second International at this point still appeared to formally adhere. Indeed he often made an unfavourable comparison between the practice of Marxists in the Russian empire and that of the German Social Democrats. Nor did he see his polemic against the Economists as setting a model for all circumstances – indeed within that polemic he occasionally referred to a radically different practice in a new phase of the class struggle.

i. Consciousness

The nature of revolutionary consciousness, and the means through which workers achieve that consciousness, must be central to the way Marxists organise themselves. Thus it is not surprising that a position on consciousness and its transformation was basic to the Social Democratic movement from its foundation by Plekhanov, and underlay all Lenin's discussion of party organisation. Nor it is surprising that his stand on this basic issue should be the most discussed and controversial aspect of that discussion.

(published in *Iskra* no. 12, December 1901, ibid., pp313-20), "Political Agitation and 'The Class Point of View'" (published in *Iskra* no. 16, February, 1902, ibid., pp337-43), and *WITBD* (ibid., pp347-527) itself.

Thus Lenin's sustained attention to organisation was provoked by the publication of the *Credo* which explicitly set out a theoretical justification for what had previously been the reflexive and largely unarticulated practice of Economism. The *Credo* was the first explicit Russian declaration that Social Democratic consciousness was, or should be, reformist consciousness:

> The party *will recognise society*, its narrow corporate and, in the majority of cases, sectarian tasks will be widened to social tasks, and *its striving to seize power will be transformed into a striving for change*, a striving to *transform* present day society on *democratic* lines *adapted to the present state of affairs* with the object of protecting the rights (all rights) of the labouring classes in the most effective and fullest way.[37] [my emphasis]

Ironically, considering the prevalence of the view that he broke with Marx, Lenin made countering this limitation on revolutionary intervention, and hence defending what was then seen as the mainstream Marxist position, the core of all his writings against the Economists. Indeed the largest section of this writing, known largely for its formulations on party structure, was actually devoted to defending Marx's original purpose of workers' self-consciousness against the threat from revisionism. Thus the statement that could be considered the opening of this campaign, "A Protest by Russian Social-Democrats" (hereafter "A Protest..."), contained nothing on tasks and structure, and opened: "A tendency has been observed among Russian Social-Democrats recently to depart from the fundamental principles of Russian Social Democracy".[38] A series of articles written for a proposed a paper raised the need for centralised organisation and the role of the paper.[39] But these articles were prefaced by a letter to editors and an article on programme in which the central role of principle was stated.[40] This was followed by a lengthy and detailed draft programme.[41] The draft article "A Retrograde Trend in Russian Social Democracy", significant for the clarity of the leading role of the "worker intelligents" within the party,[42] makes this point as part of a theoretical critique of the revisionism of the paper *Rabochaia Mysl'*. The draft critique of

---

37 ibid., vol. 4, "A Protest by Russian Social-Democrats", p173.

38 ibid., p171.

39 ibid., "Our Immediate Task", pp215-20, "An Urgent Question", pp221-6.

40 ibid., "Letter to the Editorial Group", pp207-9, "Our Programme", pp210-1.

41 ibid., "A Draft Programme of our Party", pp227-54.

42 ibid., pp280-1.

the *Profession de Foi* of the Kiev Committee[43] only raises points of organisation in the final paragraphs of an eleven-page document. In the "Draft Declaration of the Editorial Board of *Iskra* and *Zarya*",[44] as well as the "Declaration of the Editorial Board of *Iskra*",[45] the need for a centralised organisation is raised but only as the result of a struggle for Marxism within Social Democracy. In "The Urgent Tasks of our Movement"[46] the need to go beyond the limited activity of the Economists is raised but set firmly within the need to raise more general politics. Even within *WITBD* itself the first section is devoted largely to developing a theoretical critique of Economism, the second and third sections are devoted largely to criticising the limited activity of the Economists and it is only when the theoretical groundwork has been laid that Lenin turns to the need for a centralised organisation in the fourth section and the role of a revolutionary newspaper in the fifth.

Countering revisionism in the particular case of the Russian empire meant defending the view that tsarism could only be removed by a victorious insurrection. This aim could only be achieved if Marxists defended insurrection not merely in literary forums, but also through cohering an organisation comprised solely of conscious revolutionaries and wholeheartedly advocating this position. Without such a clear theoretical and organisational lead the rising workers' movement would be led by liberals who would settle for a compromise in the struggle with tsarism.

From the limited historical intervention the Economists wished to make – winning concessions within a system that remained intact – it flowed that the consciousness of workers could only be, and should only be, limited to their own immediate circumstances and interests within the current ruling order. From the far broader intervention that Lenin and other Marxists vested in the working class – an insurrection to topple tsarism – resulted the need and possibility of a far broader consciousness. An insurrection, for Lenin, involved all classes in society, and hence its leadership requires an understanding of the interests of those classes. Consequently he returned again and again[47] to the need, first promulgated by Plekhanov, for Social Democratic consciousness to be such a general understanding:

Working-class consciousness cannot be *genuine political consciousness*

---

43   ibid., pp286-96.

44   ibid., pp320-30.

45   ibid., pp351-6

46   ibid., pp281-3.

47   See for example ibid., "A Protest…", p177, "Apropos…", p291, ibid., vol. 5, "Political Agitation…", p342.

unless the workers are trained to respond *to all cases of tyranny,*
oppression, violence and abuse, *no matter what class is affected...*"[48]
[my emphasis]

As has been argued earlier, in the largely unchallenged political stability
of tsarism prior to 1905, such a general view of society could only have been
an abstraction – and such an abstraction could only have been accessible
to the most broadly critical section of an "intelligentsia". For Marxists the
physical domination of any minority ruling class both requires and then
results in the masking of the class nature of society from its participants. Thus
Lenin was only setting Marx within the context of the limited and spasmodic
struggles before 1905 when he claimed that the consciousness of the mass
of workers in struggle remained "spontaneously" capitalist. That he was not
making an overriding statement about the potential of the working class was
clear when he located the source of this "spontaneous" consciousness within
ruling class domination by stating that bourgeois ideology "has at its disposal
immeasurably more means of dissemination" [emphasis in original] than
socialist ideology. In an explanatory footnote at the foot of the same page he
elaborated on the nature of this domination:

> The working class *spontaneously gravitates towards socialism;*
> nevertheless, most widespread (and continuously and diversely
> revived) bourgeois ideology spontaneously imposes itself upon the
> working class to a still greater degree.[49] [my emphasis]

Lenin's attempt to define the Social Democratic element of this
"intelligentsia", as well as its relation to the rest of the working class, has
generated the bulk of controversy, adverse comment and allegations that he
broke with the working class self-consciousness central to Marx's own writing.
As was argued previously, Lenin's characterisation of the genesis of the
Marxist movement "outside" the working class, in fact among a section of the
radicalising bourgeois intelligentsia, closely matches the historical reality of
the Russian revolutionary movement and Marxism in general. Lenin's citation
of Kautsky in support of this genesis in general cannot be taken directly and
wholly as shifting the revolutionary subject to bourgeois intellectuals, because
Lenin did not equate the founders of Marxist theory with the party at the point
of insurrection. Consequently he could also cite Kautsky on the class nature
and weakness of bourgeois intellectuals relative to workers.

---

48 Probably the best known reference to this point, *WITBD*, ibid., vol. 5, pp412-3.

49 ibid., p386.

The weight of evidence for the critics' view of a break with Marx usually flows from an insurmountable division between the role of "worker" and "intellectual" that is here attributed to Lenin. Yet as outlined in the Introduction and elsewhere, Lenin himself used the term "worker intellectual" from his earliest polemics, and the Marxist movement in St. Petersburg was substantially based in the widely recognised "worker intelligentsia" around the Evening-Sunday Schools. Further, in the significant though unpublished early polemic against the Economists, "A Retrograde Trend in Russian Social Democracy", Lenin again recognised these "intellectuals" and argued for their role as leaders of Social Democracy.[50]

While not using the label "worker intelligent" again before 1907, Lenin several times returned to develop the conception of the party as a class conscious "intelligentsia" using other terms,[51] most notably through his qualification of the "from without" formulation in *WITBD*.[52] That argument condensed a more extended analysis of class consciousness amongst workers made in "A Retrograde Trend...". Here Lenin had equated the "intelligents" with a layer of "advanced workers". In the process of making this equation Lenin's formulation of the "worker intelligent" came closest to Gramsci's "organic intellectual" of the working class. He is also at this point defining the "intelligentsia" as those workers who "study, study, study, and turn themselves into conscious Social Democrats", who "devote themselves entirely to the education and organisation of the proletariat, who accept socialism *consciously*, and who even *elaborate independent socialist theories*". [my emphasis]

It was these "advanced workers" who led the class as a whole in struggle, and it was they who were the most politically influential force within the factories. Such workers had the inclination and ability to adopt the full program of Social Democracy, and hence become the leaders of the party. As a consequence the aim of Marxist propaganda should be to raise the political consciousness of these workers.[53]

While the "advanced workers" were distinct from the "broad stratum of average workers", as well as "the mass that constitutes the lower strata of the proletariat", Lenin's purpose here had not been not to identify a potential new

---

50   ibid., vol. 4, "A Retrograde Trend...", p281.

51   For example he speaks of advancing worker "propagandists", (*WITBD*, ibid., vol. 5, p473) and discusses the role and training of "enlightened workers" in a way that echoes his comments in "A Retrograde Trend...". (vol. 4, p500.)

52   Explanatory paragraph at the bottom of page, ibid., p384.

53   ibid., vol. 4, pp280-1. In this thesis the "intelligentsia" is more broadly defined as all workers engaged in education and political discussion – those who sustained their critical commitment to the point of becoming Social Democrats were a minority within this larger milieu.

ruling elite. Rather in seeking to raise the consciousness of the "advanced workers" or "intelligents" Social Democrats would also address the "average workers" and seek to "raise their level and help promote advanced workers from the middle stratum of workers". Indeed a process of generalisation could be extended to "the mass that constitutes the lower strata of the proletariat" through the medium of agitation and legal educational activity. This advance in all sections of the class could be facilitated provided that Social Democratic propaganda was not limited to support for local and economic struggles. Rather the party newspaper "must connect socialism and the political struggle with every local and narrow question".[54]

ii. Tasks

Lenin grounded his organisational model prior to 1905 in the defence of the traditional broadly interventionist aims of Marxism, and the consequent need for that movement to be composed of those conscious of all struggles and classes in society. Such a view was accessible to a layer that he usually termed the "advanced workers", although he initially used the term "worker intelligentsia" with an equivalent meaning. This conception of the composition of Social Democracy has contributed to the characterisation of Lenin as an elitist because it has been analysed statically and in isolation. This misinterpretation is most pronounced in the mainstream view that Lenin posed the accumulation of an isolated elite passively waiting for the moment when they would be propelled into state power. But it is also evident in the critics' judgement that Lenin's conception of the party for this phase of the class struggle created a routinist barrier to the later advance of a "spontaneously" rising labour movement.

These conclusions reflect a focus that is wholly centred on the structural elements of Lenin's argument concerning party organisation. Such a static and isolated focus is misleadingly narrow because the tasks of the conscious Social Democrats always formed an inseparable second "link" in his model of party organisation, and he paid considerable attention to it. Prior to the launching of *Iskra*, with Economism ascendant, these tasks was primarily defined in relation to workers' economic struggles – to "fuse socialism with the workers movement"[55] and divert it from its "spontaneously" channelled bourgeois direction. With the launching of *Iskra*, as well as the rise of anti-tsarist struggles, such tasks were broadened to leadership of the whole anti-tsarist movement.

---

54   ibid., pp281-3.

55   ibid., "Our Immediate Task", pp217, 219, "A Retrograde Trend", p261.

Lenin's initial outburst on the tasks of Social Democrats was a direct reaction against the localism and focus on economic concessions that flowed from an Economist political framework. Thus he advanced the position that the limited strike struggle of that time was only the germ of the class struggle – the class struggle as such could only be based on the activity of the class as a whole. This led Lenin to reverse the Economist interpretation of Marx and argue that struggle by workers was only a class struggle to the extent that it became a political struggle. Consequently the task of Social Democrats in relation to the limited and spasmodic workers' struggles of the time was one of generalising propaganda – to show the broader significance of particular sectional struggles.[56]

This task, in relation to those "advanced workers" or "intelligents" engaged in leading spasmodic economic struggles, grew to addressing the leadership of the whole anti-tsarist movement from the turn of the century. Such a broad perspective had been posed by Plekhanov in general terms from the foundation of Social Democracy. Lenin had earlier supported this view formally,[57] but from the turn of the century, and particularly in *WITBD*, this support became far more concrete and detailed. In that book Lenin took his earlier polemic a step further – to argue that strike struggles as such were only a minor part of the overall class struggle,[58] as well as that Social Democrats should seek to give a socialist lead to the struggles of all classes.[59] This position was summed up in his well-known exhortation that Social Democrats must be "tribunes of the people" and not merely "trade union secretaries".[60]

Thus the tasks, consciousness and ultimate aims of Social Democrats were directly linked. The task of leading all democratic struggles within a Marxist perspective flowed from the aim of mounting an insurrection against tsarism, but such a perspective required an understanding of the interests of all classes in Russian society. As argued earlier, the outbursts of anti-tsarist struggle, economic crisis, and rising political tension from 1900 made the possibility of this insurrection more evident. This led Lenin to begin criticising Social Democrats for "lagging behind" the mass movement and not carrying out their tasks, in a way that prefigured his appeals of early 1905.[61]

56   ibid., "An Urgent Question", p221, "The Urgent Tasks of our Movement", p368-9.

57   See for example, ibid., "A Protest…", p181.

58   ibid., vol. 5, p401.

59   ibid., pp423-4, 427-8, 433.

60   ibid., p423.

61   ibid., pp396-7.

iii. Structure

Lenin's position on organisational structure formed the third "link" of his argument on party organisation – it flowed from what he saw as the consciousness and tasks of Social Democracy in the adverse conditions prior to 1905. Thus the tasks of generalising propaganda envisaged by Lenin could only be achieved by an organisation characterised by professionalism, training and specialisation – and hence rejecting the looseness pervading Economist proposals for organisational structure. Such features of structure were always necessary, but particular aspects of their application, such as the limitation of membership and the need for conspiracy and secrecy, were justified by the particular circumstances within the Russian empire.

Up to the launching of *Iskra* Lenin was mainly concerned with the defence of Marxist orthodoxy in the two basic areas of consciousness and tasks, while his comments on organisational structure were limited to broad declarations. Thus in "A Protest…" he limited himself to re-asserting the leading role of revolutionary organisation as such,[62] as well as making a favourable reference to the *Narodnaia Volia*.[63] In "A Retrograde Trend…" he asserted the need for a "well ordered organisation" necessary for "struggle against the political police".[64] These general assertions became more detailed and pointed in an article written for *Iskra* prior to its publication. Here Lenin bemoaned the "lagging" of the Social Democrats behind the organisation of the former revolutionary movement and called for greater training and specialisation in order to confront the modern state.[65]

With the consolidation of *Iskra* and the decline of Economism as an ideological threat, Lenin devoted more attention to the detail of organisational structure. The result of this reflection was outlined in two sections in the latter half of *WITBD*. Here Lenin drew on his own experience of the inadequacies of revolutionary organisation in St. Petersburg over the early to mid-1890s, to propose a structure of organisation capable of carrying out the tasks he saw confronting Social Democrats in the early 1900s. The core of this structure was the professional revolutionary. This did not mean that the movement must be dominated by non-worker intellectuals, as has so often been assumed. Rather, given the adverse circumstances of the time, revolutionary organisation could only be based on those, either workers or their supporters from other

---

62   ibid., vol. 4, p173.

63   ibid., p181.

64   ibid., "A Retrograde Trend", p273.

65   ibid., "An Urgent Question", p222.

classes,[66] who devoted themselves full-time to revolutionary activity. Only such professionals could receive the training, as well as provide the continuity, necessary for conducting propaganda within the tsarist police state. Indeed Lenin repeatedly discussed and advocated the role of workers as professional revolutionaries and party leaders who "in regard to party activity will stand at the same level as intellectuals".[67]

For Lenin, a spirit of stringent professionalism and utilitarianism should pervade the structures that surrounded the full-time party workers at the core of the organisation. Thus selection compactness and flexibility[68] were seen as basic to effective committee composition and functioning. Direct democracy was seen as both impossible and ineffective in a clandestine context where full publicity for party conduct would be impossible.[69] For Lenin, professionalism would not substitute for workers' activity, as his critics at the time as well as later have suggested would be an inevitable outcome of his position, but rather would precisely facilitate such activity. Thus the stability and cohesion of the party committee could only raise the confidence of those workers who looked to it for leadership and were themselves subject to severe repression.[70] The specialisation of the committee members and those directed by it would in turn allow for the involvement of greater numbers in particular aspects of the committee's work.

iv. The party newspaper as party organiser

Perhaps the starkest result of the static and isolated approach taken to Lenin's ideas on party organisation has been the lack of attention paid to his argument for the newspaper as party organiser. Yet this argument was the culmination of his interventionist model of party organisation developed as a critique of the Economists. Thus professionalism in organisation would take the form of a network of full-time paper agents who would collect material and then arrange dissemination of the paper as each issue was produced. The task of "fusing socialism with the workers' movement" and being a "tribune of the people" would be achieved through the coverage of political and economic struggles in the pages of the paper, while Social Democratic consciousness would be ensured through the Marxist framework that guided this coverage. Consistent with the other elements of his overall argument in this adverse

---

66   ibid., vol. 5, p462.
67   ibid., pp370, 450, 470-1.
68   ibid., pp468, 480.
69   ibid., pp453, 477.
70   ibid., pp464-5, 475.

context, Lenin's role for the paper was one of propaganda – general political analysis and exposures, as well as polemics against the Economists, were to be given most prominence in its pages.[71]

Lenin's argument for the role of the paper built on the other elements of his argument concerning Social Democratic organisation. Thus his ideas began to develop prior to the launching of *Iskra*, and were only fully expounded in the last section of *WITBD*. Lenin's earliest mention of the role of the party press, in the polemic "Apropos (sic)...", was a general statement of the paper as the means to unite the Social Democratic movement.[72] This early general observation no doubt reflected the role of the burgeoning press in St. Petersburg in the 1890s – a phenomenon whose significance Lenin referred to on a number of occasions. In the subsequent "Draft Declaration of *Iskra* and *Zarya*" he extended this unifying role – to argue for a paper with a definite political identity, yet one within which a range of theoretical questions would be discussed.[73]

In his major article "Where to Begin",[74] as well as its augmentation in the final section of *WITBD*, Lenin fully outlined the role of the paper as the party organiser. Thus the full-time agents for the paper would collect material about workers' conditions and struggles, and in turn distribute copies of the paper to interested readers. Through this process, a layer of "enlightened workers" would form a "scaffolding"[75] by their association with the paper. In forming a distinct critical and educated layer that was amenable to Marxist propaganda, these "enlightened workers" could be considered equivalent to the "advanced workers" Lenin referred to earlier, or the political section of the "workers' intelligentsia" analysed in this thesis. This "scaffolding", comprising the professionally organised Social Democrats and their audience of "enlightened workers", would over time grow in the flexibility and capability of its intervention into political struggle.[76]

Through its reliability and frequency[77] the paper would be able to unite all study circles,[78] generalise from all local struggles,[79] and encourage the

71   ibid., vol. 4, "Draft of a Declaration of the Editorial Board of Iskra and Zarya", p324, "Declaration of the Editorial Board of *Iskra*", p353.

72   ibid., p296.

73   ibid., pp326-8.

74   ibid., vol. 5, "Where to Begin", pp13-24.

75   Term used ibid., pp23, 508.

76   ibid., *WITBD* pp513-4.

77   ibid., p508.

78   ibid., pp506-7.

79   ibid., "Where to Begin", pp20-2, *WITBD*, p499.

confidence and activity of those open to Marxism. Through the pages of the paper all who had made a contribution to the party's work, no matter how limited or peripheral, would be able to see the result of that work,[80] and all who played a leading role in the party would take responsibility for their political positions.[81] The culmination of the paper's development would be a "scaffolding" so large and flexible that it would be capable of uniting the mass of workers in the act of insurrection.[82]

What is to be Done? to the end of the Second Congress: Refinement and defence of Lenin's model of party organisation

The publication of *WITBD* marked the culmination of the struggle against the Economists. Hence the period between early 1902 and August 1903 may well be seen as one of steady and unhindered consolidation of *Iskra* influence. Such a view is bolstered by the advance of the Petersburg Committee, however hesitant and spasmodic the nature of that advance. With the Economist threat waning,[83] and an open anti-tsarist struggle looming, Lenin struggled against the other émigré leaders to make the party program for the impending Congress more concrete.[84] He also devoted considerable attention to the looming ideological threat from the recently founded Socialist Revolutionaries.[85] His articles in *Iskra* included a number of political exposures of the type he had argued for in *WITBD*, and on several occasions he again suggested the possibility of a leading "workers' intelligentsia".[86] As outlined in chapter five, in his organisational activity Lenin devoted himself to consolidating Committee support for, as well as involvement in, the Second Congress. In the course of

---

80   ibid., p501.

81   ibid., vol. 4, "Draft Declaration of *Iskra* and *Zarya*", p328.

82   ibid., vol. 5, pp22-3, 514-6.

83   ibid., vol. 6, "Preface to the Second Edition of the Pamphlet *The Tasks of the Russian Social-Democrats*", p212, "On the Subject of Reports by Committees and Groups of the R.S.D.L.P. to the General Party Congress", p294.

84   ibid., "Notes on Plekhanov's Second Draft Programme", pp37, 44, 47, 54, "Opinion on Plekhanov's Second Draft", p57.

85   ibid., "Why the Social-Democrats Must Declare a Determined and Relentless War on the Socialist-Revolutionaries", pp170-3, "Revolutionary Adventurism", pp186-205, "The Draft of a New Law on Strikes", pp215-8, "Vulgar Socialism and Narodism as Resurrected by the Socialist-Revolutionaries", pp261-8 "The Basic Thesis Against the Socialist-Revolutionaries", pp271-5, "Marxist Views on the Agrarian Question in Europe and in Russia", pp341-5, "Les Beaux Esprits se Recontrent (which may be interpreted roughly as: "birds of a feather flock together"), pp431-5.

86   ibid., "A Letter to the Northern League", pp159-60, "Revolutionary Adventurism", p198.

this work he further refined his model for organisation through his "Letter to a Comrade"[87] (hereafter referred to as "Letter..."), which examined in greater detail the structure and work of committees. His speeches at the Second Congress on the other hand marked the beginning of a new more theorised defence of his views, particularly as they related to the issues of revolutionary consciousness and tasks.[88]

"Letter to a Comrade"

The "Letter..." was written to endorse a proposed alternative committee structure to that of the Economist-influenced St. Petersburg Union of Struggle – a current now characterised by its division between worker and intellectual committees, as well its worker passivity. Consequently Lenin opened his reply by reiterating in some detail the need for professionalism and specialisation that had earlier been laboured in *WITBD*.[89] Given the widely held interpretation of these themes as substituting the intelligentsia for the working class as the revolutionary agent, it should be noted that here Lenin was even more emphatic than earlier on the role of "worker intelligents" as Social Democratic leaders. Thus he proposed that:

> We should particularly see to it that as *many workers as possible* become fully class-conscious and professional revolutionaries and members of the committee. [my emphasis]

and elaborated in a footnote:

> We must try to get on the committee revolutionary workers *who have the greatest contacts and the best "reputation" amongst the mass of workers.*[90] [my emphasis]

This desire to involve leading "worker intelligents" or "advanced workers" in the composition of the Committee did not involve a softening in Lenin's centralism as the "spontaneist" view of the critics might suggest. Thus the "Letter..." was even more direct than earlier writings in arguing that secrecy and efficiency should guide the formation and conduct of Committees rather

---

87 ibid., "Letter to our Comrade on our Organisational Tasks", pp231-52.

88 ibid., "Second Speech on the Discussion of the Party Rules", pp501-2, "Speech at the Election of the Editorial Board of *Iskra*", pp503-4.

89 ibid., "Letter to a Comrade", pp235-8.

90 ibid. p235.

than formal rules. Thus small size, expertise and division of labour in the Committee were the keys to success.[91] General meetings of all supporters should if possible be avoided, and only a few Committee members should attend those large meetings that were held. In relation to the Committee, Lenin sought to limit the number of those holding positions of responsibility, but at this point he also introduced the concept of "party information" which would later come to have greater significance. In this discussion, "party information" meant that while the size of the committee itself was limited and its members' responsibilities clearly defined, all Committee supporters should have the right to correspond with *Iskra*, and all bodies should have the right to address their resolutions to the party's leading centres and ultimately the Party Congress.[92]

Consistent with Lenin's ongoing focus on the role of consciousness and the tasks of intervention, the core of the "Letter…" deals with the propaganda tasks of the Committee. Here Lenin refined and applied his earlier comments on structure to outline the pyramid of control and responsibility with which he has been so notoriously identified in the mainstream. Thus at the peak of the pyramid would stand the Committee itself, and responsible to this central body would be a series of functional groups with particular tasks in the production and distribution of propaganda. In this way literature could be distributed frequently and regularly. As had been the case in his earlier comments, the aim of this organisational structure was not to produce a network in which students or other non-workers would predominate. Indeed even as Lenin argued for fewer and better trained propagandists, he also derided the prevailing view that students as a matter of course should be assigned a study circle. He proposed instead that, in general, practical tasks should be given to all those, including students, initially entering the movement.

Consistent with his focus on the development of workers as conscious "intelligents" and hence Social Democratic leaders, much of this discussion on the structures necessary to carry out propaganda was taken up with the role of factory circles. Here Lenin further refined his earlier distinction between the trade union activist and the political propagandist responsible to a party Committee. He suggested that the factory group or even a single agent should be appointed by the Committee and connected directly with the overseas centre of the party paper. Yet, consistent with his earlier interventionist role for the "socialist intelligentsia", the aim here was not to separate and isolate a tiny circle of Marxist scholars. Rather:

---

91   ibid., p238.
92   ibid., p239.

> [T]he factory subcommittee should endeavour to embrace the whole
> factory, the largest possible number of workers, with a network of
> all kinds of circles (or agents). The success of the subcommittee's
> activities should be measured by the abundance of such circles, by
> their accessibility to touring propagandists and, above all, by the
> correctness of the regular work done in the *distribution of literature*
> and the collection of information and correspondence. [my emphasis
> in bold, italics in original]

Given the functional centralism and specialisation in this Committee structure, the issue of the control and competence of its members must have arisen at the time, and has subsequently been raised again and again by Lenin's critics. In the "Letter..." Lenin made the first attempt to respond to this issue, and did so in two ways. The first was to point to the character of those comprising a leadership whose position is established "not by virtue of having the power, of course, but by virtue of authority, energy, greater experience, greater versatility and greater talent". Such people, if they did fail in capability or commitment, could in the first place be subject to "comradely influence" by those around them, and, were such pressure insufficient, be removed through resolutions and appeals to higher party bodies.

Lenin's other response to the issue of preserving the integrity of Social Democracy was to return to and extend the role of "party information". He now argued that information should to the greatest extent possible, and as freely as possible, flow from the sections and members of the party to the leading centres, the Congress, and hence to the party as a whole. Lenin called this dispersal of the provision of information and hence responsibility to the party "an essential prerequisite of revolutionary centralisation and an *essential corrective to it*". (italics in original) Such a flow of information would allow those most suitable for posts to be selected, and work to resume quickly after arrests. The failures of particular committees would be exposed and lessons drawn from disputes within them.[93] Indeed Lenin here goes so far as to suggest that, with regular and proper reports, rules concerning committee conduct could be dispensed with altogether.[94]

The importance that Lenin attached to "party information" could be seen in the extraordinarily detailed guide he prepared for Committees making reports to the Second Congress.[95] It should also be noted that, in contrast to the main meetings of most Western political parties, all interventions in the

---

93   ibid., pp241-50.

94   ibid., "Political Struggle and Political Chicanery", pp251-2.

95   ibid., "On the subject of Reports by Committees and Groups", pp290-300.

proceedings of RSDLP Congresses were recorded, and these minutes were published and widely distributed amongst party members. Thus members were able to make a real assessment of the party and currents within it. The role of the Party Congress, and subsequently the leading bodies, as the ultimate repository of "party information" and the authority of the party explains the enormous importance Lenin attached to their composition and conduct. Thus it was the perceived break from the organisational implications of Marxism by the central bodies after the Second Congress that explains the implacable nature of his struggle to maintain the decisions of that Congress.

The Second Congress of the RSDLP

In responding to his critics at the Second Congress Lenin made a further generalisation of his conception of the party as a socialist "workers' intelligentsia". Thus in the debate on the party program he cited the role of reformist trade unions, of which there were none operating independently in Russia at the time, in keeping the working class "spontaneously" within bourgeois ideology. In response to those who focused on the notorious passage concerning workers' spontaneously bourgeois consciousness in *WITBD* he pointed to his own record in repeatedly stating "that the shortage of fully class-conscious workers, worker-leaders, and worker-revolutionaries is, in fact, *the greatest deficiency in our movement*" [my emphasis]. Perhaps most significantly for those who argue for an authoritarian or contradictory Lenin, he concluded by declaring that his polemic against the Economists was a case of one-sided argument aimed at correcting an erroneous tendency.[96] Thus it was well before the upsurge of 1905-07 that Lenin explicitly related his pre-1905 comments on organisation to a particular context, indeed to opposing a particular current within that context.

This relativism was even more laboured in Lenin's contribution to the Congress debate on Clause 1 of the party rules. Thus it was "in the *period* of Party life that we are *now* going through"[97] [my emphasis] that membership needed to be restricted to preserve the ideological character of the party. Related to this need the dangerous confusion "between those who only talk and those who do the work" occurs in a particular circumstance:

> when political discontent is almost universal, when conditions require our work to be carried on in complete secrecy, and when most of our activities have to be confined to limited, secret circles and even to

---

96 ibid., "Speech on the Party Programme, 22 July (4 August)", pp487-9.
97 ibid., "Second Speech in the Discussion on the Party Rules, 2 (15) August, p500.

private meetings.[98]

Thus Lenin, even at the time, was very clear about the context, indeed the particular elements of that context, which limited the party to a small current within an "intelligentsia". As such it follows that when the context changed many of Lenin's particular proposals could also change, but without involving a break in the interventionism underlying his conception of Marxist organisation.

The Second Congress to Bloody Sunday: Generalising the structure and tasks of Social Democrats

Lenin's struggle between the end of the Second Congress and Bloody Sunday can well be characterised as a theorised reworking of his earlier polemic against the Economists – though now with a shift in the main focus from the nature of consciousness to questions of political tasks and organisational structure. Within Social Democracy, the Bolshevik-Menshevik split came to approximate a division between the local Committees in Russia and the émigré circles in exile. Thus support for Lenin in exile fell away, and this was the case even among his former close associates in the leading bodies established at the Second Congress. As the struggle continued, these figures began to distance themselves from Lenin and conciliate their former opponents. In contrast, within the Russian Committees, and particularly that in St. Petersburg, support at a formal level was wholehearted from the outset and remained so. Yet even here this formal support masked a lack of clarity over the political basis of the split, which led to tactical wavering and bureaucratic conciliation in the face of continuing belligerence by the local Mensheviks.

Thus Lenin's polemics in this struggle were an attempt to overcome deepening political isolation and achieve the organisational outcome that he saw flowing from the development of the Marxism in the Russian empire. They further refine and augment a position on party organisation that he had regarded as implicit in that tradition since its foundation by Plekhanov. This was done most systematically in the polemic that culminated the struggle *One Step Forward, Two Steps Back* (hereafter referred to as *One Step...*) – and in particular the discussions concerning paragraph one of the Rules[99] and the political direction of the new *Iskra*.[100] As a result this book, rather than

98 ibid., p501.

99 ibid., vol. 7, pp253-75.

100 ibid., pp377-407.

the more commonly cited *WITBD*, could well be seen as the most definitive statement of Lenin's views on party organisation prior to 1905.

"Party Spirit"

Confronted by deep hostility from those he had formerly looked to for leadership and support, Lenin sought to place the BolshevikMenshevik split in historical context as well as set limits on proper conduct in internal party disputes. He came to characterise the Second Congress as a failed attempt by Social Democrats to overcome their former "circle spirit" and rise to a new "party spirit".[101] As the struggle progressed Lenin steadily hardened in his view that the reason for this failure was the personal individualism and political opportunism of the émigré leaders, which flowed from their nature as members of the dissident bourgeois intelligentsia.[102] Implicitly, and then with increasing frequency explicitly, advocating such a position involved a call on those "anonymous activists" maintaining organisation within the empire to convene a new congress and re-establish the party.[103] That Lenin made this analysis and subsequent call shows just how distorted is the prevailing view of him as a champion of bourgeois intelligentsia dominance over workers within the Social Democratic movement.

"Party spirit" can well be analysed as two related features – the need for openness by members in informing the party of their views, combined with centralism in the conduct of party activity. All members and sections must be prepared to frankly place their position before the party as a whole for judgement, but then must also be prepared to submit to the majority in their activity if they prove to be in a minority. If members were not prepared to abide by decisions or proved to be dishonourable or incapable, they would be subject to the pressure of odium in the eyes of party "public opinion" and ultimately removed. Thus "party spirit" represents an extension of the conception of "party information". Adopted and organisationally systematised later by the Mensheviks themselves in November 1905,[104] it would be given the name by which it has become widely known – "democratic centralism".

Lenin's call for openness and discipline in party relations was a reaction to

101 ibid., p411, (*One Step Forward…*, section "R. A Few Words on Dialectics. Two Revolutions", pp407-13). See also ibid., "Account of the Second Congress of the R.S.D.L.P.", p34, "To the Party Membership", p139, "To the Party", p453.

102 See in particular the citation of Kautsky's long characterisation of intellectuals, ibid., *One Step Forward…*, pp322-4, 355, 361, 371.

103 Most particularly in the draft and formal announcement of the Bolsheviks as a faction, ibid., "What we are Working For (To the Party)", pp447-50, "To the Party", pp456-8.

104 Volobuev et al. 1996, pp147-8.

the opening phase of the struggle with the Mensheviks. Their method at this point was to make demands for organisational positions and concessions, and support these demands with abstract rhetoric rather than a discussion of the concrete issues in the split.[105] They also sought to negotiate a settlement of the dispute out of view of the party's membership. Lenin's immediate response was to challenge the Mensheviks to openly declare their positions and debate them before the whole party.[106] This may have seemed an opportune ploy on his part, given the evident support he had inside the Russian empire. Yet it was consistent with Lenin's attempts, outlined earlier in relation to the St. Petersburg Committee, to establish open and clear leadership in the conduct of leading bodies as well as in relation to the membership of other groupings moving towards the party.

Generalising from this immediate response, the role of "party information" first developed in the "Letter…" was now extended to avoiding splits and personal disputation, as well as settling issues and assessing the importance of grievances. While Social Democracy had to remain closed and secretive against penetration by the tsarist state, and this meant being selective in its membership, the greatest possible openness was to exist in relations between members of the party. Such openness reached its peak in the party congress, where all tendencies would be fully exposed, and the future course of the party settled in an open manner.[107]5

The conduct of the Mensheviks also forced Lenin to return to a question he had thought well and truly settled – the role in principle of centralism. In particular he was now forced to confront concretely the role of those who found themselves in a minority or felt personally aggrieved. This led him to reassert what must earlier have been generally acknowledged as a condition for organisation: that "considerations of place and position"[108] could not determine political conduct, and that individuals and sections of the party must submit to the will of the whole. Ultimately Lenin categorised the disruptive behaviour of the Mensheviks as a type of "anarchistic individualism"[109] or "aristocratic

105 The course of the struggle is outlined at greatest length from Lenin's point of view of view in the section "O. After the Congress. Two Methods of Struggle" in *One Step…*, *CW*, vol. 7, pp347-66. Lenin was able to cite the opinion of Struve who while sympathetic to the Mensheviks' aims found their methods disagreeable (ibid., pp484-7). Struve comments, "Only it is unfortunate that this defence is being conducted by not altogether proper, or rather altogether improper, and sometimes positively indecent means".

106 ibid., pp115-7, part of a "Letter to *Iskra*", published in *Iskra* no. 53, 25 November 1903.

107 ibid, pp114-7.

108 ibid., "Draft Resolution on Measures to Restore Peace in the Party, Moved on January 15 (28)", p147, *One Step Forward…*, pp362-6.

109 ibid., "Circumstances of Resignation from the *Iskra* Editorial Board", p194.

anarchism".[110] Having earlier cited Kautsky in support of the role of bourgeois intellectuals as the initiators of socialist ideology, he now cited him on this damaging trait of individualism that was characteristic of the layer:

> Quite different is the case of the intellectual. *He does not fight by means of power but by argument.* His weapons are his personal knowledge, his personal ability, his personal convictions. He can attain to any position at all only through his personal qualities. *Hence the freest play for his individuality seems to him the prime condition for successful activity.* It is only with difficulty that he submits to being a part subordinate to a whole, and then only from necessity, not from inclination. He recognises the need of discipline only for the mass, not for the elect minds and of course he counts himself among the latter.[111] [my emphasis]

The party as a distinct interventionist minority

In defending the need for openness and centralism in general, Lenin was not being original. Indeed it could be argued that he was merely restating the obvious conditions for any organisation of a revolutionary type – and this point was made in response to criticism by Rosa Luxemburg.[112] Yet in arguing that the party must necessarily be distinct in order to intervene, Lenin was making a clear break from the determinism predominating in the practice of the Second International. As has often been argued, the particularly severe conditions within the Russian empire made the nature of the party as a distinct grouping generally accepted there. Lenin now not only made this strategic premise explicit but defended it with arguments relevant to capitalism in general, and not merely the particularly severe circumstances in the Russian empire.

The conception of the party as a distinct element, politically separated from the class as whole in periods of unchallenged capitalist hegemony, was implicit in Plekhanov's approach to cohering the Social Democrats as propaganda circles of "intelligents". This approach was no doubt reinforced by Lenin's own experience as a propagandist among "intelligents" for the metal worker "elite" of the Nevskii district. That experience is evident in the assertion of the "socialist intelligentsia" as a distinct minority against Martov's declaration that all strikers should regard themselves as Social Democrats:

---

110 ibid., *One Step Forward…*, p407.

111 ibid., p323.

112 ibid., *One Step Forward…*, Reply by N. Lenin to Rosa Luxemburg, p474.

> We should be indulging in complacent daydreaming if we tried
> to assure ourselves and others that *every striker* can *be* a Social
> Democrat and a member of the Social Democratic Party, **in the face
> of that infinite disunity, oppression, and stultification which under
> capitalism is bound to weigh down upon such very widespread
> sections of the "untrained" unskilled workers**. [italics in original, my
> emphasis in bold][113]

Thus the nature of the party as a distinct minority of "intelligents" now resulted not merely from the repressive actions of the capitalists, but more fundamentally from the alienated nature of labour under capitalism. Yet Lenin did not mean to accept this reality in the elitist and disdainful way that has been assumed by almost all mainstream commentators. On the contrary, he now argued even more forcefully that Social Democrats should organise themselves as a distinct political force precisely in order to intervene and raise the political consciousness of workers moving towards them and thereby that of the class as whole.[114] Thus:

> to forget the distinction between the vanguard and the whole of the
> masses gravitating towards it, **to forget the vanguard's constant duty
> of *raising* ever wider sections to its own advanced level**, means simply
> to deceive oneself, to shut one's eyes to the immensity of our tasks, and
> to narrow down these tasks.[115] [my emphasis in bold, italics in original]

In fact it was those who did not organise deliberately and effectively who accepted the current consciousness of the class through their passivity. This looseness in organisation and its consequent passivity in relation to the transformation of worker consciousness Lenin now termed "tailism".[116]

Relativism

Thus, following the Second Congress, Lenin responded to hostility from the Mensheviks and prevarication from many of his own supporters, notably in St. Petersburg, by hardening his view of Social Democrats as an "elite" in terms of their consciousness, structure and tasks. Yet here there is still not a case for

---

113 ibid., p260.

114 ibid., p273.

115 ibid., p259.

116 ibid., p389, in the section "Q. The new Iskra. Opportunism in Questions of Organisation", pp377-407, in *One Step…*. See also p392.

analysing Lenin's argument as proposing an elite in anything but a contextual and temporary sense. For the relativism that Lenin introduced in the defence of his plan for organisation at the Second Congress was accentuated and amplified following the Congress. He was perhaps sharpest in response to the leftist leader of the German SPD Rosa Luxemburg:

> She repeats naked words without troubling to grasp their concrete meaning. She raises bogeys without informing herself of the actual issue in the controversy. She puts in my mouth commonplaces, general principles and conceptions, absolute truths, *and tries to pass over the relative truths, pertaining to perfectly definite facts, with which I alone operate*.[117] [my emphasis]

In a similar vein, Lenin often used the phrase "the truth is always concrete"[118] in his writing at this time and concluded *One Step...* with a critique of Plekhanov's views on dialectics.[119] Further, even as he deepened his view of the party as an elite of "intelligents", it is clear from this relativism that Lenin foresaw the possibility of the transformation of the party in a more favourable period. Thus, when writing against "tailism" and the notion that the whole class could become Social Democrats, he prefaced his comments with:

> We are the party of a class, **and therefore *almost the entire class*** (and in times of war, in a period of civil war, the entire class) should act under the leadership of our party, **should adhere to our party as closely as possible**.[120] [my emphasis in bold, italics in original]

Near the conclusion of the discussion on the debate over clause one of the Party Rules in *One Step...* he commented:

> We should never allow *support* of social democracy, *participation* in the struggle it directs, **to be artificially *restricted* by requirements (mastery, understanding etc.)**, for this *participation* itself, the very fact of it, *promotes* **both consciousness and the instinct for organisation**.[121] [my emphasis in bold, italics in original]

---

117 ibid., "Reply to Rosa Luxemburg", p475.

118 ibid., *One Step...*, p368 among others.

119 ibid., pp407-13.

120 ibid., p258.

121 ibid., p273.

These comments, which prefigure many of the supposedly "spontaneist" declarations he made following Bloody Sunday, are further evidence that prior to those events Lenin understood how a particular context set the structure and tasks of the party. He did so in a way that his Menshevik opponents, as well as many of his own supporters, did not.

The party newspaper as party organiser

As in Lenin's earlier polemic against the Economists, so in this struggle against the Mensheviks the consciousness, structure and tasks of Social Democrats found their ultimate expression in a proposal to launch a factional publication. It had been precisely because the editorial board of the party organ would be "more than a literary group"[122] for Lenin that its composition had been a question of such importance at the Second Congress. In launching a Bolshevik paper in late 1904, Lenin amplified the role of supporters of the paper as a party organiser contrary to that of the readership of a purely literary journal:

> Let everyone who regards this organ as his own and who is conscious of the duties of a Social Democratic Party member **abandon once and for all the bourgeois habit of thinking and acting as is customary toward legally published papers – the habit of feeling: it is *their* business to write and ours to read**. All Social-Democrats must work for the Social-Democratic paper. We ask everyone to contribute, and **especially the workers**. Give the workers the **widest opportunity to write for our paper**, to write about positively everything, to write as much as they can about their daily lives, interests and work – without such material a Social Democratic organ will not be worth a brass farthing and will not deserve the name."[123] [my emphasis in bold, italics in original]

Here, as throughout his writings on organisation, for Lenin the "intelligent" was defined by activity and political consciousness, not formal education or class position. Hence the aim of forming a distinct political organisation was precisely to involve workers rather than exclude them.

---

122 ibid., pp311-2.

123 ibid., "A Letter to the Comrades (with reference to the forthcoming publication of the organ of the party majority)", pp524-5.

Conclusion

For Marxists, workers' consciousness in periods of unchallenged capitalist rule must be a type of bourgeois consciousness. Both a requirement for, as well as a result of, the capitalists' physical domination of the productive process is their ideological domination over the workers engaged in that process. As a result of this domination, the consciousness of the overwhelming bulk of workers is limited to their own immediate circumstances within the current ruling order. Workers do on rare occasions engage in limited economic or political struggle, but such protests usually remain confined to a section of the class, and can be resolved without general implications for the system or a widespread challenge to the consciousness of the workers involved.

Lenin's writing on revolutionary organisation prior to Bloody Sunday sought to maintain the interventionist nature of Marxism in the adverse circumstances of such relatively unchallenged capitalist hegemony. Although developed in reaction to the determinist threat posed by Economism within the Russian empire, and drawing initially on his own experience in St. Petersburg, Lenin ultimately developed an approach to party organisation with general relevance. That approach was initially outlined in four steps or "links": the need for Social Democrats to maintain the revolutionary essence of Marxism, the consequent task of giving a lead to all struggles against the system, the need for a centralised and specialised organisational structure as the base for carrying out this task, and the role of a frequent propaganda paper as the means to do so. This plan was outlined most systematically in the widely known *WITBD*, although the principles underlying his approach were brought out more clearly in the subsequent *One Step Forward*.... It was here that Lenin defended what he termed "party spirit" – that relations between Social Democrats must be based on openness and a common purpose in settling upon their strategy and tactics, and then united activity in carrying out whatever course was decided upon.

Contrary to the usual way in which they are recounted, Lenin did not develop these positions in isolation from the Social Democratic movement. Rather, they were enunciated in three waves as Lenin drew on broadening experience within the workers' movement, and sought to give a more general lead to that movement. In his initial period of activism in St. Petersburg, as well as in the first part of his exile, he confined himself to giving general endorsement to the founders of Russian Marxism, as well as tactical advice to those attempting to sustain organisation in the repressive circumstances of the city. The emergence of Economism led Lenin to formulate a general plan for organisation in the Russian empire through the polemic that culminated in *WITBD*. Lenin thought that the convening of the Second Congress would definitively settle the main issues of principle and organisation among Social Democrats.

However the subsequent behaviour of his fellow émigré leaders forced him to generalise from the level of practice in the Russian empire to that of revolutionary organisation in general. This he did through the polemical struggle against his former associates that culminated in *One Step Forward....*

There can be no doubt that prior to Bloody Sunday Lenin envisaged Social Democrats as an elite in their generalised consciousness, centralised organisational structure, and tasks of propaganda. Yet if Lenin posed the formation of a distinct political current, he did so precisely to intervene within the political consciousness of the rest of the "worker intelligentsia" and thereby the class as a whole. It was this task that must be seen as the centre of his organisational plan, not any particular aspects of structure which were closely linked to the circumstances at the time. Indeed, even as he deepened and generalised his "elitism" in the struggle following the Second Congress, Lenin also became more explicit about the relative nature of his organisational views as well as the possibility of radical change in differing circumstances. Thus his organisational polemics prior to Bloody Sunday can best be seen as preparing the ground for, rather than constituting a break with, the apparently contrasting comments in the wake of that historical watershed. This continuity in the interventionist role of the party, though now in the ebb and flow of mass struggle, will be demonstrated in the next chapter.

Chapter 8

9 JANUARY 1905–3 JUNE 1907: LENIN'S CONCEPTION OF THE PARTY AS AN ORGANISATION OF "WORKER ACTIVISTS"

Introduction

From the morning of 9 January 1905, the scope of the labour movement, and hence the possibility for Social Democratic intervention, qualitatively broadened. Over the next two and a half years tsarism was shaken as class-wide mobilisation became the reality or expectation of the labour movement. The generalised view of class society, previously accessible only to an intelligentsia of workers through abstracted study, now pressed on a substantial layer of leading worker activists through direct experience. The leadership of the labour movement, which itself had previously been confined to a political element of the worker intelligentsia, now grew to encompass the most combative section of the activists. These activists, while not immediately joining political parties, steadily radicalised in response to tsarist attempts to co-opt and repress them. The Bolsheviks, despite persistent caution that led to repeated tactical errors, were also able to grow dramatically and transform their organisation from one of "intelligents" to one of "activists".

Associated with this transformation of the context, Lenin shifted his own conception of party organisation from a limited and defensive current of "intelligents" to an open and broad party of "activists". Most critical writers lean to the conclusion that this shift constitutes a break between an earlier authoritarianism or substitutionism and a later "spontaneism" more consistent with the working class self-consciousness essential to Marx's own views. Yet a comprehensive review of Lenin's writing following Bloody Sunday reveals a continuity from before 1905 in the nature of the party as a vehicle for conscious intervention. As was the case earlier, such an "elite" was necessary to realise the objective possibility of workers' class consciousness, through generalising from individual and sectional experience to the class nature of society as a whole. The shift in Lenin's views reflected not a break from the need for intervention but rather the now greater scope for such intervention.

The changing demands on Social Democratic intervention after Bloody Sunday, which reflected the ebb and flow of the revolution, could be seen in the changing emphasis within Lenin's "activist" conception of the party. As a result, it is possible to match the development of Lenin's own position with the historical phases of the labour movement and Social Democracy that have been outlined in the first four chapters. Thus, contrary to the argument for an over-riding break on Bloody Sunday, Lenin did not unceasingly laud a spontaneously generating consciousness over the whole course of the revolution. It is certainly true that at times when such an apparently "spontaneous" rise was evident, notably in January and October 1905 as well as June 1906 and February 1907, Lenin single-mindedly promoted the consequences of this rise for Social Democratic intervention. Yet in the relative slumps between these peaks of struggle, Lenin's comments argued a more deliberate role for Social Democrats in developing the consciousness of the "activists". Just as before Bloody Sunday, the crux of Lenin's views on party organisation lay in the task of intervention to raise consciousness, not in any particular comments on structure, which were always related to the particular context in which this task was to be carried out.

9 January–17 October 1905: Social Democracy as an element of the "activists"

January–February: Initial assessment of the Gapon Assembly

The first two months of 1905 certainly laid the basis for an "activist" approach to the organisation of Social Democracy by Lenin, and it is from this period that evidence for a supposed break from his previous views is usually taken. Earlier, particular phrases were cited in isolation to imply a substitutionist element in Lenin's understanding of leadership. Now, declarations such as "[w]ith incredible speed the broad masses of the workers have caught up with their advanced comrades, the class-conscious Social Democrats",[1] were presented with only limited context to suggest an uncritical confidence in the supposedly spontaneous advance of workers' consciousness. In fact such phrases formed part of a series of articles attempting to understand the nature of the movement that had culminated in the marches on Bloody Sunday.[2] This assessment of Gapon's supporters was aimed at developing their class consciousness and, as in all his previous writing, such a discussion of consciousness premised Lenin's position on party tasks and structure. Over

---

1   Lenin, *CW*, vol. 8, "Revolution in Russia", p71.

2   ibid., "The St. Petersburg Strike", pp90-3, "The Beginning of the Revolution in Russia", pp97-100, and especially a series of articles "Revolutionary Days", pp101-23.

January and February Lenin devoted himself overwhelmingly to making this assessment of the Gapon movement, and only later did he focus on the consequent tasks and structure of the Social Democrats.

Prior to 1905 Lenin had argued that Social Democratic consciousness could only be a full awareness of class society. The strike struggle of that time was not sufficient in itself to develop such an awareness, as it was only sectional in its demands and base. Consequently the broader Social Democratic consciousness could only be acquired through individual study by an "intelligentsia". Yet from the first news he received, Lenin sensed that the St. Petersburg strike was a qualitatively greater struggle than those occurring earlier. Due to its general nature, combative forms and motive of solidarity, Lenin implicitly counterposed this protest to earlier economic struggles by characterising the strike as: "a *political* event of tremendous importance". Reflecting his judgement of the class consciousness that could be developed within such a broad struggle, he now categorised the protest as "an outbreak of the *political class* struggle" [my emphasis].[3] Thus in contrast to those earlier limited outbursts, such a generalised struggle would develop full class consciousness as:

> this mobilisation, of course, is not be classed with demonstrations of *minor* importance in this or that municipal council…The mobilisation of the *revolutionary* forces of the proletariat in this *new and higher form* is bringing us with gigantic strides to the moment when the proletariat will even more decisively *and more consciously* join battle with the autocracy.[4] [my emphasis]

Thus through relating the breadth of struggle to the growth of workers' class consciousness Lenin's comments in the wake of Bloody Sunday mark a continuation of, not a break from, his earlier approach to party organisation.

This view of Lenin's unbroken understanding of the correspondence between the growth of consciousness and the breadth of workers' struggle is confirmed by his scathing criticism of "the sceptical *intellectual* adherents of social democracy"[5] [my emphasis]. These dissident bourgeois intellectuals had not believed conceivable, or had not been prepared to wait for, the current broad struggles that vindicated the revolutionary postulates of the Marxist tradition. As a result, such figures had been prepared to adopt the revisionist consciousness associated with lesser struggles, and consequently sought to

---

3   ibid., "The St. Petersburg Strike", p90.

4   ibid., p93.

5   ibid., "The First Lessons", p140.

subordinate Social Democracy to the liberals in the struggle against tsarism.[6] The dramatic events of Bloody Sunday "once again showed up all such *backsliding* types of the *intelligentsia* brood".[7] [my emphasis] That Lenin did not abandon his commitment to an interventionist Social Democratic consciousness is also clear from the fact that he continued without interruption his polemic against the Mensheviks. Indeed his position could be seen as hardening further when he categorised as "clearly defined" the differences between Bolsheviks and Mensheviks, with "the former representing the proletarian tendencies in our movement, the latter the tendencies of the intelligentsia".[8] These comments were part of a long article published the day after Bloody Sunday,[9] which was followed up with a pamphlet in mid-January.[10]

In the weeks following Bloody Sunday, Lenin made a more extended attempt to understand the historical causes of the Gapon movement, as well as the political nature of its leadership. Lenin's understanding of this movement as a state attempt at co-option which burst its purely economic bounds, as well as his characterisation of Gapon himself as a naive philanthropist, were necessarily schematic.[11] Yet, as outlined in the account of the movement earlier, his views have been confirmed in detail by subsequent historical research. Lenin pointed to the role of Social Democrats over the previous decades in building up a layer of "intelligents"[12] who were able to provide a lead to the movement of "activists" burgeoning around Gapon. Recent scholarship has shown that this leadership was even more profoundly "from outside" the class than Lenin grasped – that a circle of self-conscious non-party Social Democrats formed an alliance with Gapon to guide the movement in a deliberately anti-tsarist direction.[13]

In his initial writing against Economism, Lenin's basic concern had been to expose convincingly the content and source of this threat to the interventionist understanding of Marxism. He turned to the tasks of Social Democrats in countering this threat only after he had conducted that necessary preparatory

---

6   ibid., "Two Tactics of Social-Democracy in the Democrat Revolution", p75, vol. 9, p140.

7   ibid., p141.

8   ibid., "Working Class and Bourgeois Democracy" p73.

9   ibid., pp72-82.

10   ibid., "A Brief Outline of the Split in the R.S.D.L.P.", pp125-31.

11   See especially ibid., "2 Father Gapon", (in "Revolutionary Days"), pp105-6, "5 'Our Father the Tsar' and the Barricades", pp111-3, "6 The First Steps", pp114-7, "7 The Eve of Bloody Sunday", pp118-20.

12   ibid., "The St Petersburg Strike", p93.

13   As outlined earlier based on Surh's comprehensive account (Suhr 1989). For two recent Russian discussions that do not clash in substance with Surh see S.I. Potolov, "Peterburgskie rabochie i intelligentsiia...", pp530-41 in Potolov (ed.) 1997 and Ksenofontov 1996.

critique. Following a similar pattern, Lenin dealt only in passing with the tasks and structure of Social Democracy in the immediate wake of Bloody Sunday. Yet even in these preliminary comments, the germs of Social Democracy as a large body of "activists", organised around tactical leadership of generalised struggle, are clearly evident. Thus in his initial comments on Bloody Sunday, Lenin made a general call for action on the part of Social Democrats.[14] In particular, insurrection, which had earlier been the ultimate vision of Social Democrat "intelligents", now became the immediate aim of "activists".[15] Independence of Social Democracy from bourgeois liberalism, which had earlier been established in a struggle over principle within the "intelligentsia", now had to be fought out among the "activists" over the tactics to be adopted in the struggle against tsarism.[16]

From the vastly greater base of consciousness after Bloody Sunday, and hence the far broader tasks of Social Democracy, flowed Lenin's well known call for the opening of party structures. This opening was the means through which Social Democrats could provide a lead to the burgeoning mass of still incoherent though highly combative labour movement activists. That this opening was not a rejection of Lenin's former centralism is shown by the close connection he made between the call for opening Committees and that for a new Party Congress. Lenin feared, prophetically as events proved, that without such strong acts of leadership, the "activists" of the labour movement would follow rivals to the Bolsheviks such as the liberals and Mensheviks. Thus his celebrated call to:

> recruit young people more widely and boldly, more boldly and widely, and again more widely and again more boldly, *without fearing them*, while completely pushing into the background the customary, well-meant committee (hierarchic) stupidities[17] [italics in original]

was part of an exasperated plea to his closest supporters inside Russia to end prevarication and announce the Third Party Congress.[18] As outlined earlier, that Congress was intended as the culmination of Lenin's two-year struggle against the Mensheviks.

---

14   Lenin, *CW*, vol. 8, "Revolution in Russia", p71.

15   ibid., "The Beginning of the Revolution in Russia", p99, "'Our Father the Tsar' and the Barricades" (in "Revolutionary Days"), p113.

16   ibid., "Working-Class and Bourgeois Democracy", pp72-82, "Beginning of Revolution in Russia", p100.

17   ibid., "Letter to A.A. Bogdanov and S.I. Gusev", p146.

18   ibid., pp143-7.

February–August: Consolidation of structural change

As outlined in chapter four, from the end of January 1905 generalised strike activity in St. Petersburg declined to factory-based struggles, and from late February largely ceased altogether. In these circumstances the caution of Lenin's principal collaborators in St. Petersburg reasserted itself, and resistance grew to the extent of his demands for structural openness. Yet with the relative decline of struggle Lenin did not resile from his previous stand, as other Bolsheviks were inclined to do. Rather, in this period of relative calm, Lenin set out the argument for structural change in a more systematic way. This outline involved a more detailed discussion of the tasks of Social Democratic "activists" as leaders of an anti-tsarist insurrection – an insurrection that would have to be led independently of the liberal bourgeoisie. It was in the process of outlining these arguments that Lenin's often cited mid-year conflicts with the other leading Bolsheviks occurred.

The centre of contention between Lenin and the other Bolshevik "committeemen" was the recruitment of "workers" – here implicitly defined as representatives of the mass of "activists" without formal education or prior involvement in study circles. For Lenin the genuine leadership of Social Democracy by such elements was not only made possible by the depth of worker radicalisation, but was also demanded by the breadth of tasks now placed before the Social Democratic movement. Lenin sought to have "workers" co-opted directly onto committees, incorporated through the establishment of new types of organisations, and attracted through involvement in the legal labour movement. Indeed Lenin's judgement of the radicalisation was such that he suggested that groups of non-party workers should send delegates on a consultative basis to the Third Party Congress.[19]

For Lenin the mass recruitment of "workers" would not lead to the dilution of Social Democratic consciousness, as was bemoaned by some other Bolsheviks. For it seems clear that Lenin did not expect the mass of workers drawn for the first time into struggle, and still only partially class conscious, to immediately join the party. Rather it would be the smaller though still significant number of "activists" who had developed full class consciousness through leadership in mass struggle, who would pass through the now wide open doors of the party structure. Consequently for Lenin mass worker recruitment:

> **is not a question of relaxing our social democratic exactingness and our orthodox intransigence**, but of strengthening both in *new* ways, by

---

19   ibid., "A Letter to Organisations in Russia", p182.

new methods of training.[20] [my emphasis in bold, italics in original]

That Lenin sought to incorporate conscious workers as Social Democratic leaders, rather than simply make a shift in the class composition of committees, is also evident in his retort to those opposing worker membership of leading bodies at the Third Congress:

> It has been said here that the exponents of Social-Democratic ideas have been mainly intellectuals. That is not so. During the *period of Economism the exponents of revolutionary ideas were workers not intellectuals...* In my writings for the press I have long urged that as many workers as possible should be placed on the committees.[21] [my emphasis]

A draft resolution written for the Third Congress offers further confirmation that by "workers" Lenin meant a fully or near fully class conscious section of the leading "activists", rather than the mass of as yet only partially conscious participants in the labour movement:

> Only the **full** consciousness of the **advanced** workers, the complete elimination of all distinctions between intellectuals and workers within Social-Democracy, can guarantee a *Social-Democratic* class party of the proletariat. [my emphasis in bold, italics in original]

In another section of this resolution Lenin's decries Menshevik organisational proposals that:

> fail to notice the *revolutionary* independent activity of the workers and hang about the **lowest and most backward** strata of the movement.[22] [my emphasis in bold, italics in original]

Hence, as before Bloody Sunday, Lenin still identified a differentiation within the class, and sought to orient the party to incorporating those workers who were closest to it rather than the mass of the class with as yet only limited class consciousness.

Lenin continued to define Social Democratic consciousness as general

---

20   ibid., "New Tasks and New Forces", p218.

21   ibid., "On the Question of the Relations Between Workers and Intellectuals Within the Social-Democratic Organisations", p407.

22   ibid., "General Plan of the Third Congress Decisions", p186.

class consciousness, albeit now established more directly and broadly than had earlier been the case. He continued to defend the task of the party as insurrection, although now as an immediate tactical question rather than as an ultimate strategic aim. Hence Lenin continued to advocate the principles of centralism and responsibility in party structure, albeit now applied far more broadly and directly. That advocacy meant persisting with his polemic against the Mensheviks who interpreted Lenin's shift following Bloody Sunday as a turn toward their own decentralised organisational framework. For Lenin, such an interpretation of his comments:

> confounds extension of the Party's *framework* with extension of the *concept* of Party, it confounds extension of the *number of Party organisations* with extension of the Party *beyond the limits of Party organisations.*[23] [italics in original]

In countering Menshevik proposals for a loose organisation, Lenin returned to the need for centralism in relation to all party bodies, most notably the leadership,[24] as well as the related position that the party writers and press must be under the control of the party as a whole. He also repeatedly returned to the role of "party information" – considering detailed reports from local committees for the Third Congress,[25] as well as the role of fortnightly reports for the party paper.[26] Perhaps the most convincing evidence against the suggestion that Lenin precipitately abandoned his former rigorous centralism was his continuing opposition to the adoption of the direct elective principle throughout the party structure. He still saw such a measure as ineffective and damaging in the current illegal circumstances.[27]

The initial development of Lenin's approach to organisation in the new context culminated in his long defence of the Third Congress, *Two Tactics in the Democratic Revolution* (hereafter referred to as *Two Tactics...*). As suggested by the title, this book is a polemical defence of the Bolshevik view of the tasks

---

23   ibid., "The Guilty Blaming the Innocent", p311.

24   ibid., "The Third Congress", p443.

25   ibid., "Questionnaire for the Third Congress of the Party", pp200-1. While written prior to 20 February (5 March) it is not clear whether, and if so how far, this questionnaire was circulated and it was not published until 1926.

26   ibid., "Fortnightly Reports of the Party Organisations", pp357-8. While written in April 1905, this reflection was only published in 1926.

27   ibid., "General Plan of the Third Congress Decisions", p186. Clause 4 (b) in "General Plan of the Third Congress Decisions" pp184-9, p196. 4 RESOLUTION ON THE RELATIONS BETWEEN WORKERS AND INTELLECTUALS IN THE SOCIAL-DEMOCRATIC PARTY in "DRAFT RESOLUTIONS FOR THE THIRD CONGRESS OF THE RSDLP" (capitals in original), pp 191-6.

of the revolutionary movement against that of the Mensheviks. Such a defence required an explicit restatement of Lenin's historical interventionism against the deepening determinism of the Mensheviks. As such, *Two Tactics...* cannot be seen as embodying a break with the principles underlying Lenin's earlier writing, but rather should be seen as a new advance in the generalisation of those principles.

Two Tactics... opens and closes with two-sided formulations on intervention which might be interpreted as a dialectical renunciation of a former one sided elitism.[28] Such an interpretation results from viewing these passages outside their polemical context and placing no emphasis within them. Thus in the passage:

> Undoubtedly the revolution will teach us and will teach the masses of the people. *But the question that NOW confronts a militant political party is: shall WE be able to TEACH the revolution anything.* [my emphasis, capitals for increased emphasis][29]

the emphasis is clearly on the latter sentence, which reasserts the necessity for political intervention against those considering the already given process of advancing consciousness, summarised in the earlier sentence, to be sufficient. That this was Lenin's intended pattern of meaning in such passages is clear in a longer citation from the final section of the book. That section is aptly titled "CONCLUSION. DARE WE WIN?"[30] and is devoted to contrasting the general method underlying the tactics of the two Social Democratic factions. Here Lenin concludes:

> Revolutions are the locomotives of history, said Marx. Revolutions are festivals of the oppressed and the exploited. At no other time are the mass of the people in a position to come forward so actively as creators of a new social order, as at a time of revolution. At such time the people are capable of performing miracles, if judged by the limited, philistine yardstick of gradualist progress. *But it is essential that leaders of the revolutionary parties, too, should advance their aims more comprehensively and boldly at such a time, so that their slogans SHALL ALWAYS BE IN ADVANCE of the revolutionary initiative of the masses, serve as a beacon,* reveal to them our democratic and socialist ideal in all its magnitude and splendour, and show them the shortest

28 For example Molyneux 1978, p59.

29 Lenin, *CW*, vol. 9, *Two Tactics...*, p18.

30 ibid., p104. Upper case and punctuation as per the original.

258

and most direct route to complete, absolute and decisive victory.[31] [my emphasis, capitals for increased emphasis]

September–October: A further deepening of "activism"

Over the mid-year hiatus in struggle Lenin had refined his conception of Social Democratic organisation as a vehicle for conscious intervention – though now as the most combative section of the "activists" rather than as a Marxist current within the "workers' intelligentsia". In the new even broader surge of workers' struggle from mid-August to 17 October Lenin advanced the "activist" version of his conception further. He did so in response to the pressing issue of how Social Democrats could resolve a full-blown revolutionary crisis.

At this point, when the question of power itself was posed, Lenin made his main focus the tasks of Social Democrats. As outlined earlier, he now saw the principal task as exposing the Bulygin Duma, as well as advocating an "active boycott" against the elections to that body.[32] This flowed from the traditional Social Democratic position that insurrection led by the working class was the only means through which to remove tsarism, as well as the more recent conception of the "provisional revolutionary government" as the result of such an insurrection.[33] These positions were now opposed by the tactically gradualist Mensheviks, who advocated elections to "organs of revolutionary self-government" that would passively displace rather than actively disperse the tsarist state.

Such tactics reflected the deepening historical passivity of the Mensheviks, against which Lenin had come to clarify his own argument for interventionism.[34] Hence he described the establishment of "organs of revolutionary self-government" as "not the prologue to an uprising, but its epilogue".[35] This

---

31 ibid., p113.

32 ibid., "Friends Meet", pp258, "Playing at Parliamentarism", pp266, 273, "The Boycott of the Bulygin Duma, and Insurrection", pp179-87, "Argue about Tactics, but Give Clear Slogans!", pp262-4.

33 On the nature of the "provisional revolutionary government" and Social Democratic tactics in relation to it see "Social Democracy and the Provisional Revolutionary Government" (ibid., vol. 8, pp275-92) and "The Revolutionary-Democratic Dictatorship of the Proletariat and the Peasantry" (ibid., pp293-303) as well as many other references in vol. 8 and vol. 9 of the *Collected Works*.

34 See for example Lenin's polemics against the "organisation as process" theory of the Mensheviks throughout 1905 as well as his discussion of their objection to the term "fist from below" (ibid., vol. 9, "Preface to the pamphlet *Workers on the Split in the Party*", pp163-8).

35 ibid., "Oneness of the Tsar and the People, and of the People and the Tsar", p197.

was because they could not resolve the question of "sovereignty",[36] meaning here state power, which could only have been settled by a test of armed force. Flowing from this passivity, Lenin argued that the structural looseness of the Mensheviks was now being expressed tactically in their tendency to lag behind the movement rather than lead it, as well as strategically in their tendency to tail the liberal bourgeoisie rather than stand independently from them.[37]

The heightened revolutionary crisis of September and October imposed the tasks of opposing "organs of revolutionary self-government"[38] and organising an insurrection. As outlined earlier these tasks demanded concrete military preparations which the Bolsheviks, like almost all others, were reluctant to make. Responding to this equivocation Lenin returned to the themes of daring and action in party structure and activity that he had earlier raised in January.[39] As had been the case then, it was exasperation at hesitation in a decisive moment that drove Lenin to make the dramatic call:

> Go to the youth, gentlemen! That is the only remedy!... Form fighting squads *at once* everywhere, among the students, and *especially among the workers...* Do not demand any formalities, and, for heavens sake, **forget all these schemes, and send all "functions, rights, and privileges" to the devil**...make the round of *hundreds* of workers' and students' circles in a week, penetrate wherever they can, and everywhere propose a clear, brief, direct, and simple plan...but *do not wait for our help*; act for yourselves.[40] [my emphasis in bold, italics in original]

Lenin developed these points systematically in a further article, in which he suggested that a large number of small fighting squads should be formed from trusted local associates who need not necessarily belong to the same party.[41] As had been the case in January, these calls for decisive action on party tasks and structure involved a critique of the persistent caution and

---

36   ibid., "In the Wake of the Monarchist Bourgeoisie, or in the Van of the Revolutionary Proletariat and Peasantry?", p220.

37   ibid., "The Black Hundreds and the Organisations of an Uprising", pp202, "Playing at Parliamentarism", p275.

38   See for example ibid., "In the Wake of the Monarchist Bourgeoisie, or in the Van of the Revolutionary Proletariat and Peasantry?" pp212-23, "A Most Lucid Exposition of a Most Confused Plan", pp224-6, "The Theory of Spontaneous Generation", pp246-51.

39   Initially by lauding a prison raid by Social Democrats in Riga, ibid., "From the Defensive to the Offensive", pp283-5.

40   ibid., "To the Combat Committee of the St. Petersburg Committee", pp344-5.

41   ibid., "Tasks of Revolutionary Army Contingents", pp420, 423.

propagandism that pervaded the Bolsheviks, and was positively championed by the Mensheviks. Indeed in this perhaps even more decisive moment Lenin became more trenchant in his comments than he had been in January.

Thus near the conclusion of his well-known letter to the St. Petersburg Combat Committee, which included the above call, he declared: "the evil today is our inertness, our doctrinaire spirit, our learned immobility, and our senile fear of initiative".[42] And against the Mensheviks who disparaged the whole project of concrete preparation for insurrection he retorted:

> However much you may turn up your noses, gentlemen, at the
> question of night attacks and similar purely tactical military
> questions... *life goes on its way, revolution teaches, taking in hand and
> shaking up the most inveterate pedants.*[43] [my emphasis]

As had been the case in January 1905, such citations might be regarded as a reversal of Lenin's conception of the party as a vehicle for conscious intervention. Yet it is clear from other passages written at this time that the purpose of this further shift in Lenin's comments on tasks was to accelerate the spread of a Social Democratic consciousness amongst the labour movement "activists" now leading a rising general strike. Thus, in discussing a failed Moscow uprising, he wrote:

> Therefore fellow workers, *study* the lessons of the Moscow events,
> and do so most *attentively.* For it is in this way, and inevitably so,
> that matters will inevitably take their course throughout the whole
> of the Russian revolution. We must rally *more solidly than ever* in a
> *genuinely* socialist party, which will *consciously* express the interests
> of the working class, and not *drift along in the wake of the masses.*[44]
> [my emphasis]

Indeed Lenin's concern for an interventionist approach by revolutionaries reached its highest point ever with the October Strike. Now for the first time he was able to be both explicit and concrete in linking the consciousness of Social Democrats with the seizure of state power by the working class:

> The revolution has reached a stage at which it is *disadvantageous for
> the counter-revolution to attack, to assume the offensive.* For us, for the

---

42   ibid., "The Political Strike and the Street Fighting in Moscow", p346.

43   ibid., "The Black Hundreds and the Organisations of an Uprising", p203.

44   ibid., "The Lessons of the Moscow Events", p384.

proletariat, for consistent revolutionary democrats, *this is not enough.*
If **we** do not **rise to a higher level**, if **we** do not manage to **launch an
independent offensive**, if **we** do not smash the forces of tsarism, do
not destroy its actual power, then the revolution will stop half way,
then the ***bourgeoisie will fool the workers***.[45] [my emphasis in bold,
italics in original]

18 October–3 December 1905: Consciousness, tasks and structure of Social Democratic "activists" in a crisis of "dual power"

As outlined earlier, the Days of Freedom from 17 October to 3 December
marked a plateau in the breadth of workers' struggle, and consequently the
durability of "activist" organisation. Associated with this advance of the
labour movement "activists" in general, that section within the Bolsheviks
dramatically grew in number, while opening and diversifying its organisational
structure. It was at this high point of the revolution, as the working class came
closest to power and consequently its consciousness as a whole came closest
to Social Democracy, that Lenin made the most complete formulation of party
organisation as a leadership of "activists".

As in earlier historical phases, Lenin's intervention during the Days of
Freedom can best be analysed as an argument for a series of party tasks and
structures, that flowed from the given possibilities for advancing workers'
class consciousness. Thus, in the period immediately prior to his return to St.
Petersburg, Lenin sought to assess the new post-"Manifesto" circumstances in
the articles "The First Victory of the Revolution"[46] as well as the aptly-titled "The
Denouement is at Hand".[47] The assessment made in these articles underlay
the dramatic position he subsequently outlined on worker consciousness
and the Soviet in his well-known letter, "Our Tasks and the Soviet of Workers'
Deputies".[48] Following from this position on consciousness, Lenin set out his
view of Social Democratic tasks and structures in the three part article "The
Reorganisation of the Party"[49] (hereafter referred to as "The Reorganisation...").

Lenin followed up the extended argument in "The Reorganisation..." with
several shorter articles which make it clear that even at this high point of the
"activist" model of organisation he had not made a break with the principles

---

45 ibid., "An Equilibrium of Forces", p414.

46 ibid., "The First Victory of the Revolution", pp427-34.

47 ibid., "The Denouement is at Hand", pp447-54.

48 ibid., vol. 10, "Our Tasks and the Soviet of Workers' Deputies", pp17-28.

49 ibid., "The Reorganisation of the Party", pp29-39.

underlying his earlier approach to party organisation. The first of these, "Party Organisation and Party Literature",[50] generalised the role of the party paper as an organiser in the new context of virtual legality. Then, in mid-November, Lenin wrote two further articles which echoed his earlier comments about the dominance of bourgeois consciousness within the workers' movement. He did so in response to the rise of, as well as Cadet praise for, "non-partisanship" within the Soviet.[51]

In January 1905, Lenin had identified a dramatic break in workers' consciousness with the strike led by the Gapon Assembly activists. At that time he suggested that the mass of workers had been radicalised to the point of adopting the Social Democratic "Minimum Program".[52] In the far more deliberate and complete strike action of October 1905, Lenin saw a further dramatic advance in consciousness. For him, the working class as a whole had now adopted the full program of Social Democracy – the revolutionary dictatorship of the proletariat and peasantry. As a result the newly founded Soviet embodied the "provisional revolutionary government" through the adherence of its delegates to the parties that represented these two classes, and would be the vehicle for an insurrection that was clearly imminent.

The October Strike was the most complete mobilisation of the revolution and the highpoint of Lenin's understanding of consciousness arising directly from workers' immediate experience. Consequently, he rejected the view that the Soviet, the organisational reflection of this mobilisation, did not have the breadth of support or the political identity to act as a "provisional revolutionary government". For Lenin the formation of such a government:

> *has already been advanced in full by reality.* It is already recognised *in principle by all the politically conscious elements of absolutely all the classes* and sections of the population, including even Orthodox priests.[53] [my emphasis]

This estimation of universally rising consciousness led Lenin to support the inclusion of delegates holding Socialist Revolutionary views within the Soviet because:

---

50   ibid., "Party Organisation and Party Literature", pp44-9.

51   ibid., "Learn from the Enemy", pp60-1, "The Socialist Party and Non-Party Revolutionism", pp75-82.

52   See for example, ibid., vol. 8, "The St. Petersburg Strike", p92.

53   ibid., vol. 10, "Our Tasks and the Soviet", p24.

We shall have no difficulty in overcoming their inconsistency, *for our views are supported by history itself,* are supported at every step by reality.[54] [my emphasis]

But perhaps the most striking evidence of Lenin's estimation of this advancing consciousness was his judgement that those who were incomplete in their Social Democratic views should be included not only in the Soviet, but even in the party itself. Thus, on Christians, Lenin commented:

[W]e shall not expel them from the Soviet *or even from the party,* for it is our firm conviction that the *actual struggle,* and *work within the ranks,* will convince *all elements possessing vitality that Marxism is the truth,* and will cast aside all those who lack vitality.[55] [my emphasis]

As had occurred earlier in the year, Lenin's estimation of a dramatic rise in consciousness led him to broaden the tasks of Social Democracy. Since insurrection was now an immediate prospect, Social Democrats must take action to win over the army, backward workers and the peasantry, as well as prepare for the possibility of spreading the revolution to Europe.[56] Consistent with his judgement of a universal class consciousness, Lenin considered that the call for insurrection should be made by the proletariat as a whole rather than any particular section or party. It should be addressed to consistent democrats of all classes, most notably the peasantry. Thus he proposed that the text of the call to insurrection should include:

We are not trying to *impose on the people* any innovations thought up by us; we are merely taking the initiative in bringing about that without which it is impossible to live in Russia any longer, *as is acknowledged generally and unanimously.* We *do not shut ourselves off* from the revolutionary people *but submit to their judgement* every step and every decision we take.[57] [my emphasis]

Consistent with his view of the broad base for insurrection, Lenin suggested

---

54   ibid., p23.

55   ibid.

56   ibid., vol. 9, "The First Victory", pp433-4. For a discussion of Lenin's view of the revolution, and his shift towards Trotsky's position over 1905, see Schwarz 1967, pp21-7. Schwarz again here offers a "two Lenins" explanation of the apparent contradiction in Lenin's position as he does not consider the context.

57   ibid., vol. 10, "Our Tasks and the Soviet", pp26-7.

that this proposed declaration be adopted by forces far broader than Social Democracy, in fact by

> all our party organisations, *all class conscious workers*, the Soviet itself, the workers' forthcoming congress in Moscow, *and the Congress of the Peasant Union*.[58] [my emphasis]

The generalised advance of consciousness and the consequent broad base for the tasks of Social Democracy led Lenin to advocate a further opening of party structures. This he proposed in "The Reorganisation...", an article that marks a new high point in Lenin's development of a party structure for Social Democracy as a leadership of "activists". Focused on proposals to introduce an electoral regime, create new types of party bodies, and reunite with the Mensheviks, this article was also significant because it included elements of a theorisation of the difference between Social Democracy as an organisation of "intelligents" relative to one of "activists".

The first proposal Lenin argued for, the establishment of an open legal party based on the elective principle, was the one most directly linked to his understanding of the current widespread class consciousness. Thus Lenin responded to the argument that a complete opening of the party would dilute its political basis and make it the "tail" of the class:

> *[N]ow* that the heroic proletariat has *proved* by its readiness to fight, and its ability to fight *consciously* and in a body for *clearly understood aims*...it would be simply ridiculous to doubt that workers who belong to our Party...will be Social Democrats in *ninety-nine cases out of a hundred*.[59] [my emphasis]

Lenin's understanding of the current potential for massive growth in Social Democracy did not involve a renunciation of his former commitment to a clearly identified Marxism as the basis of the party. Indeed it was precisely the long established identity of Social Democracy, together with the earlier rejection of demagoguery, that would provide a guard against the danger, albeit small, that Social Democracy might be diluted by less conscious workers.

The opening and growth of Social Democracy required new types of organisational structures, as well as new types of activity within these structures. Earlier, Social Democracy had comprised an "intelligentsia" of educated dissidents and workers very much like them – "revolutionaries

---

58 ibid., p28.

59 ibid., "The Reorganisation of the Party", p32.

coming from a particular social stratum". Now, as a mass organisation of "activists", the base of Social Democracy would be "typical representatives of the masses". Such a change required that propaganda and agitation should be in "a more popular style, ability to present a question, to explain the basic truths of socialism in the simplest, clearest and most convincing manner". It would also require "more free, more loose" organisational structures as the influence of socialist ideas "is now proceeding, and will continue to proceed along paths that we very often shall be altogether unable to foresee".

The culmination of Lenin's articles on structure was a call on all Social Democratic worker "activists", most notably those supporting the Mensheviks, to force a re-unification of Social Democracy. This involved returning to his argument that the Menshevik leaders were inclined to split due to their background as intellectuals, and should be rejected by the local party leaders, just as had occurred after the Second Congress. That led him to make his most theorised formulation of the relation between intellectuals and workers within Social Democracy and hence the relation between the phases of the party as tiny circles of "intelligents" and a mass of leading "activists":

> [T]he intelligentsia is good at solving problems "in principle", good at drawing up plans, good at reasoning about the *need for action* – while the workers *act*, and transform drab theory into living reality.[60] [my emphasis]

The culmination of each round of Lenin's earlier model of the Social Democratic party as an "intelligentsia" was the conception of a propaganda paper that related particular struggles and issues to the class reality of society as a whole. In a comparable way, the culmination of his most complete formulation of Social Democracy as a layer of "activists" was the conception of the agitational paper that related the growing mass of particular struggles to the united act of insurrection. The principles that underlay the earlier task of propaganda among "intelligents" are also very marked in the new task of agitation amongst the "activists". Thus for Lenin the new legal paper would be "a free press, free not simply from the police, but also from capital, *from careerism, and what is more, free from bourgeois-anarchist individualism*".[61] [my emphasis] As before, the key to achieving this "free press" was the active supervision and involvement of worker Social Democrats – though now these workers were "activists" directly leading mass struggles rather than "intelligents":

---

60 All quotes in preceding paragraphs ibid., pp31-8.

61 ibid., "Party Organisation and Party Literature", p47.

> The *organised socialist proletariat* must keep an eye on all this work, supervise it in its entirety, and, from beginning to end, without any exception, *infuse into it the life stream of the living proletarian cause*, thereby cutting the ground from under the old, semi-Oblomov, semi-shopkeeper Russian principle: *the writer does the writing, the reader does the reading.*[62] [my emphasis]

Lenin's most complete argument for Social Democracy as a mass of "activists" could not signify the complete liquidation of the party. That became particularly evident in the second half of November, as tsarism and the capitalists returned to the offensive, but the Soviet did not adopt a concretely insurrectionary response. Prior to Bloody Sunday, Lenin had argued that the "spontaneous" view of the working class was bourgeois consciousness. Echoing that point as the movement failed to take decisive measures against tsarist initiatives, he argued that the non-partisan "independence" of such organs of struggle as the Soviet in fact signified their confinement within bourgeois limits. This was because "only a social democratic proletariat is a proletariat conscious of its *class* tasks".[63] [italics in original] Hence while Social Democrats should participate in non-party organisations, they should do so with a clear identity as party members and under the control of the party as a whole. This control would be both necessary if Social Democrats were to be distinguished from liberals, and also possible in the virtual legality of the time when positions could be openly declared and reports regularly submitted.

There can be no doubt that this shift back to an emphasis on the distinct identity of Social Democracy marks the beginning of a retreat from the highpoint of Lenin's "activist" conception of the party. This retreat was epitomised by the contrast between the defensive posture adopted to Socialist Revolutionary workers in late November[64] and the assured optimism of "Our Tasks…". It was also evident in his more measured, though still favourable, attitude to Christians joining the RSDLP.[65] With several particular interruptions, this retreat in Lenin's "activist" conception would continue to deepen with the retreat of the revolution.

---

62 ibid., p46.

63 ibid., "Learn from the Enemy", p61.

64 ibid.

65 ibid., "Socialism and Religion", pp85-7.

4 December 1905–9 July 1906: Retreat and resurgence within the model of Social Democracy as a leadership of "activists"

Between December 1905 and July 1906 the labour movement activists of St. Petersburg suffered a shattering blow, but then recovered to lead a further constrained advance. Associated with this resurgence by the activists in general, the Bolsheviks also substantially, though not completely, recovered their former membership and organisational structure. In attempting to lead the Bolsheviks in this contradictory period, Lenin was required to continue revising his position on the party as a leadership of "activists" – this time in a period of retreat followed by a limited recovery. As before, the course of this revision closely reflected the advance and retreat of the labour movement as a whole. Thus, over January and February, Lenin was forced to return to defending strategic interventionism, from February to April he was able to develop a new tactical perspective within such an approach, and over the mid-year months he returned to the argument for Social Democracy as a fully involved leadership of "activists" as a new labour upsurge gained strength.

Yet with the Bolsheviks being subject to pressure from a consolidating tsarism, Lenin was curbed in his comments on party organisation over the mid-year upsurge, and they generally mark a retreat from the assurance of the Days of Freedom. He still formally looked to the role of generalised struggle to advance the consciousness of the mass of the working class and was far from returning to Social Democracy as an "intelligentsia". Yet now he viewed party tasks and activity far more in terms of propaganda than had been the case in the high points of struggle of 1905. In contrast to the period prior to Bloody Sunday however, this propaganda would now be overwhelmingly related to immediate issues and struggles, and conducted through the newly established "democratic centralist" structures.

December 1905–January 1906

The months of December 1905 and January 1906 were ones of almost complete disarray among all sections of the activists in the wake of an apparently decisive blow from tsarism. In these circumstances Lenin was largely confined to reaffirming the possibility of successful insurrection, as well as identifying the underlying vulnerability of tsarism despite its apparent triumph. In doing so Lenin returned to his polemic against the Mensheviks, who had responded to the dispersal of the Soviet by shifting very sharply away from their radicalism during the Days of Freedom. For Lenin, a setback had certainly been inflicted in December, but in doing so tsarism had undermined its own position by dispelling illusions about the possibility for reform[66] as well as involving a mass of workers in armed struggle.[67] Furthermore continuing financial difficulties, military setbacks, and disturbances in the countryside were undermining the stability of the regime.[68]

While the long-term legitimacy of tsarism may have been undermined by the repression of December, the immediate impact of that defeat was to intimidate the mass of workers. As a consequence, Lenin returned to emphasising the role of Social Democracy as a distinct current intervening within the class rather than "tailing" it. He was compelled to do so in response to the Mensheviks' position that Social Democrats should participate in the First Duma elections. For the Mensheviks, such a position flowed from their impression that the mass of workers had now been intimidated and were prepared to submit to the consolidation of tsarist rule through the establishment of a Duma. For Lenin such an approach to the tasks of Social Democrats was erroneous because:

> the Party cannot and must not base its tactics on the *temporary weakness* of certain centres... Let the *unenlightened* and *ignorant* go into the Duma – the Party will not bind its fate with theirs.[69] [my emphasis]

This return to Social Democracy as uniting and mobilising the fully conscious element within the class, a role more predominant in its "intelligentsia" phase, was also evident when Lenin later commented that participating in the Duma elections "can only strengthen the position of the *least class conscious elements* of the mass of workers".[70] [my emphasis] Flowing from his expectation of an imminent new upsurge in struggle, Lenin made arguing for an "active boycott" of the Duma the main task of the Party. Consistent with its propagandistic nature, as well as the current repression, this basic task was associated with organisational consolidation and preparation for later struggle. Thus in his major article on perspectives in January Lenin put forward the "new task of *studying* and utilising the experience of the latest forms of struggle, the

66 ibid., "The Workers' Party and its Tasks in the Present Situation", p93.

67 ibid., p95.

68 ibid.

69 ibid., "Should we Boycott the State Duma?", p99.

70 ibid., "The State Duma and Social-Democratic Tactics", p108.

task of *training* and *organising forces* in the most important centres of the movement.[71] [my emphasis]

Consistent with the need to overcome the disarray of the labour movement as a whole, he wrote in a later article about "husbanding forces",[72] as well as showing "perseverance and patience".[73] Indeed the repression and disarray was such that Lenin suggested at one point that the return underground by the Petersburg Committee in December and January might need to continue indefinitely. Thus the recently adopted "democratic centralist" structure of an "activist" party could not be maintained unconditionally as "we must re-adapt ourselves to the national autocracy, and be able whenever necessary to go underground once more".[74]

Despite this caution Lenin did not definitively abandon his expectation of a return to mass workers' struggle, and hence the possibility of a major new advance for the Bolsheviks. Consequently he did not retreat from his commitment to unification with the Mensheviks despite the clear shift of that faction towards participation in the Duma. Such a perspective remained applicable, despite the temporarily adverse circumstances, provided that the Bolsheviks related to the experience in mass struggle of the Menshevik "activists" and "convert our polemics *into a practical setting forth* of the pros and cons, an explanation of the position of the proletariat and its class aim".[75] [my emphasis]

The division within Social Democracy accentuated the need for the contested issues to be made the centre of discussion if the "democratic centralist" structure of the party was to be effective. Consequently Lenin sought to have the Duma elections made the centre of discussion prior to the Fourth Party Congress, and subsequently the basis for selecting delegates to that meeting. That the central points of contention between the two factions of Social Democracy should be openly discussed was especially important because the Fourth Congress would formally reunite Social Democracy.[76]

---

71 ibid., p94.

72 ibid., p95, "Should we Boycott the State Duma?", p99.

73 ibid., "The Workers' Party and its Tasks in the Present Situation", pp99, "The State Duma and Social-Democratic Tactics", p105.

74 ibid., "The Workers' Party and its Tasks in the Present Situation", p95.

75 ibid., "The State Duma and Social-Democratic Tactics", p111.

76 ibid.

February–April 1906

As outlined earlier, from February to April the earlier disarray of the labour movement cleared as a plethora of sectional organisations consolidated in the easing repression. Consistent with his earlier view that the class struggle could only be a struggle by the class as a whole, Lenin does not appear to have regarded these organisations as marking in themselves the re-emergence of the working class as a political force, and he did not focus on them in his writing. For Lenin that political re-emergence occurred through the associated consolidation of Social Democracy itself, a process that culminated in the Fourth Party Congress. Consequently Lenin was overwhelmingly focused on the preparation for the Congress, and in particular the renewed tactical polarisation between Bolsheviks and Mensheviks that this preparation involved. In opposing the rightward shift of the Mensheviks, Lenin returned to many of the points developed in his polemic following the Second Congress. Indeed that shift was so marked that the Mensheviks received praise from the former Legal Marxist and Economist opponents of Social Democracy, while Lenin's own arguments recalled his earlier critique of those figures.

In the adverse circumstances leading up to the Fourth Congress, Lenin continued to argue for the role of Social Democracy in resisting rather than "tailing" the bourgeois consciousness "spontaneously" imposed on the working class. He did so in opposition to a further deepening of the shift by the Mensheviks away from their leftism in the October Strike and Days of Freedom. That trend was now reflected in the increasing influence of the abstraction and strategic passivity advocated by Plekhanov,[77] and the concurrent decline of the tactical leftism and involvement in concrete struggle advocated by Trotsky and Parvus.[78]

For Lenin, Plekhanov had generalised his celebrated condemnation of the Moscow uprising of December 1905 by citing Hegel to justify historical fatalism,[79] identifying any advocacy of insurrection with the terrorism of *Narodnaia Volia*,[80] and argued that peasant land seizure could only strengthen the reactionary nature of tsarism.[81] In making his critique Plekhanov, like the

---

77   ibid., "Report on the Unity Congress of the R.S.D.L.P. A Letter to the St. Petersburg Workers", p360.

78   ibid., p324.

79   ibid., p350.

80   ibid., p340.

81   These latter two points raised and responded to by Lenin, ibid., "Speech in Reply to the Debate on the Agrarian Question" at the Fourth Congress, pp279-88.

earlier "Legal Marxists", was very inclined to omit concrete discussion of the class struggle from his analysis of events. Consequently he came to formulate the tasks of Social Democracy in a way that strongly echoed the Economists.[82]

Lenin responded to Plekhanov, as well as the prominent Cadets who endorsed him, by again returning to the role of Social Democracy as intervening to defend the revolutionary potential and purpose of the working class. This involved repeating his earlier points that such a defence should not yield to temporary reverses,[83] prevailing pessimism,[84] or the prospect of apparent short-term gain, through sacrificing the ultimate aims of the labour movement. As a result the working class must now take an independent lead in the revolution and not become the "hanger on of the bourgeoisie"[85] and "labourer of the revolution".

In making his critique of Plekhanov, Lenin returned to many of the arguments he had made prior to 1905. Yet this did not involve returning to the model of Social Democracy as a current of "intelligents". For Lenin's arguments were still being made in relation to questions of tactics in the context of an expected return to mass struggle – not in relation to issues of principle in the wake of a defeated revolution. Despite some deterioration in the context Lenin still considered that the revolution was "in the era of its turning point"[86] to a new upsurge when, as in the highpoints of 1905:

> [A]ll *theoretical* errors and tactical deviations of the Party are most ruthlessly criticised *by experience itself,* which *enlightens and educates* the working class with unprecedented rapidity.[87] [my emphasis]

In such circumstances Menshevik activists could still be won away from their leaders, and Social Democracy could still give a lead to the activists of the labour movement.

While Lenin expected an upsurge in generalised struggle in the not too distant future, the current containment of the activists still imposed tasks of propaganda on Social Democrats. Of these the most basic continued to be the exposure of constitutional illusions in the now convened First Duma.[88] Such

82 Ibid., "Report on the Unity Congress of the R.S.D.L.P.", p365.

83 ibid., "To All Working Men and Women of the City of St. Petersburg and Vicinity", p130.

84 ibid., "The Russian Revolution and the Tasks of the Proletariat", p137.

85 ibid., p144.

86 ibid., "An Appeal to the Party By Delegates To the Unity Congress Who Belonged to the Former 'Bolshevik' Group", p311.

87 ibid., p310.

88 ibid., pp312, 314.

exposure involved a critique of the Cadets' conception of a constitutional course for the revolution,[89] as well as the consequent passivity of the Mensheviks who more and more took their lead from the Cadets. In opposing the constitutionalism of the Cadets, Lenin again raised the task of spreading propaganda among the peasantry, the base together with the working class of an insurrectionary alternative to the Cadets' constitutionalism. However at this point he did so only in a general and passing manner. The early First Duma proceedings provided the concrete material for propaganda against constitutional illusions among the activists – "Reality has already outstripped our debates"[90] commented Lenin on the impact of these proceedings.

Given the tasks of propaganda drawing on concrete topical events that he posed for Social Democrats,[91] as well as the generally constrained context, it is not surprising that Lenin made no radical proposals on party structure at this time. Rather, he sought to have the formally adopted "democratic centralist" structure actually implemented in practice. Yet the continuing split in Social Democracy, as well as its underground heritage, meant that Lenin did not think this task would be straightforward. Given his expectation of a new upsurge, as well as a continuing and fundamental split in Social Democracy, he was very thoroughgoing in his interpretation of the "democratic centralism" that now guided party structure. Thus in his "Report on the Unity Congress of the RSDLP" he declared:

> We must call upon *every* member of the party to take a conscious and critical stand on these resolutions. We must see to it that *every* workers' organisation, after making itself thoroughly familiar with the subject, declares whether it approves or disapproves of any particular decision. If we have really and seriously decided to introduce democratic centralism in our Party, *and if we have resolved to draw the masses of workers into intelligent decision of Party questions*, we must have these questions discussed in the press, at meetings, in articles and at group meetings.[92] [my emphasis].

---

89   ibid., "The Victory of the Cadets and the Tasks of the Workers' Party", pp271, 273-5.

90   ibid., "Report on the Unity Congress of the R.S.D.L.P.", p361.

91   ibid., p378.

92   ibid., p380.

May–June 1906

Over May and June 1906 despite the strikes and street protests which substantially echoed the height of the Days of Freedom, sectional organisations such as the unemployed movement and trade unions could not assume the earlier class-wide role of the Soviet. Social Democrats were again able to play a prominent role in this period of protest – indeed they were able to launch daily papers. Yet they were not able to grow as they had during the Days of Freedom, and the Mensheviks continued their drift to the right.

Lenin's comments on party organisation at this time reflected the limited contradictory nature of this spasm of struggle. With the upsurge he had anticipated now in progress, Lenin continued to expect Social Democratic consciousness to be adopted through direct experience and on a mass scale. Yet the constrained nature of the upsurge, as well as its failure to produce a class-wide organisation of struggle, was reflected in his continuing focus on the Duma proceedings and a consequent critique of the Mensheviks' passivity. In doing so, Lenin hardened his steps away from the earlier high point of his model of Social Democracy as a mass of "activists". Resulting from this hardening was a further shift in the tasks Lenin posed for Social Democrats. In early 1906 the main task had been exposing the constitutional illusions of the Cadets; now there was in addition the need to raise the revolutionary consciousness of the peasantry. Concerning party structure, the deepening split between Bolsheviks and Mensheviks hindered the full implementation of "democratic centralism", as Lenin had anticipated, and he was compelled to confine his comments to the clarification of this term.

The extent and nature of the shift in Lenin's position on party organisation was evident in his first commentary on the upsurge in an article aptly titled "A New Upswing".[93] Lenin noted and lauded the emergence of a movement among the unemployed as well as peasants and soldiers. However, in contrast to the Soviet he did not dwell on these movements, nor return to them. He suggested a widespread shift in consciousness away from the constitutional illusions of the first months of the year:

> [T]he revolution is knocking the Cadet spectacles off the noses not only of Right Social Democrats, *but also of the broad masses of the people.*[94]
> [my emphasis]

Yet his formulation of the relation between Social Democrats, the rest of

93   ibid., "A New Upswing", pp386-91.
94   ibid., p390.

the "activists" and the mass of workers had more in common with the two-sided balance of *Two Tactics...* than the one-sided assurance of January and early November 1905. Indeed the echo of his earlier view of consciousness "from outside", muted in late November 1905 and April 1906, was now becoming clearer:

> The tide is rising spontaneously, and we must do all in our power *to bring more consciousness and organisation into this upsurge* than we were able to in October and December.[95] [my emphasis]

A month later, in early June, a new wave of the upsurge broke, and was greeted by Lenin with two aptly titled articles, "The Present Political Situation"[96] and "On the Eve".[97] Here Lenin again lauded a surge of mass action, which in relation to the mobilised class forces "relentlessly reveals the basic differences of the interests involved".[98] He noted in particular a new strike wave and new forms of strike activity which he promised to return to – although it is significant that he again did not in fact do so. In "On the Eve" Lenin also noted the disillusionment with the Duma after only six weeks of its proceedings. Yet in contrast to his earlier Duma commentary, concerned overwhelmingly with the mass advance of consciousness, his conclusion now included a reassertion of the necessary ideological role of Social Democracy:

> We are on the eve of great historical events, we are on the eve of the second great stage of the Russian revolution. The Social-Democrats, *who consciously express the class struggle of the proletariat,* will stand at their posts to a man, and will perform their duty to the end.[99] [my emphasis]

Apart from the peaks of struggle Lenin's formulations were more than ever aimed at promoting the need for Social Democrats to make concretely oriented propaganda against ruling class ideology. For Lenin this task came to more and more entail opposing constitutional illusions in the Duma. Thus on 9 May he could write:

> But the masses of the peasantry and the working classes will do as they

95 ibid.
96 ibid., "The Present Political Situation", pp485-9.
97 ibid., vol. 11, "On the Eve", pp15-6.
98 ibid., vol. 10, "The Present Political Situation", p485.
99 ibid., vol. 11, "On the Eve", p16.

see fit, contemptuously throwing aside the miserable fears and doubts of the flabby bourgeois intelligentsia. *They will not support the Duma.* They will support their own demands, which the Cadet Duma has so incompletely and inadequately expressed.[100] [my emphasis]

Yet by 2 June Lenin had retreated to the position that Social Democratic views on the Duma would be vindicated "if not tomorrow, the day after tomorrow" rather than immediately.[101] On 6 June he drafted a resolution that spoke of the "damage to class consciousness" as well as the "corrupting of revolutionary consciousness" if the "Duma Cabinet" now being proposed by the Mensheviks were endorsed by Social Democracy.[102] Ultimately this view of consciousness being developed indirectly rather than in mass struggle was reflected in Lenin's formal recognition of the tasks of propaganda through the medium of the Duma proceedings. Thus on 24 May he went so far as to justify explicitly what had previously been only an implicit retreat:

> However distorted popular representation in the State Duma may be by virtue of the election law and the conditions under which the elections were held, *it nevertheless provides a fair amount of material for a study of the policies of the various classes in Russia. And it also helps to correct erroneous or narrow views on this question.*[103] [my emphasis]

By 22 June Lenin was being even more direct and prefaced a proposed Social Democratic speech in the Duma with:

> No Social-Democrat can have any doubt now that in the present situation the pronouncements of our Party members in the Duma *could be of great value to the cause of the proletariat and of the whole people.*"[104] [my emphasis]

Lenin's narrowing focus on the development of consciousness through the Duma led him to further sharpen and broaden his theoretical critique of the Mensheviks' rightward shift in relation to that body. Thus, in May, he criticised Plekhanov for seeking workers' support for the Duma, the conduct

---

100 ibid., vol. 10, "The Duma and the People", p398.

101 ibid., "Don't Gaze up, Gaze Down!", p507.

102 ibid., "Resolution (III) of the St. Petersburg Committee of the R.S.D.L.P. on the Question of a Duma Ministry", p514.

103 ibid., "Cadets, Trudoviks and the Workers' Party", p455.

104 ibid., vol. 11, "The Declaration of our Group in the Duma", p32.

of the Cadets within its proceedings, and the vagueness of his call for struggle outside those proceedings.[105] Then in a major article written in late May Lenin returned to his earliest criticisms of abstraction and passivity in a trenchant polemic against the principles underlying Plekhanov's whole approach to parliamentary bodies.[106]

This polemical reiteration of an interventionist interpretation of Marxism was deepened over June as the Mensheviks moved towards supporting a government based on the Duma, and hence dominated by Cadets. Indeed this polemic can be seen as a new generalisation in his critique of the Mensheviks, as well as a consolidation of earlier insights into the determinist premises underlying reformism. The culmination of this polemic came in late June with two articles, "Yes-men of the Cadets"[107] and "Once again about the Duma Cabinet".[108] In the latter article Lenin summarised his view of the political assumptions underlying the Mensheviks" position, as well as the consequences of these assumptions:

> "We must choose" – this is the argument the opportunists have always used to justify themselves, and they are using it now... To what conclusion does this argument inevitably lead? To the conclusion that we need no revolutionary programme, no revolutionary party, and no revolutionary tactics...
>
> What is the main flaw in these opportunist arguments? It is that *in fact* they substitute **the bourgeois theory of "united", "social" progress for the socialist theory of the class struggle as the only** *real* **driving force of history**. According to the theory of socialism...the real driving force of history is the revolutionary class struggle; **reforms are a subsidiary product of this struggle, subsidiary because they express unsuccessful attempts to weaken, to blunt this struggle**, etc. According to the theory of bourgeois philosophers, the driving force of progress **is the unity of all elements in society who realise the "imperfections" of certain of its institutions**.[109] [my emphasis in bold, italics in original]

The organisational tasks of consolidation that Lenin now posed for Social

---

105 ibid., vol. 10, "Bad Advice", pp444-9.

106 ibid., "How Comrade Plekhanov Argues About Social-Democratic Tactics", pp471, 475-6, 479.

107 ibid., vol. 11, "Yes-Men of the Cadets", pp64-8.

108 ibid., "Once Again About the Duma Cabinet", pp69-73.

109 ibid, pp69-71.

Democratic activists flowed from the need for propaganda through the medium of the Duma. Thus, with the exception of an article written in the wake of the early June peak of struggle, he did not again call for measures directly associated with insurrection.[110] Rather, the propaganda tasks associated with "mustering forces" of the proletariat came to more and more predominate in his writing.

By mid-year, as it became clear that the revolution was being contained from the countryside, Lenin posed the task of forming a revolutionary bloc with the peasantry in greater and greater detail.[111] This task could not be undertaken directly by the Bolshevik activists, still relatively few in number and largely confined to the urban areas. Rather it became a matter of arguing for the peasant-based party in the Duma, the Trudoviks, to break from the Cadets and form an alliance with the Social Democratic fraction. For such a Duma alliance to form it was also necessary for the Mensheviks, who dominated the Social Democratic fraction in the Duma, to break from the Cadets and recognise the revolutionary potential of the peasantry. As a result, it was necessary for Lenin to make a critique of the Mensheviks' determinist understanding of the revolution's progress, and in particular to justify the potential role of the peasantry in an anti-tsarist coalition.

In waging his campaign against the tendency of the Mensheviks to "tail" the Cadets in the Duma, Lenin sought to fully implement the "democratic centralist" structure adopted at the Fourth Congress. Yet, as he had feared, most of his attention was taken up with disputes of interpretation within the now deeply divided Social Democratic movement. Thus on 20 May he criticised a circular from the Menshevik dominated Central Committee which sought to limit discussion of party policy – no doubt in view of the evident opposition to the official party policy now being pursued in the Duma. This circular also sought to limit the discipline with which action should be carried out – almost certainly in the expectation of a new more revolutionary policy being adopted in the near future.[112] On 1 June he reiterated the position, argued earlier in the year, that all members should be involved in the resolution of the Duma policy and that delegates to the forthcoming St. Petersburg Conference should be elected on the basis of their declared position on this issue.[113] Late in the month he also returned to his earlier arguments concerning the need for leadership accountability and organisational openness.[114]

---

110 ibid., "Unity!", p22.

111 ibid., vol. 10, "The Peasant, or 'Trudovik', Group and the R.S.D.L.P.", p413.

112 ibid., "Freedom to Criticise and Unity of Action", pp442-3.

113 ibid., "Let the Workers Decide", p504.

114 ibid., vol. 11, "Among Newspapers and Periodicals", p75.

It may be argued that Lenin's position at this time was largely an opportunistic one – as a leader in opposition it was in his own interest to have the greatest organisational openness through which to win undecided elements to his strategy. Yet these structural positions were also the outcome of his long-held views on party centralism and responsibility, and were related to the context of an upsurge that he thought would deepen into a full-blown revolutionary crisis. In such a crisis, Social Democracy would be fully mobilised and return very sharply and completely to an "activist" model of party organisation.

10 July 1906–3 June 1907: A further retreat towards an "intelligentsia", but still within the "activist" approach to party organisation

For the labour movement and Social Democracy the period between dissolution of the First and Second Dumas substantially repeated the cycle of recovery between the end of the Soviet and the dissolution of the First Duma. However in this second historical cycle there were significant variations from the first. The labour movement did recover over the second half of 1906 and burst into struggle in early 1907. Yet this recovery was even more constrained than that earlier, and the new upsurge was largely confined to symbolic political protests. As a result the Duma became even more central to Lenin's perspectives on party organisation. In these constrained circumstances the Bolsheviks made a limited recovery in the latter half of 1906, even though they were hindered by their inability to give a lead in major struggles. Then over the first half of 1907 their support for Lenin's turn to propaganda through the Duma allowed the faction to make major gains among the embittered labour movement activists.

Lenin's views on Social Democratic organisation reflected the contradictory and halting decline of the revolution. Responding to the deteriorating circumstances for the workers' movement, he more and more returned to elements of his former "intelligentsia" approach, yet still refused to definitively abandon the prospect of a party of "activists" whose consciousness had been raised in mass struggle. Thus in the wake of the First Duma dissolution he expected a new upsurge, yet also argued for participation in any forthcoming Duma elections, should these be held. Over the second half of 1906, it became clear how limited the revival of the labour movement would be, and he focused more and more on tasks of propaganda – albeit still related to daily events and hence addressed to worker leaders as "activists".

From the end of 1906 Lenin's attention was focused almost entirely on the Second Duma elections and proceedings. He still saw Social Democrats as "activists", but now more than ever saw consciousness being established through the exposure of classes via the medium of parliamentary debate, rather than in direct confrontation. In making such exposures Lenin continued his polemic against the deepening reformism of the Mensheviks, and returned to the role of "party spirit" in guiding organisational behaviour. Yet this shift still did not amount to a return to a model of the party as an "intelligentsia". For over the period of the Second Duma there was still the prospect of mass struggle, and consequently issues of principle continued to be expressed as disputes over tactics between the leading labour movement "activists".

Second half of 1906–early 1907

In the months following the Duma dissolution, as following the repression of the Soviet, Lenin was compelled to return to the defence of the possibility of successful insurrection. Thus he argued that the prospect for revolution was not finished, but on the contrary improved by the loss of constitutional illusions within the anti-tsarist movement.[115] In doing so he restated yet again, in fact was more emphatic than ever about, the role of major political events in raising the consciousness of the mass of workers. However in a substantial and significant revision of his earlier expectation this advance would now be through a process of stages rather than directly:

> The logic of life is stronger than the logic of textbooks on constitutional law. **Revolution teaches**... The people has gained – they will say – by losing one of its illusions... – all these are events of serious political significance; **they all mark stages in the revolutionary development of the *people*...** Cast a general glance at the main stages of the great Russian revolution and you will see how, ***through experience,* the people, step by step, approached the slogan of a Constituent Assembly.**[116] [my emphasis in bold, italics in original]

These declarations from Lenin's initial response to the Duma dissolution were repeated in more measured terms in subsequent articles.[117] Consistent with Lenin's renewed expectation of generalised class consciousness, most of his discussion of party tasks concerned the immediate lead of labour movement activists in decisive confrontation with the state. Thus in his initial

---

115 ibid., "Before the Storm", p135.

116 ibid., "The Dissolution of the Duma and the Tasks of the Proletariat", p112-4.

117 ibid., "Before the Storm", pp135, 137, "The Political Crisis and the Bankruptcy of

response to the Duma dissolution he suggested that the possibility of joint action by all anti-tsarists was increasing[118] and proposed the formation of a "military organisation".[119] In subsequent articles Lenin declared that "[a]n explosion is inevitable and may be near at hand".[120] Reinforcing this position, Lenin used a review of the Moscow uprising to criticise passivity in winning over troops, and repeated his perennial criticism that at a decisive moment leaders lagged behind the mass of workers.[121] Perhaps the most striking evidence of Lenin's return to direct struggle in party tasks was his response to the emergence of guerrilla warfare:

> On the whole, we consider that the instigation of guerrilla warfare in Russia after the dissolution of the Duma *is a gain.* A ruthless guerrilla war of extermination against the government's perpetrators of violence appears to us *to be timely and expedient.*[122] [my emphasis]

Such an aggressive approach was counterposed to an attitude among other Social Democrats, most notably the Mensheviks, of "a proud smugness and a self-exalted tendency to repeat phrases learned by rote in early youth about anarchism, Blanquism and terrorism".[123] Yet even within this return to party tasks of leadership in mass struggle, Lenin also considered the possibility of an approach focused on propaganda in a series of subsidiary articles. He did so primarily through his defence of participation in elections for the Second Duma, should these be held. Such a course flowed from the conclusion he had reached, and which he now repeated, concerning the role the sessions of the First Duma had played in raising consciousness:

> History has ruthlessly confuted [sic] all constitutional illusions and all "faith in the Duma"; *but history has undoubtedly proved that institution is of some, although modest, use to the revolution as a platform for agitation,* for exposing the true "inner nature" of the political parties, etc.[124] [my emphasis]

Opportunist Tactics", p150.

118 ibid., "The Dissolution of the Duma and the Tasks of the Proletariat", p131.

119 ibid., p126.

120 ibid., p139.

121 ibid., "Lessons of the Moscow Rising", pp. 173-5.

122 ibid., "The Events of the Day", p168.

123 ibid., "Guerrilla Warfare", p221.

124 ibid., "The Boycott", p145.

By October, the balance of Lenin's understanding of consciousness and tasks had been reversed in the absence of any generalised protest against the dissolution of the First Duma in July. Thus in an article on the Cadet Party Congress, Lenin spoke of the new upsurge as a possibility, rather than the certainty that had been his judgement earlier.[125] As a consequence the organisational tasks of Social Democrats again became preparation to take the lead in mass struggles at some future date rather than concrete measures for immediate insurrection.[126] Associated with this shift he came to see class consciousness being formed less and less through the impact of direct experience. With the exception of a short period after the elections to the Second Duma this drift would continue until the definitive crushing of the revolution in June 1907.

Initially Lenin's arguments had only a general focus and reiterated basic points against revisionism. Thus on 18 October he published an article on opportunism reiterating his views that this trend reflected the role of the bourgeois intelligentsia within the workers' movement, and subordinated the historical interest of the class to immediate reforms.[127] This argument was extended on 29 October, when Lenin made an analysis of the shift to the right by the Cadets and Mensheviks. Here he returned to his earliest points concerning the need for an analysis of classes that was concrete, as well as the role of Social Democracy as the preserver and defender of the Marxist tradition.[128]

From late October 1906 this general critique was narrowed to countering the Menshevik proposal to form an electoral bloc with the Cadets in the Duma.[129] Such a bloc was associated with a plan to convert Social Democracy into a reformist party or "Labour Congress".[130] These proposals could be seen as representing in practice the tactical application of the leadership of the liberal bourgeoisie in the revolution, as well as the consequent limitation of workers' struggles to economic demands, first outlined in the Economist *Credo*. Lenin did not immediately draw this conclusion explicitly, but his critique of the Mensheviks now became broader, and the tone of his articles returned to the trenchancy of 1904. Thus on 23 November 1906 he

---

125 ibid., "The Results of the Cadet Congress", p243.

126 ibid., p245.

127 ibid., "The Russian Radical is Wise after the Event", pp239-40.

128 ibid., "Philinstinism in Revolutionary Circles", p255.

129 Most notably in ibid., *The Social-Democrats and Electoral Agreements*, pp275-301, "Blocs with the Cadets", pp307-19.

130 For Lenin's critique of this proposal see ibid., vol. 12, "Angry Embarrassment, The Question of the Labour Congress", pp320-32

commenced a significant article:

> The sanction of blocs with the Cadets *is the finishing touch that
> definitely marks* the Mensheviks as the opportunist wing of the party.[131]
> [my emphasis]

Then on 25 January 1907 he concluded an article on the disarray within the Mensheviks after the Duma elections with the declaration:

> Part of the social democrats *has fallen under the hegemony* of the
> bourgeois ideologists... Let the workers *expel the very spirit* of
> Menshevism from the Party![132] [my emphasis]

These dramatic political conclusions flowed from what Lenin saw as the class nature of the Mensheviks, which was now being clearly exposed in the course of the electoral campaign for the Second Duma. Thus he commented in an analysis that was also published on 25 January:

> We could not even dream of better confirmation than that provided
> by the course of political events, of our constant assertion that the
> Mensheviks are the ***opportunist, petty-bourgeois*** section of the
> workers' party, **and that they are as unprincipled and vacillating as the
> petty-bourgeois in general**.[133] [my emphasis in bold, italics in original]

To defend the electoral and organisational independence of Social Democracy against the Menshevik turn in tactics to Economism, Lenin himself echoed his own earlier interventionist critique of the determinism underlying the "legal Marxists" and Mensheviks. Thus in a major article analysing Menshevik tactics, Lenin suggested a "theory of passivity" that underlay their approach to political activity.[134] This "theory of passivity" could be shown to have a similar meaning to the term "objectivism" with which Lenin characterised the "legal Marxists" in 1893-94, as well as the terms "tailism" and "organisation as process" with which he had characterised the Mensheviks prior to November 1905. This common meaning is evident in a retort to Larin,

---

131 ibid., "Angry Embarrassment. The Question of the Labour Congress", p320.

132 ibid., "The St. Petersburg Elections and the Crisis of Opportunism", pp60-1.

133 ibid., "The Social-Democratic Election Campaign in St. Petersburg", p25.

134 ibid., vol. 11, "The Crisis of Menshevism", pp 341-64. Note: Lenin here uses inverted commas around the term. The "theory" is dealt with in part II, pp348-53. The article as a whole was published on 7 December 1906 in *Proletary*, no. 9.

a prominent Menshevik publicist in late 1906:

> No, Comrade Larin, if you had mastered the *spirit* of Marxism, and
> not *merely its language,* you would know the difference between
> *revolutionary* dialectical materialism and the opportunism of
> "*objective*" historians.[135] [my emphasis]

Further evidence that Lenin saw a common underlying principle is the
parallel he drew between arguments now being made by the Mensheviks and
those formerly made by the Economists.[136] Echoing his position in *One Step...*
Lenin now made frequent references to the intellectualism of the Mensheviks
as the source of their current tactics.[137]

Yet this defence of an interventionist interpretation of Marxism did not yet
involve a full return to the model of Social Democracy as an "intelligentsia".
Certainly Lenin conceived the tasks of Social Democrats more completely
in terms of propaganda than at any other time since Bloody Sunday – thus
he uses the term "explain" repeatedly in the period leading up to the Second
Duma elections.[138] Yet this "explanation" drew on current events to concretely
expose the class nature of the parties in the electoral contest. Hence Lenin
repeated his arguments that the manoeuvres of the parties within the electoral
contest reflected their class interests,[139] and that the campaign itself was only a
respite prior to the resumption of the direct class struggle.[140]

In a parallel with the role of the "activists" in that direct struggle, Lenin
argued that Social Democrats should orient to the 10 percent of workers most
interested in the electoral contest. These leaders would be the most responsive
to party propaganda, and the rest of the working class electorate would follow
them in voting for Social Democratic candidates.[141] In a comparison with the

---

135 ibid., p351.

136 ibid., pp353, "Plekhanov and Vasilyev", p421, "The Social-Democrats and the Duma
Elections", p449, "When You Hear the Judgement of a Fool...", p456.

137 ibid., "The Crisis of Menshevism", p356, "Plekhanov and Vasilyev", p420, ibid., vol. 12, "The
Elections in the Worker Curia in St. Petersburg", p67.

138 ibid., "The Social-Democrats and Electoral Agreements", pp294-5, "A Dissenting Opinion
Recorded at the All-Russian Conference of the Russian Social-Democratic Labour Party By the
Social-Democratic Delegates From Poland, The Lettish Territory, St. Petersburg, Moscow, The
Central Industrial Region and the Volga Area", p300, "The Political Situation and the Tasks of the
Working Class, p394, "The Working-Class Party's Tasks and the Peasantry", p396.

139 ibid., vol. 12, "The Social-Democratic Election Campaign in St. Petersburg", p21.

140 See for example ibid., "Draft resolution for the Fifth Congress of the RSDLP", p135.

141 ibid., vol. 11, in "When You Hear the Judgement of a Fool...", pp456-74. Published in January
1907 as a pamphlet.

language used earlier in leading the direct class struggle, Lenin now argued that in their electoral propaganda the Bolsheviks:

> must speak simply and clearly, in a language comprehensible to the masses. Without flamboyant phrases, without rhetoric, but with facts and figures, they must be able to *explain* the questions of socialism and of the present Russian Revolution.[142] [italics in original]

As outlined earlier, the Bolsheviks participated in the Second Duma elections with unprecedented enthusiasm and success. In doing so they developed an organisational structure that marked the high point of "democratic centralism" to that time. In turn Lenin was required to further develop the meaning of that term at decisive points of struggle. As in the case of the political paper he counterposed Social Democratic decision-making to that in bourgeois society:

> The bourgeois parties settle big political questions from case to case by the simple ruling of *one or other party "authority"*, which *secretly* concocts various political nostrums for the people… Only the workers' party, when marching to battle, demands *from all its members a well considered, straight and clear answer* to the question whether a certain step should be taken and how it should be taken.[143] [my emphasis]

In a polemic on the Duma elections shortly thereafter Lenin returned to his earlier call for full and direct involvement of all members in settling the central questions of the moment:

> In order that the settlement of a question may be really democratic it is not enough to call together the elected representatives of the organisations. It is necessary that **all the members of the organisation** in electing their representatives, should at the same time *independently, and each for himself,* express their opinion on the point at issue before the whole organisation. Democratically organised parties and unions cannot, on principle, dispense with such canvass of the opinion of every member without exception in the most important cases at any rate, and especially when it is a question of a political action in which the *masses* act independently, e.g., a strike, elections,

142 ibid., "The Social-Democrats and Electoral Agreements", p294.

143 ibid., "The Workers' Party Election Campaign in St. Petersburg", p426.

the boycott of some important local institution etc.[144] [my emphasis in bold, italics in original]

Contrary to the popular and academic impression of the two antagonists within Social Democracy as open Mensheviks and scheming Bolsheviks, this extreme position on leadership responsibility and membership involvement was here, as it had been in 1903-04, a reaction against the practice of the Mensheviks. Lenin was obviously irritated at the imperious standing of Plekhanov who, holding no party post and seeking no endorsement from any party body, could set the tone of Menshevik pronouncements through statements in the Cadet press.[145] It was also a matter of distaste for Lenin that two other leading Mensheviks conducted their disputes through non-party publications.[146] The Menshevik-dominated Central Committee ignored these clear breaches of "party spirit", yet sought to divide the St. Petersburg Conference in an organisational manoeuvre that Lenin argued was an illegitimate attempt to gain factional advantage.[147] In an associated development, in some sub-districts the Mensheviks sought to have delegates elected to the Conference without discussion and representation based on the issue of the Duma.[148]

For Lenin the Mensheviks had definitively broken from Marxism through seeking an electoral bloc with the Cadets. In doing so they had raised the prospect of a split yet, contrary to the way he has been stereotyped as well as his demands in the circumstances of 1904 and the early party of 1905, Lenin now opposed such a step. He justified this hesitance on three grounds that flowed from his expectation of a new upsurge, and hence the revival of a full-blown "activist" Social Democracy. Firstly, clearly contrary to Marxism as the bloc with the Cadets was, it had only just been embarked on "unsteadily and uncertainly".[149] Indeed the Menshevik leader Martov had recently repudiated such a move. Secondly, Lenin expected the bloc to quickly shatter and be discredited among workers moving towards Social Democracy – including those activists who still accepted a lead from the Mensheviks. Perhaps of greatest significance, the formally unified structure of Social Democracy did

---

144 ibid., "The Social-Democrats and the Duma Elections", p435.

145 ibid., "The New Senate Interpretation", p333.

146 ibid., "Martov's and Cherevanin's Pronouncements in Bourgeois Press", pp262-3.

147 ibid., "The Social-Democrats and the Duma Elections", pp441-4.

148 This led to the credentials of the delegates from these districts being challenged. For Lenin's account see ibid., vol. 12, "Report to the Fifth Congress of the R.S.D.L.P. on the St. Petersburg Split and the Institution of the Party Tribunal Ensuing Therefrom", pp433-41.

149 ibid., vol. 11, "Party Discipline and the Fight Against the Pro-Cadet Social-Democrats", p321.

not prevent the Bolsheviks from pursuing their own policy in areas where they predominated – most notably in the cities of Moscow and St. Petersburg.[150] Underlying these clearly limited and circumstantial arguments was Lenin's desire to keep open the possibility of winning over the mass of Menshevik worker activists. For him such a possibility existed as long as there was even the faintest hope of a new upsurge in the revolution.

After the Second Duma elections

The results of the Second Duma elections appeared to vindicate Lenin's hopes, and he returned to arguing that a new wave of struggle reflected a resurgence of consciousness. Thus, in the immediate wake of the election results, Lenin could conclude:

> Events are moving at a pace which can only be called revolutionary...
> *Revolution is a good teacher.* It forces back on the revolutionary
> track those who are continually going astray either from weakness of
> character or weakness of intellect... The Mensheviks wanted blocs
> with the Cadets, unity in the opposition... Nothing came of it. *The*
> *revolution is stronger than opportunists of little faith think.*[151] [my
> emphasis]

Two weeks later the disturbances around the opening of the Second Duma convinced Lenin that

> "the seemingly unruffled surface of political life has concealed a quiet,
> inconspicuous, but deep-going process *in the growth of understanding*
> *among the masses.*[152] [my emphasis]

Lenin recognised the deep bitterness that underlay the election result and expected a new wave of struggle in the future. Yet in the very short term he also recognised the intimidated passivity of workers, and hence increased the role of propaganda in the tasks of Social Democrats. Thus, in stark contrast to the drift of his comments in previous moments of optimism, he now warned against premature action on several occasions.[153] Corresponding to this caution he continued to discuss tasks in terms of the preparation for, rather

---

150 ibid., pp321-3.

151 ibid., vol. 12, "The Second Duma and the Second Revolutionary Wave", pp113-6.

152 ibid., "The Opening of the Second State Duma", p152.

153 ibid., "The Second Duma and the Tasks of the Proletariat", p159.

than the launching of, a decisive struggle.[154]

In the wake of the Duma opening, relative political stability returned to St. Petersburg and was reinforced by the consolidation of tsarist rule over the rest of the empire. In such circumstances Lenin resumed his defence of an interventionist Marxist consciousness, implicitly making a further shift away from the highpoint of Social Democratic organisation as a mass of "activists". Thus on 24 February he criticised Plekhanov's call for a "responsible ministry" as "a slogan of this kind will *corrupt* not enlighten, **the minds of the people**; it will confuse, not revolutionise – *demoralise,* not educate".[155] [my emphasis in bold, italics in original] Then on 19 March he published a major article that culminated with a discussion of this demand as a case of reformism.[156] In April he resumed his critique of the Labour Congress, now analysing the conception as the product of a demoralised intelligentsia seeking to unite a non-party labour movement under the ideological tutelage of the bourgeoisie. Indeed he now went so far as to explicitly draw the parallel between the strategy of the Labour Congress and the principles enunciated in the Economist *Credo*.[157]

These polemics culminated in Lenin's substantial critique of the Mensheviks' determinist understanding of the role of the peasantry and liberal bourgeoisie in the democratic revolution. It was this extended critique which formed the core of his contribution to the Fifth Congress of the RSDLP.[158] With the revolution now in evident decline, they mark a strident return to Lenin's very earliest arguments concerning Social Democratic consciousness. In particular Lenin again laboured the need for a concrete understanding of, as well as intervention within, the class struggle. He did so against the liberal leader Peter Struve, whose current tactical position reflected the abstraction and determinism which had characterised his writings as a legal Marxist.[159]

The escalating polarisation with the Mensheviks compelled Lenin to return concretely to issues of party structure, and in particular the conduct of party leaders. Thus in late February the possibility that the Social Democratic group in the Duma would form a bloc with the Cadets led Lenin to threaten a split with the Mensheviks.[160] This implacable opposition to those who led

154 ibid., "The Bolsheviks and the Petty Bourgeoisie", p180.

155 ibid., "On the Tactics of Opportunism", p177.

156 See points (4) and (5), ibid., "How Not to Write Resolutions" pp236-9.

157 ibid., "Angry Embarrassment", pp330-1.

158 See in particular ibid., "Speech on the Attitude towards Bourgeois Parties, May 12 (25)", which is point 6 in "The Fifth Congress of the Russian Social-Democratic Labour Party", pp456-68.

159 ibid., "The Attitude to Bourgeois Parties", pp 507-9.

160 ibid., "What the Splitters Have to Say About the Coming Split", pp170-2.

the Mensheviks as the revolution declined was in marked contrast to Lenin's earlier anxiety to maintain contact with the Menshevik worker activists when a new upsurge had been expected. Thus near the conclusion of his threat Lenin declared:

> The unity of the party is most dear to us. But the purity of the principles of revolutionary social democracy is dearer still. We submit as we have always done to the will of the majority at the Party's Stockholm Congress. We consider it imperative to carry out all its decisions. *But we demand that these decisions be carried out by the central leading organs of the Party.*[161] [my emphasis]

This severity in relation to the Menshevik leaders reflected the gravity of their actions in making a break from the "party spirit" of centralism. For Lenin the impact of such a break was greatest in the case of a formal split, and following such action the "party spirit" that formerly guided party relations no longer applied. This was made clear in his reply to charges of uncomradely polemic against the 31 Menshevik leaders from St. Petersburg, who had split from the city wide Conference in January to form a bloc with the Cadets:

> What is **impermissible** in members of a **united** party is **permissible and obligatory** for sections of a party that has been split. It is wrong to write about party comrades in a language that systematically spreads among the working masses hatred, aversion, contempt, etc., for those who hold other opinions. But *one may and must write* in that strain about an organisation that has seceded. Why must one? Because when a split has taken place it is one's duty *to wrest* the masses from the leadership of the seceding section.[162] [my emphasis in bold, italics in original]

Associated with this hostility to those leaders who breached centralism was a desire to involve the leading party activists as directly as possible in controlling local activity. Thus Lenin lauded the convening of a directly elected and ongoing St. Petersburg Conference to conduct the party work in the city. For Lenin the advantage of such a Conference was that it "makes possible and inevitable the participation of the *majority of outstanding*

---

161 ibid., p172.

162 ibid., "Report to the Fifth Congress of the R.S.D.L.P. on the St. Petersburg Split and the Institution of the Party Tribunal Ensuing Therefrom", p425.

workers in the guidance of *all the affairs* of the *entire* local organisation.[163] [my emphasis] This Conference elected a 16-person executive to direct the work of the now highly diversified St. Petersburg organisation. Such centralised and responsible structures were counterposed to a Menshevik proposal which omitted the executive body entirely. For Lenin, such a structure could have only been suitable for Social Democrats functioning as a circle of abstract propagandists within the Mensheviks' proposed Labour Congress. Thus at the height of "democratic centralism" after Bloody Sunday, the principles of centralism and responsibility underlay party relations, just as they had under the earlier far less formalised structure guided by "party spirit".

Conclusion

For Marxists, the possibility of socialism lies in the transformation of workers' consciousness – a transformation that can only occur in the generalised struggles that wrack the crisis-prone system of capitalism. Yet in periods when bourgeois hegemony is not challenged most workers respond to the physical domination of the capitalist class by adopting a version of capitalist consciousness. It is only when that domination is challenged by generalised struggle that the mass of workers will be open to the socialist consciousness that reflects their own interest. Thus, if the containment of limited struggles permits the predominance of reformist consciousness among workers, then the rise of generalised struggle creates the possibility of a fully revolutionary consciousness.

Lenin's comments on party organisation were a response to the resistance of those defending the physical domination of the old ruling class. As such they refined the intervention of revolutionaries aimed at realising the objective possibilities for workers' consciousness. In the adverse circumstances prior to Bloody Sunday, such an intervention could only be carried out by a tightly knit and clearly Marxist current within the "worker intelligentsia". More than any other leading figure, Lenin was implacable in struggling for such a party organisation through which a leadership could be prepared for the time when the explosion of class struggle, which he foresaw, actually came. Given the intensity of his focus in the adverse period it is not surprising that Lenin, perhaps more than any other Russian Social Democrat, recognised the shift in consciousness associated with the mass struggle following Bloody Sunday. In order to intervene within this dramatic, though not complete and uniform, shift in consciousness, Lenin now developed a model of party organisation which could well be analysed as the most consistently combative section of

---

163 ibid., "Reorganisation and the End of the Split in St. Petersburg", p396.

the "worker activists" leading the labour movement.

Lenin's model of party organisation as a leadership of "activists" continued the principle of conscious intervention which underlay his conception of the "intelligentsia". Consequently his views on party organisation after Bloody Sunday, just as earlier, can be analysed as a series of party tasks and structures demanded by the possibilities for raising workers' consciousness. As earlier, the fundamental task of the party was to generalise from the current workers' struggle in order to raise consciousness to that objectively possible. Prior to Bloody Sunday, that generalisation occurred mainly through propaganda to explain sectional grievances and protest within an understanding of society based on Marxist principles. After Bloody Sunday, that generalisation occurred mainly in struggle, through agitation aimed at advancing from mass strikes to a united blow against the state. Party structure now needed to open in order to incorporate a mass of radicalising workers, as well as adopt directly democratic forms of decision-making. Yet this "democratic centralism" in organisational forms was an advance on, not a break from, the "party spirit" of centralism and responsibility which had earlier guided conduct between supporters of the party. The main external expression and organisational medium of the party, the political paper, shifted from a clandestine weekly propaganda organ to a legal daily newspaper of agitation. But its active control by, as well as production and distribution through, the party as a whole continued as before.

This continuity in the underlying principle of conscious intervention is evident in the changing balance of Lenin's views as the struggle rose and fell over the course of the revolution. In January and most completely in November of 1905, as well as in mid-1906 and early 1907, Lenin responded to peaks in struggle by labouring the consequences of spreading class consciousness for party organisation. Between these high points his views became more balanced and, particularly with the decline of the revolution from December 1905, mark a trend to once again labour the necessity of deliberate intervention by a distinct Marxist current if consciousness was to be raised.

This principle of conscious intervention is evident in the form of Lenin's comments as a polemic against the deepening historical passivity of the Mensheviks. Thus the "organisation as process" principle that Lenin had criticised in the phase of the "intelligentsia" became the strategic "theory of passivity"[164] to be opposed among the "activists". In opposing the Mensheviks' dramatic slide into passivity as the revolution declined, Lenin generalised and deepened his own understanding of the determinist premises underlying

---

164 This is how Lenin summarised the tactical views of Yurii Larin, a leading Menshevik figure, in December 1906 (ibid., vol. 11, p348; part of the article, "The Crisis of Menshevism", from

reformism. As such his polemic could be seen as a the culmination of an advance in the understanding of the role of intervention which had begun with the initial conception of a "worker intelligentsia" by Plekhanov and Axelrod.

Lenin's comments on party organisation after Bloody Sunday do not, then, represent a continuity of interventionism albeit now "freed of the elitist foundation"[165] of his earlier model. And it would be a very one-sided exaggeration to say that, in contrast to his earlier views, Lenin, "having submitted himself to learning from the experience of the revolution…acknowledged the merits, occasional but fundamental, of proletarian spontaneity and initiative".[166] Rather, Lenin's comments over the mass struggles of 1905-07 represent a broadening in the role of the intervention that was first developed in the earlier period of limited and spasmodic protest. Following Bloody Sunday the base for this advance existed in the actual generalised and permanent agitation of workers. This change in the context made possible the shift of the labour leadership, the Bolsheviks' and Lenin's conception of the party from a small "intelligentsia" to a large layer of "activists".

which the citation concerning Larin's "objectivist" interpretation of Marxism, has already been cited).

165 Molyneux 1978, p60.

166 Liebman 1975, p49.

Chapter 9

CONCLUSION

For Marxists, the historical advance of human society has ultimately been generated by a material agency – the advance of the productive forces humans wield to secure their physical survival. In this materialism, Marxism is distinguished from earlier idealist views of history, which saw that progress as a result of random causes or the mental activity of an elite. In viewing this physical source as changeable, indeed inclined to advance, Marxism envisaged history as the product of mass involvement in decisive events, whereas earlier views had confined the great bulk of humans to unavoidable passivity.

In locating the source of historical progress within the advance of productive forces, Marxism identifies a physical base for human society and claims to make the study of that society a science. Yet within this study the role of human consciousness cannot be directly and simply related to the advance of productive forces, and hence the course of history cannot be determined in the way that much of physical nature can. For Marxists the scarcity resulting from the lack of productive forces is the ultimate basis for the division of human society into antagonistic classes, and the struggle between these classes makes history a process of advance and retreat rather than a linear and logical advance. Within this process the old ruling class resists the transformation of productive relations impelled by the advance of productive forces, and hence this transformation is determined by the degree to which the ruled can centralise to overcome their rulers. For this reason, a common revolutionary consciousness, the base for a centralised struggle by the ruled, becomes more decisive as the contradiction between rising productive forces and existing productive relations becomes greater, and consequently the struggle between ruled and ruling classes more severe. Yet the advance of consciousness is itself part of the process of struggle, resulting not merely from evident material reality, but also from the efforts of ruling and ruled classes to promote their own interests within that reality.

To recognise an ultimately decisive role for consciousness, and hence conscious intervention, in determining the outcome of class struggle involves rejecting an interpretation of Marxism in which history is directly and "absolutely" determined by the rise of productive forces alone. Within that view, historical advance is irresistible, and any role for conscious intervention is limited or denied. Consequently, within the transition from capitalism to socialism, the advance of the working class is no longer to be won in struggle, and hence the revolutionary party can only reflect workers' consciousness and not intervene to advance it. Ultimately the party does not lead the class in smashing the state and establishing a new structure of power, but rather takes over the existing state to administer the inevitable evolution of capitalism into socialism.

The case for an understanding of Marxism which incorporates an ultimately decisive role for conscious intervention is well supported by an analysis of the class struggle in St. Petersburg between the Emancipation (1861) and the Stolypin coup (3 June 1907). As the focus of industrial development in the Russian empire, the city encompassed a massive advance in productive forces to become one of the most modern and concentrated industrial centres in the world. In the process, one of the most educated working classes of the time was gathered within its boundaries. As such the development of the city, as well as the contradictions within that development, could be seen as the forerunner of the modern system of imperialism emerging on a world scale, rather than as a remnant of Russia's feudal heritage.

The culmination of St. Petersburg's post-Emancipation development was the First Russian Revolution, which began on Bloody Sunday (9 January 1905), and was only definitively crushed by the Stolypin coup. Taking only a general overview, it might have appeared from this conflagration that the contradictions of modernising tsarism had induced a generalised revolt without conscious intervention to lead that uprising. It might indeed have appeared that, despite the repression of the ruling class, workers were able to organise a labour movement, and then challenge for power, without the intervention of a Marxist party. Flowing from such a view, the only revolutionary role for such a party would have been to reflect, rather than intervene within, the inevitably advancing consciousness of workers. As a result, Lenin's interventionist approach to party organisation could only hinder the advance of the class to power.

Yet the apparently unconscious "spontaneity" in the overall forms of workers' advance screens a process of conscious intervention to both advance and repress the labour movement. Thus, confronted with the evidence of worker protest rising against it, the tsarist state and capitalists did not submit, but responded with greater and greater force in an attempt to crush that movement. Hence Bloody Sunday did not mark a break between periods of complete passivity and irrepressible revolt, but rather a massive acceleration and generalisation of an earlier process of advance and retreat by the labour movement. That acceleration and generalisation certainly had dramatic consequences for the way in which, as well as the extent to which, class consciousness developed among workers. Yet despite the radical difference in the forms of struggle, there was just as much a vital role for deliberate intervention in the advance of consciousness among workers after Bloody Sunday as before.

The necessary role of conscious intervention in the fomenting of workers' struggle was evident from the earliest protests in post-Emancipation St. Petersburg. Such disputes certainly reflected the rise of productive forces in the city and a consequent rise in the skill, education and self-confidence of workers. Yet these disputes, no matter how limited, required the articulation of grievances by conscious leaders. From the first, that articulation was facilitated by the intervention of educated figures "outside" the working class, through which the most aggrieved workers could understand their grievances within a general view of the world. Initially turning to radical liberals, worker leaders went on to critically appropriate the view of Narodniks, Marxists, and in the wake of the textile strikes, revisionist theorists. Clearly a certain level of productive advance was necessary for workers' struggle, and the actual rise of such struggle reflected the fulfilment of those requirements. Yet a necessary catalyst for this struggle was the development of conscious worker leaders through the interaction of aggrieved workers with a wider anti-tsarist intelligentsia. Thus the development of such a broader intelligentsia was also a condition for an advancing level of workers' struggle.

In developing a general view within which to articulate grievances these conscious worker leaders were part of a broader "worker intelligentsia". Like the workers' struggle which it facilitated, this intelligentsia ultimately resulted from the advance of the productive forces which created a demand for an educated "elite" of workers. Yet the formation of the intelligentsia also required the intervention of anti-tsarist intellectuals, who taught in Evening-Sunday Schools as a way of promoting the democratic movement against tsarism. Thus the workers' struggle in St. Petersburg, from its earliest and most basic forms, was a conscious process, not a destructive delinquency or determined advance as has been suggested by most historians of the period. Consequently, in addition to the development of industry and other economic factors, the ideological balance between revolutionaries and the tsarist state within the student and worker intelligentsia was also a vital consideration in the course and outcome of workers' struggle.

Prior to 1905, the consciously leading "intelligents" were on the whole isolated from workers in general, as well as ideologically dominated through repression, concession, and co-option by the tsarist state. In the crisis of that state after Bloody Sunday, this leadership grew to a large layer of radicalising activists with a firm base among the now mobilised mass of workers. In contrast to the "intelligentsia", these "activists" generalised their understanding through relating theory very directly to their own experience of leading struggle "within" the class. Whereas the "intelligents" had been driven into clandestinity and isolation by the state, the "activists" were able to openly organise a base of agitated workers in confrontation with tsarism. Thus the celebrated Soviet of late 1905 was the culmination of the whole history of the labour movement to that time.

Yet if the struggle after Bloody Sunday was a dramatically accelerated and generalised version of that of an earlier period, then the role of conscious leadership in determining its course and outcome was perhaps even greater than before. Thus the "activists" cohered around the traditional base of the "intelligentsia" in the Nevskii district, and it was the opening of the universities just prior to the October Strike that provided the greatest boost to the numbers and confidence of these leaders. If the generally incomplete – from a Marxist view – consciousness of the leading "intelligents" had earlier led to the fragmentation and co-option of the labour movement, then now the incomplete radicalisation of most activists prevented the Soviet from taking power, and hindered the subsequent defensive struggles which could have become the base for a new challenge to the state. Earlier abstracted issues of principle in the debate between Marxism and revisionism had divided the intelligentsia "outside" the class. The same fundamental issues divided the activists "within" the class, though now in the form of concrete questions of tactics in a mass struggle against the state.

If the formation of a conscious labour leadership required intervention "from outside" prior to 1905, then the formation of a Marxist current within that leadership was even less determined than the formation of the workers' leadership as a whole. For the consciousness of a Marxist current was even more generalised than that for the movement as a whole, and was therefore initially more "outside" the class. Indeed, before Marxism could begin to gain an organised base among the "intelligents" of St. Petersburg, it had to be developed as a theory relevant to the Russian empire within the radical democratic critique of tsarism. This was only achieved by Plekhanov some 20 years after Emancipation. Over the rest of the 1880s, the exiles around Plekhanov succeeded in fostering a growing interest in Marxism among the students and "worker intelligents" of St. Petersburg. Yet while this general sympathy for Marxism grew, so too did the alarm of the state, which repressed the Marxists as soon as they appeared to be reaching an audience of workers.

As a result, it was not until the late 1880s that the first substantial and enduring Marxist propaganda group was established around the student Brusnev. Usually criticised for its insularity and academicism, the clear political identity of the Brusnev group was a necessary base for later advance, despite the group's evident limitations. Indeed it was the pioneers of the Brusnev group who provided the organisational focus for the strategy of "agitation" in the early to mid-1890s, when Marxists for the first time centralised across the city and intervened within workers' struggles. Yet this breakthrough proved to be abortive as state pressure resulted in the dominance of Economism within the movement as a whole and confined those adhering to a traditional Marxist view to a series of sectarian groups. Then the apparent success in re-establishing a united Marxist movement around *Iskra* proved to be a further disappointment when the split at the Second Party Congress was replicated in St. Petersburg.

The containment of the Marxist movement reflected above all the pressure of the tsarist "superstructure". For if the generalisation necessary for an "intelligentsia" to lead a labour movement posed an implicit threat to the tsarist state, then the broader generalisation embodied in a Marxist current posed an even greater and clearer threat. Hence the pervading repression against the labour movement was especially severe against the Marxists. The result was that, if prior to 1905 the general labour leadership could only be an intelligentsia "outside" the class, then this was even more the case for the Marxist current. Seeking to embody the historical reality of struggle by the class as a whole, the Marxists were limited to propagating a defence of workers' potential in the absence of widespread worker protest. Yet in doing so they succeeded in preserving and refining Plekhanov's original application of Marxism to the Russian empire. The success, however, could not have been a determined process. Rather it was the result of a series of struggles waged by an exile leadership against those who wished to return Marxism to liberal democracy, or who were not capable of fulfilling the organisational measures necessary to maintain the identity of Marxism in such difficult circumstances.

If the relative passivity prior to 1905 isolated Marxism "outside" the working class, and demanded a persistent struggle to sustain its revolutionary character, then the generalised struggle after Bloody Sunday created the possibility for massive growth among the radicalising activists. In fact, the Bolshevik faction did grow dramatically – most notably during the heightened radicalism of the Days of Freedom as well as the deepening bitterness of the first half of 1907. As a result, the faction became a mass party of "activists" within the comparable transformation of the general labour leadership. Yet this transformation, like that of the general labour leadership, was very far from being direct and determined.

The preservation of Marxism as the abstracted memory of generalised struggle had earlier been the result of intervention by Lenin and other exiles against the "spontaneous" tendency to liquidate the current into revisionism. Now the advance of the Bolsheviks was the result of a struggle for the faction to organisationally orient to the greater opportunities for intervention and advocate a strategy culminating in insurrection. Yet if his earlier intervention had been hindered by difficulties and setbacks, now many of the proposals advocated by Lenin and other central leaders were adopted only belatedly and gradually in the advances and retreats of the revolution. As a result, while the faction made an enormous advance over the course of the revolution, it failed to determine the outcome of that generalised confrontation with the state.

The formation of a labour leadership required the generalised understanding of workers' particular grievances to articulate a lead to collective struggle. The formation of a Marxist current within that leadership required the further generalisation of the experience of collective struggle to the historical reality of class society, and hence the potential of workers to seize and exercise state power. Lenin's comments on party organisation sought to generalise the results of this attempt to link collective workers' struggle to the historical possibility of workers' power. As such, his comments could only have been grounded in the current reality of workers' struggle, and sought to advance that struggle towards a political challenge to state power.

For this reason, Lenin's particular comments on organisation, for the period covered by this thesis, can only be understood as a circumstantial response to the workers' movement in the Russian empire, and particularly its focus in St. Petersburg. Yet Lenin was at the same time fundamentally committed to the Marxist potential of the working class and sought above all to realise that potential. For this reason, these circumstantial reflections were always in turn circumscribed by a principled framework that was directed toward achieving Marx's ultimate aim of workers' self-conscious exercise of power. As such, the essence of Lenin's approach to party organisation lay not in any particular formulations on structure or consciousness, as these were always contextual, but rather in the essential task of intervention within the consciousness of workers, together with the adoption of appropriate structures to complete that intervention.

Prior to 1905 the general labour leadership was confined to a section of the "worker intelligentsia" "outside" the reality of capitalist domination experienced by most workers. The Marxists, embodying a broader generalisation, were even more confined "outside" the class than the general labour leadership. Hence, Lenin's model for party organisation in such a period could only have been a politically defined intelligentsia "outside" the class. For him, Marxists needed to organise defensively as they were largely limited to propagating a view with little if any connection to the day to day experience of the mass of workers. Over a period when ruling ideas were very much "the ideas of the ruling class", Lenin refined an interventionist model of party organisation against those, from Peter Struve in the early 1890s to the Mensheviks after the Second Congress of the RSDLP, whose determinism was leading them to organisationally and politically liquidate Marxism into liberal democracy. Far from breaking with the Marxist view of the working class and its potential, it was precisely Lenin who emerged as the principal defender of that view, and consequently the principal advocate of an organisation capable of leading the class in a struggle for power when the opportunity came. Through the three cycles in this defence of Marxism, he refined a theoretical break with the determinism that had come to dominate the practice of the Second International.

The crisis of the tsarist state that both precipitated, and was then dramatically deepened by, the massacre on Bloody Sunday, transformed the nature of intervention by the general labour leadership , the Marxist current, and hence also Lenin's approach to party organisation. With the hold of ruling class consciousness now evidently undermined, the former leading labour "intelligentsia" became a large layer of "activists" "within" the class leading generalised and persistent struggle by the mass of workers. This connection between those intervening to foster collective struggle and the class as a whole reached its high point in the Soviet, a structure which united workers against the state. Within this process, the Marxist current also grew dramatically to itself become an organisation of "activists" seeking to lead the now generalised struggle in a final assault on state power. Thus the Bolsheviks grew most "within" the class during the period of the Soviet, as well as the first half of 1907 when a mass of radicalised activists sensed that the historical opportunity for power could be lost without organisation.

Lenin's comments on party organisation now reflected the possibility for Marxists to intervene among the activists "within" the class. Whereas earlier the party needed to be closed against revisionism and propagate the abstract possibility of class power, now the party had to be open to radicalising workers and agitate for the realisation of such power. Before, an influx of workers had represented a threat to the basic principles of the party; now, the realisation of those principles demanded an influx of workers. Whereas earlier the party could only have been a small part of the intelligentsia, now the party had to become the predominant section of the activists.

In the accelerated advance and retreat of workers' struggle after Bloody Sunday, the relation of Lenin's comments to the radicalisation of the leading labour activists was clearly evident. Thus his focus on the organisational consequences of the heightened struggle became deeper over 1905, and this tendency reached its peak at the highest point of struggle near the end of the year. In the halting retreat of the revolution, Lenin also made a halting retreat away from his most full-blown formulation of an "activist" party, and began leaning towards his earlier view of an "intelligentsia". It was through the process of this advance and retreat that he developed the tactical flexibility, within a framework of firm principle, with which he would come to be identified. Thus the First Russian Revolution was a "dress rehearsal" for 1917, not only in the forms and organisation of workers' struggle as well as the role of conscious revolutionaries, but also in Lenin's understanding of that role and its organisation through a party.

Footnote references

Abramov 1900, *Nashi Voskresnyia Shkoly*, Tipografiia M. Merkyshena, St. Petersburg.

Acton et al. 1997, "The Revolution and its Historians: the *Critical Companion* in Context", in Edward Acton, Vladimir Iu. Cherniaev, William G. Rosenberg (eds.), *Critical Companion to the Russian Revolution*, Arnold, London.

Andronov 1978, *Bol'shevistskaia Pechat' v Trekh Revoliutsiiakh*, Politizdat, Moscow.

Antoniuk et al. 1979-91, *Perepiska V.I. Lenina i pukovodimykh im uchrezhdenii RSDRP s partiinymi organizatsiiami 1905-1907 gg.*

Ascher 1986, "Soviet historians and the revolution of 1905", in Francois-Xavier Coquin, Céline Gervais-Francelle (eds.), *1905, La Première Révolution Russe*, La Sorbonne/Institut D'Etudes Slaves, pp475-96.

Ascher 1988, *The Revolution of 1905*, 2 vols., Stanford University Press, Stanford.

Baron 1963, *Plekhanov, The Father of Russian Marxism*, Stanford University Press, Stanford.

Bater 1976, *St. Petersburg, Industrialization and Change*, Edward Arnold, London.

Blackburn 1991, "Fin de Siecle: Socialism after the Crash", *New Left Review*, no. 185, January-February, pp5-66.

Blackwell 1968, *The Beginnings of Russian Industrialization, 1800-1860*, Princeton University Press, Princeton.

Blackwell 1970, *The Industrialization of Russia*, Thomas Y Crowell, New York.

Bondarevskaia 1975, *Peterburgskii Komitet RSDRP v Revoliutsii 1905-1907 gg.*, Lenizdat, Leningrad.

Bondarevskaia et al. 1982, *V.I. Lenin i Piterskie Rabochie 1893-1924*, Lenizdat, Leningrad.

Bondarevskaia et al. 1986, *Peterburgskii Komitet RSDRP, Protokoly i materialy zasedanii, Iul' 1902-febral' 1917*, Lenizdat, Leningrad.

Bonnell 1983, *Roots of Rebellion. Workers' Politics and Organizations in St. Petersburg and Moscow, 1900-1914*, University of California Press, Berkeley.

Brusnev 1923, "Vosniknovenie perbykh sotsial-demodraticheskikh organizatsii", *Proletarskaia Revoliutsiia*, vol. 14, no. 2, pp17-32.

Bukharin 1976, *Imperialism and World Economy*, 2nd impression, Merlin, London.

Burns 1982, *The Marxist Reader*, Avenel Books, New York.

Callinicos 1983, *The Revolutionary Ideas of Karl Marx*, Bookmarks, London.

Callinicos 1989, *Against Postmodernism*, Polity Press, Cambridge.

Callinicos 1996, *Party and Class*, (2nd edition), Bookmarks, London.

Carew Hunt 1954, *Marxism Past and Present*, Geoffrey Bles, London.

Carew Hunt 1957, *The Theory and Practice of Communism*, Geoffrey Bles, London.

Cliff 1975-78, *Lenin*, 4 vols., Pluto Press, London.

Cliff 1988, *State Capitalism in Russia*, Bookmarks, London.

Cliff, 1989-99, *Trotsky*, 4 vols., Bookmarks, London.

Conquest 1972, *Lenin*, Fontana, London.

Dan 1964, *The Origins of Bolshevism*, Secker and Warburg, London.

Davidheiser 1990, "The world economy and mobilizational dictatorship: Russia's transition, 1846-1917", PhD, Duke University.

Diakin et al. 1972, *Istoriia Rabochikh Leningrada, Tom Pervyi*, 1703-febral' 1917, «Nauka», Leningrad.

Falkus 1972, *The Industrialization of Russia, 1700-1914*, Macmillan, London.

Gatrell 1986, *The Tsarist Economy, 1850-1917*, B.T. Batsford, London.

Gatrell 1994, *Government, industry and rearmament in Russia, 1900-1914*, Cambridge University Press, Cambridge.

Gavrilov 1933, *Ocherki po Istorii Vyborskoi Partorganizatsii*, Lenizdat, Leningrad.

Geary 1987, *Karl Kautsky*, Manchester University Press, Manchester.

Getzler 1967, *Martov. A Political Biography of a Russian Social Democrat*, Melbourne University Press, Parkville.

Girault et al. 1974, *Sur 1905*, Editions Champ Libre, Paris.

Gurevich 1939, "My chasto obsuzhali s uchashchimisia voprosy prepodavaniia", in *Shkola vzroslykh*, no. 1., pp38-40.

Guroff 1970, "The State and Industrialization in Russian Economic Thought 1909-1914", PhD., Princeton University.

Haimson and Tilly (eds.) 1989, *Strikes, wars, and revolutions in an international perspective*, Cambridge University Press, Cambridge.

Harding 1976, "Lenin and his Critics: Some Problems of Interpretation", *European Journal of Sociology*, vol. XVII, pp366-83.

Harding 1977-81, *Lenin's Political Thought*, 2 vols., Macmillan, London.

Harding 1996, *Leninism*, Macmillan, London.

Harding 1999, "Lenin as Doctrinaire: Ripe and Unripe Time", in Ian D. Thatcher (ed.), *Regime and Society in Twentieth-Century Russia*, MacMillan, London.

Harding (ed.) 1983, *Marxism in Russia*, Cambridge University Press, Cambridge.

Harman 1986, "Base and Superstructure", *International Socialism*, series 2, no. 32, Summer, pp3-44.

Haynes, "Social History and Russian Revolution", in Rees (ed.) 1998, pp57-80.

Hoare and Smith 1971, *Selections from the Prison Notebooks of Antonio Gramsci*, International Publishers, New York.

Hogan 1993, *Forging Revolution*, Indiana University Press, Bloomington/Indianapolis.

Ivanov 1966, *Rabochii klass i rabochee dvizhenie v Rossii, 1861-1917*, Nauk, Moscow.

Jakubowski 1990, *Ideology and Superstructure in Historical Materialism*, Pluto Press, London.

Kaiser 1987, *The Workers' Revolution in Russia, 1917. The View from Below*, Cambridge University Press, Cambridge.

Keep 1963, *The Rise of Social Democracy in Russia*, Clarendon Press, Oxford.

Kochakov (ed.) 1956, *Ocherki Istorii Leningrada*, vol. 2, Izdatel'stvo Akademii Nauk SSSR.

Kochakov (ed.) 1957, *Ocherki Istorii Leningrada*, vol. 3, Izdatel'stvo Akademii Nauk SSSR.

Kreidlina 1970, "Deiatel'nost", Peterburgskogo Komiteta Bol'shevikov po Rasprosraneniiu i Propagande Proizvedenii V.I. Lenina Nakanune i v Khode Pervoi Russkoi Revoliutsii (1903-07 gg.), Avtoreferat Dissertatsii na soisskanie uchenoi stepeni dandidata istoricheskikh nauk, Leningrad.

Kudelli 1939, "Dom no. 65 po shlissel'burgskomy trakty", *Shkola vzroslykh*, no. 1, pp34-7.

Lane 1981, *Leninism: a sociological interpretation*, Cambridge University Press, Cambridge.

Le Blanc 1990, *Lenin and the Revolutionary Party*, Humanities Press International, New Jersey.

Lenin, *Collected Works* 1977-78, vols. 1-12, fourth edition, fourth printing, Progress Press, Moscow.

Liebman 1975, *Leninism under Lenin*, Merlin, London.

Listovki Peterburgskikh Bolshevikov 1902-1917, Tom Pervyi 1902-1907, OGIZ Gosudarstvennoe Isdatel'stvo Politicheskoi Literatury, Leningradskii Institut Istorii VKP (b), Moscow-Leningrad, 1939.

Lukács 1971, *History and Class Consciousness*, Merlin, London.

McKean (ed.) 1990, *St Petersburg between the Revolutions*, Yale University Press, New Haven/London.

McKean 1992, *New Perspectives in Modern Russian History*, MacMillan, London.

Marx and Engels 1977, *Manifesto of the Communist Party*, Progress Press, Moscow.

Marx and Engels, *Collected Works* 1975-, Lawrence and Wishart, London.

Mel'nikov 1975, *Khranitel' partiinykh tain*, Politizdat, Moscow.

Meyer 1964, *Communism*, Random House, New York.

Meyer 1970, *Marxism: The Unity of Theory and Practice*, Harvard University Press, Cambridge.

Meyer 1972, *Leninism*, Praeger, New York.

Mikhailov 1995, "Peterburgskii Soviet Bezrabothykh i rabochee dvizhenie v 1906-1907" gg, "Avtoreferat dissertatsii nasoiskanie uchenoi stepeni kandidata istoricheskikh nauk", Saint Petersburg.

Molyneux 1978, *Marxism and the Party*, Pluto Press, London.

Molyneux 1981, *Leon Trotsky's Theory of Revolution*, Harvester, Sussex.

Molyneux 1995, "Is Marxism deterministic?", *International Socialism*, series 2, no. 68, Autumn, pp37-73.

Offord 1986, *The Russian Revolutionary Movement in the 1880s*, Cambridge University Press, Cambridge.

Pateman (ed.) 1972, *Counter Course*, Penguin, London.

Pipes 1963, *Social Democracy and the St. Petersburg Labor Movement, 1885-1897*, Harvard University Press, Cambridge.

Pipes 1990, *The Russian Revolution*, Alfred A. Knopf, New York.

Potolov (ed.) 1997, *Rabochie i intelligentsiia Rossii v epohky peform i revoliutsii 1861-febral'* 1917 g., St. Petersburg Branch Institute of Russian History/«Blits», St. Petersburg.

Rees 1998, *The Algebra of Revolution*, Routledge, London.

Rees (ed.) 1998, *Essays on Historical Materialism*, Bookmarks, London.

Rozanov 1976, *Obukhovtsy*, Lenizdat, Leningrad.

Rubanov 1982, *Krasnaia papka*, Lenizdat, Leningrad.

Sablinsky 1976, *The Road to Bloody Sunday*, Princeton University Press, Princeton.

Sassoon 1987, *Gramsci's Politics* (2nd edition), University of Minnesota Press, Minneapolis.

Schapiro 1970, *The Communist Party of the Soviet Union* (2nd edition), Eyre and Spottiswoode, London.

Schneiderman 1976, *Sergei Zubatov and Revolutionary Marxism*, Cornell University Press, Ithaca.

Schwarz 1967, *The Russian Revolution of 1905: the workers' movement and the formation of Bolshevism and Menshevism*, The University of Chicago Press, Chicago.

Service 1979, *The Bolshevik Party in Revolution: A Study in Organizational Change 1917-1923*, Macmillan, London.

Service 1985, *Lenin: A Political Life*, vol. 1, Indiana University Press, Bloomington.

Share 1987, *The Central Workers' Circle of St. Petersburg: A Case Study of the "Workers' Intelligentsia"*, Garland Publishing, New York/London.

Shaw 1975, *Marxism and Social Science*, Pluto Press, London.

Shub 1976, *Lenin*, Penguin, London.

Shuster 1976, *Peterburgskie rabochie v 1905-07 gg.*, Lenizdat, Leningrad.

Smith 1983, *Red Petrograd: revolution in the factories 1917-1918*, Cambridge University Press, Cambridge.

Smith 1994, "Writing the History of the Russian revolution after the Fall of Communism", *Europe-Asia Studies*, vol. 46, no. 4, pp563-78.

Spirin (ed.) 1984, *Na Barrikadakh, Vospominaniia uchastnikov revoliutsii 1905-1907 gg. v Peterburge*, Lenizdat, Leningrad.

Suny 1983, "Toward a Social History of the October Revolution", *American Historical Review*, vol. 88, no. 1, February, pp31-52.

Suny 1994, "Revision and Retreat in the Historiography of 1917: Social History and Its Critics", *The Russian Review*, vol. 53, April, pp165-82.

Surh 1989, *1905 in St. Petersburg*, Stanford University Press, Stanford.

Tiutiukin 1991, *Iiul'skii politicheskii krizis 1906 g. v rossii*, «Nauka», Moscow.

Tovstukhi 1934, *Listovki Peterburgskogo «Soiuza Bor'by za Osvobozhdenie Rabochego Klassa», 1895-97 gg.*, Partiinoe Izdatel'stvo, Moscow.

Tretii S'ezd RSDRP, Aprel'-Mai 1905 goda, Protokoly, 1959, Gosudarstvennoe Izdatel'stvo Politicheskoi Literatury, Moscow.

Trotsky 1982, *The Permanent Revolution/Results and Prospects*, New Park, London.

Tucker 1975, *The Lenin Anthology*, W.W. Norton and Company, New York.

Tucker 1978, *The Marx-Engels Reader* (2nd edition), W.W. Norton and Company, New York.

Tugan-Baranovsky 1970, *The Russian Factory in 19th Century*, Richard D. Irwin, Ontario.

Ulam 1965, *Lenin and the Bolsheviks*, Secker and Warburg, London.

Venturi 1966, *Roots of Revolution. A History Of The Populist And Socialist Movements In Nineteenth Century Russia*, Grosset and Dunlap, New York.

Volin et al. 1969-70, *Perepiska V.I. Lenina i redaktsii gazety «Iskra» s sotsial-demokraticheskimi organizatsiiami v Rossii 1900-03 gg.*, 3 vols., «Mysl'», Moscow.

Volin et al. 1974-1977, *Perepiska V. I. Lenina i rukovodimykh im uchrezhdenii RSDRP s partiinymi organizatsiiami 1903-1905 gg*, Mysl', 7, Moscow.

Volobuev et al. (eds.) 1996, *Mensheviki, Dokumenty i materialy, 1903-fevral' 1917 gg.*, ROSSPEN, Moscow.

Von Laue 1963, *Sergei Witte and the Industrialization of Russia*, Columbia University Press, New York.

Wildman 1967, *The Making of a Workers' Revolution: Russian Social Democracy, 1891-1903*, University of Chicago Press, Chicago.

Zakharov (ed.) 1980, *Ocherki Istorii Leningradskoi Organizatsii KPSS, Tom Pervyi 1883-1917*, Lenizdat, Leningrad.

Zelnik 1965a, "An Early Case of Labor Protest in St. Petersburg: The Aleksandrovsk Machine Works in 1860", *Slavic Review*, vol. 24, no. 3, (September), pp507-20.

Zelnik 1965b, "The Sunday School Movement in Russia, 1859-1862", *Journal of Modern History*, no. 37, pp151-70.

Zelnik 1971, *Labor and Society in Tsarist Russia*, Stanford University Press, Stanford.

Zelnik 1997, "Rabochie i intelligentsiia v 1870-kh gg.", in Potolov 1997, pp464-97.

Zhuikov 1975, *Peterburgskie Marksisty i Gruppa «Osvobozhdenie Truda»*, Lenizdat, Leningrad.

Zhuikov (ed.) 1977, *Marksizm-Leninizm i Piterskie Rabochie*, Lenizdat, Leningrad.

Bibliography

Editor's note: The editor and the subeditor are not Russian specialists. We have corrected errors which occurred in footnotes and the bibliography only with an eye for accuracy. However, we have not changed any Russian language references. Readers can find the whole, unedited thesis online at minerva-access.unimelb.edu.au/handle/11343/38767.

Reference and primary sources

Lenin, V.I., *Collected Works*, vols. 1-12, fourth edition, fourth printing, Progress Press, Moscow, 1977-78.

Marx, Karl, and Frederick Engels, *Collected Works*, Lawrence and Wishart, London, 1975-.

——, *Manifesto of the Communist Party*, Progress Press, Moscow, 1977.

General Reference Material

Bol'ahevistskaia Periodicheskaia Pechat' (Dekabr' 1900-Oktiabr 1917), Bibliograficheskii ukazatel', Politizdat, Moscow, 1964.

Bovykin, V.I. (chair of editorial board) et al., *Rabochee dvizhenie v Rossii., 1895-febral' 1917 g., Khronika Vyn. 1. 1895 god*, Moscow, 1992.

Bystrianksogo, V.A., *Khronika revoliutsionnogo rabochego dvizheniia v Peterburge*, Lenizdat, Leningrad, 1940.

Dash, Barbara L., *The American Bibliography of Slavic and East European Studies for 1988*, The American Association for the Advancement of Slavic Studies, Stanford, 1990.

Egan, David R., Melinda A. Egan, Julie Anne Genthner, *V.I. Lenin, an annotated bibliography of English language sources to 1980*, Scarecrow Press, Metuchen, 1982.

Kantor, R.M., *"Katorga i SSylka" za desiat' let (1921-1930), Sistematicheski-Predmetnyi*

Ukazatel', Tipografiia Profizdata, Moscow, 1932.

Kir'ianov, Iu. I. (managing editor) et al. 1993, *Rabochee dvizhenie v Rossii, 1895-febral' 1917 g., Khronika, Vyp. II 1896 god*, «Blits», Moscow-St. Petersburg.

——, *Rabochee dvizhenie v Rossii, 1895-febral' 1917 g., Khronika, Vyp. III 1897 god*, «Blits», Moscow-St. Petersburg, 1995.

——, *Rabochee dvizhenie v Rossie, 1895-febral' 1917 g., Khronika, Vyp IV, 1898 god*, «Blits», Moscow-St. Petersburg, 1997.

Kirianov, Iu. I. and S.I. Potolov (chief editors), *Rabochee dvizhenie v Rossii v period revoliutsii 1905-1907 gg., (Materialy dlia «Khronika rabochego dvizheniia»)*, Glavnoe arkhivnoe upravlenie pri Kabinete Ministrov SSSR, Moscow, 1991.

Maichel, Karol, *Guide to Russian Reference Books*, Hoover Institution of War Revolution and Peace, Stanford, 1964.

"V. Revoliutsionnaia Bor'ba Rabochikh obukhovskogo zavoda", Tsentralnyi Gosudarstvennyi arkhiv Sankt Peterburga, fond 9672, opis' 1, delo 247, listy 1-7.

Ruble, Blair A., Vladimir Vinogradov (project supervisors), *A Scholars' Guide to Humanities and Social Sciences in the Soviet Successor States*, M.E. Sharpe, New York, 1993.

Vasilii Andreevich Shelgunov – professional'nyi revoliutsionep-marksist, uchenik V.I. Lenina/1867-1939/, Cpisok literatury, Respublikanskaia tsentral'naia biblioteka dlia slepykh, Moscow, 1967.

Vladimir Il'ich Lenin, Biograficheskaia Khronika, 1870-1924, Politizdat, Moscow, 1970.

Vol'tsenburg, O.E. (collator), *Bibliograficheskii Putevoditel' po Revoliutsii 1905 goda*, Gosudarstvennoe Izdatel'stvo, Leningrad, 1925.

Archival and Library Guides

Carpenter, Kenneth E. (compiler), *Russian Revolutionary Literature Collection, Houghton Library, Harvard University, A Descriptive Guide and Key to the Collection on Microfilm*, Research Publications, Inc., New Haven, 1976.

Getty, Dzh. A., V.P.Kozlov, *Kratkii Putovoditel" fondy i kollektsii, sobrannye Tsentral'nym partiinym arkhivom*, "Blagovest", Moscow, 1993.

Grimstead, Patricia Kennedy, *A Handbook for Archival Research in the USSR*, IREX/Kennan Institute, New York, 1989.

——, *Archives in Russia 1993, A Brief Directory, Part 1 Moscow and St. Petersburg*, IREX/State Archival Service of Russia, Moscow/Washington, 1993.

Guide to the Boris I. Nicolaevsky Collection in the Hoover Institution Archives, Part I, compiled by Anna M. Bourgina and Michael Jakobson, Part II compiled by Michael Jakobson, Hoover Institution, Stanford University, Stanford, 1989.

van der Horst, Atie and Elly Koen (eds.), *Guide to the International Archives and Collections at the IISH, Amsterdam*, International Institute of Social History, Amsterdam, 1989.

Obzor arkhivnykh materialov Baltiiskogo Sudostroitel'nogo i Mekhanicheskogo zavoda v Leningrada. /Dopolnitel'nyi/', Tsentralnyi Gosudarstvennyi arkhiv Sankt Peterburga, *fond 9672, opis' 1, delo 1, listy 1-18.*

Raskin, D.I. (chief compiler), *Fondy rossiiskogo gosudarstvennogo istoricheskogo arkhiva*, Russian State Historical Archive, St. Petersburg, 1994.

Wakefield, E., *Microform Collections in the University of Melbourne Library*, The University of Melbourne Library, Parkville, 1989.

Statements, Articles and Minutes of Local Meetings

Bol'sheviki vo Glave Vserossiisskoi Politicheskoi Stachki v Oktiabre 1905 goda, Sbornik Dokumentov i Materialov, Gosudarstvennoe Izdatel'stvo Politicheskoi Literatury, Moscow, 1955.

Bondarevskaia, T.P. (director), T.A. Abrosimova, E.T.Leikina, *Peterburgskii Komitet RSDRP, Protokoly i materialy zasedanii, Iul' 1902-febral' 1917*, Lenizdat, Leningrad, 1986.

Ivanov, L.M. (chief editor), *Rabochee dvizhenie, v Rossii v 1901-1904 gg.*, «Nauka», Leningrad, 1975.

——, *Rabochii klass i rabochee dvizhenie v Rossii, 1861-1917*, Nauk, Moscow, 1966.

"Kraskolu partii", *Proletarskaia Revoliutsiia*, vol. 11, no. 34, pp43-61.

Listovki Peterburgskikh Bolshevikov 1902-1917, Tom Pervyi 1902-1907, OGIZ Gosudarstvennoe Isdatel'stvo Politicheskoi Literatury, Leningradskii Institut Istorii VKP (b), Moscow-Leningrad, 1939.

"Proklamatsii Petersburgskogo Komiteta i Peterburgskoi Gruppy R. S.-D. R. pIanvarskikh Dnei 1905 Goda", *Krasnaia Letopis'*, no. 1, 1922, pp162-83.

Tovstukhi, I. (ed.), S.N. Valk (collator), *Listovki Peterburgskogo «Soiuza Bor'by za Osvobozhdenie Rabochego Klassa», 1895-1897 gg.*, Partiinoe Izdatel'stvo, Moscow, 1934.

Volobuev, O.V. et al. (eds.), *Mensheviki, Dokumenty i materialy, 1903-fevral' 1917 gg.*, ROSSPEN, Moscow, 1996.

310

Correspondence

Antoniuk, D.I. et al., *Perepiska V.I. Lenina i pukovodimykh im uchrezhdenii RSDRP s partiinymi organizatsiiami 1905-1907 gg.*, 5 volumes planned but only 4 published (the first three of two books each). Access was gained to the printer's copy of the fifth volume, «Mysl'», Moscow, 1979-91.

Marx, Karl and Frederick Engels, *Selected Correspondence, 1846-1895*, Lawrence and Wishart, London, 1941.

Volin, M.S. et al., *Perepiska V.I. Lenina i redaktsii gazety «Iskra» s sotsial-demokraticheskimi organizatsiiami v Rossii 1900-1903 gg.*, 3 vols., «Mysl'», Moscow, 1969-70.

——, *Perepiska V.I. Lenina i pukovodimykh im uchrezhdenii RSDRP s partiinymi organizatsiiami 1903-05 gg.*, 3 vols., «Mysl'», Moscow, 1974-77.

Perepiska cem'i Ul'ianovykh, 1883-1917, Politizdat, Moscow, 1969.

Party Meetings and Congresses

Chetvertyi (Ob'edinitel'nyi) S'ezd RDSRP, Aprel" (Aprel'-Mai) 1906 goda, Protokoly, Gosudartsvennoe Izdatel'stvo Politichestkoi Literatury, Moscow, 1959.

Pearce, Brian (translator and annotator), *1903, Second Ordinary Congress of the RSDLP*, New Park, London, 1978.

"Peterburgskii «Coiuz bor'by za osvobozhdenie rabochego klassa» (1893-1896)", *Krasnyi Arkhiv*, no. 1, 1934, pp75-117.

"Pervoe maia v tsarskoi Rossii (1892-1903 gg.)", *Krasnyi Arkhiv*, no. 3, 1937, pp164-92.

Pervyi S'ezd RSDRP, Mart 1898 goda, Dokumenty i Materialy, Gosudarstvennoe Izdate'stvo Politicheskoi Literatury, Moscow, 1958.

Piatyi (Londonskii) S'ezd RSDRP, Aprel'-Mai 1907 goda, Protokoly, Gosudarstvennoe Izdatel'stvo Politicheskoi Literatury, Moscow, 1963.

Tretii S'ezd RSDRP, Cbornik Dokumentov i Materialov, Gosudarstvennoe Izdatel'stvo Politicheskoi Literatury, Moscow, 1955.

Tretii S'ezd RSDRP, Aprel'-Mai 1905 goda, Protokoly, Gosudarstvennoe Izdatel'stvo Politicheskoi Literatury, Moscow, 1959.

Vtoroi S'ezd RSDRP, Iul'-Avgust 1903 goda, Protokoly, Gosudarstvennoe Izdatel'stvo Politicheskoi Literatury, Moscow, 1959.

Memoirs

Bedoshitskaia, Ol'ga Evgen'evna, "O Kornilovskoi shkole", Tsentral'nyi Gosudarstvennyi arkhiv istoriko-politiche skikh dokumentov Sankt-Peterburga, fond 4000, opis' 5, delo 177 listy 1-2.

Brusnev, M.I., "Vosniknovenie perbykh sotsial-demodraticheskikh organizatsii", *Proletarskaia Revoliutsiia*, no. 2 (14), 1923, pp17-32.

Dunken, I.A., "Shkola sdelala nas bortsami za sotsialisticheskuiu revoliutsiiu", *Shkola vzroslykh*, no. 1, 1938, pp43-4.

Gurevich, A. Ia., "My chasto obsuzhali s uchashchimisia voprosy prepodavaniia", *Shkola vzroslykh*, no. 1, 1939, pp38-40.

Kanatchikov, S.I., "Moi vospominanii o Smolenskoi shkole/ili Kornilovskoi shkole/", Tsentral'nyi gosudarstvennyi arkhiv istoriko-politicheskikh dokumentov Sankt-Peterburga, fond 4000, opis' 5, delo 150 listy 1-4.

Karelin, A.E., "Deviatoe Ianvaria i Gapon", *Krasnaia Letopis'*, no. 1, 1922, pp106-16.

Karelina, V.M., "Na zare rabochego dvizheniia v S.-Peterburge", *Krasnaia Letopis'*, no. 1, 1922, pp12-20.

Krasin, L.B., "Dela davno minuvshikh dnei (1887-1892)", *Proletarskaia Revoliutsiia*, no. 3, 1923, pp3-28.

Krupskaia, N.K., "Piat' let raboty v bechernikh Smolenskikh kursakh", Tsentralnyi gosudarstvennyi arckiv istoriko-politicheskikh dokumentov Sankt-Peterburga, fond 4000, opis' 5, delo 58, listy 1-15, 30/3/23.

Kudelli, P.F., "Dom no. 65 po shlissel'burgskomy trakty", *Shkola vzroslykh*, no. 1, 1939, pp34-7.

Onufriev, E.P., "Na urokakh skladyvalis' i krepli nashi revoliutsionnye ubzhdeniia", *Shkola vzroslykh*, no. 1, 1939, pp41-2.

Peres, B., "K istorii Peterburgskogo 2-go Sovieta Rabochikh Deputatov", *Proletarskaia Revoliutsiia*, no. 4 (16), 1923, pp112-6.

Samoilov, F., "Pervyi Soviet rabochikh deputatov v 1905 g." *Proletarskaia Revoliutsiia*, no. 35 (4), 1925, pp125-37.

Smidovich, I., "Rabochie massy v 90-kh godakh", *Proletarskaia Revoliutsiia*, no. 1, 1925, pp161-97.

Sulimov, "Vospominaniia obukhovtsa", *Proletarskaia revoliutsiia*, no. 12, 1922, pp145-69.

312

Tsytsarin, V.S., "Kornilovskaia shkola", Tsentral'nyi gosudarstvennyi arkhiv istoriko-politicheskikh dokumentov Sankt-Peterburga, fond 4000, opis' 5, delo 138, listy 1-5.

"Vospominaniia Chlena Peterburgskogo Sovieta 1905 goda *Anisimova I. I.* Ot Sestroretskogo Oruzheinogo zavoda", Tsentral'nyi Gosudarstvennyi arkhiv Sankt-Peterburga, fond 9618, opis' 1, delo 21 listy 38-50.

Zarubkin, A.P., "Moia uchitel'nitsa", *Shkola vzroslykh*, no. 2, 1939, pp9-12.

Secondary sources

Abramov, Ia. V., *Nashi Voskresnyia Shkoly*, Tipografiia M. Merkyshena, St. Petersburg, 1900.

Acton, Edward, "The Revolution and its Historians: the *Critical Companion* in Context", in Edward Acton, Vladimir Iu. Cherniaev, William G. Rosenberg (eds.), *Critical Companion to the Russian Revolution*, Arnold, London, 1997.

Adler, Alan (ed.), *Theses, Resolutions and Manifestos of the First Four Congresses of the Third International*, Ink Links, London, 1980.

Anderson, Thornton, *Masters of Russian Marxism*, Meredith, New York, 1963.

Andronov, Sergei Antinovich, *Bol'shevistskaia Pechat' v Trekh Revoliutsiiakh*, Politizdat, Moscow, 1978.

Angrand, Pierre, *La revolution russe de 1905*, Récherches Soviétiques, book 5 (preface), Paris, 1956.

Arutiunov, Akim, *Fenomen Vladimira Ul'ianova*, Prometei, Moscow, 1992.

Ascher, Abraham, "Soviet historians and the revolution of 1905", in Francois-Xavier Coquin, Céline Gervais-Francelle (eds.), *1905, La Première Révolution Russe*, La Sorbonne/Institut D'Etudes Slaves, Paris, 1986, pp475-96.

——, *The Revolution of 1905*, 2 vols., Stanford University Press, Stanford, 1988.

Aveniri, Shlomo, *The Social and Political Thought of Karl Marx*, Cambridge University Press, Cambridge, 1970.

Avseenko, V.G., *Istoriia goroda S.-Peterburga v litsakh i kartinakh*, Sotis, St. Petersburg, 1993.

Barker, Colin (ed.), *Revolutionary Rehearsals*, Bookmarks, London, 1987.

——, "Comments from Colin Barker" (on Chris Harman's account of base and superstructure), *International Socialism*, series 2, no. 34, Winter 1987, pp118-22.

Baron, Samuel H., *Plekhanov, The Father of Russian Marxism*, Stanford University Press, Stanford, 1963.

313

——, *Plekhanov in Russian History and Soviet Historiography*, University of Pittsburgh Press, Pittsburgh/London, 1995.

Bater, James H., *St. Petersburg, Industrialization and Change*, Edward Arnold, London, 1976.

Bazanov, M., "Bol'sheviki Metallicheskogo Zavoda v Revoliutsii 1905-07 gg. (Iz materialov po istorii partorganizatsii Vyborgskogo paiona)", *Krasnaia Letopis'*, no. 1, 1936, pp168-86.

Billington, James H., *Mikhailovsky and Russian Populism*, Oxford University Press, New York, 1958.

Blackburn, Robin, "Fin de Siecle: Socialism after the Crash", *New Left Review*, no. 185, January-February 1991, pp5-66.

——, "Reply to John Rees", *International Socialism*, series 2, no. 55, Summer 1992, pp107-12.

Blackwell, William L., *The Beginnings of Russian Industrialization, 1800-1860*, Princeton University Press, Princeton, 1968.

——, *The Industrialization of Russia*, Thomas Y Crowell, New York, 1970.

Blumenberg, Werner, *Karl Marx, An Illustrated Biography*, New Left Books, London, 1972.

Boggs, Carl, *Gramsci's Marxism*, Pluto Press, London, 1977.

Bondarevskaia, T.P., "V.I. Lenin i ukreplenie Bol'shevistkoi organizatsii Peterburga" in *V.I. Lenin i mestnye partiinye organizatsii rossii (1894-1917)*, Perm, Permskoe Knizhnoe Izdatel'stvo, 1970, pp286-99.

——, *Peterburgskii Komitet RSDRP v Revoliutsii 1905-1907 gg.*, Lenizdat, Leningrad, 1975.

Bondarevskaia, T.P. and A.Ia. Velikanova, "Peterburgskii Soviet rabochikh deputatov v 1905 gody", *Voprosy Istorii KPSS*, no. 1, 1958, pp55-71.

Bondarevskaia, T.P., Z.S. Mironchenkova and Kh.M. Astrakhan (eds.), *V.I. Lenin i Piterskie Rabochie 1893-1924*, Lenizdat, Leningrad, 1982.

Bonnell, Victoria E., *Roots of Rebellion. Workers' Politics and Organizations in St. Petersburg and Moscow, 1900-1914*, University of California Press, Berkeley, 1983.

Bornstein, Sam and Al Richardson, *War and the International*, Socialist Platform, London, 1986.

Bradley, Joseph, *Guns for the Tsar*, Northern Illinois University Press, Dekalb, 1990.

Briggs, Asa, *Marx in London. An Illustrated Guide*, BBC, London, 1982.

Brighouse, Harry, "A Reply to Smith and Mandel: Rights in Socialist Society", *Against the Current*, vol. 6, March 1991, pp35-6.

Bukharin, Nikolai, *Economics of the Transformation Period*, Bergman Publishers, New York, 1971.

——, *Imperialism and World Economy* (2nd impression), Merlin, London, 1976.

Burgess, William Francis, "The Istpart Commission: The Historican Department of the Russian Communist Party Central Committee, 19201928", PhD, Yale University, 1981.

Burns, Emile (commentary and notes), *The Marxist Reader*, Avenel Books, New York, 1982.

Callinicos, Alex, "The Rank-and-File Movement today", *International Socialism*, series 2, no. 17, Autumn 1982, pp1-38.

——, *The Revolutionary Ideas of Karl Marx*, Bookmarks, London, 1983.

——, "Comments from Alex Callinicos" (to Chris Harman's account of base and superstructure), *International Socialism*, series 2, no. 34, Winter 1987, pp122-5.

——, *Against Postmodernism*, Polity Press, Cambridge, 1989.

——, *Trotskyism*, Open University Press, Milton Keynes, 1990.

——, "Premature Obituaries: A Comment on O'Sullivan, Minogue, and Marquand", *Political Studies*, vol. XLI, Special Issue 1993, pp57-65.

——, *Party and Class* (2nd edition), Bookmarks, London, 1996.

Carew Hunt, R.N., *Marxism Past and Present*, Geoffrey Bles, London, 1954.

——, *The Theory and Practice of Communism*, Geoffrey Bles, London, 1957.

Carlo, Antonio, "Lenin on the Party", *Telos*, no. 17, Fall 1973, pp2-40.

——, "Trotsky and the Organization Problem", *Critique*, no. 7, Winter 1976-77, pp19-30.

Cherniaev, V.Iu. (chief editor) et al., *Anatomiia revoliutsii, 1917 god v Rossii: massy, partii, vlast'*, «Glagol'», St. Petersburg, 1994.

Chernobaev, A.A. (chief editor), *Iz istorii marksistskoi mysl'*, Moscow, Institut Marksizma-Leninizma pri TsK KPSS, Otdel istorii sotsial'no-politicheskikh teorii, 1990.

Cliff, Tony, *Lenin*, 4 vols., Pluto Press, London, 1975-78.

——, "The balance of class forces in recent years", *International Socialism*, series 2, no. 6, Autumn 1979, pp1-50.

——, *Neither Washington nor Moscow. Essays on revolutionary socialism*, Bookmarks, London, 1982.

——, *State Capitalism in Russia*, Bookmarks, London, 1988.

——, *Trotsky*, 4 vols., Bookmarks, London, 1989-99.

Conquest, Robert, *Lenin*, Fontana, London, 1972.

Cooper, Julian, Maureen Perrie, E.A Rees (eds.), *Soviet History, 1917-1953, Essays in Honour of R.W. Davies*, St. Martin's Press, New York, 1995.

Coquin, Francois-Xavier, Céline Gervais-Francelle (eds.), *1905. La Première Révolution Russe*, Paris, La Sorbonne/Institut D'Études Slaves, 1986.

Dan, Theodore, *The Origins of Bolshevism*, Secker and Warburg, London, 1964.

Davidheiser, Evelyn B., "The world economy and mobilizational dictatorship: Russia's transition, 1846-1917", PhD, Duke University, 1990.

Daxton, Lawrence E., "Lenin and the Working Man", *Sbornik*, no. 1, 1975, pp28-31.

Day, Richard B., *Leon Trotsky and the Politics of Economic Isolation*, Cambridge, London, 1973.

Diakin, V.S. (managing editor) et al., *Istoriia Rabochikh Leningrada, Tom Pervyi, 1703-febral' 1917*, «Nauka», Leningrad, 1972.

Donald, Moira, *Marxism and Revolution*, Yale University Press, New Haven, 1993.

Doroshenko, Nikolai, "Sotsial-Demokraticheskaia Bol'shevistskaia Organizatsiia raiona Peterburgskoi Storony vo Btoroi Polovine 1905 goda", *Krasnaia Letopis'*, no. 3 (27), 1928, pp173-91.

Edelstein, David J., "Politics Under Socialism", *Against the Current*, vol. 6, April 1991, pp23-6.

Efremtsev, G.P., *Istoriia Kolomenskogo Zavoda*, «Mysl'», Moscow, 1973.

Eissenstat, Bernard W., *Lenin and Leninism*, Lexington Books, Lexington, 1971.

Elster, Jon, *Making Sense of Marx*, Cambridge University Press, Cambridge, 1985.

Erman, L.K., *Intelligentsiia v Pervoi Russkoi Revoliutsii*, «Nauka», Moscow, 1966.

Evans, Michael, *Karl Marx*, George Allen and Unwin, London, 1975.

Falkus, M.E., *The Industrialization of Russia, 1700-1914*, Macmillan, London, 1972.

Farber, Samuel, *Before Stalinism*, Polity Press, Cambridge, 1990.

——, "In defence of democratic revolutionary socialism", *International Socialism*, series 2, no. 55, Summer 1992, pp85-96.

Fenin, Aleksandr I., *Coal and Politics in Late Imperial Russia, Memoirs of a Russian Mining Engineer*, Northern Illinois Press, DeKalb, 1990.

Finkel, David, "Defending 'October' or sectarian dogmatism?", *International Socialism*, series 2, no. 55, Summer 1992, pp97-106.

Fisk, Milton, "Why Social Context is Crucial", *Against the Current*, vol. 6, July-August 1991, pp36-7.

Flaherty, Patrick Anthony, "Lenin and the Russian Revolution, A Study on the Dialectics of Revolutionary thought and Plebeian Social Mobilization", PhD, Harvard University, 1984.

Fomicheva, L.N. (collator), *Nadezhda Kontstantinova Krupskaia* (2nd edition), "Plakat", Moscow, 1988.

Forgacs, David, *An Antonio Gramsci Reader*, Schocken Books, New York, 1988.

Gallili, Z., A. Nenarokov (executive editors) 1994, *Men'sheviki v 1917 gody, Tom 1, Ot ianvaria do iiul'skikh sobytii*, "Progress-akademiia", Moscow.

Ganin, N.I. (director of editorial collective), *Istoriia KPSS: Kurs lektsii. Vypusk 1*, «Mysl'», Moscow, 1983.

Gapon, George, *The Story of My Life*, Chapman and Hall, London, 1905.

Gatrell, Peter, *The Tsarist Economy, 1850-1917*, B.T. Batsford, London, 1986.

——, *Government, industry and rearmament in Russia, 1900-1914*, Cambridge University Press, Cambridge, 1994.

Gavrilov, I., *Ocherki po Istorii Vyborskoi Partorganizatsii*, Lenizdat, Leningrad, 1933.

Gaza, I.I., *Putilovets v Trekh Revoliutsiakh*, Gosudarstvennoe Isdatel'stvo «Istoriia Zavoda», Moscow, 1933.

Geary, Dick, *Karl Kautsky*, Manchester University Press, Manchester, 1987.

Geras, Norman, "Lenin, Trotsky and the Party", *International*, vol. 4, no. 2, 1977, pp3-8.

Getzler, Israel, *Martov. A Political Biography of a Russian Social Democrat*, Melbourne University Press, Parkville, 1967.

——, "The Bolshevik Onslaught on the Non-Party 'Political Profile' of the Petersburg Soviet of Workers' Deputies October-November 1905", *Revolutionary Russia*, vol. 5, no. 2, December 1992, pp123-46.

Gibson, Ralph, *The People Stand Up*, Red Rooster, Melbourne, 1983.

Gill, Graeme, *The Rules of the Communist Party of the Soviet Union*, MacMillan, London, 1988.

——, "Bolshevism and the Party Form", *The Australian Journal of Politics and History*, vol. 34, no. 1, April 1988, pp51-73.

Gil'gulin, M. (ed.), *Yelena Dimitrievna Stasova, Stranitsy Zhizni i Bor'by*, Politizdat, Moscow, 1957.

Girault, René et al., *Sur 1905*, Editions Champ Libre, Paris, 1974.

Glickman, Rose L., *Russian Factory Women*, University of California Press, Berkeley/Los Angeles, 1984.

Gluckstein, Donny, *The Tragedy of Bukharin*, Pluto Press, London, 1994.

Gollan, D.E., "Bolshevik Party Organisation in Russia 1907-1912", MA thesis, Australian National University, 1967.

Gordon, Maks, "Dvizheniia na Putilovskom zavode («Krasnyi Putilovets») v 1901-17 g.g.", in *Arkhiv istorii truda v Rossii*, books 11-12, pp132-48.

Gorelov, I.E. (ed.), *Bol'sheviki, Dokumenty po istorii bol'shevizma s 1903-po 1916 god byvshego Moskovskogo Oxkrannogo Otdeleniia*, Politizdat, Moscow, 1990.

Gourfinkel, Nina (tr. Maurice Thornton), *Portrait of Lenin*, Herder and Herder, New York, 1972.

Guidelines on the Organizational Structure of Communist Parties, on the Methods and Content of their Work, Resolution of the Third Congress of the Communist International, Prometheus Research Library, New York, 1988.

Guroff, Gregory, "The State and Industrialization in Russian Economic Thought 1909-1914", PhD, Princeton University, 1970.

Gusiatnikov, P.S., *Revoliutsionnoe studencheskoe dvizhenie v Rossii 1899-1907*, «Mysl'», Moscow, 1971.

Haberkern, Ernest, "On 'Leninism' and Reformism", *Against the Current*, vol. 7, March-April 1992, pp50-2.

Haimson, Leopold H., *The Russian Marxists and the Origins of Bolshevism*, Beacon Press, Boston, 1955.

——, and Charles Tilly (eds.), *Strikes, wars, and revolutions in an international perspective*, Cambridge University Press, Cambridge, 1989.

Hallas, Duncan, *The Comintern*, Bookmarks, London, 1985.

——, "Comments from Duncan Hallas" (in response to Chris Harman's account of base and superstructure), *International Socialism*, series 2, no. 34, Winter 1987, pp125-7.

Hammond, Thomas Taylor, *Lenin on trade unions and revolution, 1893-1917*, Columbia University Press, New York, 1957.

Harding, Neil, "Lenin's Early Writings – The Problem of Context", *Political Studies*, vol. XXIII, no. 4, December 1975, pp442-58.

——, "Lenin and his Critics: Some Problems of Interpretation", *European Journal of Sociology*, vol. XVII, 1976, pp366-83.

——, *Lenin's Political Thought*, 2 vols., Macmillan, London, 1977-81.

——, *Leninism*, Macmillan, London, 1996.

——, "Intellectuals and socialism: making and breaking the proletariat", in Jeremy Jennings and Anthony Kemp-Welch, *Intellectuals in Politics*, London, Routledge, 1997, pp195-224.

——, "Lenin as Doctrinaire: Ripe and Unripe Time", in Ian D. Thatcher (ed.), *Regime and Society in Twentieth-Century Russia*, MacMillan, London, 1999.

Harding, Neil (ed.), Richard Taylor (tr.), *Marxism in Russia*, Cambridge University Press, Cambridge, 1983.

Harman, Chris, "Crisis of the European Revolutionary Left", *International Socialism*, series 2, no. 4, Spring 1979, pp49-87.

——, *The Lost Revolution: Germany 1918 to 1923*, Bookmarks, London, 1982.

——, "The Revolutionary Press", *International Socialism*, series 2, no. 24, Summer 1984, pp3-44.

——, "Base and Superstructure", *International Socialism*, series 2, no. 32, Summer 1986, pp3-44.

——, *The Fire Last Time: 1968 and After*, Bookmarks, London, 1988.

——, "From feudalism to capitalism", *International Socialism*, series 2, no. 45, Winter 1989, pp35-88.

Hoare, Quinton and Geoffrey Nowell Smith, *Selections from the Prison Notebooks of Antonio Gramsci*, International Publishers, New York, 1971.

Hogan, Heather, "Labor and Management in Conflict: The St. Petersburg Metal-Working Industry, 1900-1914", PhD, University of Michigan, 1981.

——, "Industrial Rationalization and the Roots of Labor Militance in the St. Petersburg Metalworking Industry, 1901-1914", *The Russian Review*, vol. 42, 1983, pp163-90.

——, "Scientific management and the changing nature of work in the St. Petersburg metalworking industry, 1900-1914", in Haimson and Tilly (eds.), 1989, pp356-79.

——, *Forging Revolution*, Indiana University Press, Bloomington/Indianapolis, 1993.

Hoare, Quinton, and Geoffrey Nowell Smith, (eds. and trs.), *Prison Notebooks*, New York, International Publishers, 1971.

Holmes, Larry Eugene, "Soviet Historical Studies of 1917 Bolshevik Activity in Petrograd", PhD, University of Kansas, 1968.

Il'in-Zhenevski, A., "Putilovskii Zavod", *Krasnaia Letopis'*, no. 3 (36), 1930, pp192-222.

Istoriia Kommunisticheskoi Partii Sovetskogo Soiuza, Bypusk pervyi. 1883 g.-febral' 1917g., Gospolitizdat, Moscow, 1962.

Iukhneva, N.V., "Nakanune Obukhovskoi Oborony", *Vestnik Leningradakogo Universiteta*, no. 2, 1961, pp57-67.

Jakubowski, Franz, *Ideology and Superstructure in Historical Materialism*, Pluto Press, London, 1990.

Jeffreys, Steve, "Striking into the 80s – modern British trade unionism, its limits and potential", *International Socialism*, series 2, no. 5, Summer 1979, pp1-53.

Kaiser, Daniel H., *The Workers' Revolution in Russia, 1917. The View from Below*, Cambridge University Press, Cambridge, 1987.

Kalekina, O.P., *Ocherki po izdanii marksistskoi literatury v Rossii (1870-1917)*, Moscow, 1962.

Kargalitsky, Boris, "Between the Hammer and the Anvil", *Against the Current*, vol. 6, January-February 1992, pp39-40.

Keep, J.L.H., *The Rise of Social Democracy in Russia*, Clarendon Press, Oxford, 1963.

Kerzhentsev, P., *Life of Lenin*, Cooperative Publishing Society of Foreign Workers in the USSR, Moscow, 1937.

Khenderson, Robert, "Lenin v biblioteke Britanskogo Musei", *Voprosy Istorii KPSS*, no. 4, 1991, pp118-26.

Kindersley, Richard, *The First Russian Revisionists. A Study of "Legal Marxism" in Russia*, Clarendon Press, Oxford, 1962.

Kirillov, V., *Bol'sheviki vo glave massovykh politicheskikh stachek v period pod'ema revoliutsii 1905-1907 gg.*, Moscow, 1961.

"K Istorii Zarozhdeniia Biuro Komitetov Bol'shinstvo", *Proletarskaia Revoliutsiia*, vol. 10, no. 93, 1929, pp80-95.

Kitanina, T.M., *Voenno-infliatsionnye kontserny v Rossii 1914-1917 gg.*, Isdatel'stvo «Nauka» Leningradskoe otdelenie, Leningrad, 1969.

——, "'Shestidesiatniki' i dvizhenie za voskresnye shkoly dlia rabochikh. 1859-1869 gg.", in S.I. Potolov (editor in chief) et al., *Rabochie i Rossiiskoe obshchestvo*, Sankt-Peterburg, Glagol", 1994, pp17-29.

320

——, (editor in chief), N.N. Smirnov, B.I. Kolonitskii, *Intelligentsiia i Possiiskoe Obshchetsvo v nachale XX veka*, St. Petersburg branch, Institute of Russian History, Russian Academy of Science, Saint Petersburg, 1996.

Kochakov B.M. (chief editor), *Ocherki Istorii Leningrada*, vol. 2, Izdatel'stvo Akademii Nauk SSSR, 1956.

——, *Ocherki Istorii Leningrada*, vol. 3, Izdatel'stvo Akademii Nauk SSSR, 1957.

Kostin, A.F. (director of editorial board), *General'naia Repetitsiia Velikogo Oktiabria, Pervaia burzhuazno-demokraticheskaia revoliutsia v Rossii*, Izdatel'stvo politicheskoi literatury, Moscow, 1985.

Kozyrev, Z.P., V.N. Molchanov, (chief editors), *Istoriia Tyl'skogo Oruzheinogo Zavoda, 1712-1972*, «Mysl'», Moscow, 1973.

Kratkaia Istoriia Rabochego Dvizheniia v Rossii, Moscow, Politicheskaia Literatura, 1962.

Kreidlina, L.M., "Deiatel'nost", Peterburgskogo Komiteta Bol'shevikov po Rasprosraneniiu i Propagande Proizvedenii V.I. Lenina Nakanune i v Khode Pervoi Russkoi Revoliutsii (1903-1907 gg.), Avtoreferat Dissertatsii na soisskanie uchenoi stepeni dandidata istoricheskikh nauk, Leningrad, 1970.

——, "V.I. Lenin-Organizator revoliutsionnoi propagandy v vecherne-voskresnykh shkolakh Peterburga (1895-1906 gg.)", in *Vestnik Leningradskogo Universiteta*, vypusk 2, no. 8, 1970, pp75-83.

Krivoshena, Evg., "O vtorom Peterburgskom Soviet Rabochikh Deputatov", *Proletarskaia Revoliutsiia*, no. 53 (6), 1926, pp181-96.

Krupskaia, N.K., *Remininscences of Lenin*, International Publishers, New York, 1970.

Kruze, E.E., *Usloviia Truda i Byta Rabochego Klassa Rossii v 1900-1914 godakh*, «Nauka», Leningrad, 1981.

Ksenofontov, I.A., *Georgii Gapon, Bymycel i Pravda*, ROSSPEN, Moscow, 1996.

Kuraev, A.N., "Diskussiia o Sovetakh na Stranitsakh Gazety «Novaia Zhizn'» (1905 g.)", *Voprosy Istorii KPSS*, no. 8, 1991, pp71-82.

Kurochkin, B.A. and O.P.Khaneev, *Zavod i liudi*, Lenizdat, Leningrad, 1971.

Lane, David, *The Roots of Russian Communism. A Social and Historical Study of Russian Social-Democracy 1898-1907*, Royal Van Gorcum, Assen, 1968.

——, *Leninism: a sociological interpretation*, Cambridge University Press, Cambridge, 1981.

Latyshev, A.G., *Rassekrechennyi Lenin*, Mart, Moscow, 1996.

Le Blanc, Paul, *Lenin and the Revolutionary Party*, Humanities Press International, New Jersey, 1990.

Lekovich, Dragutin, "Lenin i Stalinizm", in *Voprosy Istorii KPSS*, no. 3, 1991, pp64-75.

Lenin and the Vanguard Party, New York, Spartacist Publishing Co., 1997.

Lepetiukhin, V.F. (collator), *Zaria Nadezhdy*, Lenizdat, Leningrad, 1982.

Lewin, Moshe, *Lenin's Last Struggle*, Pluto Press, London, 1975.

Liebich, Andre, "Mensheviks Wage the Cold War", *Journal of Contemporary History*, vol. 30, 1995, pp247-64.

Liebman, Marcel, "Lenin in 1905: A Revolution That Shook a Doctrine", in Paul M. Sweezy, Harry Magdoff (eds.), *Lenin Today*, *Monthly Review*, New York, 1970, pp57-76.

——, *Leninism under Lenin*, Merlin, London, 1975.

Lipilin, V.G., *Absoliut*, Lenizdat, Leningrad, 1990.

Lukács, Georg, *Lenin*, New Left Books, London, 1970.

——, *History and Class Consciousness*, Merlin, London, 1971.

Lunev, Vasilii, Shilov Stepanov, Vladimir Vasil'evich, *Nevskii Raion*, Lenizdat, Leningrad, 1970.

McAuley, Mary, *Bread and Justice*, Clarendon Press, Oxford, 1991.

McKean, Robert B. (ed.), *St Petersburg between the Revolutions*, Yale University Press, New Haven/London, 1990.

——, *New Perspectives in Modern Russian History*, MacMillan, London, 1992.

McLellan, David, *Karl Marx, His Life and Thought*, Harper and Row, New York, 1973.

Mandel, Ernest, "Liebman and Leninism", *The Socialist Register*, 1975, pp95-114.

Margolis, Iu. D. (ed.), *Novoe Revoliutsii 1905-1907 gg. v Rossii*, Izdatel'stvo Leningradskogo Universiteta, Leningrad, 1989.

Marot, John Eric, "Alexander Bogdanov, Vpered, and the role of the Intellectual in the Workers' Movement", *The Russian Review*, vol. 49, 1990, pp241-64.

Martin, Rosalie G., "Lenin's Concept of Proletarian Class Consciousness (Especially in the Period 1917-1923)", B.A. Hons thesis, University of Tasmania, 1980.

Maslov, N.N., *Istoriia KPSS, kurs lektsii, vypusk 1.* «Mysl'», Moscow, 1983.

Mayer, Robert, "Lenin and the Concept of the Professional Revolutionary", *History of Political Thought*, vol. XIX, no. 2, Summer 1993, pp249-62.

——, "Marx, Lenin and Corruption of the Working Class", *Political Studies*, vol. XLI, December 1993, pp636-49.

Mehring, Franz, *Karl Marx*, George Allen and Unwin, London, 1966.

Mel'nikov, A.B., *Khranitel' partiinykh tain*, Politizdat, Moscow, 1975.

Meyer, Alfred G., *Communism*, Random House, New York, 1964.

——, *Marxism: The Unity of Theory and Practice*, Harvard University Press, Cambridge, 1970.

——, *Leninism*, Praeger, New York, 1972.

Mikhailov, Nikolai Vasil'evich, "Peterburgskii Soviet Bezrabothykh i rabochee dvizhenie v 1906-1907" gg, "Avtoreferat dissertatsii nasoiskanie uchenoi stepeni kandidata istoricheskikh nauk", Saint Petersburg, 1995.

Minutes of the Second Congress of the Communist International, New Park, London, 1977.

Mitel'man, M., B. Glebov, A. Ul'ianskii, *Istoriia Putilovskogo Zavoda*, 3rd edition, Izdatel'stvo Sotsial'no-Ekonomicheskoi Literatury, Moscow, 1961.

Molyneux, John, *Marxism and the Party*, Pluto Press, London, 1978.

——, *Leon Trotsky's Theory of Revolution*, Harvester, Sussex, 1981.

——, "What is the real Marxist tradition?", *International Socialism*, series 2, no. 20, Summer 1983, pp3-54.

——, "Is Marxism deterministic?", *International Socialism*, series 2, no. 68, Autumn 1995, pp37-73.

Morgan, Anne, "The St. Petersburg Soviet of Workers' Deputies", PhD, Indiana University, 1979.

Murav'eva, A., I. Sivolap-Kaftanova (tr. Jane Sayer), *Lenin in London*, Progress Press, Moscow, 1983.

Murray, Patrick, *Marx's Theory of Scientific Knowledge*, Humanities Press, New Jersey, 1988.

Mushtukov, Viktor Efimovich, Petr Erofeevich Nikitin, *Zdes' zhil i rabotal Lenin*, 5th edition, Lenizdat, Leningrad, 1969.

Naarden, Bruno 1992, *Socialist Europe and Revolutionary Russia*, Cambridge University Press, Cambridge.

Na putiakh k Oktiabriu: bor'ba partii bol'whevikov za massy i demodratizatsiiu strany (Materialy nauchnoi konferentsii, 30-31 oktiabria 1989g.), Leningradskaia ordena Oktiabr'skoi Revoliutsii vysshaia partiinaia shkola, Leningrad, 1990.

Nekrich, Aleksandr, *Forsake Fear,* Unwin Hyman, Boston, 1991.

Offord, Derek, *The Russian Revolutionary Movement in the 1880s,* Cambridge University Press, Cambridge, 1986.

Ol'khovskii, E., *Proletarskii Prolog, Vospominaniia uchastnikov revoliutsionnogo dvizheniia v Peterburge v 1893-1904 godakh,* Lenizdat, Leningrad, 1983.

——, Manifest Bol'shevizma, *Leningrad,* «Znanie», 1984.

——, "Formirivanie rabochei intellingentsii v Rossii v kontse XIX – nachale XX v.", in Potolov 1997, pp77-95.

"150-letie Kirovskogo zavoda (Materialy dlia dokladov i beced)", roneod notes from the Museum of the Kirov Factory, no author or publisher given, March 1951.

Paialin, N., *Zavod imeni Lenina, 1857-1918,* Gosudarstvennoe Sotsial'no-Ekonomicheskoe Izdatel'stvo, Moscow-Leningrad, 1933.

——, "Bol'sheviki Nevskoi zastavy nakanune pervoi russkoi revoliutsii (Iz materialov po istorii partorganizatsii Volodarskogo raiona)", in *Krasnaia Letopis',* no. 1, 1936, pp157-67.

——, *Nevskaia Zastava ,* Molodaia Gvardiia, 1938.

——, "Nevskii Zavod v 1903-190 gg.", *Krasnaia Letopis',* no. 4, pp207-15.

Pankratova, A.M., *Rabochii Klass Rossii,* «Nauk», Moscow, 1983.

Pateman, Trevor (ed.), *Counter Course,* Penguin, London, 1972.

Pokrovskii, M.N., *Russia in World History,* The University of Michigan Press, Ann Arbor, 1970.

Pipes, Richard, *Social Democracy and the St. Petersburg Labor Movement, 1885-1897,* Harvard University Press, Cambridge, 1963.

——, *Revolutionary Russia,* Harvard University Press, Cambridge, 1968.

——, *The Russian Revolution,* Alfred A. Knopf, New York, 1990.

——, *The Unknown Lenin,* Yale University Press, New Haven/London, 1996.

Pospielovsky, Dimitry, *Russian Police Trade Unionism,* LSE/Redwood Press, London, 1971.

Potolov, S.I., (editor in chief), *Rabochie i Rossiiskoe Obshchestvo,* «Glagol'», St. Petersburg, 1994.

——, (editor in chief), *Rabochie i intelligentsiia Rossii v epohky peform i revoliutsii 1861-febral'1917 g.,* St. Petersburg Branch Institute of Russian History/«Blits», St. Petersburg, 1997.

——, "Peterburgskie rabochie i intelligenstiia nakanyne revoliutsii 1905-1907 gg." «Sobranie russkikh fabrichno-zavodskikh rabochikh g. S.-Peterburga», in Potolov (ed.) 1997, pp530-41.

Pustarnikov, V.F. (managing editor), *N. G. Chernyshevskii v Obshchestvennoi Mysli Narodov SSSP*, «Nauk», Moscow, 1984.

Pomper, Philip, *The Russian Revolutionary Intelligentsia*, 2nd edition, Harlan Davidson, Wheeling, 1993.

Ransome, Paul, *Antonio Gramsci, A New Introduction*, Harvester Wheatsheaf, London, 1992.

Rees, John, "Dedicated followers of fashion", *International Socialism*, series 2, no. 55, Summer 1992, pp113-26.

——, "In defence of October", *International Socialism*, series 2, no. 52, Autumn 1991, pp3-82.

——, *The Algebra of Revolution*, Routledge, London, 1998.

—— (ed.), *Essays on Historical Materialism*, Bookmarks, London, 1998.

Riddell, John (ed.), *The German Revolution and the Debate on Soviet Power*, Pathfinder, New York, 1986.

——, *Workers of the World and Oppressed Peoples Unite!*, Pathfinder, New York, 1991.

"Rol' putilovtsev-kirovtsev v sozdanii promyshlennogo i sel'sko-khoziaistvennogo potentsiala sovietskogo soiuza", roneoed document from the Museum of the Kirov Factory, no author, publisher or date given.

Rosen, Bernard, "A Balanced View: Of Lenin and Leninism", *Against the Current*, vol. 7, May-June 1992, pp45-7.

Roslova A.C., "Pervye massovye politicheskie vystupleniia peterburgskikh rabochikh", *Voprosy Istorii*, no. 2, 1956, pp88-95.

Rossanda, Rossana, "Class and Party", *The Socialist Register*, 1970, pp217-31.

Rozanov, M.D., *Obukhovtsy*, Lenizdat, Leningrad, 1965.

——, *Vasilii Andreevich Shelgunov*, 2nd edition, Lenizdat, Leningrad, 1976.

Rubanov, S. and S.Neginskii, *Krupskaia v Peterburge-Leningrade*, Lenizdat, Leningrad, 1975.

Rubanov, S., *Krasnaia papka*, Lenizdat, Leningrad, 1982.

Sablinsky, Walter, *The Road to Bloody Sunday*, Princeton University Press, Princeton, 1976.

Saralieva, Z.Kh., *"Kapital" K. Marksa i rabochee dvizhenie Rossii (1895-1917 gg.)*, «Mysl'», Moscow, 1975.

Sassoon, Anne Showstack, *Gramsci's Politics* (2nd edition), University of Minnesota Press, Minneapolis, 1987.

Schapiro, Leonard, *The Communist Party of the Soviet Union* (2nd edition), Eyre and Spottiswoode, London, 1970.

Schneiderman, Jeremiah, *Sergei Zubatov and Revolutionary Marxism*, Cornell University Press, Ithaca, 1976.

Schwarz, Solomon M., *The Russian Revolution of 1905: the workers' movement and the formation of Bolshevism and Menshevism*, The University of Chicago Press, Chicago, 1967.

Scott, Mark Chapin, "Her Brother's Keeper: The Evolution of Women Bolsheviks", PhD, University of Kansas, 1980.

Semenov-Bulkin, F., "Ekonomicheskoe polozhenie rabochikh-metallistov do 1905 goda", *Arkhiv Istorii Truda v Rossii*, book 9, pp77-98.

Seniavskii, S.L., *Rost rabochego klassa SSSR (1951-1965 gg.)*, Izdatel'stvo «Nauka», Moscow, 1966.

Service, Robert, *The Bolshevik Party in Revolution: A Study in Organizational Change 1917-1923*, Macmillan, London, 1979.

——, *Lenin: A Political Life*, 3 vols., Indiana University Press, Bloomington., 1985-95.

——, "Did Lenin lead to Stalin?", *International Socialism*, series 2, no. 55, Summer 1992, pp77-84.

Share, Michael, *The Central Workers' Circle of St. Petersburg: A Case Study of the "Workers' Intelligentsia"*, Garland Publishing, New York/London, 1987.

Shaw, Martin, *Marxism and Social Science*, Pluto Press, London, 1975.

Shelokhaev, V.V. (director of editorial board), *Pervaia Rossiiskaia, Cpravochnik o revoliutsii 1905-1907 gg.* Politizdat, Moscow, 1985.

——, (director of board of authors) et al., *Politicheskaia istoriia Rossii v partiiakh i litsakh*, TERRA, Moscow, 1994.

Sherrer, Iu., B.V. Anan'ich (eds.), *Russkaia Emigratsiia do 1917 goda – Laboratoriia Liberal'noi i Revoliutsionnoi Mysli*, Evropeiskii Dom, St. Petersburg, 1997.

Shipler, David K., *Russia, Broken Idols, Solemn Dreams*, Times Books, New York, 1983.

Shub, David, *Lenin*, Penguin, London, 1976.

Shukman, Harold, *Lenin and the Russian Revolution*, Capricorn Books, New York, 1968.

Shuster, U.A., *Peterburgskie rabochie v 1905-1907 gg.*, Lenizdat, Leningrad, 1976.

Sidorov, A.L. (chairman of the Principal Editorial Board), *Revoliutsiia 1905-1907 gg. v Rossii, Dokumenty i Materialy*, Moscow, 1963.

Simon, Lawrence (ed.), *Karl Marx*, Hackett Publishing Company, Indianapolis, 1994.

Smith, S.A., "Craft Consciousness, Class Consciousness: Petrograd 1917", *History Workshop Journal*, issue 11, Spring 1981, pp33-58.

——, *Red Petrograd: revolution in the factories 1917-1918*, Cambridge University Press, Cambridge, 1983.

——, "Spontaneity and Organization in the Petrograd Labour Movement in 1917", Discussion Paper Series no. 1, January 1984, Russian and Soviet Studies Centre, University of Essex.

——, "Writing the History of the Russian revolution after the Fall of Communism", *Europe-Asia Studies*, vol. 46, no. 4, 1994, pp563-78.

Sokolov, O.D., *Na zare rabochego dvizheniia v Rossii*, 2nd edition, «Mysl'», Moscow, 1978.

Spirin, L.M. (scientific editor, T.P. Bondarevskaia and N.I. Priimak, collators), *Na Barrikadakh, Vospominaniia uchastnikov revoliutsii 1905-1907 gg. v Peterburge*, Lenizdat, Leningrad, 1984.

Stalin, Joseph, *Leninism*, George Allen and Unwin, London, 1933.

——, *History of the Communist Party of the Soviet Union/Bolsheviks/Short Course*, Current Book Distributors, Sydney, 1942.

——, *Problems of Leninism*, Foreign Languages Publishing House, Moscow, 1953.

——, *Works*, vol. 2, 1907-13, Foreign Languages Publishing House, Moscow, 1953.

Stepanov, Z.V. (managing editor) et al., *Rabochie Leningrada, 1703-1975, Kratkii Istoricheskii Ocherk*, «Nauka», Leningrad, 1975.

Suny, Ronald Grigor, "Toward a Social History of the October Revolution", *American Historical Review*, vol. 88, no. 1, February 1983, pp31-52.

——, "Revision and Retreat in the Historiography of 1917: Social History and Its Critics", *The Russian Review*, vol. 53, April 1994, pp165-82.

Surh, Gerald D., *1905 in St. Petersburg*, Stanford University Press, Stanford, 1989.

Svalov, A.N., *Postigaia Lenina*, Akademiia obshchestvennykh nauk pri TsK KPSS, Kafedra istorii KPSS, Moscow, 1990.

Swain, Geoffrey, "Bolsheviks and Metal Workers on the Eve of the First World War", *Journal of Contemporary History*, vol. 16, 1981, pp273-91.

——, *Russian Social Democracy and the Legal Labour Movement, 1906-14*, MacMillan, London, 1983.

Sweezy, Paul M. and Harry Magdoff, "Lenin Today", *Monthly Review Press*, New York, 1970.

Tiutiukin, S.V., *Iiul'skii politicheskii krizis 1906 g. v rossii*, «Nauka», Moscow, 1991.

——, "RDSRP na Demokraticheskom Etape Revoliutsii (1905-1917 gg.)", in *Voprosy Istorii KPSS*, no. 1, 1991, pp31-41.

——, "Rossia, 1905-i…", in *Svobodnaia Mysl'*, no. 5, 1995, pp75-86.

—— (collator), *Men'sheviki. Dokumenty i materialy. 1903-febral' 1917 gg.*, ROSSPEN, Moscow, 1996.

——, and V.V. Shelokhaev, "Pervaia rossiiskaia revoliutsiia 1905-1907 gg.", in *Voprosy Istorii KPSS*, no. 7, 1991, pp50-66.

Trotsky, Leon, *The Permanent Revolution/Results and Prospects*, New Park, London, 1962 (3rd impression 1982).

——, *The History of the Russian Revolution*, Pluto Press, London, 1977.

——, *The Lessons of October*, Bookmarks, London, 1987.

Tucker, Robert C. (ed.), *The Lenin Anthology*, W.W. Norton and Company, New York, 1975.

——, *The Marx-Engels Reader* (2nd edition), W.W. Norton and Company, New York, 1978.

Tugan-Baranovsky, Mikhail I., *The Russian Factory in 19th Century*, Richard D. Irwin, Ontario, 1970.

Twiss, Tom, "Leninism Revisited (Review of Paul Le Blanc, *Lenin and the Revolutionary Party*)", *Against the Current*, vol. 6, May-June 1991, pp46-7.

Ugriumov, A.L. and N. V. Romanovskii, *Leninskaia Partiia v Revoliutsii 1905-1907 godov v Rossii*, «Znanie», Moscow, 1975.

Ulam, Adam B., *Lenin and the Bolsheviks*, Secker and Warburg, London, 1965.

Urilov, I. Kh., *Iu. O. Martov, Politik i Istorik*, «Nauka», Moscow, 1997.

Valentinov, N., *Maloznakomyi Lenin*, «Smart», St. Petersburg, 1991.

Varhall, Gregory, "The Development of V.I. Lenin's Theory of the Dictatorship of the Proletariat", PhD, University of Notre Dame, 1982.

328

Venturi, Franco, *Roots of Revolution. A History Of The Populist And Socialist Movements In Nineteenth Century Russia*, Grosset and Dunlap, New York, 1966.

Volin, M.S. (ed.), *Rabochii Klass Rossii ot Zarozhdeniia do Nachala XX v*, «Nauk», Moscow, 1983.

Volkogonov, Dmitri, *Lenin, A New Biography*, The Free Press, New York, 1994.

Von Laue, Theodore H., *Sergei Witte and the Industrialization of Russia*, Columbia University Press, New York, 1963.

Walker, Angus, *Marx, His Theory and its Context*, Rivers Oram Press, London, 1989.

Wilde, Lawrence, *Marx and Contradiction*, Avebury, Aldershot, 1989.

Wildman, Allan K., *The Making of a Workers' Revolution: Russian Social Democracy, 1891-1903*, University of Chicago Press, Chicago, 1967.

Wohlforth, Tim, "In The Grip Of Leninism", *Against the Current*, vol. 6, June 1991, pp41-5.

——, "Response to Ernest Haberkern: Revolutionary as Conservative", *Against the Current*, vol. 7, May-June 1992, pp43-4.

Wolfe, Bertram D., *An Ideology in Power*, Stein and Day, New York, 1969.

——, *Three Who Made a Revolution*, Stein and Day, New York, 1984.

Wynn, Charters, *Workers, Strikes, and Pogroms*, Princeton University Press, Princeton, 1992.

Yakovlev, N.N., *Narod i partiia v pervoi russkoi revoliutsii*, «Mysl'», Moscow, 1965.

Yegorov, A.G. (director of the editorial board) et al., *Vladimir Il'ich Lenin, Biografiia, Tom 1, 1870-1917*, Politizdat, Moscow, 1987.

Yerofeev, N. D., "Chislennost i sostav sotsial-demokratov, privlekavshikhsia k doznaniiam v 1892-1902 gg.", *Voprosy Istorii KPSS*, no. 11, 1990, pp118-33.

Zakharov, V.G. (chair of editorial collegium, Z.S. Mironchekova, collator), *Ocherki Istorii Leningradskoi Organizatsii KPSS, Tom Pervyi 1883-1917*, Lenizdat, Leningrad, 1980.

Zelnik, Reginald E., "An Early Case of Labor Protest in St. Petersburg: The Aleksandrovsk Machine Works in 1860", *Slavic Review*, vol. 24, no. 3, September 1965, pp507-20.

——, *Labor and Society in Tsarist Russia*, Stanford University Press, Stanford, 1971.

——, "Populists and Workers. The First Encounter between Populist Students and Industrial Workers in St. Petersburg, 1871-74", *Soviet Studies*, no. 26, 1972, pp251-69.

——, (editor and translator), *A Radical Worker in Tsarist Russia*, Stanford University Press, Stanford, 1986.

——, "Rabochie i intelligentsiia v 1870-kh gg." in Potolov (ed.) 1997, pp464-97.

——, "The Sunday School Movement in Russia, 1859-1862", *Journal of Modern History*, no. 37, 1965, pp151-70.

Zel'tser, V., "Iz istorii «rabochego obrazovaniia» v Rossii v nachale XIX v.", *Istoriia Proletariata SSSR*, no. 4 (16), 1933.

Zeveleva, A.I. (ed.), *Istoriia politicheskikh partii Rossii*, «Vyshaia shkola», Moscow, 1994.

Zhuikov, G.S., *Peterburgskie Marksisty i Gruppa «Osvobozhdenie Truda»*, Lenizdat, Leningrad, 1975.

—— (ed.), *Marksizm-Leninizm i Piterskie Rabochie*, Lenizdat, Leningrad, 1977.

Zotova, Z.M., "Tsentralizm i demokratiia na etape formirovaniia RSDRP", *Voprosy Istorii KPSS*, no. 3, 1991, pp112-24.

Zuckerman, Fredric S., "Political Police and the Revolution: The Impact of the 1905 Revolution on the Tsarist Secret Police", *Journal of Contemporary History*, vol. 27, 1992, pp279-300.

Index

Assembly of Russian Factory Workers (Gapon Assembly) 10-6, 250, 262
Axelrod (Akselrod), Pavel 11, 73, 100, 154n, 215-7, 225, 291

Babushkin, Ivan Vasil'evich 159, 161, 169, 169-70n
Bernstein, Eduard 7-9, 30, 30n, 56, 100, 100n
Black Repartition 147, 147n
Blagoev, Dimitri Nikolaevich 12, 17, 83n, 89n, 152, 149
Bogdanov, Alexander Aleksandrovich 185, 193, 253n
Bouncer 169-70, 174
Brusnev group 153, 153n, 155, 296
Brusnev, Mikhail Ivanovich 14, 17, 90-1, 90n, 153, 153n, 296

Central Students' Circle 90, 90n
Central Workers' Circle 14-5, 89-91
Chernyshevskii, Nikolai Gavrilovich 143-5, 143-5n
Cliff, Tony 3-6, 9-10, 10n, 14, 24n, 32n, 49-50n, 53, 53n, 59, 59n, 63-6, 63-4n, 68, 68n, 71
Council of the Unemployed 129-30, 132

Doroshenko, N.V. 188n, 193

Egorov, I.I. 169
Engels, Friedrich (Frederick) 16-7, 19, 23, 23n, 25-29, 25-29n, 48n, 67-8, 144n, 148n, 152, 221, 221n
Essen, M.M. 188n, 191n, 193, 195, 195n

Federated Committee (of Bolsheviks and Mensheviks) 187, 190-1, 193, 199-200, 210
Fighting Groups 201

Gapon Assembly (Assembly of Russian Factory Workers) 10-6, 250, 262
Gapon, Sergei 105-6, 105n, 113n, 118, 118n, 131, 252
Group of 20 165
Gusev, Sergei Ivanovich 180-2n, 181, 185, 253n

Harding, Neil 47n, 49-50n, 51-2, 52n, 59, 59n, 63, 73-4, 73-4n, 79n, 81n, 88n, 92n, 95n, 99n, 154n, 159-60n, 162-3n
Harman, Chris 8, 9n, 24-5n, 32n, 34n, 63n
Hegel, Georg Wilhelm Friedrich 25,

25-26n, 28, 52n, 144n, 270

Iskra 7, 7n, 19, 104, 126n, 150, 166-71, 168-70n, 173n, 216, 224, 224-5n, 227, 230, 232, 234-5, 234-36n, 237, 240, 242n, 244n, 296

Kalinin, M.I. 10, 99
Kautsky, Karl 4, 7-9, 16, 19, 26-7, 29-31, 30n, 33n, 71, 228, 241n, 243
Khalturin, Stepan 11-2, 12n, 17, 79-81, 80n, 83n
Knuniants, Bogdan Minaevich (also known as Bogdan Radin) 193, 193n, 195n, 198
Krasin, Leonid Borisovich 153, 153n, 155-6, 156n, 219
Kremer, Arkadi 154n, 216-7
Krupskaia, Nadezhda 86, 153n, 159-61, 161n, 170-1, 170-1n, 173, 173-4n, 181n, 187-8n

Land and Freedom 144, 147-8, 147n
Larin, Yurii 282-3, 290-1n
Lassalle, Ferdinand 149, 149n
Le Blanc, Paul 50n, 53-4, 60n, 69n
Liberation of Labour 147-9, 151-2, 162, 164
Liebman, Marcel 5, 47n, 49-50n, 57, 59-65, 59-60n, 69n, 71, 112n, 180n, 219n, 291n
Lukács, György 30, 31n
Luxemburg, Rosa 8, 16, 28, 31, 33n, 61, 63, 243, 243n, 245, 245n

Martov, Julius 15, 19, 154-7, 154-5n, 169, 171, 216-7, 243, 285, 285n
Marx, Karl 4-6, 15-17, 19, 23-31, 23-9n, 31n, 32, 34, 34n, 36, 38, 42, 45-6, 48, 49-50n, 50, 52, 52n, 54-8, 55n, 60-1, 63-4, 67-8, 71, 71n, 73-5, 84, 93, 106,

142, 144, 144n, 146, 148-9, 148n, 151-2, 214, 221, 225-6, 228-9, 231, 249, 257, 297
Metal Workers' Union 135-6
Meyer, Alfred G. 4, 49-50n, 54-8, 54-6n
Molyneux, John 3, 5-6, 25n, 27-32n, 50n, 53, 60n, 66-72, 257n, 291n

Narodnaia Volia (The People's Will) 12-3, 15, 17, 232, 270
Nekrasov, N.A. 144
Nemtsov, N.M. 192, 193n, 198
Northern Union (of Russian Workers) 11, 13, 79-81, 79-80n, 83, 83n, 89, 106, 148
Novaia Zhizn' 189n, 193n, 194

Obnorskii, Victor Pavlovich 11-2, 79, 147n

Parvus, Alexander Lvovich 190, 270
Pavlov, Platon 85n, 144
People's Universities 138
Petersburg Committee 19-20, 166, 168-70, 170n, 172, 172n, 174, 174n, 180-4, 183-4n, 186, 186-7n, 189n, 190-5, 191n, 195-6n, 197-202, 198-9n, 201-4n, 204-8, 204n, 206n, 208-11n, 210, 235, 242, 259n, 269, 275n
Petersburg Group (of the Party of Russian Social Democrats) 12, 174, 174n, 196n
Petersburg Workers' Leaflet 162
Pipes, Richard 47n, 49n, 53n, 95, 95-7n, 99-100n
Plekhanov, Georgii 10-1, 13-4, 16-19, 61, 73, 99, 147-50, 148n, 151n, 152-4, 154-5n, 158, 162, 165, 171, 173, 215-7, 219, 221, 225, 227, 231, 235n, 240, 243, 245, 270-1, 275-6,

276n, 283n, 285, 287, 291, 295-6
Proletarii 188, 210
Proudhon, Pierre Joseph 69
Rabochaia Mysl' (Workers' Thought) 10, 97-100, 100n, 104
Radchenko, Stepan Ivanovich 14, 18, 91, 91n, 155-6, 155-6n, 159-63, 167-8, 168-70n, 219
Radin, Bogdan (pseudonym of Bogdan Minaevich Knuniants) 193, 193n, 195n, 198
RSDLP (Russian Social Democratic Labour Party) 16, 19, 24n, 26, 70, 89, 104-5, 104n, 126n, 134-5, 137, 150, 162-3, 167, 171, 173n, 180n, 185, 188n, 190, 193, 198-9, 200n, 202n, 205n, 211-3, 216, 239, 256n, 266, 272, 283n, 287, 287n, 298

Service, Robert 53, 53n
Shidlovskii Commission 115n, 116, 119-20, 119n, 181
Sil'vin, M.A. 159-60, 161n
Smith, Steve 48n, 53, 53n, 68n
Social Democratic Workers' Library 165
Sovremennik 143-4, 143n
SPD (Sozialdemokratische Partei Deutschlands/German Social Democratic Party) 8, 26-7, 29, 149n, 245
Stasova, Yelena Dimitrievna 169-71n, 170-1, 173, 173n
Stolypin, Pyotr 35, 293
Struve, Peter 218-20, 242n, 287, 298

Takhtarev, K.M. 10, 99, 99n, 156n
Tochiiskii, Pavel Varfolomeivich 13-4, 16, 83n, 90, 90n, 152, 152n
Trotsky, Leon 11, 24n, 31, 37n, 52-3n,

53, 61, 63, 126, 126n, 190, 263n, 270

Unemployed Council 195
Union of Struggle for the Liberation of the Working Class (Union of Struggle) 104, 158-65, 161n, 167-9, 167n, 236

Venturi, Franco 78-81n, 79, 143-4n, 146-8n
Vyshnegradskii, Ivan Alekseevich 86

Weitling, Wilhelm 69
Witte, Sergei 36n, 37, 42, 86, 98, 101
Workers' Flame 19, 163, 165, 168n
Workers' Organisation 104, 164

Zarya 12, 227, 234, 234-5n
Zelnik, Reginald 41-2n, 78-83n, 80-1, 85n
Zinoviev, Boris 159
Zubatov, Sergei 98, 100-1, 105, 131

www.ingramcontent.com/pod-product-compliance
Lightning Source LLC
Chambersburg PA
CBHW060308030426
42336CB00011B/970